SANTA-TIZING

What's wrong with Christmas
and how to clean it up

by
Robin Main

Xulon PRESS

Copyright © 2008 by Robin Main

Santa-tizing
What's wrong with Christmas and how to clean it up
by Robin Main

Printed in the United States of America

ISBN 978-1-60791-115-9

All rights reserved solely by the author. The author guarantees all contents are original and do not infringe upon the legal rights of any other person or work. No part of this book may be reproduced in any form without the permission of the author. The views expressed in this book are not necessarily those of the publisher.

Unless otherwise indicated, Bible quotations are taken from The HOLY BIBLE, NEW INTERNATIONAL VERSION®. (NIV)® of the Bible. Copyright © 1973, 1978, 1984 by International Bible Society. Used by permission of Zondervan. All rights reserved.

www.xulonpress.com

TABLE OF CONTENTS

ଔ

- 1 - Supernatural Encounters 11
    - Word Up 13
    - New Dimensions of Freedom 19
    - Holiness to the Lord 22
    - Glory Departs or Dwells in You 23
    - Fill It Up Full of Meaning 26
    - What's Wrong? 27

- 2 - The Land of the Merchants 31
    - Sacred Frenzy 31
    - Materialism Is the Name 33
    - Kingdom of Self 35
    - Clean It Up 37

I – **Come out of Babylon (Past)** 41

- 3 - Babylon and Beyond 43
    - The Original Nimrod 43
    - Babel 45
    - To Repeat Childhood 46
    - Trying to Reach Heaven 47
    - Come out of Babylon 51
    - The Source of Sun Worship 52
    - The Sun God and His Sacred Bull 53
    - By Babylon's Sorcery 55
    - Abraham's Baptism of Fire 59

Shem on Nim 60
  Semiramis—The First Babylonian Queen of
      Heaven 64
  Yuletide Season 65
  Mock King 69
  Service to the Dead and Death 71

4 - Age-Old Foundation 73
  One New Man 73
  Noahiac Commandments 75
  The Essential Commandments for All Believers ...77
  Heavenly Requirements for Holy Matrimony 80
  Biblical Time-Keeping 90
  Changing the Marks of Time 91
  Destroying People's Sense of Time 95
  Greco-Roman Marks on Time 97
  Triggers for Idolatrous Practices 100

5 - The Golden Snare 103
  Tradition of Man 103
  Coming Full Circle 106
  Solomon's High Place 108
  Constantine Compromises 110
  Ancient Idolatry Made Modern 119
  An Idol in the Form Of 123
  The Cosmic Christmas Tree 126
  Reformation Hits a Holiday 130

6 - The Golden Calf 137
  Contending With God 137
  The Original Golden Calf 141
  The Christmas Connection 143
  The Father of Christmas 146
  Critical Mass—Christmas 150
  The Promised Land 156

II – Lay Down Christmas (Present) 161

7 - This Is Radical! 163
The Word of My Testimony 163
A Way Out 165
It's Good Enough for Me 169
The Feasts of the Lord 171
Being Brought Together 175
Ardent Reformation 179

8 - Fullness of Time 183
The Kingdom 183
Temple of Sons 185
In the Dispensation of the Fullness of Time 186
Draw Closer and Go Up 191
In the Midst 194
Fullness of Him 195
Seismic Shift 196

9 - The One to Be Sacrificed 201
The Spirit of Elijah 201
Christmas I Have Loved 203
Colonial History of the Festival of Laughter 207
The Holiday That Trade Built 209
His Will Entirely 216
Sacrifice of Laughter 217

III – Pure and Spotless Bride (Future) 221

10 - Here Comes the Bride 223
Passionate Love 223
Spending Ourselves 226
You Are Cordially Invited 227
Righteous Readiness 229
Unfaithful Friend 231
Surrendering All 234
Sanctification—Clean Hands and Pure Heart 237

11 - I Thee Wed 241
       With This Wine and Bread, I Thee Wed 242
       Seasoned Bridal Company 247
       Genu-wine 249
       The Wayward Wife 251
       Extreme Tribulation 255
       Baptism of Fire 258
       Bridal Mysteries 260

12 - Epilogue 263

    Index 267

    Glossary 291

    Bibliography 317

    Notes 325

DEDICATION

To the One
who makes all things possible.

To John and Cody
for your
incredible support and love.

1

SUPERNATURAL ENCOUNTERS

☙

> And they overcame him because of the blood of the Lamb
> and because of the word of their testimony,
> and they did not love their life even when faced with death.
> —Revelation 12:11 NASB

Christmas. Mention the word and most Americans are filled with a feeling of joy and warmth. They are transported to a happy place surrounded by nostalgia and anchored in tradition. Its magical appeal is felt deep down inside and never lets us forget the season. It transports us into a timeless cycle that's a living piece of ancient culture—an authentic Yuletide atmosphere. It's the crowning of the year. It's an expression of deep-seated loyalty and worldwide unity. People seem to be linked together by big hearts and a common love. Almost nothing can quench the desire to do the right thing by Christmas. It's impressive both in its scope and association, where a set of bonds has us looking homeward and to one another. Many people believe that Christmas embodies everything that is good. There's an impression that things are simply right with the world, evidenced by the avalanche of charitable giving, well wishes, and generosity of the soul. How could anyone in their right mind be opposed to such a glorious occasion? Yet, every single one of us experience various distasteful fruits of this season and wonder, at least occasionally, whether it's all that we have cracked it up to be.

Even the term *Christmas* expresses two opposites ends of a spectrum. In the mental health world, this condition is called bi-polar. When Americans say the word *Christmas,* they are either discussing: (1) the religious events, which commemorate Jesus' birth or (2) the secular celebrations—annual traditions that predate Christ's birth—characteristic of midwinter celebrations: the lights, the evergreen decorations, the gift giving, the music, the food, the chance to get together with family and friends, and the special feeling of warmth that this season brings.[1] From its inception, the Christmas celebration has been a concoction of preexisting pagan winter revels *mixed* with Christian subject matter; and because of this, it never was, nor can it ever be, the pure spiritual holiday that so many wish it would be.

This fact may surprise some people, but it also confirms other's observations. I have noticed that Christmas is so well loved that when its name is mentioned, people automatically go to that place in their minds that is well-defended. We have built a fortress of self-protection around it. It's the same phenomenon that happens with any label where people hear the word and then immediately pigeon-hole anything related to it. We almost instantly turn off our thinking mechanisms, and in general, don't look at the substance behind the labels.

It's important to note, for those who lay claim to a Judeo-Christian heritage, that the Hebraic culture is our most primordial foundation. Its language is ideogramic, where many pictures are used to describe a word. Each letter of the Hebrew alphabet is actually a picture, and together these letters, which are pictures, reveal a pictograph. For example: The ideogram or pictograph for the Hebrew word *humble* tells us that humility comes when we "destroy the fence or wall (i.e., self-protection is done away with)."[2] My past reveals that I have put a wall around myself when I have been mad at my husband or abused by a friend, and so have you when you have felt threatened, vulnerable, or angry. It's a natural, almost automatic, action. But these walls of self-protection hold us captive in our own prisons, where not only do we shut out the one who's hurt us, but we are hedged in from receiving good things in the very areas where we unhealthily guard ourselves. Effort is required to walk humbly before God and man. Sometimes extreme effort. Some of our most daunting obstacles to being humble and teachable are our walls of self-protection. Labels are just one of the ways that people go into self-protection mode.

Had I not been confronted with a mind-blowing reality and been given the task to tell the church its ramifications, I would be amongst the majority in hearing the label "Christmas" and then placing it where I was taught it belonged. I am no better than anyone else. I have just been given something very difficult to do; and for the past ten years, the process has slowly chipped away at some cracks in my belief system. I will shortly go into how I was given the assignment to look into what's wrong with Christmas. But first, I will simply ask you to put on your critical thinking cap. Be a Berean: "And the people of Berea were more open-minded than those in Thessalonica, and they listened eagerly to Paul's message. They searched the Scriptures day after day to see if Paul and Silas were teaching the truth" (Acts 17:11 NLT). Don't let the label trap trip you up from examining the truth behind what you believe.

WORD UP

Now to how I came to write this book on this highly controversial subject: As sure as I know that my daddy loves me, I know that the Word of the Lord came to me twice on two separate occasions. While I do not put these revelatory words of the Lord (i.e., *rhema*[3]) on par with Scripture, I greatly value anything God would like to share with me, especially anything close to His heart. I also check any *rhema* word against Scripture, for I believe that God does not contradict His written Word.

The first Word of the Lord, which is important for the context of this book, happened in the month of December. The year was 1998. Jesus came to me in an apparition.[4] He had tears in His eyes when He told me: "The mixture of Christmas grieves my heart." He paused momentary to let this bombshell sink in; then added: "Come out of Babylon and lay down Christmas, for I *will* have a pure and spotless Bride." As all things truly of God are, these words were utterly life changing.

As a side, please allow me to explain that I am not trying to appear to be more spiritual than others by sharing the words, experiences, or visions I have received from the Lord. The Lord has created me to be a seer, and visions are a regular way the Lord communicates with me. Other believers have different, and just as important, gifts given by the grace of God as articulated in the Bible. My husband is an excellent example of this. John has the gifts of practical knowledge, profound discernment, and sound wisdom, which encourage, ground, and balance everyone around him. John tells me that he has never directly communicated with the Lord. When, in reality, he issues forth a steady stream of God's living water, due to his efforts to live a right life before his Creator. Although some individuals may have a hard time accepting any spiritual (i.e., supernatural) experience, it is important to note that they are biblical and that our God is a supernatural God.

To help you understand what an unlikely candidate I was, know that in 1998 I loved the beauty of the Christmas season. I liked Christmas songs, Christmas teas, and Christmas cheer. Quite frankly, I'd be one of the last persons to be sour or dour toward any celebration. Growing up in northwestern Montana in the 1960s and '70s, my family annually would go Christmas tree hunting. All five of us would pile into Dad's big, green Ford pick-up and head out to the abundant supply of evergreens on national forest land west of Kalispell. It was a wonderful all-day event. We'd bring an axe, our sleds, and a thermos full of hot cocoa. My dad would dangerously drag our sleds behind his truck. I shouldn't tell you that it was tons of fun! We sang, and sometimes yelled, carols via the PA system of my dad's CB radio to any deer, bear, or squirrel that would listen. I'd have to say that Christmas tree hunting is still one of my favorite memories. Extravagant parties are my forte too. Just ask any friend who has been to one of my tea parties. Additionally, when I got my first job out of college in southern California, I was a computer programmer/analyst by day and a sole proprietor of a handmade greeting card company by night. Let's just say that I thoroughly took pleasure in putting a personal and affectionate touch to my annual Christmas cards. I also had a reputation for getting just the right gift.

Even today, gift-giving and being involved in philanthropic efforts are two of my favorite things to do.

In 1998, I enjoyed the sights, sounds, smells, textures, and tastes related to Christmas. It's safe to say I liked, even loved, it all. Yet way back, even when I was a child, somewhere deep inside of me, I sensed that something was amiss. And like Halloween, I shelved the "feeling," remembering it only when the Lord chose to unveil the reason for my uneasiness.

I was totally cognizant that when the Lord said: "Come out of Babylon and lay down Christmas," I would either choose to not obey; and thus, not believe and move toward an ever increasing compromised and useless Christian life—or—I would chose to hear God and seek understanding, so I could obey the dictates of the Lord's heart; and thus, ever increase in knowing Him and His ways. The only option for my sold-out heart was to respond with a feeble, but genuine heart cry: "Lord, I want to. Help me. Show me the way. My husband's not ready for this. Give me, give us a way out."

Little did I expect the response to my prayer to be so dramatic and so soon. Within a few hours our beautiful Christmas tree, decorated to the hilt with so many sweet memories, was infested with hundreds, if not thousands, of tiny spiders. I didn't take the time to count! As you probably could have guessed, I could have been diagnosed with arachnophobia at the time. I recount this story in chapter 7, but for now the shortened version of my story goes something like: It was the day of the winter solstice December 21, 1998. My husband was in an important all-day meeting, so a good friend and I dismantled my family's Christmas tree without his knowledge. I thought something to the effect: Those spiders with "their" tree are outta here! As soon as the tree was out of our home, miraculously and instantaneously, all the spiders were gone. When my family room was cleared of its infestation, I placed all our beautifully wrapped gifts in the bare corner of the room where the tree used to reside. When I told my husband what happened, I was amazed at how fast he agreed that the entire situation was of God. I should let you know that my husband is extremely analytical and rarely agrees quickly to anything. He's quite pensive and our family is better off for it.

Prior to our spousal heart-to-heart, I had been staring at our presents; and even though I felt an *incredible* spirit of joy and peace, I still felt a void. It was like having a rug being pulled out from beneath you. I had lost my footing, so I sought the Lord. I said something similar to: "There's a *big* hole in our life now. What are we to do?" I distinctly heard Jesus say: "Do what I did. If Chanukah was good enough for Me, it's good enough for you." My first response was: "What?" At that time, I honestly never even had thought of that possibility. I went to my *Strong's Concordance* and found the scriptural reference I needed under the word *winter*.[5] But of course, Jesus grew up and lived as a Jew while He was here on earth: "Then came the Feast of Dedication at Jerusalem. It was winter, and Jesus was in the temple area walking in Solomon's Colonnade" (John 10:22-23). Chanukah also can be spelled "Hanukkah." It has several additional names, including the Feast of Dedication, the Feast of Miracles, and the Feast of Lights.

So in 1998, our family set out to celebrate Chanukah. We were just like little children trying to please our parent with a clumsy, yet sincere, stab at doing what Jesus did. That year, December 21st was the last day of Chanukah; therefore, the last day of the official eight-day Chanukah season was the first day we actually celebrated as Jesus did. I thought it interesting that the Lord would reveal his heart about Christmas and Chanukah on the final and eighth day of Chanukah, because the number eight in Scripture speaks of new beginnings. For eight consecutive days, our cozy, little family lit a nine-branch lampstand at sunset, and read devotions from *Matthew Henry's Commentary of the Bible* furnished by Robin Scarlata and Linda Pierce's book: *A Family Guide to the Biblical Holidays*.

As I stated before, December 21, 1998, was also the day of the winter solstice, which was the actual day pagans originally celebrated Christmas under various other names. So . . . on the eighth day of Chanukah according to the biblical calendar and on the day of the winter solstice according to man's marks of time, my family and I began a new and joyous journey. For us, God ordained this crossover date to switch our family from celebrating Christmas to His biblical celebration of Chanukah. There will be more about

Chanukah being one of God's ordained occasions of celebrating in section II of this book.[6]

The second Word of the Lord that is relevant to this book was shared with me about a year later on December 4, 1999, at an event in Colorado Springs. This time it was the first day of Chanukah when I had a supernatural encounter of the divine kind. It was another apparition.

In fact, in hindsight, I was graced with a season of divine appearances. A week prior to my arrival at the Intercession Conference in Colorado Springs, my Beloved appeared to me and asked me to marry[7] Him—to be with Him eternally as a devoted best friend and to be full of love. A goal all believers should strive for. Yeshua[8] literally appeared to me out of the blue. Shocked is a word that comes to mind. In a moment, many thoughts flashed through my mind: What? What do you mean? Like this? Thoughts, which He could instantaneously read. What can I say? Yeshua was messing with my paradigms. My Beloved smiled, and even chuckled a little, as I realized that all was so silly compared to the Beauty before me. He was here, and He had asked me to marry Him! How many marriage proposals would I personally get from the King of Kings? I wasn't taking any chances. After I exclaimed, "Yes! Of course!" I fell back while reclining as Yeshua whipped out a celestial wedding ring. Yeshua asked me for my left hand. When I extended it to Him, He placed this glorious supernatural ring on my finger. My whole being resonated with His voice, "With this ring I thee wed." I knew I was to repeat the phrase after Him, "With this ring I thee wed." After my Beloved slipped His eternal ring on my finger, He asked me, "Where would you like to go on our honeymoon?" Completely blowing right past my mind, I was again dumbstruck with amazement. It seemed like an eternity that I just stared deeply into His eyes before I stammered, "I . . . I . . . I . . . I . . . don't know. Whhhhhaaat do you think?" Yeshua told me that He would like us to go down to the Intercession Conference in Colorado Springs. My slightly mischievous side recovered quickly and playfully replied, "Don't you think that will be a little crowded?" He laughed the most perfect laugh, and I knew that He was taking me to a place that was full of bridal hearts. I was excited! The sole reason I am sharing this very personal experience with you is that the church needs to know that first we must obey our Beloved by coming out of Babylon and laying down Christmas before He literally will ask us to become a part of His pure, spotless, and most glorious Bride. Each one of us must qualify individually before we will become His special corporate one, and we will need some divine intervention to make it happen, which is illustrated throughout my 1998-1999 bridal journey. Please join me as I continue with my testimony about how I got down to Colorado Springs.

As I prepared to go to the Intercession Conference the next weekend, John made sure that my vehicle was up-to-snuff. My Barbie truck, which can't be missed because of its raspberry metallic sheen, had been slowly leaking anti-freeze into the oil. Any mechanic will tell you that this is not good. The morning I was to leave for my heavenly honeymoon, my earthly husband insisted that I go to the dealership to get my engine checked out. The diagnosis was terrible—in fact fatal. The mechanic told me that if I didn't check my truck in immediately, I would ruin my engine. Not good news. My heart didn't sink that much, for I was still fresh from my divine wedding encounter; and I just knew that my Beloved would work it out. So I mentally and spiritually tuned into my Bridegroom, for His manifest presence was near indeed. I immediately heard, "Get in the truck. Get on the highway. Lay your hand on the dashboard and I will heal it." I would like to have reported that I immediately obeyed; but the truth is I reacted with a "Yikes! Are you kidding me?!" I screamed silently in my head, "My husband will literally KILL me if this doesn't work!" Yeshua gently repeated His instructions verbatim. What choice did I have? Really? Stay home and please my practical, caring husband or go on a divine honeymoon and get to see a healing miracle on a truck, no less. So . . . I thanked the mechanic. As he topped off my radiator, the mechanic proceeded to remind me of the disastrous consequences for such foolishness. In my spirit I was getting tickled way deep down inside at the thought of Jesus healing my truck. It would save us hundreds of dollars; and I would need a miracle to get down to Colorado Springs. It sounded like God to me. I grinned and thanked the mechanic again as I slid into the driver's seat and steered for Interstate 25. As soon as I merged with traffic, I laid my hand on the dashboard. I merely reminded my Beloved of His promise, "I have gotten in the truck. I am driving on the highway. Now I ask You to heal my truck." Period. Just like that. I believed His Word; and it was done. My Barbie truck is still going strong nine years later; and tragically, I am beginning to want a new vehicle.

The experience in Colorado Springs was wonderful; most of the encounter will have to wait for another time. Yeshua had several messages for me, but there was one that particularly pertains to this book. I distinctively heard, "Christmas will be the golden calf of America." At the time, Yeshua asked me, "Will you tell them?" three times, in regard to speaking to a church full of people. When Jesus asked me the first time, "Will you tell them?" I thought of the speaker two sessions ago, who was the pastor of the church where we were having the conference. He had just talked so eloquently about how the beauty of the Christmas tree spoke of the eternal truths of Christ. I looked around at a room full of bridal hearts who celebrate Christmas. I fidgeted in my mind and half-heartedly, yet sincerely, told Jesus, "You know, Lord . . . I will do anything for You." Jesus asked me a second time, "Will you tell them?" "Yes, Lord. If you want me to, I will," I said a little more confidently. The third time Yeshua asked me, "Will you tell them?" I told my Beloved, "Yes, I will tell them. But . . . I will not buck authority. You will have to have the speaker call me up to the pulpit sovereignly; and I will tell them what You have shared with me." I breathed a sigh of relief when my Beloved dropped the subject. At the time, I thought that was the end of the subject; but even my quick little mind slowly comprehended that my Beloved did not tell me that Christmas will be the golden calf of America for no good purpose.

NEW DIMENSIONS OF FREEDOM

This book is the culmination of my historical and biblical search to understand my Beloved's heart. The first two years were an exploration made solely so I could explain what the Lord was requiring of my family, which eventually led me to comprehend that this book was how I was going to fulfill "telling them" (i.e., the church) that

"Christmas will be the golden calf of America." Hopefully, without sounding super spiritual, I'd like to declare that I write this book in obedience to my Lord, my Savior, my King, and my God.

I have died many deaths in writing this book—to myself and my desires and to other people and theirs. Literally, I have had to lay down everything for this project—my time, my energy, and my ambition. Had it been my personal choice, I never would have taken this path. Without God's enabling grace, who would be so audacious to touch the church's sacred cow? Really.

As I have journeyed on this narrow path, I have come to love my Lord, His heart, and His Word, even more. The Lord Jesus Christ really does want our good when He tells us to do or not do something. Additionally, I have discovered deep, bottomless peace and new dimensions of freedom. I deeply appreciate the heavens opening and His sharing revelatory information with me. I pray that you hear the Lord's heart through His Word, history, and my testimony—prayerfully in Him. Even though I have purposely limited my personal testimony in this book, know that I have endeavored to recount accurately any of my experiences through referencing my journals. I also have endeavored to limit the scope of this work to what the Lord has revealed: Specifically, how God wants His pure and spotless Bride to come out of Babylon, and how His people can lay down the golden calf of America. Coming out of Babylon is a new concept for many people. Fundamentally, Babylon can be likened to the kingdom of self with its unholy trinity of me, myself, and I. We will get into this subject more in chapter 3.

The message contained within is meant for the church in the nations (i.e., the Gentile church), primarily the church in the United States of America, although my goal is that it will be reader-friendly for anyone who picks up this volume. Please be aware that when I mention a particular person or organization, religious or otherwise, I do so with one purpose—to discover the substance behind what has been cast as Christmas. Our focus zeroes in on western Christianity due it being the main influence on Christmas in America.

All the questions contained within reflect my own soul-searching journey. I have included them to assist you in your quest for clarity. If any question in this book offends you, try to get your focus off yourself and any personal condemnation you may feel. Everything in *Santa-tizing* is meant to guide us in an honest assessment of God's truth. Unfortunately, feelings often trump the truth in the American church today.

Please try to have an open mind when you read *Santa-tizing*, for it is beneficial when change is involved in any shape, form, or matter. When I ask you to aim at having an open mind, I am asking your mind to be open to the Spirit of the living God and the way of Truth articulated in His Word.

One of my greatest concerns is that some person or some group will take the message articulated in this book and try to beat people over the head with it. Over the last two millennia, history is littered with organized religion forcibly imposing "the truth." I believe this contradicts some very basic tenets of the Christian faith: compassion, grace, kindness, et cetera. Without the sanctifying work of the Spirit of Truth teaching each of us the genuineness of the enclosed message, a sincere heart change will be impossible. An authentic move of the Holy Spirit literally will be required.

Holiness is our aim. Simply put, we are to become more and more like Jesus. Christ's Bride will look like Him. We will be totally genuine and sincere, pure and spotless. I hear from Christians that we are already holy, because Jesus died for our sin and He is in us. Yes. A seed of holiness exists within every believer when they accept Him as their Savior; but remember that after a person is saved, the Lord Jesus Christ cleanses us from our sin after we confess it (1 John 1:8-9). Once we sin, we have sullied our holy state. We must go back to Jesus, so He can cleanse us again and again until we mature to the point where we have done away with our sin. It's a place where a particular sin no longer compels or attracts us. Our will becomes enthroned in His love. Our nature has matured in that particular arena to be holy as He is holy. Holiness is our inevitable consummation as we choose Him and His ways. With the enabling power and grace of the Spirit of the living God coupled with our obedient devotion, God's people will become the dwelling place for the King.

HOLINESS TO THE LORD

Holiness means to be set apart from the ordinary. "If an object is holy, it has a degree of sanctity that forbids its use for ordinary pleasures. If a person is holy, he is on a higher level than others."[9] People are not innately holy. They become holy as man reflects God's absolute sanctity and purity. The Hebrew sage R' Hirsch reveals that man's sanctity literally results from a mastery of all his instincts and inclinations where they're placed at the disposal of God's will.[10] The Lord our God remains holy whether man venerates Him or not; because man's conduct has no effect on God's supremely infinite and unchanging holiness. Man only can influence the manifestation of God's holiness on earth. When man spends quality time communing with God, a by-product is produced in and through our lives—His *shekinah* glory. This is the same *shekinah* that used to arise as a cloud of glory over the ark of the covenant in the wilderness tabernacle. It is also the same *shekinah* that used to radiate from Moses' face after he had spent time in the midst of God's presence.[11] God's *shekinah* glory and His holiness are so closely related that the Bible tells us that His *shekinah* literally requires holiness:

> I saw the glory of the God of Israel coming from the east. . . . The glory of the Lord entered the temple through the gate facing east. . . . I heard someone speaking to me from inside the temple. He said: 'Son of man, this is the place of my throne and the place for the soles of my feet. This is where I will live among the Israelites forever. The house of Israel will never again defile my holy name—neither they nor their kings—by their prostitution and lifeless idols of their kings at their high places. *When they placed their threshold next to my threshold and their doorposts beside my doorposts, with only a wall between me and them, they defiled my holy name by their detestable practices.* So I destroyed them in my anger. Now let them put away from me their prostitution and lifeless idols of their kings, and I will live among them forever. Son of man, describe the temple to the people of Israel, . . . so they may be faithful to its design and follow its

regulations. *This is the law of the temple: All the surrounding area on top of the mountain will be most holy.* Such is the law of the temple.

—Ezekiel 43:2-12, emphasis mine

When a person has faith in Jesus, he or she is considered holy because Christ then dwells in him or her—"the hope of glory" (Col. 1:27). Our holy deposit of Christ in us is called "the hope of glory" for a reason. First and foremost, Christ is the one in whom our hopes of glory are centered, and it is from Christ that the glory literally flows, "... because by one sacrifice he has made perfect forever those who are being made holy" (Heb. 10:14).

People have tried to boil holiness down to a formula of dos and don'ts. This is partially correct. Doing what the Bible prescribes for holiness taps into the prerequisites for which God's presence can dwell among us. We also must take into account that our hearts must be engaged when we seek to obey God. Christians need to consider that the *shekinah* glory dwelt in the midst of Israel for generations: "The people of Israel. Theirs is the adoption of sons; theirs the divine glory . . ." (Rom. 9:4). First century believers understood the biblical holiness requirements, which facilitated God's dwelling presence. When the Holy Spirit fell at Pentecost, the church experienced His manifest presence. They additionally sustained a multigenerational revival for more than three hundred years, because they understood how to live in God's presence. For the church to sustain His awesome presence today, we need to accurately grasp His *minimum* requirements for purity and their relevant application in our lives. Purity is like a guardian for worship of the One True God. "Only those whose hands and hearts are pure, who do not worship idols and never tell lies. They will receive the Lord's blessing and have right standing with God their savior. They alone may enter God's presence and worship the God of Israel" (Ps. 24:4-6 NLT).

GLORY DEPARTS OR DWELLS IN YOU

We need to comprehend that God's dwelling presence departed from the Christian church around the time when pagan holidays were assimilated into it. As I just demonstrated, the Bible shows us that the Lord's special dwelling presence—His *shekinah*—requires certain prerequisites to stay. Probably the most important conditions are spelled out in Ezekiel 8-11. Please note, as you personally read this passage, that God's presence slowly and sorrowfully departed, for He longs for His people to repent so His presence may return. "Son of man, do you see what they are doing . . . things that will drive Me far from My sanctuary?" (Ezek. 8:6). The idolatrous practices listed in Ezekiel 8 originated in Babylon. We will dig into the following points throughout section I. For now, let's merely note which idolatrous practices are detestable to God. Please notice that these are listed in increasingly detestable order:

1. The idol that provokes to jealousy at the entrance to the north gate of the inner court (Ezek. 8:3-5) coincides with the primary access to the Babylonian shrine summit of most ziggurats.[12]
2. All the idols of the house of Israel with seventy elders leading prayers each at the shrine of his own idol (Ezek. 8:9-12) coincides with the footprint of Babylon—the Kingdom of Self.
3. The women sitting at the north gate of the house of the Lord mourning for Tammuz (Ezek. 8:14) coincides with the death of Nimrod and his resurrection/reincarnation in Semiramis's supposedly "immaculate" son—Tammuz, who also died a gruesome death.
4. At the entrance to the temple, between the porch and the altar, about twenty-five men have their backs to the temple of the Lord and their faces bowing down to the rising sun (Ezek. 8:16). This coincides with the worship of the sun gods, especially on their most ancient and noteworthy birthday of December twenty-fifth.

The fourth and most detestable practice was performed in the inner court of the house of the Lord between the portico and altar. The inner court symbolizes those who are intimately acquainted with God. The portico is a place of traversing back and forth. It can be akin to a heaven to earth connection. The altar was a platform of sacrificial worship, where worshipers endeavored to meet with their God.[13] So the twenty-five or so men, who were bowing down to the sun with their backs toward the temple of the Lord, were His close companions. They were people who knew and loved the Lord; yet they still grievously bowed down to and worshiped the sun, whether they acknowledged the fact or not.

It is not until Ezekiel 9:3 that the departure of God's presence begins. His *shekinah* glory moves from the inner court to the threshold of His sanctuary. The Lord hesitates there to see if His people will notice His leaving. Will they repent and welcome His manifest presence back? He waits, then in Ezekiel 10:19 God's glory moves further away to the eastern gate. He waits again. His people still won't repent of their idolatry, so God's *shekinah* moves out of Jerusalem across the Kidron Valley to the Mount of Olives (Ezek. 11:23). There God waits again for the people to turn from their idols.

When the Lord says that "Christmas will be the golden calf of America," He is telling us that it's idolatry in His eyes. The Lord has given each of us the responsibility to prepare a place for Him. "Everyone who has this hope in Him purifies himself, just as he is pure" (1 John 3:3). His *shekinah* glory cannot dwell where there is idolatry; therefore, His dwelling presence can not, and will not, coexist with this golden calf we call Christmas. Christians should not be offended by the multicultural displays being promoted at Christmastime. The non-Christian (i.e., secular) elements have always existed and preceded the Christian ones. Christmas has become a humungous amalgamation of pagan and Christian customs. Our traditions are based in Babylon. The profane has become irreparably intertwined and mixed with the sacred.

The rabbis tell us that Abraham originally shared the idolatrous practices of his father,[14] but as the story goes he cast off his idols. "According to the Talmud, Abraham was 13-years old when he rejected the idol worship practiced by his father. From then on he became a servant of God."[15] Anyone who accomplishes the noteworthy feat of breaking with the idolatry of their family and surroundings will receive the same reward as Abraham. The bonus includes a close personal relationship with the Lord and God identifying Himself by your name.

FILL IT UP FULL OF MEANING

The Bible tells us: "We know that we have come to know Him if we obey His commands. The man who says, 'I know him,' but does not do what he commands is a liar, and the truth is not in him. This is how we know we are in Him: Whoever claims to live in Him must walk as Jesus did" (1 John 1:3-6).

Jesus Himself tells us in Matthew 5:17: "Do not think that I have come to abolish the Law or the Prophets; I have not come to abolish them but to fulfill them." If we are to do what Jesus did, we are called to fulfill the commandments of God. Please stick with me. My goal is to bring purity and balance to our Christian walk, not to promote legalistic behavior.

Jesus came to set us free and to fulfill the law (i.e., the Bible). That means He came to fill it full of meaning. The concept of "fulfill" is the exact opposite of abolish. Yeshua converted His law into reality, when He fully and consistently demonstrated the first and greatest commandment, and the second one that is like it: "Love the LORD your God with all your heart and with all your soul and with all your mind . . . Love your neighbor as yourself" (Matt. 22:36-40). Jesus perfectly made the fullness of the commandments known. He demonstrated for us what the manifestation of perfection looks like in mature believers: ". . . whoever keeps the word, in him the love of God has been truly been perfected" (1 John 2:5). This message permeates the Bible. It is very meaningful that the Lord equates a new heart and a new spirit within His people with their keeping His permanent rules, which are prescribed practices in order to facilitate the culture and climate of life. "And I shall give them one heart, and shall put a new spirit within them. And I shall take the heart of stone out of their flesh and give them a heart of flesh, that they may walk in My statutes and keep My ordinances, and do them. Then they will be My people, and I shall be their God" (Ezek. 11:19 NASB).

The lives of those who follow the Lamb wherever He goes will embody the truth that not only must God's people keep the faith of

Jesus, but sanctified saints also will abide by the commandments of God (Rev. 14:12). This is a practical key for end-time believers. The Bride of Christ shall operate in the Lord's perfect will, not His permissive will. Both Jews and Gentiles in Christ will have law-abiding conduct, which translated means that they will remain in His extravagant love. "For this is the love of God, that we keep His commandments; and His commandments are not burdensome" (1 John 5:3 NASB). To function in God's perfect will, we must first discern what it is. Due to the staggering strength of the delusion involving Christmas, I would suggest that Christians first lay Christmas on God's altar; otherwise, you will probably hear the Lord your God through the idols of your own heart. Another helpful hint in discerning the Lord's perfect will in this regard is: It is best not to ask "Could I celebrate Christmas?" or "Should I celebrate Christmas?" These types of questions are easily influenced by our desires. I believe that a better approach is to ask Jesus direct questions like: "Do You consider Christmas to be a golden calf?" "Does the mixture of Christmas grieve Your heart?" "Will You require me to lay down Christmas to become part of Your pure and spotless Bride?"

WHAT'S WRONG?

The paganism of Christmas and holiness message contained within *Santa-tizing* is not a new message, but I believe that some new revelatory light has been shed on it. For the past fifteen hundred to seventeen hundred years, the Lord has talked to His church about coming clean from the paganism of Christmas—exemplified in the writings of the early church fathers, Protestant-led England and Scotland, plus the Pilgrims and the Puritans in America. Since the Reformation, and even before, people in the church have sanctified things for God. In this kingdom day, our sanctifying things for God is no longer acceptable. The time has come when the Lord is leading His people to revisit any unholy practice that exists within the church, for He *will* have a pure and spotless Bride. "I remember the devotion of your youth, how as a bride you loved Me and followed Me through the desert . . . Israel was holy to the LORD, the first fruits of His harvest . . . But My people have exchanged their Glory for worthless idols . . . you said, 'It's no use! I love foreign gods, and I must go after them.' Does a maiden forget her jewelry, a bride her wedding ornaments? Yet My people have forgotten Me, days without number" (Jer. 2:1-32).

Many of us believe that we have sanctified Christmas as unto the Lord through our taking out Santa and doing what we feel would please Him. But in this kingdom day, we will *not* sanctify things for the Lord; He will sanctify Himself in us. "For I the Lord, who sanctifies you, am holy" (Lev. 21:8 NASB). This is a time of separation—a time that the Lord is extracting the precious from the vile.

You will notice when you peruse my bibliography that I don't have an abundance of Christian sources. This is because I could not find many accurate facts in regards to Christmas in Christian resources, except for Catholic materials and more ancient texts. The church has been like a contortion artist, shaping Christmas so Christians can feel we have rightly sanctified our Christmas worship. We cite historical references that support our belief system and traditions without considering their background. Incredulously, I found more accurate information about Christmas in books written by atheists and pagans. For this reason alone, Christians need to examine the enclosed evidence about Christmas and how it affects the Bride of Christ. We can't make changes in the church unless we are willing to take risks and confront what is wrong. Enclosed is evidence that certainly demands a verdict for those who continually seek first His kingdom and His righteousness. I received the bulk of my information from the Bible or from historically-based books from academia.

Know that I am merely a messenger. I deeply appreciate and support the concepts of individual liberty and freedom of expression *for everyone*. What's wrong with Christmas? Plenty. This book shines some light on various troubling issues involved in celebrating a Christian Christmas. How to clean it up? This will be determined by you and your family. Each Christian will have to choose for themselves a point on a spectrum when it comes to cleaning up Christmas. That continuum runs from "I am fine just the way I am" to "I'm going to throw it out." Since we have an abundance of traditions, memories, and reasons to stay just the way we are, *Santa-tizing* primarily will explore the opposite. Know that in God's kingdom no person is forced to do anything against their will.

Please be prayerful and patient as you read this book, for we will be endeavoring to walk a fine line between coming out of compromises while staying out of legalism. Please know that I have been guilty of every fault I mention in this book. God's grace is so incredible! So let the mountains of human obstacles become mere molehills. May the dynamic power of the Spirit of the living God help everyone become part of the Bride of Christ.

I pray that the Lord's unmerited favor undergirds this work and you as you, the reader, seek to become more like Him. And may you *especially* respond as the Holy Spirit leads in obedience to the dictates of the Lord's heart. "For all who are being led by the Spirit of God, these are sons of God" (Rom. 8:14 NASB).

୯ଌ

2

THE LAND OF THE MERCHANTS
ଔ

> You also multiplied your harlotry with the land of merchants,
> Chaldea, yet even with this you were not satisfied.
> How languishing is your heart," declares the Lord GOD, "while you do all
> these things, the actions of a bold-faced harlot.
> When you built your shrine at the beginning of every street and made your high
> place in every square, in disdaining money, you were not like a harlot.
> —Ezekiel 16:29-31 NASB

SACRED FRENZY

My title, *Santa-tizing*, is obviously a play on words. "Santa" is short for Santa Claus—the mischievous, magical, and generous red-suited father figure of Christmas. Santa is a product of the industrial age, which was a by-product of the Reformation. I believe that Dell deChant hit the nail on the head when he says: "He has become the god of postindustrial culture."[16] Santa Claus is literally the cultural deity in America's capitalistic, consumer-based society.

If Americans were to be completely honest, Santa, not Jesus, signals the beginning of the Christmas "holy day" cycle. Whether we believe in Santa or not, he is real. Santa is a compelling figure, who commands our attention during the grand festival of consumption. Christmas would simply not be Christmas without its commercial winter wonderlands in department stores and malls, where Santa sits enthroned among his helpers and followers. In fact, Santa's arrival marks the beginning of our devout consumption.

Santa Claus was sold to the American public around 1822. Our modern red-suited icon began in New York City with John Pintard's efforts to establish St. Nicholas Day. His version never completely took, but two of Pintard's friends helped him out. Washington Irving weaved a beguiling setting for a benevolent, yet mischievous figure, which was later heralded by Clement Clarke Moore's poem *A Visit From St. Nicholas* (better known as *A Night Before Christmas)*. In Leigh Eric Schmidt's book *Consumer Rites,* he links the rise of the American Christmas as the primary gift-giving holiday with the creation of Santa Claus as a cultural myth and icon.

America's Christmas festival, which has been exported throughout the entire world, is such a pervasive and inescapable part of our culture that it all but consumes our calendar from Thanksgiving to New Year's Day. It consumes huge chunks of our wallets too. The Christmas season signals the time to acquire, and we do. Russell Belk, a professor of business at the University of Utah, reports that by the time the Christmas shopping season was over in 2006, an average of $500 for every man, woman and child had been spent in America.[17] Christmas is such a significant part of America's economy that many retailers live or die according to the profits connected to the Yuletide season. Cable business news shows inform us about the progress of the annual Christmas shopping spree on a daily basis. One commentator has noted that America's Christmas is bigger than the gross national product of Ireland. So deeply enmeshed are America's economy and her calendar, our holidays are scarcely recognizable without the trappings of the marketplace. Just look at how Christmas and Easter provide the occasion, timing, and inspiration for shopping. Notice how sales are announced around various holidays.

Also, note for now that Babylon is referred to as "the land of merchants" in Ezekiel 16:29.[18] Perhaps you can recognize the marketing/making of Christmas in "the land of merchants" title given to Babylon—specifically Chaldea, the place where sorcery, sun god worship, and its associated "land of merchants" status originated.[19] We will examine Chaldea more in chapter 3. We are first told in Ezekiel 16:29-31 that the land of merchants is a place where God's people multiply their harlotry against the Lord; but they still are not satisfied. It can be recognized by its shrines that are built at the beginning of every street and in the high place in every town square. Is there any other time when America's streets and town squares are so lavishly decorated? Evergreen boughs, wreaths, lights, ribbons, banners, and trees come to mind. Additionally, this scripture tells us that the harlotry associated with "the land of merchants" status has a general disdain for frugally spending money when it comes to its worship.

MATERIALISM IS THE NAME

If you want to pull out the root of all evil from your life, then go back to Babylon—the land of the merchants[20]—where they loved commerce, merchandise, and money more than God.[21] "For the love of money is the root of all evil" (1 Tim. 6:10 KJV). Rick Joyner so aptly articulates: "Money tests some of the ultimate issues of the human heart. Idolatry is one of the ultimate offenses against God. Money is one of the primary idols in the world today. An idol is not just something that people fear or worship, but what they put their trust in. Many sincere Christians still have idolatry in their hearts in relation to money, because they trust more in their job or bank account than they do in the Lord."[22]

"In a way, the world is a great liar. It shows you it worships and admires money, but at the end of the day it doesn't."[23] The illusion that money, fame, or power brings ultimate fulfillment is shattered at funerals. When death so rudely awakens us, we find ourselves returning to a basic reality, which at least temporarily shakes loose the scales of deception. We don't eulogize money. We speak of what's perpetually important: love, kindness, goodness, generosity, self-sacrifice, mercy, and honesty. These virtues of a good life lived is what people really admire; because a seed of eternity has been placed in every man's heart. The measure of light given to all men causes us to seek the source of our creation, and we tend to seek most when confronted with death—ours or another's. Ironically, at the same time we come face-to-face with a person's legacy, many families grapple over the inheritance. One would think facing one's mortality would elevate thoughts and behaviors; but, in reality, the character a person cultivates prior to the funeral most often carries them through the settlement of the estate. Too many times, selfishness, masked as greed, raises its ugly head; and money becomes an earthen wedge in a time when families should draw closer. At the time of a loved one's passing, we come to a crossover place where the eternal and temporal realms intersect. Fights over assets are juxtaposed next to eternal virtues. Too bad we don't remember that gold is akin to pavement in heaven. A much-used cliché declares: You can't take it with you. Even though this is oh-so-true, our carnal nature still craves what money can buy.

It takes only a cursory glance to see "the land of merchants" connection to Christmas. In my opinion, Stephen Nissenbaum has written one the best historical accounts of Christmas. He became a Pulitzer Prize finalist in History in 1997 after he wrote *The Battle for Christmas*. He documents: "Christmas was consciously used by entrepreneurs as an agent of commercialization, an instrument with which to enmesh Americans in the web of consumer capitalism."[24] It's obvious to the most casual observer that Americans are materialistic about Christmas. Our preoccupation with material things appears to be the name of the game. We seem to be caught up in a sacred frenzy. As the ancients participated in rituals at temples and shrines, Americans participate in similar rituals at malls and department stores.[25] For many Americans, Christmas is not a Christian holiday, but a secular one.

I see Christians wrestling to balance what we call the true spirit of Christmas with the spending demands, which come with the season. The true spirit of Christmas always has been rooted in the land of the merchants, and its fruits of spending oneself or one's money always has been intimately involved in its celebration. The observation of a news commentator is more than telling: "Retailers are hoping the holiday spirit overtakes the people and they will spend more than last year."[26]

Making money is essential for everyone's survival. Capitalism is not bad in and of itself. Many important benefits are a result of it, including: allowing people to rise out of poverty, extending human life, and encouraging wonderful innovations. I am not against capitalism. I am against people manipulating and being manipulated with a mask of spirituality, especially if that façade is Christian.

KINGDOM OF SELF

One of the greatest tests of the last days will revolve around the mark of the beast. From Revelation 13:17, we know that the mark of the beast is an economic symbol; because no one can buy, sell, or trade in the world's economic system unless they have received the beast's mark.[27] We also know from the preceding verse that worshiping the image of the beast will accompany his mark. What beastly image will people be worshiping in these last days? There are many answers to this question, but I believe that the simplest explanation is we will either worship God or ourselves.

The first commandment of *The Satanic Bible* could be boiled down to: Do unto thy self. Although this commandment is not listed in their little black book, the high priest of the Church of Satan and author of *The Satanic Bible*, Anton LaVey, promoted a doctrine of self-indulgence, self-satisfaction, self-gratification, and self-rule. LaVey's predecessor, Aleister Crowley,[28] is "often referred to as the father of modern Satanism."[29] In Crowley's *Book of the Law*, he proclaims: "In this new age, the only moral commandment will be, 'Do what thou wilt shall be the whole of the law.'"[30] Therefore, the satanic kingdom can be equated to the kingdom of self. When I mention the kingdom of self in this book, know that I am also referring to the satanic kingdom at the same time, as well as Babylon, for they are all focus on self. "The Babylonians, that ruthless and impetuous people, who sweep across the earth . . . They are a law to themselves . . . whose own strength is their god" (Hab. 1:6, 7, 11). Just keep in mind that the Hebrew pictograph for the word "pride" tells us that pride is to lift up yourself by your own strength,[31] while humility comes when you destroy your wall of self-protection.[32] Notice that "self" is the key ingredient that determines whether one is full of pride or humility.

The mark of the beast starkly displays the reality of the kingdom of self. Infamously, everyone seems to know about the number God has assigned to the beast—666. Our living God is literally speaking to us through this number. He is telling us the character of the beast, and it corresponds to the image worshiped. We have been told that 666 is the number of the name—the name of a person called the Antichrist, which is one aspect of the truth. Also, "666 was the *secret symbol* of the ancient pagan mysteries connected with the worship of the Devil."[33, 34, 35, 36] Both man and the serpent were created on the sixth day. Satan has been described as being "man-centered" (as opposed to God-centered): "And He turned and said to Peter, 'Get behind Me, Satan! You are a stumbling block to Me; for you are not setting your mind on God's interest, but man's" (Matt. 16:23 NASB). Thus the devil's number appears to be a twist on man's number.

Let's regard the number 666 by looking at the meaning of the number 6 repeated three times. E.W. Bullinger's book *Number in Scripture* tells us that the number 6 stands for man's world with man's enmity to God or man adding to God's grace by perverting and corrupting it.[37] Multiply the intensity of man's enmity to God through the corruption of God's grace three times, and we understand one aspect of the character of the beast. The beast exists within you and me. It's equivalent to a completely selfish man. This is an image people worship when they take the mark of the beast. "But mark this: There will be terrible times in the last days. People will be lovers of themselves, lovers of money . . . lovers of pleasure rather than lovers of God" (2 Tim. 3:1-2). One aspect of truth is that the "beast" is the personification of Satan in those who have given their will over to the things of this world. All of us have the choice each day to be or not to be part of the beast's system.

Believers have spent an enormous amount of time and energy trying to figure out how the mark of the beast will come. The bottom line, in regards to the mark of the beast, is that everyone must choose to serve and live in the kingdom of God or in the kingdom of self. Our primary objective should be to hit God's mark, not the beast's. The mark of the beast is like focusing on a sand trap while golfing. If we focus on the sand trap rather than the true goal, we'll hit it. Let's focus on pressing on toward the goal for the prize of the heavenly call of God in Christ Jesus (Phil. 3:14). Let's not be enemies of the cross of Christ, whose god is their belly, and who set their minds on earthly things (Phil. 3:18-19).

Rick Joyner remarks in his book *Overcoming the Spirit of Poverty*: "The only way we will not take the mark of the beast, regardless of whether we know what it is or not, is to have the mark of God. If we are marked by God we will never have to fear taking the enemy's mark."[38] The Bible makes it clear that a great many troubles are coming upon the earth in the last days, which corresponds with Paul telling us that "we must through many tribulations enter the Kingdom of God" (Acts 14:22 NKJV). Entering the kingdom of God is a process, and its path is the narrow road that Jesus walked. We are to do as Jesus did. We must journey to our personal Garden of Gethsemane and take ourselves to the cross daily to crucify our selfish desires by choosing not my will, but Yours be done (Matt. 26:39; Mark 4:36; Luke 22:42). Believers will be prepared for these difficult times through seeking the kingdom of God first (Matt. 6:33). Kingdom life boils down to obeying the King. In these end days, God's kingdom will not be shaken. Scripture declares that it cannot be shaken; therefore, if we build our lives upon it, neither can we.

CLEAN IT UP

Primarily, *Santa-tizing* is meant to make one think about the concept of sanitizing. My *Webster's Collegiate Dictionary* tells me that to sanitize something means to clean it up, to sterilize it, or to make it more acceptable by removing unpleasant or undesired features. Think about the body of Christ in regards to sanitation. Sanitation promotes hygiene in the body. It prevents disease through the maintenance of holiness.

This book endeavors to expose mixture within the church that is considered unacceptable to the Holy One of Israel. In fact, the first words of Yeshua's statement relate the primacy of the mixture issue. Remember, Jesus told me: "The mixture of Christmas grieves My heart. Come out of Babylon and lay down Christmas, for I *will* have a pure and spotless Bride." Examining mixture in the church is central to understanding the Lord's grief in this hour.

We are in a new season in God's timetable, and some things that God permitted His people to do in this past season will no longer be winked at if Christians want to come into agreement with the kingdom of Christ and God. This coming holiness move will be a work of the Holy Spirit or it will merely be wind, because flesh and blood cannot inherit the kingdom of God (1 Cor. 15:46, 49-50). Examining idolatrous practices within the sphere of Christianity is only one facet of His sanctifying work in this hour.

Revelation 18 calls God's people to come away from Babylon. Listen, if you will, to portions of Revelation 18 according to *The Living Bible* and see how much Babylon sounds like our American Christmas: ". . . businessmen throughout the world have grown rich from her luxurious living . . . She was their [the merchants of the earth] biggest customer . . . the dainty luxuries and splendor that you prized." Nissenbaum appears to support this supposition: "Producers and merchants were not slow to grasp these connections. They recognized that it was possible to exploit the season by offering a plethora of 'fancy goods . . .'"[39]

The Lord our God created us to love celebrations. God created beauty. He created fun. He also created us with the capacity for addiction, so we could be totally and utterly devoted to Him. When our God-given capacity for addiction becomes twisted through our fleshly appetites, disaster and destruction are its results. We will witness throughout *Santa-tizing* that Christmas literally holds people captive in a spellbinding potion of the sacred commemoration of Christ's birth mixed with a plethora of profane traditions associated with its celebration. We only need to examine the term "Christmas" to see this reality. Remember how I discussed that the word "Christmas" is a bi-polar term Americans use to discuss either the religious nativity or the secular celebration. Most Christians will be shocked to learn that their definition of getting back to the true meaning of Christmas goes back before Christianity, including the religious focus of a nativity. Pagan mysteries reveal that many of the various sun gods were born in a cave, and their birth was called "The Nativity." Unfortunately, almost everything associated with Christmas has been rooted and grounded in pagan[40] rituals. Charitable giving and joyous get-togethers with family and friends are definitely part of the true meaning of Christmas. It's just questionable whether this "true meaning" is a truth affirmed in the Bible. Obviously, giving to charity and gathering with family and friends are not bad practices in and of themselves. In fact, they are marks of a more fulfilled life. The questionable part comes when these rituals center around a pagan holiday supposedly made Christian.

God's people are in bondage. We are being manipulated through our own desires. The majority of American Christians are so grossly sensual in nature that we vehemently come to defend our Christmas traditions without doing our homework. The majority of us don't know where Christmas came from or where it's been.

The recent war over saying "Merry Christmas" versus "Happy Holidays" should make Christians stop and think. What are we getting so worked up about? In our defense of Christmas, we should ask ourselves if we are exhibiting the nature of Jesus. Could anyone take Christ out of Christmas if He did not allow it? What if it is actually the Lord Jesus Christ who is taking His name out of Christmas?

I never would have investigated Christmas being the golden calf of America, let alone written about it, had it not been for the unequivocable word from the Lord: "The mixture of Christmas grieves my heart. Come out of Babylon, and lay down Christmas, for I *will* have a pure and spotless Bride." You will undoubtedly see in this historical and biblical account that our Christian Christmas has been fashioned in the exact same image as Aaron's golden calf. We would all do well to heed the word of the Lord (backed by substantial scriptural evidence) that "Christmas will be the golden calf of America." Galatians 5:19-21 reveals that idolaters will not inherit the kingdom of God. Let's keep turning the pages to gain understanding of how Christmas is considered idolatry, and how we can lay it down so we will come out of Babylon to not take part in her sins. When this book encourages getting rid of anything in the church (i.e., in your life), it is because of His great love for us. It is not so we can earn His love.

08

SECTION I

COME OUT OF BABYLON

(Past)

☙

3

BABYLON AND BEYOND

☙

> In those days they made a calf and brought a sacrifice to the idol,
> and were rejoicing in the works of their hands.
> But God turned away and delivered them up to serve the host of heaven;
> as it is written in the book of the prophets,
> "It is not Me that you offered victims and sacrifices forty years
> in the wilderness, was it, O house of Israel?
> You also took along the tabernacle of Moloch and the star of the god Rompha,
> the images which you made to worship them.
> I also will remove you beyond Babylon."
> —Acts 7:41-43 NASB

THE ORIGINAL NIMROD

Exotic Babylon . . . the land just outside the original Garden . . . the place where war and earthly kings came into existence. To understand Babylon, we must comprehend some important features of the man who started it all. Before Nimrod, there were neither wars nor reigning monarchs. He subjugated all the people of Babylon, which was the entire world population at that time, until they crowned him (Gen. 10:10).[41] Nimrod's ruling territories extended into Assyria. Along with Babylonians, the Assyrians were an ancient civilization that both influenced and troubled God's people.

The Bible tells us that Nimrod was Noah's great-grandson and Ham's grandson; both of whom survived God's judgment of the flood encased within God's ark of protection. The Bible also says that Nimrod was "a mighty hunter"[42] (Gen. 10:9). In his day, Nimrod was a warrior with such extraordinary ability that he had no precedent. It appears that he controlled and conquered everything around him.[43] Nimrod not only was mighty in war, his strength and incredible hunting skills must have provided much meat for the people he desired to rule. From what is known of Nimrod's character, his generous provision of food must have had strings attached; and it must have been a potent negotiating tool for marshalling an army and gathering "loyal" followers. Undoubtedly, this provider must have been elevated in the eyes of his community[44]—at least by those who demonstrated some defiance toward God.

Most Jewish Bible commentators interpret the phrase "a mighty hunter" figuratively.[45] For example, R' Hirsch comments, "Nimrod ensnared men with his words and incited them to rebel against God. He was the forerunner of all hypocrites who drape themselves in robes of piety in order to deceive the masses."[46] Paula A. Price assesses Nimrod's name: "His name designates him as a tyrannical warrior who governed his land with cruelty and rebellion against the Most High God. He was apparently bent on establishing himself as god and instituting religious forms and worship that deposed the Lord God in the minds of His creatures. The name Merodach or Marduk is synonymous with Nimrod and so designates the wild, ruthless hunter as a deity himself. The words for his history, as simply stated in the Bible, refer to one who used violence to profane, pollute, and desecrate the holy and sacred. Nimrod did this by instituting Marduk and Ishtar worship, among many other deities of the Babylonian pantheon. He injected full-scale ritual sexuality and idolatry into the mainstream of human culture. He defiled everything and anything that could be named God and trampled his Creator's covenant under the pollution of sin. Nimrod violated and vilified anything that stood in his way and slaughtered and wounded thousands in building and subduing his kingdoms."[47, 48]

Nimrod's military might was complemented by his architectural acumen, ecclesiastical genius, and political savvy. If God had gifted anyone to impact the world, it was this man. When one analyzes Nimrod's name via Hebrew pictographs and the symbology associated with the letters of his name, we get the message that Nimrod was the first and supreme man to open the door to a massive and mighty spread of chaos.[49] The Jewish sage Ramban notes that Nimrod's generation attempted to "mutilate the shoots," which means they disrupted the unity between God and His creation; therefore, Ramban said it was an appropriate punishment for God to disrupt "their" unity,[50] which was earthy, sensual, and even demonic (James 3:15).

BABEL

Nimrod's first conquest was the ancient city of Babel. The Bible calls Babel "the beginning of Nimrod's kingdom" (Gen. 10:10). Its primitive Hebraic root means to overflow or to mix.[51] This book will zero in on the concept of mixture—the essence of Babylon.[52] It's the place where a group of people began to indiscriminately mix the sacred with the profane. Combining the sacred with the profane brought confusion, which, understandably, is Babel's primary definition.[53]

Nimrod spearheaded mixing the sacred with the profane. He was the mighty leader who first institutionalized idolatry; but it would have been very difficult to introduce and promulgate idolatry in one fell swoop due to the flood still being fresh in the people's minds. Nimrod's generation had living testimonies among them, because Noah and many of his descendants were still alive.

To mix something means to combine or blend two different elements into one mass. At Christmastime, commerce and religion are commingled,[54] which is not always a bad combination; but the comingling of worship and entertainment—the sacred and the sensual—is. My *Webster's Collegiate Dictionary* also defines the word *mix* as crossbreeding, which results in a hybrid. It's an offspring of two different genera that involves crossing two different breeds. In Nimrod's case he mixed the truths of God's sacred kingdom with the lies of Satan's demonic one. *Santa-tizing* focuses its sights on the mixture instituted way back in Babylon. When the Lord tells us: "The mixture of Christmas grieves My heart. Come out of Babylon and lay down Christmas, for I *will* have a pure and spotless Bride," He is giving us a precious glimpse into His heart. This book focuses on the mixture of Christmas, because the Lord has confirmed over and over again the accuracy of this message. Additionally, God emphasized this truth by revealing that "Christmas will be the golden calf of America." The Lord our God does not utter anything insignificant.

Hold onto your hats, folks, and keep an open mind, for our quest is a holy one. I have prayed that our guide is none other than the Holy Spirit. I honestly could not have deciphered the tangled web that Nimrod and company have weaved without the enabling power of the Spirit of the living God.

TO REPEAT CHILDHOOD

Genesis 11:1-9 tells us that the Tower of Babel was on a plain in Shinar. Therefore, Babylon is in Shinar. Although the origin of the word *Shinar*[55] is said to be unknown, the late Reverend Alexander Hislop extrapolates that "Shinar" implies the idea of repeating childhood,[56] so let's explore the concept that Babylon is in the practice of repeating childhood.

Let's acknowledge that being nostalgic is not bad in and of itself. A problem occurs when the emotional pull of anything keeps us from maturing. This is when nostalgia can be unhealthy. The Bible tells us to put away childish ways and move unto perfection (1 Cor. 13:11-13). We cannot put away childish ways if we value them so highly; we refuse to let them go. God's people must hold onto Him tighter than to any other thing in this world. Dr. Neil Chadwick relates: "Often when people call the church looking for financial assistance at Christmastime, they may say, 'It's just not right that the children won't have any Christmas.' Most of the time we associate Christmas with giving presents, especially giving them to children. Yes, Christmas is for children—but we all are children."[57] Kate West, High Priestess of a Wiccan coven in Cheshire, said that: "Many Pagans do celebrate Christmas, but mainly for the children."[58] "Not very much has changed in the way Christmas is celebrated from the way pagans observed the day (under a different name) centuries before the birth of Jesus!"[59]

Natalie Constanza-Chavez's column entitled "Grace notes" speaks about: "If you believe in Santa Claus, he is real." She concludes, "Perhaps God gave us an imagination so things unexplainable and unlikely could live and breathe and feed our soul when we need them most. And so we can teach our children that things unseeable can still be very real and that not every part of us needs to grow up and grow old."[60] Generally speaking, America, as a society, is stuck on not wanting to grow up or old. Our culture is fixated on youth and play. It is in a word "childish" in many ways. Our bumper stickers proclaim, "He who dies with the most toys wins" or "I'd rather be fishing . . . hiking . . . dancing."

Who does not vicariously relive their childhood during the Christmas season? Raise your hands. If we are honest, when someone mentions Christmas, we are flooded with the nostalgia of trimming the Christmas tree, Santa Claus, playing that part in the Christmas pageant, et cetera. If you had Santa Claus amongst your holiday traditions, you probably went to the mall to sit on Santa's lap. You probably wrote a letter to Santa addressed to the North Pole. You probably made out a Christmas wish list. You probably set out milk and cookies for Santa, so he would have enough energy to get gifts to all the children in the world in one magical night. You probably thought you heard sleigh bells before you feel asleep on Christmas Eve, and you probably thought that the best thing about Christmas was waking up on Christmas morning and finding at least one of your best presents under the tree. I can say all this, because I grew up immersed in it all.

I encourage each of us to take into account the question: Who would have a harder time laying down Christmas in your family? Grandparents, parents, or children? By the way, my five-year-old son had no problem whatsoever.

TRYING TO REACH HEAVEN

Babylon was the ancient Mesopotamian city founded by Nimrod. It was originally called Babel or confusion. As even children know, it was the place that the Lord confused words' meanings.[61]

According to Jewish literature,[62] Nimrod was the primary force behind the plan to build a tower of earth that ascended into heaven. To his eventual demise, Nimrod followed in the Father of Lies' footsteps. He tried to be like God and took pride in his own God-given abilities to such an extent that he felt he actually could lead the people's rebellion against God.

The year of the dispersion of the seventy nations from the Tower of Babel has been recorded to be 340 years after the flood. Noah, Shem, Ham, and Japheth were all still alive at this time; and Abraham was forty-eight years old.[63]

We are told that Abraham had already begun to relate to his Creator.[64] "Abraham, the father of the Jews,[65] came from Chaldea and was recognized by the God Most High as one of Babylon's highly trained prophets. He was initially groomed under the Babylonian's supernatural dominance."[66] Historians relate how Abraham originally shared the idolatrous practices of his father;[67] Terah actually manufactured and sold idols.[68] We will get around to that story soon enough. For now, let's journey back to the Tower of Babel and the dispersion.

All the people of the earth, which became the national families, were concentrated in present-day Iraq. They all spoke one language. The Hebrew sages call the "one language" the holy tongue, by which the world was said to be created.[69]

It seems ludicrous to us that these people, who spoke the holy tongue and who had firsthand witnesses of the flood among them, could rationalize a way to bypass God's control. The period when Nimrod lived was a time when the patriarchal faith was still fresh due to the cataclysmic deluge. God must have seemed very near to the earth. The grand aim of those who loved God and had the best interests of the human race in mind was to maintain the union between heaven and earth (keep it as close as possible). I know that this is my aim today as well. The maintaining of any union between heaven and earth caused an implicit restraint from pleasures of sin, which every carnal, natural mind craves. Those who chose to be alienated from God and godliness felt the convicting presence of heaven, and its influence was intolerably near. They had no freedom to walk after "the lust of the flesh and the lust of the eyes and the boastful pride of life" (1 John 2:16 NASU). From this "bondage" Nimrod emancipated people. By the apostasy he introduced and the "free" life he developed, Nimrod helped put God and the strict spirituality of His law at a distance; and thus, he became the "elevator of the heavens," making men feel and act as if heaven was far off from earth, as if the God of heaven and earth was not able to see.[70] "Have you seen what the elders of the house of Israel are doing in the darkness, each at the shrine of his own idol? They say, 'The LORD does not see us; the LORD has forsaken the land'" (Ezek. 8:12).

Amazing as it may seem, many people turned away from their Creator to Nimrod and their own self-aggrandizement and power. The capacity for man to sin should never be underestimated, but always remember that the Bible says: "where sin increased, grace increased all the more" (Rom. 5:20).

Man's capacity for self-deception in the face of cold hard facts could have begun in Babylon. The Hebrew word that speaks of deception or betrayal is *ree-mah*; its word picture tells us that deception and/or betrayal comes from the man of chaos.[71] Recall that Nimrod was the first and supreme man to open the door to a massive and mighty spread of chaos. "Yes, they knew God, but they wouldn't worship him as God or even give him thanks. And they began to think up foolish ideas of what God was like. The result was that their minds became dark and confused. Claiming to be wise, they became utter fools instead. And instead of worshiping the glorious ever-living God, they worshiped idols made to look like mere people, or birds and animals and snakes. So God let them go ahead and do whatever shameful things their hearts desired. As a result, they did vile and degrading things with each other's bodies. *Instead of believing what they knew was the truth about God, they deliberately chose to believe lies.* So they worshiped the things God made, but not the Creator himself, who is praised forever, Amen" (Rom. 1:21-25 NLT, emphasis mine).

This capacity for self-deception in the face of cold hard facts should not astonish us. It is one of the oldest sins in the Book. When humans turn from God, we typically negate reality according to our own choosing and try to build false substance around an illusion that we'd like to be true. By the end of section I, you should be able to recognize the elements of deception, manipulation, and idolatry with regard to Christmas. Deception is usually self-chosen; but sometimes it is generational, especially when it comes to traditions. We will get more to this subject later in chapter 5.

The Bible says that the people of Babel exerted a tremendous amount of energy building a tower of bricks[72]—lest they be disbursed. What they feared actually happened. When God descended to examine the deeds of man, He was not uninformed prior to His descent. God's descent speaks of Him coming to earth as a judge. He observed man's condition and then rendered a verdict that would facilitate a culture of life. Our God is a God of life, not death. The Hebrew word for "judge" is *dan*,[73] and its word picture communicates that the judge is the door of life.

Remember that man is created in the image of God. Twice in Bible times, when men forfeited their own image of God by denying His existence, people's temperaments and character changed dramatically, where men began to act no better than animals. The first time man exchanged the image of God for an image like corruptible man was "in the generations of Enosh, when people began making idols and call them gods. The second time was when people built the Tower of Babel and tried to gain mastery over the human race and to dispense with God."[74]

God articulates over and over again: "Be holy, because I am holy" (Lev. 11:44-45; 19:2; 20:7; 1 Pet. 1:16). Many believers tell me that we can never attain God's holiness, which our natural eyes seem to testify as true. But if we truly walk by faith, not by sight, we need to take God at His Word. When He says: "Be holy as I am holy," He means it.

The Tower of Babel was a satanically-inspired man-made effort to counterfeit the mountain of God. When Satan was cast out of heaven, he built his own mountain to be like God, which is "the mount of assembly in the recesses of the north" (Isa. 14:12-13 NASB). Satan's polluted city is on top of his profane mountain, and it's called Mystery Babylon where the Antichrist is revealed, where one reaps corruption, where one eats with demons, where one hordes wealth, where one hates God and his brother, where one is a slave to sin, where one walks according to the flesh, where one abides by the law of sin and death, and where the spirit of the world dwells.⁷⁵ It's the mountain that corrupted man still tries to climb.

God's spiritual mountain is beautiful in elevation, the joy of the whole earth—Mount Zion (Ps. 48:1-2). The city of the Great King—the New Jerusalem—is on top of the mountain of God. This is a place of holiness where the Messiah is revealed, where one reaps eternal life, where one eats with God, where one shares wealth, where one loves God and his brother, where one is a slave of righteousness, where one walks according to the Spirit, where one abides by the law of life in Christ Jesus, and where the Spirit of God dwells.

COME OUT OF BABYLON

The first time God's people came out of Babylon, they had been trying to make a name for themselves. The next time God's people will endeavor to display His glorious name through presenting their bodies as a living and holy sacrifices (Rom. 12:1). The next time the people of God come out of Babylon, they also will have one heart and one mind; but this time, unlike the first time, God's people will truly be set on loving the Lord our God with all their heart, all their soul, and all their strength. This bridal company will be one with a common purpose to make God's name great—totally surrendering all to Him and His kingdom ways. Coming out of Babylon in this kingdom day will result in bringing the One New Man (Jew and Gentile) in the Messiah together.⁷⁶ To do this, we will have to forsake all, but the Lord; and then He will, incredibly and wondrously, make heaven and earth His people's oyster. We will be able to scale celestial heights united with Him. We will have boundless, even creative, potential in the domain God has given man—the earth and all that is in it.

This corporate reality probably won't be made manifest for some time, but the option of fully uniting in love with our Beloved is available to us, individually, right now. Christians sing: "All for Jesus . . . our precious Jesus."⁷⁷ Do we really mean it?

THE SOURCE OF SUN WORSHIP

In keeping with the Lord's statement: "Come out of Babylon and lay down Christmas," we should find that Babylon is where sun worship originated. Antiquity reveals that December twenty-fifth was reserved to celebrate the sun god's birthday throughout the world;[78] and as modern-day Americans know, it is also the date we celebrate Christmas. Although the twenty-fifth no longer designates midwinter, due to the Roman shift to our Western calendar, we will see later how it still retains its "glory" as the birth date of the sun gods. In chapter 5, we will delve into sun gods and their association with December twenty-fifth in greater detail. But for now, let's concentrate on the seat of early sun worship, which was in the ancient city of Chaldea.[79]

Nimrod founded the four oldest cities of the world: Babel (Babylonia), Erech (Uruk), Accad (Akkad), and Calneh (Nippur). Corporately, they all made up the land of Shinar (Gen. 10:10), which is a code name for ancient Babylonia.[80] The ancient city in the southern region of Babylonia, which came to be considered Babylon, was called Chaldea. That's why, for clarity's sake, one can substitute "Chaldea" for "Babylonia" when we read Scripture; but when the Bible designates "Chaldea," it is more precisely pointing out the place where sun god worship and its associated land of merchants status originated.

Chaldea arose from Sumeria and biblical Accad.[81] It was the place where sun worship was first prevalent. Couple this with the fact that Nimrod's deific name, Marduk,[82] was known as the Assyrian/Babylonian sun god,[83] and we can extrapolate that sun worship began in Babylon. I know that when the Lord says, "Come out of Babylon and lay down Christmas," God is revealing that Babylon is at the root of our Christmas worship.

Therefore, the first people-approved earthly king, Nimrod, initiated exchanging the glory of the immortal God for an image made to look like mortal man. In this case, the mortal man was Nimrod. The image he made was an image of self displayed as Marduk: What a picture of the kingdom of self being perpetuated by a prideful man.

THE SUN GOD AND HIS SACRED BULL

My aim in this section is to produce a good case for Nimrod being the original sun god and his deification being given the recognizable form of a sacred bull, so the spiritual force he represented did not seem so abstract to the masses. This same idea of a sacred bull was associated with the Roman and late Hellenistic solar cult of Mithras. In chapter 5, you'll see that Mithra's Winter Festival is the most immediate predecessor of our modern Christmas day celebration. We will also investigate the history of the sacred bull (specifically the Apis) to lay some groundwork for it being the forerunner of the golden calf.

The worship of the sun and the sacred bull were the most widespread cults throughout the ancient world. A revered animal in Egypt was considered to be the incarnation of a particular god; therefore, the sun god and the sacred bull were synonymous. I believe that it makes the most sense that their origins began with Nimrod before the dispersion at the Tower of Babel. There is constant confusion between pagan gods and their associated sacred animals. Confusion and mixture is Babylon's modus operandi. Confusion comes from being concentrated in Babylon.

Remember that Nimrod was the first earthly king, who opened the door to the colossal spread of chaos throughout the then-known world. Additionally, remember that the deific name of Nimrod was Marduk (i.e., biblical Merodach). The ruins of the ancient city of Babylon speak of fifty-five chapels dedicated to its patron deity.[84] Consider that Marduk assumed fifty names.[85] Talk about confusing! Earthly, sensual gods were given different names and different forms to represent their different facets. For instant, in Egypt, the sun god was spoken of as a beetle, and the sun was described as his (the sun god's) eye. In one sentence in immediate sequence the sun god is spoken of as Re, Khepre, Horus, etc.[86]

The oldest civilization that our Bible primarily discusses beyond Babylon is Egypt. Egypt is actually a metaphor for the world or slavery. Its land is named after the patriarch of Nimrod's clan—Ham. Let us take a deeper look into the land of Ham to decode the mystery of the sun god and the sacred bull. To the Egyptian there was no god of higher standing than the sun god. Under the name of Ptah, the sun god was regarded as the apostate sole creator and ruler of the world. The sun god often was addressed as a bull.[87] The oldest and most popular object of worship in Egypt was probably the sacred bull called the Apis.[88] Mankind has not been able to trace why Apis attained such an honor.[89]

Assuming Nimrod is the original sun god seems to explain what is otherwise confusing and inexplicable: "The ancients believed that the powerful bull represented the personality of the king"[90] — the first earthly king was Nimrod. It is recorded that Nimrod wore bull's horns, which is the predecessor of our modern crowns. Also, note that the first idolatrous "Bel" or "Baal,"[91] which means owner or lord, was originally identified as the sun.[92]

Marduk was given the epithet Bel (i.e., Baal). He created a new world order. He also informed the assembly of gods that the center of the cosmos was Babylon.[93] The *1911 Encyclopedia* identifies Marduk as the patron deity of Babylon with the original character of a solar deity.[94] Some sources define Marduk's name to mean either the "bull calf of the sun"[95] or "the solar calf."[96]

It often has been held that the golden calf worshiped by the Israelites was an imitation of the worship of the Apis bull of Memphis, Egypt. I believe this is a correct assumption. The *Encyclopaedia Biblica* states that only living bulls were worshiped, but that statement appears to be incorrect.[97] A sacred Apis bull was identified by distinct markings: The black calf had a white diamond shape on its forehead, an image of an eagle on its back, double the number of hairs on its tail, and a scarab mark under its tongue.[98] Once a bull was proclaimed to be a god incarnate, it was taken to the temple compound where it was purified, fed the best foods, and then given a herd of extremely fine cows.[99] In Egypt, the first Apis bull was considered to be an incarnation of the sun god Ptah, symbolizing the creator of the universe and a master of destiny. Thus, it was believed that in Apis dwelt the soul of Ptah.[100] Later the Apis became widely known as the incarnation of the sun god Osiris.[101]

Only one bull was considered to be to be a sacred Apis at a time. If one of these bulls died, the Egyptians believers held that sun god transferred himself to another bull, and therefore, the Apis lived anew.[102] Any new Apis was transported to Memphis on a boat housed in a specially built golden cabin.[103] While alive, the kings of Egypt worshiped the Apis by providing for them in every way with great sumptuousness and cost.[104]

The grandiose extended to the Apis in death. When an Apis bull died, his body was embalmed and entombed with great ceremony that usually would be afforded to royalty.[105] Reverence for these Apis bull tombs were carried so far that the dead oxen had even funerary figures to work for them in the next world.[106] At Apis's death, the pious wore mourning garments and ate nothing but vegetables and water for sixty days till his burial was accomplished.[107]

When the Apis bull was embalmed, it had artificial eyes inserted. In addition, its horns and face were significantly gilded or covered with a gold leaf mask. It then was covered with a shroud.[108] In death, the Apis mummy was given all the formalities due a deity. Alive, an Apis bull was conveyed to its sanctuary in a golden cabin; in death, his head was coated with gold. I wonder where those Israelites, who came out of Egypt, got their idolatrous idea for a golden calf.

BY BABYLON'S SORCERY

Chaldea was not only the seat of earliest sun worship, but it was also the primordial center of sorcery: "For all the nations were deceived by your sorcery" (Rev. 18:23 NASB). The definition for *sorcery* to which I will be referring is stated in *The Prophet's Dictionary:* "The practice of manipulating creation, humans, or events to provoke manifestations of what is desired by the occultist."[109]

The title "Chaldeans" was used for Babylonian experts in divination and magic, and its label goes way back to early Babylonia, if not further. They were the highest priestly caste of the ancient pagan world. Their superior occultic powers and mysterious knowledge were famous throughout the ancient world. Chaldeans were renowned for sophisticated systems of divination; they used various manipulative means of accessing supernatural knowledge, like: omens, augury, dream interpretation, spell binding and casting, horoscopy, and sorcery. "Magic was their main divinatory tool. The Chaldean mindset was set toward nature worship. How it operated and its times and seasons of operation were essential to the success of their magic formulae."[110]

"Magic includes sorcery, witchcraft, incantations, enchantments, wizardry, spells and spell casting, and demonism of all kinds."[111] During the 2007 Christmas season, the ABC Family TV channel kicked off its twenty-five days of Christmas with three Harry Potter movies. The first one was entitled: *Harry Potter and the Sorcerer's Stone*. It was advertised as the magic of Christmas.[112] Practitioners of magic claim that there are two types: white magic and black magic. White magic is supposed to be harmless, while black magic is harmful. Harmless white magic seems to coincide with little white lies, like: Old St. Nick putting his finger to the side of his nose and up the chimney he goes, or Santa knowing who is naughty or nice, or his eight flying reindeer. On the surface white magic appears innocent (even though they are lies) until one realizes that the operation and object of the two are essentially the same. The only difference is the varying degrees of manipulation for both aims at using the supernatural for purely selfish reasons. Their object is to use people. Their operation takes what is not given to conjure up what is not earned. They seek to influence a person through oppressive or coercive actions,[113] and for this reason alone, magic can be classified as harmful to those controlled.

The Battle for Christmas makes a profound case for how Santa Claus, the Christmas tree, and gift-giving traditions were brought into America's culture to control people's beliefs and, therefore, their behavior. Control and manipulation were used to intimidate the raucous elements of American society. Prior to the introduction of Santa Claus or the Christmas trees as pervasive fundamental practices, Christmas was a rowdy carnival celebration. It was reminiscent of our modern-day Halloween in many ways. Hallmarks of the carnival Christmas included: lawlessness (i.e., inversion of the social order); aggressive, sometimes threatening, begging; clamorous noise; and much alcohol with its accompanying vices. It should come as no surprise that when one digs deep enough into the founts of Christmas, the Mardi Gras (i.e., carnival) spirit is at its root. The carnival Christmas was the norm in America and Western Europe prior to the 1820s, and it was ruled by the Lord of Misrule.[114]

The Lord of Misrule was appointed on All Hallow's Eve (October 31) for the Christmas to come. Known also as the "Master of Merry Disport," "Abbot of Unreason," and "Christmas King." The man acting as the Lord of Misrule was the personification of the spirit of disorder, fun, and merriment. This jester was the principle ingredient in the medieval celebration of Christmas. This servant-made-king was a recreation of the purple robed Mock King from Babylon, which Roman society adopted in their Saturnalia and the Roman Church parodied in their Feast of Fools.[115]

Even though our modern-day Christmas celebration became domesticated during the 1820s to 1840s, the spirit of lawlessness remains part of Christmas, for it is the Lord of Misrule's holy day, as many of its fruits attest. Christmas always has been a holiday of excess. Evidence is produced by merely looking at our own households and the selfish, greedy, and spoilt dispositions Christmas encourages within our own children and grandchildren. Christmas merely morphed into a supposedly better and acceptable form. Instead of an outward societal endorsement of carnival, Christmas turned inward toward the home and children. Materialism, consumerism, and domestication appeared as its new fruit, which seemed to look all good and well on the surface; but in reality, Christmas became domesticated because the wealthy men of New York City (i.e., patricians) wanted to stop the poor from hassling them during the winter holiday season, so they instituted Santa Claus.[116] In actuality, we can see more clearly the most ancient shamanistic (i.e., witchcraft) roots of the Lord of Misrule through his newly cast image of Santa. More on this subject will be revealed later. Just mentally check for now that since the fourth century, when the grossly sensual roots of Christmas periodically got out of hand, efforts were made by the religious and some non-religious to sanitize it.

Basically, these patricians subtly manipulated the poorer masses with a charming emotional cocktail of Old Saint Nick, his eight tiny reindeer, and stockings hung by the chimney with care. These wealthy men wanted to keep the masses from intimidating them once a year, so they turned the tables by shifting popular culture to make their rowdy carnival tradition outmoded. The raucous masses were unsettled when the wealthy forged Christmas into a renewed façade of tranquility. Children replaced the poor as Christmas's primary focus.

According to the social historian Nissenbaum, the Christmas tree tradition is a direct outgrowth from parents being concerned over putting children at the center of Christmas. We are told that the Christmas tree tradition came to America through several possible sources. Ultimately, the Christmas tree was brought to the domesticated Christmas to manipulate the behavior of children at Christmastime. As a side note, Santa Claus was, and still is, used to manipulate children's behavior too. Remember, he knows if you are naughty or nice. With the introduction of the Christmas tree in America, the focus of Christmas was supposed to shift from the children to the tree.

Unbeknownst to most Christians, the evergreen element returns us full circle to Christmas' original root. Today, the ancient idol of a tree is the most common Christmas symbol in America. With much satisfaction, we erect the beautifully adorned images in our homes, businesses, schools, churches, and town squares. In antiquity, a fir, palm, or evergreen tree were used in conjunction with celebrating various pagan sun gods' birthdays, which I just mentioned fell on the ancient winter solstice—December 25.

Just as Santa cannot hide Christmas's commercial root, so our beautiful Christmas trees cannot hide its idolatrous root. Note that the commercial segment of Christmas is connected to political Babylon while the idolatrous part is linked to religious Babylon. Our seemingly joyful and harmless celebration of Christ's birth is more than what we have assumed it to be. Christ's birth is biblical, and therefore, to be honored. But as you will discover—historically and biblically—Christ is definitely not the reason for the Christmas season. Recently, Christians have heard many cases against Christmas and have brushed these "attacks" off as mere secular hogwash. Truly, the quickest way to find out if the church is off in any area is to ask anyone outside of it. The reality is . . . the integrity of our Christian message has been compromised. Every other group seems to be able to see our hypocrisy before we do. Blindness has a way of keeping people from seeing. Thank God that the veil is taken away whenever anyone turns to the Lord (2 Cor. 3:16). Christians are no bigger hypocrites than anyone else, but don't you think that we should cleanse our hands and our hearts from anything that grieves the Lord's heart? This book is a clarion call for Christians to put on our thinking caps and reexamine the Christian significance of Christmas. A sincere examination will require intellectual honesty.

Revelation 18 tells us that Babylon will be thrown down with violence, and it will no longer be found. Translation: Its roots of sun worship, sorcery, and manipulative merchandising will come to a painful end sooner or later. "And the light of a lamp will not shine in you any longer; and the voice of the bridegroom and bride will not be heard in you any longer; for your merchants were the great men of the earth, because all the nations were deceived by your sorcery" (Rev. 18:23 NASB). Our heavenly Bridegroom will bring His Bride out of Babylon by her consent. Any form of exploitation is not acceptable for God's people.

ABRAHAM'S BAPTISM OF FIRE

Let's explore a couple stories that include our old friend Nim (i.e., Nimrod). Through them, we hopefully will get a clearer picture about the roots of Babylon and the various mysteries that flow from its idolatrous fountain.

Remember that Nimrod, the first earthly monarch, was the primary force behind the rebellion at the Tower of Babel. Nimrod was also the man other idolaters went to for help. Godly people probably consulted Noah, Shem, or Abraham.

In Genesis 11:28, it says Abraham's brother Haran died in the lifetime of his father Terah. The Hebrew sage Rashi translates verse 28 as Haran died in the presence of his father. This phrase signifies that Haran died "because of" Terah. As we have already observed, Terah was a manufacturer and seller of idols. He complained to Nimrod that his son, Abraham, had smashed his wares. When King Nimrod had Abraham thrown into a fiery furnace, Haran was challenged to choose sides between Abraham and Nimrod.[117] By all natural accounts, death appeared to be swallowing Abraham up in the fire. Haran was afraid to choose sides, so he decided to wait until he saw who came out victorious. His choice was between the physically strong and seemingly all-powerful Nimrod and his spiritually-attuned brother, who followed in the righteous footsteps of those who survived the flood.

When Abraham was miraculously saved from the furnace, many moons before Shadrach, Meshach, and Abendego,[118] Haran sided with his brother, whereupon the furious Nimrod had Haran thrown in the furnace, and he died. Rashi notes that Haran defied Nimrod, not because he believed in the God of Abraham, but because he expected a miracle; therefore, he was unworthy of one. Thus Haran died in *Ur Kasdim*, which literally means the fire of the land of Kasdim (i.e., Chaldea or Babylon).

SHEM ON NIM

There has been a battle between good and evil since Adam and Eve's fall. During our stay on earth, every person is the object of a struggle between the forces of holiness and evil. Evil's hold over Nimrod is quite apparent. Probably the most well-known story about him deals with his demise. Nimrod's body was chopped up into pieces and sent throughout the land as a warning to anyone who would follow in Nimrod's footsteps.

Much of what I relate in this section comes from several sources, but I want to acknowledge the incredible work of the late Reverend Alexander Hislop entitled: *The Two Babylons*. It is a challenging, yet very rewarding, study on Babylon in the world and in the church. Please refer to *The Two Babylons* for a much more extensive study on the following subject. I have rewritten[119] those parts of *The Two Babylons* that I feel is necessary to understand the Babylonian (pagan) roots of Christmas . . . so stick with me as we partake of this small slice of history of Babylon and beyond.

"According to an ancient Jewish tradition, it was Noah's righteous son Shem, who slew Nimrod and scattered his body parts throughout the land of Shinar."[120] Shem was one of the eight people on Noah's ark from whom "the nations spread out over the earth after the flood" (Gen. 10:32). Abraham was a direct descendant of Shem. Shem was 390 years old when Terah became the father of Abram, Nahor, and Haran (Gen. 11:10-26). This was nine generations after the flood. Shem was still alive. Shem's lifespan was for a full half of a millennium—500 years—with the first 98 of those years being before the flood.

Scripture is silent as to how Nimrod actually died, but in the following account you will see that the primitive Egyptian Hercules overcoming giants remarkably coincides with the death of Osiris, which also maps back to Nimrod being killed by Shem. As a side note, the ordinary way in which the favorite Egyptian divinity Osiris was mystically represented was in the form of a young bull or calf—the Apis calf—from which the golden calf of the Israelites was borrowed. The golden calf seems to be the anchoring knot that allows Christmas and Babylon to be woven together. Osiris in Egypt and Nimrod in Babylon are one and the same, with some slight cultural differences and mutations added to the mix. Osiris was celebrated as the strong chief of the buildings. This strong chief of the buildings originally was worshiped in Egypt with every physical characteristic of Nimrod. Nimrod, as the son of Cush, was a black man. There was a tradition in Egypt, recorded by Plutarch, that "Osiris was black," which, in a land where the general complexion was dusky, must have implied something more than ordinary in its darkness."[121] Also, we find that Osiris was arrayed in a leopard's skin or spotted dress—an indispensable part of the sacred robes of his high priest—which identifies Osiris with Nimrod. Nimrod was recorded to have worn bull's horns and a leopard skin.

Let's take a look at Shem and the ancient tale of the Egyptian Hercules. One of the names of the primitive Hercules in Egypt was *Sem*.[122] This most ancient Egyptian Hercules was known as having "by the power of the gods" (i.e., the Spirit of the Lord God Almighty) fought against and overcome giants. The pagans later gave Hercules erroneous homage as the grand deliverer or Messiah, and stigmatized Hercules' adversary as the giants who rebelled against heaven. The real giants alluded to in the primitive Egyptian story of Hercules were Nimrod and his party, who actually rebelled against heaven. The "giants" were just the "mighty ones" of whom Nimrod was leader.[123]

If Sem or Shem was the primitive Hercules, who overcame the giants not by mere physical force but by "the power of God" (the influence of the Holy Spirit), it entirely agrees with his character. Moreover, it remarkably agrees with the Egyptian account of the death of Osiris. The Egyptians say that the grand enemy of their god did not overcome him with open violence, but he obtained power to put Osiris (i.e., Nimrod) to death from seventy-two of the leading men of Egypt. Seventy-two represented the Egyptian judicial system of the time. It was just the number of the judges (both civil and sacred) who, according to Egyptian law, were required to determine the punishment of one found guilty of such a high offense. In determining such a case, two tribunals were necessary. First, there were thirty ordinary judges who had the power of life and death; then there was a tribunal—over and above—consisting of forty-two judges. The forty-two determined whether a body should be buried or not when anyone was condemned to die. In Egypt, everyone had to pass the ordeal of this forty-two-judge tribunal after death. As burial was refused Osiris, both tribunals would be concerned; and thus, there would be exactly seventy-two persons that condemned him to die and to be cut into pieces. The great opponent of the idolatrous system convinced these judges as to the enormity of Osiris's transgression. Both Egyptian tribunals gave up Osiris to an awful death and to ignominy after it as a terror to anyone who might tread in his steps afterwards. They cut Osiris's dead body into pieces and sent the dismembered parts to the different cities of the kingdom. This story parallels the Levite's concubine story in Judges 19:29. He cut her dead body into pieces and then sent a severed part to each of the twelve tribes. It is also similar to a step taken by Saul when he chopped two yoke of oxen asunder and sent them throughout all the coasts of his kingdom. Commentators admit that both the Levite and Saul acted on a patriarchal custom where vengeance would be dealt to those who failed to come to the gathering when they were summoned in such a way. Saul fearfully declared vengeance in so many words when the parts of the slaughtered oxen were sent among the tribes: "Whosoever cometh not forth after Saul and after Samuel, so shall it be done to his oxen" (1 Sam. 11:7). In like manner, when the dismembered parts of Osiris were sent among the cities by the seventy-two supreme judges of the kingdom ("conspirators" according to the Mysteries[124]), it was equivalent to a solemn declaration in their name that whosoever should do as Osiris had done, so should it be done to him—he would also be cut to pieces.

When the idolatrous system arose again, but in secret as the "Mysteries of Egypt," the leader of the Egyptian tribunals was stigmatized as Typho—the Evil One. Egyptian expert Wilkinson admits that while different individuals have bore this hated name in Egypt, one of the most noted names by which Typho was known was Seth.[125] Shem seems to have been known in Egypt as Typho, not only under the name of Seth, but also under his own name. The names Seth and Shem are alike, both signifying "the appointed one."[126]

Egypt is known as the land of Ham in the Bible. Mizraim is the also the scriptural name of the land of Egypt, being derived from the name of Ham's son (Gen. 10:6). According to this Egyptian story in the land of Ham, Ham's brother Shem persuaded the judges (tribunal courts) to kill Nimrod—Ham's apostate grandson. Ham's lack of honor toward his father (Gen. 9:22) caused not only his son Canaan to be cursed, but also made his descendants more susceptible to sin. Perhaps that is a root to the reason why Egypt is scripturally equated with worldliness and the deeds of the flesh, like idolatry, witchcraft, et cetera. But still, both Shem and Ham were actual eyewitnesses to the flood and the forging of the Noahiac Covenant (Gen. 6:9-9:19).

Consider this: History teaches that an absolute monarch governed Babylonia, which means that the king was active as legislator, judge, administrator, and warlord.[127] So . . . if Nimrod was an absolute monarch, how did Egypt not only get to judge the Babylonian king, but also execute vengeance against such a mighty one? I have a hypothesis. At Babel, all nations were one nation under God and indivisible—until the rebellion. What if? Could it be possible that the seventy-two "Egyptian" judges were actually something like a world court? Could seventy of the tribunal representatives have come from the seventy nations documented as having scattered from Babel and the remaining two judges were Shem and Ham? It's just a theory. There is the problem with getting the people with different languages to understand one another. But all these nations would have understood who was responsible for the scattering of the nations. They could have wanted to see justice served for this egregious error. Justice facilitated through the righteous leader of then-known civilized world—Shem.

As an example as how the various Mysteries throughout the earth flow from Babylon, we can follow the death of Nimrod, which is also the Egyptian Osiris, into Greek mythology. The myth that makes Adonis perish by the tusks of a wild boar is unraveled when one understands that a "tusk" is regarded as a horn according to the symbolism of idolatry. The boar's tusks were the symbol of spiritual power. Nimrod wore bull's horns as a symbol of his physical power; therefore, a tusk or a "horn in the mouth" means the power in the mouth. In other words, it's the power of persuasion—the very power with which *Sem*, the primitive Hercules was endowed—this is how Adonis (equivalent to Nimrod) perished. What a beautiful illustration of the persuasive power of the Holy Spirit, which enabled Shem, and those on his side, to withstand the tide of evil when it was rushing in upon the world like a flood.[128]

I can cite example after example to show you how all the world's Mysteries have come from Babylon. Today, God is calling Gideon's army. He is calling those who will withstand this current tide of evil rushing in upon our world in our day, and we must go to the root of the problem, which the Bible earmarks as the corrupt system of Babylon.

SEMIRIAMIS—THE FIRST BABYLONIAN QUEEN OF HEAVEN

Our buddy Nimrod founded Babylon. He founded man-made governments based on a viciously competitive economic system. Although the great apostasy Nimrod started morphed and existed in various forms through numerous cultures throughout time, its final form can be reviewed in the book of Revelation in chapters 17 and 18 (religious and political Babylon).

Nimrod had a wife, Semiramis, who was exalted alongside her influential husband. Truth be told, Semiramis probably had as much personal ambition as Nimrod. As you have just witnessed, the ringleader of the rebellion against God met with a violent death. He was cut into pieces, and parts of him were sent as a warning throughout the then-known world. The various Mysteries testify to these facts through their legends, which are sometimes also called traditions. After Nimrod's fateful death, Semiramis[129, 130] had to create a scheme so she could retain her exalted position. She began to lie, and were they whoppers! She told anyone willing to listen to her that Nimrod had actually chosen willingly to die for all mankind. Not only did Nimrod willingly sacrifice his body, but he had come back from the dead in the form of her son—Tammuz. Semiramis told the world that Nimrod had been reincarnated in Tammuz through her own immaculate conception. Almost too close for comfort. Isn't it? What did Lucifer see before he fell? He lived in eternity with God, outside of time and space. Lucifer must have been able to see into time and space, for many false marks that mimic the Messiah can be tracked throughout paganism centuries before Christ came to earth.

The mother-child cult grew up out of Semiramis's immaculate conception lie. We will go into more detail in chapter 5. Let's note for now that the pagan mother-child cult has been consistently represented as a woman holding a baby son in her arms—the Madonna and child. This cult, which originated in Babel, justified the worship of Semiramis as the first mother goddess by saying the work of redemption (manifested through Tammuz—the begotten son) could not have been accomplished without her. Therefore, Semiramis was elevated, by self and man, to the status of "deity" and given the title of "The Virgin Mother."

YULETIDE SEASON

There were many rituals and symbols that accompanied the mother-child cult of antiquity (an integral part of religious Babylon) included was the Yule log tradition. It is no mere coincidence that the burning of the Yule log was at one time one of the most well-established traditions of Christmas.[131]

Before we hop out of the Babylonian frying pan into the Yuletide fire, let's understand the word *Yule*.[132] In the ancient Chaldean language of Babylon, the word *Yule* is the name for an infant or little child.[133, 134] Therefore, the very name by which Christmas is also known—Yule-day or the Yuletide season—is literally linked to its

Babylonian origin. Far and wide, in the realms of ancient paganism, the birth of the son of the Babylonian Queen of Heaven was celebrated at the time of midwinter (i.e., the winter solstice), which in antiquity equated to the date of December twenty-fifth.[135] Take for example how the twenty-fifth of December was called "Yule-day" by the pagan Anglo-Saxons long before they came in contact with Christianity.[136] Remnants of this ancient root are still evident in the Nordic people of Norway and Sweden. They declare: "God Jul" (pronounced *good yewl* or *good yeul*,) when they say the equivalent to Merry Christmas.

Part of the birth celebration of the original Babylonian Queen of Heaven's son consisted of bringing in a Yule log on December twenty-fourth. The Yule log symbolized Nimrod being cut down in the prime of his life and in the height of his power, then cut into pieces and burned.[137] The Yule log ceremony celebrated the sun during the winter solstice.[138] The word *solstice* comes from the word *sun*, and it means to "stand still" as it appears to do on the shortest day of the year as the sun gets nearest to the southern horizon.[139] The date of December twenty-fifth was designated the highest holy day of the pagan year, because it was originally associated with the mother-child cult. Still today, one of the eight Wiccan/Pagan holidays is called Yule, and it celebrates the shortest day of the year.[140] The southernmost descent of the sun on the ancient calendar was said to portray the death of Nimrod, while the coming back of the sun portrayed his rebirth.

The Yule log was such an integral part of Christmas for centuries upon centuries that it's hard to understand why it's virtually nonexistent in the United States today.[141] As recently as the nineteenth century, bringing the Yule log in was as much a part of Christmas as putting up an evergreen tree is today.[142]

Everything to do with Yule logs was fraught with pagan rituals and superstitions. As a side, please note that "superstition has occult principles at the core."[143] "While superstition is defined by the dictionary as an 'irrational belief,' when we connect it with an ungodly supernatural belief system it becomes occult superstition."[144] Please recall that Babylon (specifically Chaldea) was the primordial center of sorcery. This means that superstition was, and is, an occultic system to its core. Babylonian systems have been inspired by Satan, because the god of this world controls any unbiblical spiritual practice, including superstitions. Satan gets empowered in our own lives through our beliefs. It is no mere marketing ploy when advertisers and greeting card artists tout "believe" in Santa; there is a deeper spiritual root behind it. We will discuss this issue later.

Let's concentrate, for now, on superstitions practiced through the Yule log tradition. Please pay attention to words like: misfortune, luck, talisman, and omen. On December twenty-fourth, an enormous freshly cut log would be brought from outside into the house with great ceremony.[145] The first Yule log *superstition* involves believing that one's Yule log should never be bought.[146] *Lucky* ones were obtained from one's own land or from a neighbor.[147] The master of the house placed the Yule log in the hearth, followed by *making libations* by sprinkling the wood with oil, salt, and mulled wine, accompanied by suitable prayers.[148] (By the way, making libations is considered to be an act of worship, which is forbidden by the second commandment [Exod. 20:3-6]. Please refer to the section in chapter 5 called "An Idol in the Form Of" for more information.) To light the Yule log, one had to catch fire to the log in the first attempt or else it was considered a *bad omen* for the year ahead.[149] It was a *sign of misfortune* coming to the family.[150] Once the log was lit, it had to be kept burning for twelve hours a day throughout the twelve days of Christmas; otherwise, *bad luck* would visit the household.[151] This was not always easy, for it was forbidden to tend the Yule log during the lengthy festive supper on December twenty-fourth, so caution and much effort went into preventing this mishap.

We should note that the ancient Egyptians got their rebirth of the sun celebrations from Babylon. They set the length of the festival at twelve days to reflect the twelve months or divisions of the sun calendar.[152] Additionally, in AD 567 Christians officially co-opted the twelve-day midwinter festival. Roman Catholic leaders proclaimed the twelve days from December 25 to Epiphany a "sacred" festive season.[153]

As the Yule log burned, the people told ghost stories.[154] Funny how the people hoped to keep evil spirits away by burning the Yule log,[155] yet they told ghost stories, which brought them near.

In the Greek culture, there is the story of the *Kallikantzaroi*[156]—ugly monsters of chaos—who are forced underground most of the year; but during the twelve days of Christmas, the demons are said to roam freely on the earth's surface. Once again, we find that the Greeks held to the superstitious practice of keeping their Christmas logs burning to scare evil spirits away.[157]

Not only did the superstitious people tell ghost stories as they were futilely trying to scare evil spirits away, they also scrutinized the shadows cast by the fire. Any headless shadow was supposed to foretell a person's death. Doesn't this sound like Halloween? For several years now, I've noticed that Christmas merchandise has been mixed with Halloween paraphernalia in most stores. Spiritually speaking, this gives us a clue. Additionally, several years ago, I drove past a local psychic's storefront every day on my way to and from school. As I prayed for her one day, the Lord told me to pay attention to how she decorates for the holidays. I was amazed that Psychic Kay decorated more for Christmas than for Halloween, followed by every major holiday except Thanksgiving. My observations remarkably coincide with Disneyland's Haunted Mansion's Nightmare Before Christmas ride, which cleverly combines Christmas and Halloween.

Today, the Yule log has transformed itself. It has become something sweet, just like other Christmas traditions. It's a pastry called the French Christmas cake or *Buche de Noel* to be exact. This delicious sponge cake is rolled up and decorated to look like a Yule log. In France, this scrumptious *buche de noel* takes part in the French Christmas eve meal called *reveillon*, which takes place after midnight mass.[158] Christians would do well to remember that part of the idolatrous mother-child worship consisted of the burning of logs, the pouring out of libations, and the making of cakes for the Queen of Heaven (Jer. 7:17-18). The Lord our God has made no secret that this activity does not glorify Him (Jer. 7:17-20; 44:20-30). While the pagan mother-child cult has been active since Babel, it is easily documented that this idolatrous worship did not enter the church until the third century. General buy in for the pagan Christmas, *magically* made Christian by a man-made decree, did not happen until the fourth century.

Notably, the favorite word for idols in the book of Ezekiel is *gillulim*. Rabbinical interpreters of Scripture connect it with the word for "dung," or "dungy gods" (Ezek. 4:12, 15). Others remarkably prefer to connect this word with the Hebrew word *gal*, meaning a stone heap. Its primary root means to "be round." It is the idol contemptuously called a mere log.

MOCK KING

For years after the church woefully assimilated Christmas, a man acting as the Lord of Misrule presided over the revels of Christmas. Temporary subversion of order was one of the themes of the midwinter festival that carried over from Babylon and beyond. The church needs to understand that it was the custom in Babylon for masters to be subject to their servants, and one of them ruled the house clothed in purple garments.[159] This Mock King was dressed in royal robes, allowed to enjoy the real king's concubines, and after reigning for five days was stripped, scourged, and killed.[160] It's not merely a coincidence that a purple-robed Mock King was called the "Lord of Misrule" in the Dark Ages. As mentioned before, the Lord of Misrule presided over the carnival Christmas in Christian countries. Prior to the 1820s, the carnival Christmas was the norm in America too. We can find remnants of drunkenness and promiscuity in the United States, even in our current domesticated Christmas. I recently asked a man who owns a liquor store: "What day do you sell the most alcohol?" He told me: "Christmas Eve." Hislop reveals that: "The wassailing bowl of Christmas had its precise counterpart in the 'drunken festival' of Babylon; and many of the other observances still kept up among ourselves at Christmas came from the very same quarter."[161]

Masters became slaves, and slaves became masters with one being crowned king—the Mock King. This tradition was practiced during the Roman Saturnalia, the immediate predecessor of the Christmas season. "A record of one such celebration has survived: In 303 A.D. a young conscript named Dasius had the misfortune of being picked as the king of the Saturnalia by soldiers of the Roman legion stationed in a distant province. As such he was to be provided with all the trappings of royalty . . . finally, at the conclusion of the festival, he was to be sacrificed to *Saturnus* [i.e., Saturn]. But Dasius happened to be a Christian and therefore refused the honor, with some dire consequences."[162] He was promptly martyred.

It would have been natural for Roman participants at a crucifixion to expect a prisoner from a distant province to be made into a mock king by Roman soldiers and be killed in the end.[163] Listen to these words penned by the Greek historian Dio Chrysostom about the Persian festival *Sacaea:* "They take one of the prisoners condemned to death and make him sit on a royal throne; they dress him in royal robes . . . but in the end they undress him and hang him."[164] A crucifixion was generally described as a hanging. The *Sacaea* midwinter festival was a counterpart to the Roman Saturnalia. The Saturnalia was a direct descendant of the merged Egyptian and Persian mother-child/sun traditions, both of which came from Babylon. It formed the basis for the festival dedicated to the ancient god of seed (i.e., agriculture) and time (i.e., Saturn).[165] As we will see in chapter 6, Saturn is simply another name for Satan.

All four gospels give us an account of Jesus being beaten and mocked by Roman soldiers while in Pilate's custody. Could it be that the real Mock King—Satan—wanted to mock the King of Kings? From the book of Mark we know that the mockery of Jesus took place in the open courtyard of the *praetorium*.[166]

The Roman soldiers had brought Jesus into an area where people had gathered. They had put a purple robe and a crown on Jesus, which was the traditional practice for crowning the Lord of Misrule too. As we know Jesus' crown consisted of thorns, not gold. After the Roman soldiers forced the brutal crown on Jesus' head, the Bible says that they paid homage to Jesus and spit on Him (Mark 15:19). The purple, royal, seamless robe must have been taken off of Jesus before the scourging; else no one would have wanted to cast lots for such a fine garment. Therefore, the incident of the drawing of lots belongs with the mockery scene, which perfectly corresponds to how the king of the Saturnalia was chosen by drawing lots.

Just as Satan instigated an inversion of order by making Jesus Christ of Nazareth the mock king before Jesus went to the cross, he is trying to perpetuate the same tomfoolery today. Satan is trying to pass off the pagan sun child born at Christmastime as God incarnate. He has, so far, greatly succeeded in perpetuating and disseminating this bait and switch in America. We have bought, and we passionately defend, the great lie first spread through Semiramis. Even a causal glance at the facts of Jesus' birth reveals that he was not born in December. Shepherds do not watch their flock in the Holy Land at this time of year; and the wise men did not visit Jesus at a manger, but as a toddler at a house. Yes, it has been a long held tradition to celebrate Jesus Christ's birth at this season, but it's a man-made tradition that started out as an effort to link paganism and Christianity.

The fact of Jesus' virgin birth is too precious to cheapen by assimilating it with the pagan traditions of yesteryear. This type of mixture is Satan's formula, not Christ's.

SERVICE TO THE DEAD AND DEATH

The theme of death flows through the various customs associated with the ancient winter solstice festival. This makes sense, for Nimrod's death is the root of this entire farce, and the lord of death—Satan—is its promulgator and promoter.

We have seen how Nimrod's death is commemorated in the Yule log ceremony: As an evergreen tree he springs up into new life (as Tammuz) from a dead tree stump, which was chopped up and burnt. During this same festive season, we also see death promoted in the gladiator extravaganzas of Rome. "Augustus decreed that gladiator fights should be held every year with fixed dates in December and March. Shows were to take place from 2 to 8 December and then from 17 to 23 December during the celebration of Saturnalia."[167] "The ancient Romans believed they were performing a service to the dead by putting on these shows. Originally Roman funerals would have involved a much more cold-hearted kind of human sacrifice... . Festus a second century writer, who says quite simply: . . . 'It was the custom to sacrifice prisoners at the gravesites of brave warriors;[168] when the cruelty of this habit became known, they switched to gladiator fights beside the grave.'"[169] "The earliest Roman gladiator fights were part of elaborate funeral rites for important people."[170]

This could possibly be a mutation of Nimrod's sacrifice, and the sacrifices required for his death.

Saturnalia was said to be a reenactment of the happy age when *Saturnus* reigned the earth as its first king. Take your pick. In the natural realm, the earth's first king was the mighty one Nimrod, in the spiritual realm this equates to Satan (i.e., Saturn). Gladiators fought to the death in Saturnalia funeral games. Today, the ancestor of the worship of Saturn has death as its fruit too. The Christmas season is known as the heart attack season in hospitals. It is also known for having the highest suicide risk of the year.[171] Statistically, springtime has the highest suicide rate, but the greatest time for suicide risk is still the winter holiday season. Mental health professionals have been on their toes for years now in an effort to lessen suicides and depression during Christmas. Some of Christmas's bad fruit can be associated with bruising, like: getting worn down, getting sick, or getting in debt. But some of the bad fruit is much more destructive—heart attacks and suicide—which minimally warrants a more serious inspection of our Christian Christmas.

God calls us to be fruit inspectors: "by their fruit you will recognize them" (Matt. 7:20). His Word says, "No good tree bears bad fruit" (Luke 6:43). Hum. Probably the most predominant bad fruit of Christmas is financial ruin or difficulty,[172] which is a result of people operating under the world economic system called Babylon.

ଓଃ

4

AGE-OLD FOUNDATION

> Then they will rebuild the ancient ruins,
> they will raise up the former devastations;
> And they will repair the ruined cities, the desolations
> of many generations.
> —Isaiah 61:4 NASB

The Ancient of Days is calling us to return to His ancient ways. I will only touch on three desolations of many generations, which specifically relate to the focus of this book: the One New Man in Christ, the Essential Commandments for All Believers, and biblical time-keeping.

Before the Messiah returns, His church will reclaim these lost age-old elements. These three are foundational elements that have been established through God's Word and by the Christian church's first apostles and disciples. These three were first-order practices performed for over two hundred years. These three are also necessary to understanding what Yeshua meant when He declared that the mixture of Christmas grieves His heart.

ONE NEW MAN

In chapter 8, you will be more fully introduced to the One New Man in the Messiah concept and how it's time to discover some new facets to God's plans that always have been in the Bible, but the requirements for their manifestation have not been revealed, or necessary, until now. We also will discover how we have just entered a new season where there has been a divine shift in earth's administration. When the dispensation of Abraham was held supreme, prior to God coming with skin on, the Jews submitted to the ceremonial law of not keeping company with those of another nation; because when Jews mingled with the idolatrous nations, it corrupted them and God's message through them. But when Yeshua came, a new dispensation was instituted where Jesus crucified in His flesh the enmity caused by the law so that He might create in Himself One New Man—Jew and Gentile—in a single body by means of the cross (Eph. 2:15-16). The cross was a natural, objective manifestation where Jesus (perfectly natural and supernatural) began the process of reconciliation of Jew and Gentile into one body. On earth, we have yet to see the enmity (or feud) end between Jews and Gentiles; but we have entered the dispensation of the fullness of time where it will occur. Now is the time for the spiritual manifestation for God's temple to come forth. We will see how its perfection is the One New Man positioned in the New Jerusalem as the Bride of Christ.

History has well documented that Christianity and Judaism share a common heritage. A specialist in early Christianity and early Judaism articulates: "They were actually inseparable before 60 C.E. (perhaps until the middle of the second century)."[173] Christianity was regarded as a "sect" within Judaism first known as "The Way" (Acts 2:5, 14).[174] Many sources reveal that the earliest Christians in Rome were Jews and God-fearing Gentiles.[175] They were the first fruits of Ephesians 2:15-16: "by abolishing in His [own crucified] flesh the enmity [caused by] the Law with its decrees and ordinances [which He annulled]; that He from the two might create in Himself *one new man* [one new quality of humanity out of the two], so making peace. And [he designed] to reconcile to God both [Jew and Gentile, united] in a single body by means of His cross, thereby killing the mutual enmity and bringing the feud to an end" (AMP, emphasis mine).

The earliest Christians never knew, nor did they imagine, a Christianity that was not closely connected to the Jewish community. As late as the fourth and fifth century, we have evidence of

Christians still existing within Jewish communities and members of the Christian communities participating in Jewish (i.e., biblical) festivals. Beyond the borders of Constantine's empire, these influences persisted even longer.

The preacher of Antioch and later Constantinople, John Chrysostom, complained in a series of eight sermons to his congregation: "You must stop going to the Synagogue. You must not think that the Synagogue is a holier place than our churches are."[176] In my research of Christmas, I found that many Christians who defend their celebration of Christmas usually cite John Chrysostom. This is understandable, because while he was the church patriarch of Constantinople, December twenty-fifth became a fixed festival for the church. We should note, however, that he promoted separating the united Jewish and Gentile believers, which caused the woeful separation of the One New Man in Christ.

Chrysostom's sermons line up with what was proclaimed in AD 325 at the Council of Nicaea. "We ought not have anything in common with the Jews . . . our worship follows a more legitimate and more convenient course . . . we desire, dearest brethren, to separate ourselves from the detestable company of the Jews . . ."[177] "We desire" is the optimal phrase here. It was not what God preferred, for this statement blatantly contradicts God's Word. I agree with the Apostolic Creed crafted by the Nicene Council, but if the Christian Church were to practice literally not having anything in common with the Jews, we would be forced to throw out the very foundation we stand on—the Bible and even Jesus, for He came to earth as a Jew.

NOAHIAC COMMANDMENTS

While the earliest Gentile believers weren't expected to become Jews (as clearly articulated through Paul and the Jerusalem Council), they were expected to obey the first century requirements for the "Righteous Gentile." Righteous Gentiles also were known as God-fearers. They did not keep the Jewish Law;[178] but prior to the Apostolic Decree of Acts 15 (what I call "The Essential Commandments for All Believers"), they did maintain the Noahiac commandments.[179] These commandments were linked to the rainbow covenant with

Noah (Gen. 9:1-18). They dealt with monotheistic issues, such as the rejection of idolatry, and were binding on all of Noah's descendants, whether Jew or Gentile. "Rabbis believed that six of the seven Noahiac commandments had already been given to Adam and his descendants, with the seventh added to Noah, to refrain from eating flesh with blood in it."[180] This *truly* is an age-old foundation. The following are the Noahiac commandments,[181] which address matters relating to:

1. **Adjudication.** You shall set up an effective judiciary to enforce the following six laws fairly. (Requirement to have just laws and establishment of courts of justice.)
    a. No false oaths (Gen. 21:23)

2. **Idolatry.** You shall not have any idols before God.
    a. No idolatry (Gen. 2:16)
    b. To pray only to God (Gen. 20:7)
    c. To offer ritual sacrifices only to God (Gen. 8:20)

3. **Blasphemy.** You shall not blaspheme God's name.
    a. To believe that God is one (Gen. 2:16)
    b. No blasphemy (Gen. 2:16)
    c. No consulting oracles (Deut. 18:10)
    d. No divination (Deut. 18:10)
    e. No astrology (Deut. 18:10)
    f. No interpreting omens (Deut. 18:10)
    g. No witchcraft (Deut. 18:10)
    h. No conjuration (Deut. 18:10)
    i. No necromancy (Deut. 18:10)
    j. No consulting of mediums (Deut. 18:10)
    k. To honor one's father and mother (Gen. 9:22-23)

4. **Sexual Immorality.** You shall not commit adultery.
    a. No adultery—defined only as a married woman having sex with someone other than her husband (Gen. 20:3)

    b. Formal marriage via bride price and marriage gifts (Gen. 34:12)
    c. No incest with a sister (Gen. 12:13)
    d. No bestiality (Gen. 2:24)
    e. No crossbreeding of animals (Gen. 8:20)
    f. No castration (Gen. 5:16)
    g. No homosexuality (Gen. 2:24)

5. **Bloodshed.** You shall not murder.
    a. No murder (Gen. 9:5-6)
    b. No suicide (Gen. 9:5-6)
    c. No Moloch worship—infant sacrifice (Deut. 18:10)

6. **Robbery.** You shall not steal.
    a. No theft—including kidnapping (Gen. 2:16; 6:11)

7. **A limb torn from a living animal.** Dietary Law.
    a. Not to eat a limb torn from a creature while it is still living (Gen. 9:4)
    b. Not to eat or drink blood (Gen. 9:4)
    c. Not to eat carrion (Gen. 9:3)

In the middle of the first century, the Jerusalem Council simplified the legal purity requirements for Righteous Gentiles to address the particular needs of the new Jewish movement called "The Way."

THE ESSENTIAL COMMANDMENTS FOR ALL BELIEVERS

The Christian purity requirements detailed in Acts 15 applied to Gentiles who chose to become part of the believing community, but also became the holiness requirements for Jews living outside Israel among pagan Gentiles.[182] Gentiles turning to faith in the Messiah of Israel need not become Jews. However, equally, they could not remain pagan either. Pagans were the embodiment of what Christians were not.

Gentiles attending synagogue in the first century were expected to adopt minimal purity practices, which demonstrated both respect for the righteousness of God and respect for Jewish sensitivities, due to their adherence to God's Word. Polite and considerate behavior was appreciated from Gentiles, who were merely pagan guests; but the expectations for Gentiles claiming to "fear" the God of Israel as the God of the nations was much greater. God-fearers were expected to exhibit behavior that showed they had turned from idolatry to worship the One True God. Gentile believers accomplished this feat by putting off their former deeds of darkness and adopting a simplistic version of those enlightened—the Apostolic Decree of Acts 15. This was the primordial practice for the earliest Christians.

In the second century, when the young Christian church gradually included a growing number of Gentiles with no prior contact with Judaism, they increasingly were dependent on their mother soil. A distinct demarcation line had to be firmly drawn between right and wrong Christianity, as well as between Christianity and paganism. Christians had to go back to how the gospel was preached to them in the beginning—just as Paul and Jesus preached it. And it just happened to coincide with the points Christians share with Jews: biblical monotheism, ethics, and rejection of idolatry.[183] Today, it seems that clear-cut line has become blurred once again. Many times the world is having a difficult time distinguishing between those who are Christian and those who are not.

Practicing Jews still keep the essential commandments decreed in Acts 15; therefore, it remains for Gentile believers to restore these ancient ruins long since devastated in our own lives. Historically, we know that Christians observed the Essential Commandments for All Believers through a stirring document preserved by the ancient historian Eusebius, which was entitled *Ecclesiastical History*.[184] It is a letter written about the cruel persecution of some forty-eight citizens of Lyons, France, dating from AD 177. While a Christian girl was being tortured, she is recorded to have indignantly voiced, "How can those eat children, who are forbidden to eat the blood even of brute beasts?" This is a clear sign that the Christian community of Lyons still observed the apostolic decrees set up in Jerusalem.[185]

The Essential Commandments for All Believers actually demonstrate a person's rejection of idolatry; hence, our connection to the golden calf of America—Christmas. It is necessary to emphasize that Christmas will not be the only idolatrous practice that the Lord will require His people to lay down in these last days, but it will probably be one of the most difficult. I personally believe that if a Christian can come out of Babylon and lay down Christmas, they can come out of just about anything. I have been truly amazed at the incredibly strong emotional hold it has had on me. The attachment to Christmas seems magnetic, almost irresistible. Not to mention the incredibly strong societal pressure.

The Essential Commandments for All Believers prohibit things that had or have connections with pagan customs and/or traditions. They are abstinence requirements to live a holy life, just as abstinence before marriage preserves the sanctity of holy matrimony. These abstinence requirements for the Bride of Christ preserve the sanctity of holy matrimony to our Bridegroom. "Blessed are those who wash their robes, that they may have the right to the tree of life and may go into the city. Outside are . . . the idolaters and everyone who loves and practices falsehood" (Rev. 22:14-15).

The holiness requirements for the Lord's living stones (i.e., you and me) are so important that they were mentioned twice when the founding church fathers were discussing what the nations needed to do to become part of God's household. Then, incredibly, Paul repeats them again in Acts 21:25 when he arrives in Jerusalem after his third missionary journey. These were Paul's last days. He topped off his final missionary efforts (gathering funds for the church in Jerusalem) with a final exhortation to the people in the nations to keep the Essential Commandments for All Believers.

When something is repeated twice in Scripture, God is emphasizing that the matter has been decreed by God and that it will happen soon (Gen. 41:32). *The significance of the Essential Commandments for All Believers being repeated three times in the Bible is momentous.* E.W. Bullinger says that the number three points us to what is solid, real, essential, perfect, substantial, complete, and divine.[186] This is one of the reasons I call the Apostolic Decree of Acts 15 the "Essential Commandments for All Believers." The other reason is that the word *essential* is expressed in the accurate New American Standard Version of Acts 15:28: "For it seemed good to the Holy Spirit and to us to lay upon you no greater burden than these essentials."

The Essential Commandments for All Believers are complete. They represent divine perfection and were first taught in Moses' writings. Even today, the proper comprehension of Leviticus 17-18 can help one measure a person's heart. Don't be surprised. Jesus tells us in John 5:46-47: "For if you believed Moses, you would believe Me; for he wrote of Me. But if you don't believe his writings, how will you believe My words?" God has written His new covenant as well as the Law and the Prophets on His people's hearts. Come. Let us learn more and move onto perfection.

We already have learned that these holiness requirements for God's household are in reality abstinence requirements, which bind God's people in holy matrimony to our beloved, heavenly Bridegroom. It's noteworthy that these abstinence requirements for holiness were the *only* burdens the Holy Spirit led the Jerusalem Council to specifically place upon Gentile believers. In reality, they regulate chaste behavior for those who are the temple of the living God.

HEAVENLY REQUIREMENTS FOR HOLY MATRIMONY

Let's take a more specific look at the four Essential Commandments for All Believers as an apostolic decree from Jesus' first apostles and elders. Keep a sharp eye out for *things* sacrificed to or contaminated by idols throughout *Santa-tizing*. The truth is that all of the Roman holidays are modern holdovers of ancient pagan practices. They came out of Babylon via Rome. Here are all three scriptural references for the Essential Commandments for All Believers:

> Therefore it is my judgment that we do not trouble those who are turning to God among the Gentiles, but that we write to them that they abstain from [1] things contaminated by idols and [2] from fornication and [3] from what is strangled and [4] from blood.
> —Acts 15:19-20 NASB

For it seemed good to the Holy Spirit and to us to lay upon you no greater burden than these essentials: that you abstain from things sacrificed to idols and from blood and from things strangled and from fornication; if you keep yourself free from such things, you will do well.
—Acts 15:28-29 NASB

But concerning the Gentiles who have believed, we wrote having decided that they should abstain from the thing sacrificed to idols and from blood and from what is strangled and from fornication.
—Acts 21:25 NASB

1. **Abstain from things contaminated by idols—**

In this sub-section, we will mainly explore the angle of abstaining from food polluted by idols, due to this being a common way the first Essential Commandment is translated in Christian Bibles. But know that the most accurate translations of the Bible declare that the first essential commandment is: abstaining from *things* sacrificed to or contaminated by idols. Please notice in the next two chapters that almost every single Christmas custom or tradition is a thing saturated with paganism (i.e., contaminated by idols).

In Rome, the dominant world power at the time of the Jerusalem Council, Jews found the association with idolatry almost unavoidable when among Gentiles, particularly when sharing meals. Like Daniel IN BABYLON (Dan. 1:8-13), Jews refrained from meat and wine, when questionable. They just ate vegetables and drank water, or brought their own food and wine. Often their lifestyle offended Gentiles, and they became a source of ridicule and scorn.[187]

In the first century, idolatry was woven throughout the very fabric of Roman society. At the time, "for most people, meat was a thing never eaten and wine never drunk save as some religious setting permitted. There existed no formal social life in the world . . . that was entirely secular. Small wonder, then, that Jews and Christians holding themselves aloof from anything the gods touched, suffered under the reputation of misanthropy [i.e., hatred and distrust]!"[188] Acting as a peacemaker, Paul addressed the "strong" directly in Romans 14:1-15:4, asking them to forego their perceived freedoms from Judaic customs in matters of food in view of the priorities of the kingdom of God.[189] "For he who serves Christ in these things is acceptable to God and approved by men" (Rom. 14:18 NKJV).

Before Christians adopted the Christmas season, it was called the Feast of Saturn—Saturnalia—in Rome.[190] Several sources say that Saturnalia was a seasonal festival, which began in the middle of December continuing until January first. I have adopted this definition to simplify our understanding, but in actuality, by the fourth century the Romans celebrated three pagan festivals:

1) **The Saturnalia** lasted for three to seven days or even longer. One of the common ways to find it defined is as a general time period extending from December 17 to December 23.
2) Halfway through Saturnalia, the idolatrous birth worship of the sun god—*Sol Invictus*—was celebrated on December 25. *Sol Invictus's* solar worship merged with a different pattern of sun worship from the Orient—Mithraism—which became known as *Sol Invictus Mithra*. Roman emperors following Aurelian were connected to this religion of the sun. Initially, the birth celebration was not an all-encompassing tradition for the masses, especially when compared to the Saturnalia and Kalends. The elite of Rome practiced secret rituals under the name of **"The Nativity"** or "The Nativity of the Sun" or "The Nativity of the Unconquered Sun."
3) **The January Kalends** was a New Year's party. Today, Western civilization still follows the Kalends' tradition of singing and heavy drinking on New Year's Eve. A fourth century writer, Libanius, describes the

Roman January Kalends: "The impulse to spend seizes everyone. . . . People are not only generous towards themselves, but also towards their fellow-men. A stream of presents pours itself out on all sides . . . The Kalends festival banishes all that is connected with toil, and allows men to give themselves up to undisturbed enjoyment."[191]

Since the focus of this book is the circumstances surrounding Christmas, I don't emphasize the January Kalends, but I generally include it in my definition of the Saturnalia and the Christmas season. Just note that the gift-giving tradition connected to this ancient Roman New Year's festival still existed in New York City when Christmas was forged into its modern image in the 1820s. The overwhelming element of our modern Christmas—shopping—was transported into America's renewed image of Christmas via merchants and the Americanized Santa Claus tradition.

By the way, it also has primordial roots that reach back into Babylon's twelve-day New Year's festival (i.e., *Akiti*) coupled with the magical appeal of its December sun god birth observance. Christmas acts like a homing device or talisman[192] that never fails to point us back to the sensual place where mixture is its modus operandi. Christmas's homing signal draws people together, reminding us to look not just to our immediate friends and family, but toward Babylon. The Yuletide season is the high tide for the year when the world is of one mind. The people of the earth are busy building a tower by our own desires and design, to get for ourselves what we believe is a slice of heaven. Remember that the Babylonian "land of merchants" status is exemplified by: harlotry, a continual lust for more, disdain for frugal spending, and shrines at the beginning of every street and in the high place of every town square. Very similar to today, history records that evergreens were used to decorate during the Roman Saturnalia and January Kalends. For now, let's just center in on the wildly popular Saturnalia to see a few of its many idolatrous connections.

The Saturnalia began with the *sacrificium publicum,* in which a young pig was sacrificed in the temple of Saturn in the Forum.[193] It was literally said that, "this boar will make you a good Saturnalia." A libation offering of a special mulled wine went with the sacramental gift of the Saturnalia swine. Knowing this, I can understand why the "weak" Jewish Christians would have had a problem with the merger of the former, and originally, pagan festival of Saturnalia into The Way. Even church fathers of the faith at the time of the merger, like Tertullian, lamented about the inconsistency of the disciples of Christ. Tertullian recognized that the celebration of Christmas was just a spin off the Feast of Saturn, calling it "the heathen being faithful to their religion."[194] Only a small remnant of upright saints did not become submerged under pagan superstition and celebration.

To this day ham or swine is a traditional Christmas dinner for many people throughout the world. For example, unlike the rest of southern Asia, Christianity is the leading religion in the Philippines. Filipinos on Christmas Day have a traditional holiday dinner, which includes a roast pig.[195]

Additionally, 2 Corinthians 8 tells us that compromised faith is like meat sacrificed to an idol. Faith in the Lord is essential and non-negotiable, which brings us to the Hebraic concept that the primary violation when one sins against God is the breach of the first commandment—belief in God—before one trespasses any of the second through fifth commandments.

"You shall have no other gods besides Me" (Exod. 20:3). Can anyone protest that "to have and hold" another god basically equates to a compromised belief in God? Casual concessions or compromises are made in relation to the One we can always confidently trust. Why do we cavalierly write off our relationship with the King as if it doesn't matter and it won't hurt Him? Perhaps because of His awesome, endless love, kindness, and grace or the fact that "the heart is deceitful above all things, and it is exceedingly perverse and corrupt and severely, mortally sick! Who can know it [perceive, understand, be acquainted with his own heart and mind]?" (Jer. 17:9 AMP).

2. **Abstain from fornication**—Leviticus 18

Next we turn our focus upon the general trait of sexually immorality rather than on the more specific topic of fornication—consensual sexual intercourse between two people not married to each other. 1 Corinthians 6:18 tells us to "Flee from sexual immorality. All other sins a man commits are outside his body, but he who sins sexually sins against his own body." If we are part of the church of the Lord Jesus Christ, we are members of His body (1 Cor. 12:12-14; Eph. 4:15-16). Hebrews 10:10 NKJV says that, "we have been sanctified through the offering of the body of Jesus Christ once for all." If, being members of His body, we sexually sin, then we are actually sinning against the body of Christ (i.e., our own body as well as Christ's). A sobering thought indeed. "Do you not see and know that your bodies are members (bodily parts) of Christ (the Messiah)? Am I therefore to take the parts of Christ and make [them] parts of a prostitute? Never! Never!" (1 Cor. 6:15 AMP). Sexual immorality has a strong connection to cultic prostitution and its promotion of promiscuity. Is it merely a coincidence that sexual immorality is rampant in American society today?

The author Lucian tells us: "There are no ancient [pagan] rites of initiation without dancing."[196] "In the Greek *mysteria* there are dancing and instrumental music, the dancers to be dismissed as 'prostitutes,' i.e. professionals."[197] "It is God's will that you should be sanctified: that you should avoid sexual immorality; that each of you should learn to control his own body in a way that is holy and honorable, not in passionate lust like the heathen, who do not know God" (1 Thess. 4:3-5).

Galatians 5:19-21 says that sexual immorality is an act of the sinful nature and "those who live like this will not inherit the kingdom of God" (Gal. 5:21). "Do you not know that the unrighteous and the wrongdoers will not inherit or have any share in the kingdom of God? Do not be deceived (misled): neither the impure and immoral, nor idolaters, nor adulterers, nor those who participate in homosexuality, nor cheats (swindlers and thieves), nor greedy graspers, nor drunkards, nor foulmouthed revilers and slanderers, nor extortioners and robbers will inherit or have any share in the kingdom of God" (1 Cor. 6:9-10 AMP). Forgiveness is available for any of these sins for anyone who turns to God with sincerity. However, unrepentant sin is another matter. Any sexually immoral person or any idolater *whatsoever* will not inherit the kingdom of God. Probably one of the most shocking passages for believers is: "Not everyone who says to me, 'Lord, Lord,' will enter the kingdom of heaven, but only he who does the will of My Father who is in heaven. Many will say to Me on that day, 'Lord, Lord, did we not prophesy in Your name, and in Your name drive out demons and perform miracles?' Then I will tell them plainly, 'I never knew you. Away from Me, you evildoers!'" (Matt. 7:21-23).

3. **Abstain from the meat of strangled animals—**

It is not kosher (i.e., fit and proper), according to Hebraic dietary law, to strangle an animal. The preferred method for killing pigs in the Old Testament was strangling them as they were tied to a tree. Many of the kosher laws are about the sanctity of life. We are to have respect for the life that God made—whether animal or human. I had a close encounter with death once, and the Lord told me to choose life, even if I am on my way out (of this world).

"Strangled meat played a role in some pagan cults."[198] Origen[199] wrote that blood, including that in strangled meat, was said to be the food of demons: "If we were to eat strangled animals, we might have such spirits feeding along with us."[200] Strangling was a pagan custom in Alexandria.[201]

4. Abstain from blood—

Hebrews 9:22 NKJV notifies us that, "according to the law almost all things are purified with blood, and without shedding of blood there is no remission." Couple that with Leviticus 17:10-14 being a kosher law: "because the life of every creature is its blood. That is why I have said to the Israelites, 'You must not eat the blood of any creature, because the life of every creature is its blood; anyone who eats it must be cut off'" (Lev. 17:14). Blood is sacred to life, and if the Lord of Life says anyone who eats blood will be cut off from Him, and therefore, His Kingdom, I would definitely not take this essential commandment lightly.

Abstaining from blood in the first century CE most probably had connections with refraining from practices of an idolatrous pagan religion. "It was a pagan who described, 'the priest himself [who] stands there all bloody and like an ogre carves and pulls out entrails and extracts the heart and pours the blood about the altar.' . . . The great bulk of the meat eaten in the ancient world had been butchered in temple precincts, most of which, [were] ill-supplied with water."[202] Accumulated ugly piles of offal were placed in corners and supported not only clouds of flies, but stray mongrels as well.

Haima [blood] refers to the bloody rites of pagan sacrifices.[203] It was one of their most prominent features. It was also the custom in some cults to drink the blood of the victim.[204] The drinking and eating of blood is hard for me to image when I think of the blood disorders and disease carried in humans: anemia, hemophilia, HIV/AIDS, leukemia, and sickle cell. "For the life is in the blood" (Lev. 17:10). Lethal diseases can be transferred through the blood, like the infamous blood-borne disease of the human immune system, HIV/AIDS. The HIV/AIDS pandemic is tragically decimating the continent of Africa, causing millions of children to be without parents. Leukemia often is referred to as cancer of the blood, a malignant condition affecting the immature blood-forming cells in the bone marrow. You get the idea.

At first I thought that these four essential commandments were not required for salvation, but a love (i.e., purity) issue. Like a loving parent, the Father wants His kids, His family, protected from those things that would harm them, and He is infamously known to be a jealous God. But as I have meditated upon these Essential Commandments for All Believers requiring abstinence from four things, I wonder if these decrees are required for salvation or not. Romans 10:9 says: "If you confess with your mouth, 'Jesus is Lord,' and believe in your heart that God raised him from the dead you will be saved." Since when has mere verbal assent been okay with God? Has the American church become like the Pharisees? "These people honor me with their lips, but their hearts are far from me. They worship me in vain; their teachings are but rules taught by men" (Matt. 15:8-9). If we confess, "Jesus is Lord," it means that Jesus is our Master, our Lord, our King, and our God. Jesus led His church in the first century to include these four essential commandments as legal requirements for all believers. If we throw out this portion of His Word, which demarcates pure-hearted worshipers who worship the Father in spirit and truth (John 4:23-24), do we truly submit to Him as our Lord?

I know that God extends a tremendous amount of grace when it comes to people's ignorance, but once He has spoken personally to you or me about an issue of our life or an issue of the heart, He expects obedience. "And having been perfected, He became the author of eternal salvation to all who obey Him" (Heb. 5:9 NKJV). God is <u>not</u> after legalistic behavior. He wants us to pursue the way of love. He wants us to turn to Him with all our heart, soul, mind, and strength; and exhibit His Lordship in our lives by forsaking all but Him. If you are not "there" yet, it's okay. Start with an honest request like: "I want to be willing to obey, Lord, please help me," or "I am willing, but I don't know how. Please help me." A heart like that—a heart of David that turns to God—will always get His attention and assistance. I have literally told my Beloved: "I don't know how to love. Please help me. Please show me." I have found that He thinks that sort of heart is simply irresistible.

Jesus Christ filled the commandments articulated in the Old Testament full of meaning, signifying that the Messiah has redeemed us from the legalistic requirements of the law; but there are still principles that Christ's followers must abide by being yielded to the dictates of the Lord's heart, which brings life. For example, Jesus filled the Ten Commandments full of meaning when He said and demonstrated that all the Law and the Prophets hang on two commandments: Love the Lord God with all your heart, soul, and strength; and love your neighbors as yourself (Matt. 22:37-40). That does not mean that the Lord sanctions false witnesses, murder, and the like; but living your life in love will keep you from sin. We have learned that the Apostolic Decree, listed in Acts 15:20, Acts 15:29, and Acts 21:25, contains four essential abstinence commandments for all believers in the Lord Jesus Christ. They are the minimal requirements for holiness for the sons of the living God.

Of special note, I want to emphasize an important point. *Please do not measure people who are not Christians with these same standards* (Matt. 7:1-2). We are to seek and save, not accuse and abuse.

> I don't want you to forget . . . what happened . . . in the wilderness long ago. . . . These events happened as a warning to us, so that we would not crave evil things as they did or worship idols as some of them did. For the Scriptures say, "The people celebrated with feasting and drinking, and they indulged themselves in pagan revelry." . . . If you think you are standing strong, be careful, for you, too, may fall into the same sin. But *remember that the temptations that come into your life are no different from what others experience.* And God is faithful. He will keep the temptation from becoming so strong that you can't stand up against it. When you are tempted, He will show you a way out so that you will not give in to it. *So, my dear friends, flee from the worship of idols.* . . . What am I trying to say? Am I saying that the idols to whom the pagans bring sacrifices are real gods and that these sacrifices are of some value? No, not at all. What I am saying is that these sacrifices are offered to demons, not to God. And I don't want any of you to be partners with demons. . . . You say, "I am allowed to do anything"—but not everything is helpful. You say, "I am allowed to do anything"—but not

everything is beneficial. . . . Whatever you eat and drink or whatever you do, you must do all for the glory of God.
—1 Corinthians 10 NLT, emphasis mine

BIBLICAL TIME-KEEPING

The first thing God called holy is the Sabbath (Gen. 2:3). It was the perfect establishment of a measurement of time. Our Bible also calls a burning bush holy, Mount Sinai holy, and the Holy of Holies. What makes these things holy is the same thing that makes people holy—God's presence.

We must understand that our heavenly Father's timetable is laid out in the Bible according to His calendar, and its time and seasons always point to the Messiah. As God's people, we should be pointing to the Messiah too. So returning to this age-old foundation of biblical time-keeping should be an instinctive process for believers. The Sabbath sets His people's weeks. The New Moon sets their months. The feasts of the Lord set their years (Isa. 29:1b). Due to the focus of this book, we will only be exploring the feasts of the Lord, which situates a year in the dimension of time; but please allow me to state a few points about the concept of measurement first. Every player in a game of sports plays by the same rules (2 Tim. 2:5). We just need to understand that in the spiritual realm, it's God's rules by which everyone plays, including the devil. Time is one of the closest things we have on earth to the spiritual realm. When God created weeks, months, and years, He gave them as gifts to mankind. His measurements of time help us understand where we are in the process of life. Life is progressive. These measurements of time are not there to make us feel bad or condemned. They simply help us make sure that we are not stagnant or stunted. As time goes by, we see our children growing up, and we periodically ask ourselves: Am I better than I was a year ago? Time helps us see if our growth is heading in the proper direction—maturity.

What society calls the Jewish feasts, God calls "the feasts of the Lord," and significantly He emphasizes: "they are <u>My</u> feasts" (Lev. 23:2). They have been called the Jewish feasts because remnants of Jewish people have faithfully rehearsed the feasts of the Lord since they have been instituted. All believers of the first century celebrated the feasts of the Lord. It is the Christian church's primordial practice. For example, Paul exhorted the Gentile believers in Corinth: "Therefore purge out the old leaven, that you may be a new lump, since you truly are unleavened. For indeed Christ, our Passover, was sacrificed for us. Therefore *let us keep the feast*, not with the old leaven . . . but *with* the unleavened bread of *sincerity and truth*" (1 Cor. 5:7-8 NKJV, emphasis mine).

The Lord Jesus Christ and the early church continued to observe the rituals and feasts of the Torah because they understood that they portrayed the Messiah. These observances were not done for righteousness' sake, for the early church embraced Yeshua's sacrifice on the cross as the only way in which they could obtain their right standing in and before God.

CHANGING THE MARKS OF TIME

Man's movement of the marks of time has had the intent to glorify the Lord; but like the incident of the golden calf, something said to honor Jehovah is not necessarily as we say. The Lord will be the judge. Be encouraged. The ancient Hebrew pictograph for the word *judge* means the door of life. Biblical faith always includes the call to judgment from a heart of love. Judgment is actually the opposite of despair and death.

> Great are Your tender mercies, O LORD; revive me according to Your judgments.
> —Psalm 119:156 NKJV

> Let my soul live, and it shall praise You; and let Your judgment help me.
> —Psalm 119:175 NKJV

God's righteous judgments reveal our actions as they actually are. He already sees us as we are, and loves us nevertheless—forever and always. God's love is unconditional. Please remember, in God's judgment, there is forgiveness, which is why there is no reason to fear the truth. Our faith in the goodness and forgiveness of God makes self-criticism possible.

A genuine confession of sin is revealed not merely in words, but also in deed. To truly repent of idolatry requires that we purge its practices from our midst. Authentic repentance presumes desisting from sin. Simply put, repentance makes change necessary. I personally believe that the church is currently going through the greatest change since its passage from a Jewish sect to a Greco-Roman religion. The church, with its many members, needs to be ready to acknowledge mistakes wherever they are identified.

Sometime between the second and the fourth century, the Christian church began to marginalize the Essential Commandments for All Believers. It most probably happened in the fourth century, when the birth of Christ was officially designated as a separate festival on the basis of the Roman calendar. To this day, the basic fourth century structure still determines the church's ecclesiastical year.[205] Further testimony may possibly be the change in the calendar to measure time against the birth of Jesus Christ. Throughout Christendom, years began to be numbered as *anno Domini* (i.e., A.D.).[206] It was not just the past that was being redefined, but our present and future too.

Man's declaration of "the year of the Lord," as in *anno Domini,* meaning that the Lord has dominion over time, seems like an admirable practice, except for one thing. The Lord had already set His dominion over time in the beginning;[207] and even before time began, for God is eternal, sovereign, and immutable (i.e., never changes). "Time marks the beginning of created existence, and because God never began to exist it can have no application to Him."[208] "Jesus Christ is the same yesterday and today and forever" (Heb. 13:8). Time is contained in Him. "God dwells in eternity but time dwells in God. C.S. Lewis suggests that we think of a sheet of paper infinitely extended. That would be eternity. Then on that paper draw a short line to represent time. As the line begins and ends on that infinite expanse, so time began in God and will end in Him."[209] Originally, in 526, Dionysis Exiguus[210] insisted that the reckoning from the incarnation served solely to locate his Easter cycles in time. By the way, Easter has as much pagan-Christian mixture as all the Roman holidays. *Anno Domini* owed its custom to people recording significant events in the blank spaces of calendars.[211] Harmless it seems; but as you will see, man, via the church, has had to work extremely hard to perpetuate worshiping God through mixed means and measures. It's too bad that the church hasn't always stuck to God's biblical calendar. Let's examine how man's effort to be in command of time has been an abysmal failure.

It is the spirit of the Antichrist, which intends first to change God's appointed times and then His laws. "He will speak against the Most High and oppress his saints and try to change the set times and the laws" (Dan. 7:25). We will see how the changing of biblical time-keeping has caused His people to modify some of what needed to be kept in God's Word—like the Essential Commandments for All Believers.

We would do well to be students of history. Before the Roman Empire, the Jewish people already had experienced a person and a world-impacting movement, who strove to change God's times and law. This person was a Seleucid General named Antiochus Epiphanes IV. History infamously classifies him as an antichrist. The world-impacting movement he promoted was called Hellenism. By the way, when Greek culture mixed with the culture of the Middle East, it created a new hybrid—Hellenism—whose influence on the Roman Empire, Christianity, and Western civilization has been monumental.

When Alexander the Great overthrew Persia, Judea became subject to him. Alexander was a kind and generous ruler to the Jews. He canceled the Jewish taxes during Sabbatical years, and even offered animals to be sacrificed on his behalf in the temple.[212] When Alexander died, in 323 BC, he had succeeded in conquering the important lands around the eastern Mediterranean; and he had also laid the foundation of a cultural revolution that would forever change the world. "Alexander himself had envisaged a synthesis between the classical Greek culture and the old cultures of the Orient"[213] (i.e., the ancient Middle East). In the wake of the Alexandrian takeover, a new way of defining a person's identity appeared. Prior to Alexander's program of cultural conquest, it was rare for any "ism" to exist. Now, people who were not Greeks by descent began to talk, dress, and live like Greeks in Greek-style cities. This new way of life was called *hellenismos*[214] in Greek, and it was probably the first "ism" in recorded history. No longer did a person's descent and territory merely define their identity, but now a person could choose to identify themselves by one set of values or ideals or another. Jews responded by beginning to call their way of life *ioudaismos*[215] (Judaism). This term was most likely first used by the author of the book of Second Maccabees.[216] Judas Maccabees and his brothers "fought bravely for Judaism" (2 Maccabees 2:21). Just as non-Greeks could become Hellenists by transferring their allegiance to Hellenism, so could non-Jews become adherents of Judaism. "In fact, we encounter the first known examples of conversion to Judaism in the days of the Hasmoneans."[217] This new development of conversion was a very important pre-condition for an early Christian's self-understanding and mission: "Therefore go and make disciples of all nations" (Matt. 28:19).

After Alexander died, his kingdom was divided among his four generals. Judea, as usual, was caught in the middle, and eventually ended up in the Seleucid Dynasty in 199 BC with its ruler Antiochus IV.[218] The ruling dynasty in Syria, the Seleucids, had Greek origins from the time of Alexander the Great.

In 168 BC, the heathen—in this instance the Syrian Greeks—sacrificed a pig on God's altar and put a statute of Zeus in the sanctuary, which for all intents and purposes dedicated God's temple to the worship of Zeus. A pig, as many people know, is the ultimate non-kosher animal; so this was not a compliment, but a statement of utter contempt and degradation to the Jews and their God. An interesting aside is that many ancient cultures offered a pig as a sacrifice once a year at a feast. Those pagan festivals, throughout the world, mainly harmonize with today's Christmas celebration. Turkeys are traditional for a Thanksgiving feast. What is traditional for Christmas? Ham. In the 1800s, boar's head was still a standing dish in England at the Christmas dinner, when the reason of it was long since forgotten.

DESTROYING PEOPLE'S SENSE OF TIME

Antiochus Epiphanes IV is rightly portrayed as an antichrist, for he polluted the altar of God by offering up swine on it, knowing that this was against the Law of Moses.[219] Antiochus also forced God's people to bow before the false Greek god, Zeus, under penalty of death. Many innocent people were massacred. The survivors were heavily taxed. This type of religious persecution was unknown up to its time, because the attitude of polytheism was relativistic. Your truth is your truth. My truth is mine. The pluralism of the polytheistic world says that one person's religion was as good as another's. History tells us that the Greek and Roman mythology, which were their religions, blended together, with Zeus becoming Jupiter, Artemis becoming Diana, et cetera. No one in the ancient world died for their religion. No one, except the descendants of Abraham, Isaac, and Jacob.

Before the church changed the explanation of time and before the marginalization of the Acts 15 Apostolic Decrees, there was another ruler who endeavored to change biblical time-keeping. Antiochus IV issued an unheard-of decree. He outlawed another people's religion—both the teaching and practicing of Judaism. The book of the Maccabees tells us: "Not long after this, the king sent an Athenian senator to compel the Jews to forsake the laws of their fathers and cease to live by the laws of God" (2 Maccabees 6:1).[220] The Greeks' brutal persecution of the Jews triggered the first religious and ideological war in history—The Maccabean Revolt. The book of Maccabees calls this period a "reign of terror." We would do well to remember that Antiochus, who took the name Epiphanes—God manifest—took four deliberate steps between 169 and 167 BC to Hellenize the people of The Book.[221]

1. Antiochus first dealt with the seat of Jewish power—the high priest. He removed the sitting high priest, whose name meant righteous peace, and replaced him with a Jew who would do man's (i.e., Antiochus's) bidding. By the way, from this point on, the high priesthood in Israel largely became a corrupt institution.

2. Secondly, Antiochus tried to dissolve the biblical calendar, for he felt these people were time obsessed. They tried to keep their time holy. If Antiochus destroyed the Jews' sense of time, he felt that he destroyed their ability to practice their religion. Therefore, Antiochus forbid the observance of Shabbat, New Moon, and festivals (*Passover, Shavuot, Rosh HaShana, Yom Kippur, Sukkot,* etc.), which set their weeks, months, and years according to God's timetable.
3. Antiochus forbade studying Torah (the Word of God) and keeping kosher (respecting the sanctity of life). Torah scrolls were publicly burnt and pigs were sacrificed over God's Word to defile them. Antiochus even forced the high priest to institute swine sacrifices in the temple in Jerusalem, as well as permitting worship of various Greek gods (1 Maccabees 1:41-64).
4. Lastly, Antiochus forbade circumcision. To Jews, this was their physical sign of their covenant of faith with God (i.e., Abrahamic covenant). Circumcision was the most abhorrent to Greeks, who worshiped the perfection of the human body. Greeks saw circumcision as mutilation.

For the purposes of this book, let us focus on this antichrist's second deliberate step to corrupt God's people, which involved dissolving God's calendar and His people's sense of time. It is *very* important to note that a pronounced antichrist figure felt that if he could destroy God's people's sense of time, he would destroy their ability to practice their holy faith. Notice also that this was after Antiochus first removed God's chosen high priest by replacing him with his own. Prophetically, this is a picture of us setting ourselves up, as God manifest in our temples (i.e., our bodies) dethroning our great High Priest, Jesus, from the seat of our hearts. When Antiochus set out to change God's people's sense of time, he prohibited the observance of three things: Sabbath, New Moon, and festivals. We shall observe that this was the same mistake the church carried out in subsequent centuries. "He will defy the Most High and wear down the holy people of the Most High. He will try to change their sacred festivals and laws, and they will be placed under his control for a time, times, and half a time" (Dan. 7:25 NLT). I believe that this is where the earthly, selfish door opened to enable the eventual institutionalization of the Roman pagan festivals (i.e., holidays) in the church. Thus, instead of time being sanctified as God designed in His Word, it became triggers for idolatrous behavior.[222]

GRECO-ROMAN MARKS ON TIME

There is supporting evidence that lends credence to the claim that the Greeks have led the charge to change biblical time. It is seen with Julius Caesar's establishment of the Julian year, and, additionally, at Constantine's Council of Nicaea. The church in Constantine's day, and after, had a problem with the date of Easter, due to their changing God's set times and ways. In Constantine's effort to unify a divided empire, he forced the bishops at Nicaea to resolve the Asian church difference in Easter from the Roman-African church, by declaring the Quartodeciman practice of the Asian church heretical.[223] Quartodeciman meant the "fourteenth day." The Asian church did as Jesus and His first-century believers did, as defined in the Bible. They celebrated God's holy feast called Passover[224] on the fourteenth day of *Nisan*, followed by the Feast of First Fruits[225] on seventeenth day of *Nisan*. The Feast of First Fruits was encompassed by the Festival of Unleavened Bread,[226] celebrated on the fifteenth through twenty-first days of *Nisan*, as prescribed by the Lord Himself[227] and fulfilled in Christ. Constantine's practice of setting up a difference-obliterating universalism that swallowed up all religious distinctiveness in a triumphant Christianity sided with the Roman-African practice of choosing the closest Sunday to the first full-moon after the spring equinox as the day all Christian communities should celebrate Easter. Thus, Constantine and his compromising cohorts led the movement that no longer looked to Scripture as the last word. This was later affirmed by Pope Paul III, when his council stipulated that Scripture be understood in light of tradition.[228] When Constantine's Nicene Council declared the Quartodeciman practice heretical, they came against what God prescribed as perpetual in His eternal Word. The exact date that God established His Passover Feast was tweaked by the church. Now, to come up with the universal time for Easter, Constantine turned to the wise men of Alexandria, Egypt, to compute Easter and inform the rest of the world of its given time.[229] Alexandria was the center of mathematical learning in the Hellenistic world, which was the same cultural influence being propagated by Antiochus Epiphanes IV.

Heilbron's excellent, albeit very technical, book entitled *The Sun in the Church* informs us: "The Romans began with a calendar that tried to respect both sun and moon, But the arithmetic and the politics of intercalation became so entangled that Julius Caesar had to make the year now called 44 B.C. 445 days long to restore the spring equinox to its traditional [Roman] calendar date of 25 March. He decided to keep it there by detaching the lengths of the months from the motions of the moon."[230] Remember, that a spirit of antichrist, made manifest through people, will aim to first alter God's times and then His law. Gentiles (i.e., the nations) may not like it, but the key to God's time(s) was given to the Hebrews, and even then, they had to take their cues solely from Him. The Lord instructed His people to begin a month by sighting the new moon at dusk, which could not be predicted far in advance. The rulers of the Jewish people—the Sanhedrin of Jerusalem—appointed an official sighting committee to determine the onset of the month via the astronomical moon. So, the Hebrews followed God's instructions by employing the moon to specify the times of civil and religious transactions. God's people had to rely on Him by looking up at His dusky sky to see the sign of His time. The Romans, after Caesar, picked the sun to specify civil and religious time. The Christians *mixed* the two, compromising between Jewish and Gentile practices of using the moon and the sun to specify a calendar year.

Notably, there is an eleven-day difference between the solar and lunar year.[231] The number eleven in Scripture is said to represent disorder, disorganization, imperfection, and disintegration.[232] The "eleventh hour" in Scripture (Matt. 20:6, 9) is proverbial as being contrary both to what is right in order and what is right in arrangement. I believe this reveals that orderly time can only be done God's way. When God made everything on earth according to measure and number, He purposely chose difficult ones for astronomy. "He assigned 29.53059 days for the moon to fulfill its phases, and

365.2422 days for the sun to run from one vernal equinox to the next."[233] Perhaps. Just perhaps. God wants us dependent upon Him to get our time and timing, not on man-made formulas. Time is in perpetual motion. However the days are distributed among the months, they will *never* sum to a year.[234] Can you say, "We are dependent on God to show us His time?"

To keep the vernal equinox on, or as close to 25 March as possible, Caesar also brought an Alexandian astronomer named Sosigenes to Rome. Recall that Alexandria was the center of mathematical learning in the Hellenistic world.[235] Sosigenes brilliantly came up with the formula for the Julian year, which gave a year 326.25 days. Sosigenes set a year at 365 days, with every fourth year containing 366 days, so the vernal equinox would stay put in the calendar. This Julius Caesar practice of setting a year was so good that we still use the Julian year model in America today. But, was it good enough? Sosigenes made the year too long by about eleven minutes. Eleven minutes? Yes, eleven minutes. A Roman year, set according to the dictates of Julius Caesar, is eleven minutes too long. And a solar year is eleven days too long.

The Roman Catholic Church gave the greatest amount of money to the study of astronomy for six centuries during the late Middle Ages into the Enlightment, not because of its love for science, but because the date of Easter throughout the ages was very screwed up.[236] Let go into greater depth by diving into how man's establishment of Christ's resurrection, on the basis of the pagan holiday of Easter, resulted in disorder, disorganization, imperfection, and disintegration.

The church insisted on celebrating Easter on a Sunday close to the first full moon of spring.[237] By the way, "there is a hint of the anti-Jewish spirit of the Nicene fathers in their ban of the celebration of Easter in the same week as Passover."[238] By the twelfth century, the date of Easter was no longer in harmony with the heavens, which destroyed the image of the miracle of the solar eclipse at the crucifixion.

As time rolled on, the errors in the reckoning of Easter compounded.[239] In 1276, man's computations for setting Easter displayed its incompetence to the entire world by erring by a whole month.²⁴⁰ The calculated Easter differed from the set date by eight days in 1345, a month in 1356, five weeks in 1424, and one week off in 1433 and 1437.²⁴¹ "The professional astronomers then took the matter in hand, calculating not from average, but from real moons."²⁴² The church tried to square its year with the astronomy of the sun, and its Easter to the moon in 1511; but to no avail. Martin Luther recommended that the problem be dissolved by nailing Easter in the calendar like Christmas.²⁴³ When the Catholic-Protestant split happened to the church, they each followed different calendars. During the seventeenth century, correspondence between Europeans usually bore two dates, for example, "10/20 January."²⁴⁴ The Catholic Easter had coincided with the Anglican Easter less than half the time (thirty-six years out of eighty), despite placing both of their vernal equinox on the same day of 21 March. In the seventeenth century, the Catholic Easter preceded the Anglican one by one week twenty-six times, by four weeks five times, and by five weeks thirteen times. This sounds like an acute case of disorder to me. All mathematicians knew that the discrepancies would only grow worse in the eighteenth century. The civil calendars would diverge by *eleven,* count them, eleven days rather than ten, owing to the Gregorian suppression of the Julian leap day of 1700.²⁴⁵ The religious calendars of the church were moving further and further out of step, which is a progressive phenomenon that happens when man makes calculation errors. In hindsight, we could say that when the church chose to run itself according to an earthly kingdom rather than God's kingdom, it made a calculated error. "Moreover, man does not know his time: like fish caught in a treacherous net, and birds trapped in a snare, so the sons of men are ensnared at an evil time when it suddenly falls on them" (Eccles. 9:12 NASB).

TRIGGERS FOR IDOLATROUS PRACTICES

Christ's church has been set adrift upon the sea of Greco-Roman forgetfulness where, in general, we have lost much of our sense of time according to God's biblical calendar—according to His time. Easter and Christmastime triggers ancient idolatrous practices in and out of the church. The ancient festival from which the world derives today's Christmas season is the Roman Saturnalia. Saturnalia itself developed from the older rituals of midwinter (i.e., the winter solstice) and goes all the way back to Babylon in the ancient land of Mesopotamia, where the midwinter king's (initially Tammuz) birthday was celebrated on December 25.[246] As the name "Saturnalia" suggests, the celebration was in honor of Saturn. It is no mere happenstance that Saturn is defined as the Roman god of time as well as agriculture.[247] "He . . . shall intend to change times and law . . ." (Dan. 7:25 NKJV).

This is not the most ancient path of the Ancient of Days; but the path of antiquity, which glorifies man and feeds his flesh. Materialism, sensual gratification, and carnal pleasure, readily apparent at Christmastime, cannot, and do not, satisfy one's soul, for these vices are earthly and sensual. It leaves people lusting for more as the manic shopping of December twenty-sixth attests. The kingdom of God is in direct opposition to the kingdom of self. How will the American church be able to stand before God justifying our Babylonian practices and our Greek mind-sets? Instead of time being sanctified as God designed and desires, it became triggers for idolatrous behavior, and shows us a worldly pattern for assimilating God's people into pagan practices and thus corrupting God's priesthood, who are supposed to be holy, with customs associated with idols.

CR

5

THE GOLDEN SNARE
☙

> But they mingled with the Gentiles and learned their works;
> they served their idols, which became a snare to them.
> Thus they were defiled by their own works,
> and played the harlot by their own deeds.
> —Psalm 106:35-36, 39 NKJV

TRADITION OF MAN

In this chapter, we will explore the idolatrous roots of Christmas and how it came to be a "Christian" holy day. If you are analytical, like my husband, you already have asked yourself: How can the majority of Christians and church leaders be wrong in their endorsement of Christmas? I have been surprised as I have personally asked various church leaders about the pagan roots of Christmas. They all seem to know about the pagan roots and rituals of Christmas; and yet, they simply brush off these facts as if they are small things. Just when does passivity become collaboration anyway? I should not be surprised, because they, like I, have become entangled in a tradition of man.

> All too well you reject the commandment of God, that you may keep your tradition. . . . making the word of God of no effect through your tradition which you have handed down.
> —Mark 7:9, 13

I cannot help but think that church leaders are trying (at least to some degree) to please those who pay their salaries. "The fear of man brings a snare, but he who trusts in the LORD will be exalted" (Prov. 29:25 NASB).

That the Christian celebration of Christmas will be a snare is no doubt. My *Webster's Collegiate Dictionary* defines a *snare* as something by which one is entangled, involved in difficulties, or impeded. It is something deceptively attractive. It makes something complicated. It is a position or situation from which it is difficult or impossible to escape. One is caught as if in a trap or lured into a compromising statement or act. "If they have escaped the corruption of the world by knowing our Lord and Savior Jesus Christ and are again entangled in it and overcome, they are worse off at the end than they were at the beginning. It would have been better for them not to have known the way of righteousness, than to have known it and then to turn their backs on the sacred command that was passed on to them" (2 Pet. 2:20-21).

We literally have learned about Christmas through traditions. Yeshua warned His disciples that traditions spread by religious leaders are like leaven[248] (Matt. 16). Once it has mingled with the dough (i.e., the body of Christ) traditions cannot be naturally removed. "What is impossible with men is possible with God" (Luke 18:27); and all He requires is a humble, teachable heart.

Michael Rood exposes that the English word "tradition" is derived from the Latin word *tradiere*, which means to lay into the hands of another. When someone, especially a parent, lays something in a child's hands, one expects the gift to be good. Family members and church leaders, most likely, did not intentionally mislead us; but nonetheless they, and therefore us, can be misled.[249] Sincerely, but hopelessly, misled. The Bible declares that love covers a multitude of sins. The positive edge to this verse has to do with forgiveness and confidentiality. The other end of this two-edged sword communicates what happens with ungodly traditions—soulish love literally covers up the sin its likes.

Traditions are accepted, and usually given, with sincerity and innocence, which is probably why Proverbs 20:25 says it's a snare not to use caution or deliberation when devoting something as holy.

"It is a snare for a man to devote rashly something as holy and afterwards to reconsider his vows" (Prov. 20:25 NKJV). I don't believe that it's merely a coincidence that the New King James Version uses the word "rashly."[250] A rash is an eruption on the body. Hence, sin in the body of Christ causes it not to be holy or healthy. Additionally, 2 Timothy 3:4 tells us that in the last days people will be rash. "But mark this: There will be terrible times in the last days. People will be lovers of themselves, lovers of money, boastful, proud, abusive, disobedient to their parents, without self-control, brutal, not lovers of the good, treacherous, *rash*, conceited, lovers of pleasure rather then lovers of God—having a form of godliness but denying His power" (2 Tim. 3:1-5, emphasis mine).

Traditions, in the eyes of the people who practice them, appear to be good; but the Word of God says: "There is a way that seems right to a man, but its end is the way of death" (Prov. 14:12 NKJV). The book of James says that every good and perfect gift comes from the Father above. It is the responsibility of maturing believers to inspect each gift to see if it is indeed good and perfect. The reality is that a tradition can be either good or evil or a mixture of both. Christians need to measure all of our traditions by the Bible. "Beware lest anyone cheat you through philosophy and empty deceit, according to the traditions of men, according to the basic principles of this world, and not according to Christ" (Col. 2:8 NKJV). All traditions are portrayed as good, but it's naïve to assume that they all are.

Most devout believers who celebrate Christmas will probably tell you that they have sanctified their Christmas traditions. But the question remains: Have you sanctified Christmas or has the Lord? And how can you sanctify something He does not consider holy?

For some 1,750 years or so, Jesus Christ has allowed His Christian church to dedicate some things to Him that are impure, because we have been permitted to operate in an immature, first principles state (Heb. 6:1-2). At Mount Sinai, God's people were told how to prepare for Jehovah's visit. On the first day, which we can equate with first principles, the people were told to sanctify themselves. On the second day, they were told to consecrate themselves, which speaks of the second principles of setting yourself apart for God's exclusive use or setting yourself apart as holy being devoted for sacred use. God's people sanctified themselves and consecrated themselves, because on the third day He was/is coming down (Exod. 19:10-11). It's time to put away childish things (1 Cor. 13:11). In this third day, the Lord Himself will sanctify Himself in and through us. The Lord our God is moving His holy priesthood onto perfection. He is calling us to Him—to His Kingdom—where the mature head of Jesus Christ will be laid on His mature body. Therefore, let us lay aside our childish traditions and practices—"let us throw off everything that hinders and the sin that so easily entangles, and let us run with perseverance the race marked out for us. Let us fix our eyes on Jesus, the author and perfecter of our faith" (Heb. 12:1-2).

COMING FULL CIRCLE

This is a time when the Lord is leading His people to revisit any unholy practice within His church. Things are coming full circle in our day. We are coming full circle to the Puritan origins of America and the pagan origins of Christmas. Many signs are pointing to this fact. Christians must be careful to not resist the One in whom we say we have faith.

Puritans are given credit for being the earliest founders of America and for bringing the gospel to the United States. Many Americans greatly admire the settlers, who came over on the Mayflower; but in 1621, Christmas was just another day for the pilgrims.[251] The Puritans adamantly disagreed with the practice of Christmas, due to its pagan origins. Paul Harvey calls them "Pagan hunting Puritans."[252] Being a fruit of the Reformation, Puritans were in charge of Cromwellian England. When the Puritans came to power in England, attention was repeatedly given to Christmas. In June 1647, Parliament passed legislation abolishing Christmas and other Roman holidays.[253] "In 1659, England fined people five shillings if they were caught celebrating Christmas."[254]

Puritan opposition to Christmas is widely recognized, but what is often overlooked is that many people living in different nations also espoused the same opposition. A significant portion of the American colonial population (Presbyterians, Baptists, Quakers, and Methodists) joined them in eliminating or deemphasizing the observance of Christmas. (Please refer to the "Ardent Reformation" section in chapter 6 for a more information on the Pilgrims and Puritans.)

I know that this examination of Christmas being the golden calf of America is uncomfortable. It has been for me. To the dismay of many, God is transporting us out of our comfort zones. I don't know about you, but I don't want comfort at the expense of truth or solace at the cost of ignorance. Deception needs both ignorance and obstinance to exist. "Rebellion is as bad as the sin of witchcraft, and stubbornness is as bad as worshipping idols" (1 Sam. 15:23 NLT). To begin with, we each must repent for stubborn hearts; we are all guilty to one extent or another for wanting to stay in our comfort zone. In this day, God is dealing with our ignorance in many capacities—the roots and fruits of Christmas are just one facet of this work. It's difficult to comprehend that our mothers, fathers, and religious leaders could have been misleading us all our lives. The Word of God isn't surprised: "Instead, they have followed the stubbornness of their hearts; they have followed the Baals, as their fathers taught them" (Jer. 9:14).

I feel I must reiterate that celebrating Christmas is not a salvation issue, but the Word of God says that the sin of idolatry will affect our eternal rewards, as well as our inheritance in the kingdom of God. It's a bridal heart issue. By following the traditions of pagans, we set ourselves up to be stripped of the reward for which we have worked an entire lifetime. Many people aren't cognizant that we are normally deceived one little compromise at a time. Many times we will follow after seemingly harmless things of this world, without even realizing that we have been led away from following the Messiah. We will have been tricked out of our eternal reward. The Bible says that salvation is by grace, but rewards are earned through obedience and pure-hearted service. ". . . O great and powerful God, whose name is the LORD Almighty, great are your purposes and mighty are your deeds. Your eyes are open to all the ways of men; you reward everyone according to his conduct and as his deeds deserve" (Jer. 32:18-19).

SOLOMON'S HIGH PLACE

King Solomon was the chosen son of the man after God's own heart. He erred in the same way that our American church has. Not long after, the Lord came to Solomon and granted him his heart's desire for wisdom and knowledge, so he could rule and judge God's people justly: "Solomon did evil in the sight of the Lord, and did not follow the Lord, as did his father David. Then Solomon built a high place for Chemosh the abomination of Moab on the hill that is east of Jerusalem, and for Molech the abomination of Ammon" (1 Kings 11:6-7 NKJV). The following verse says: "He did likewise for all his foreign wives, who burned incense and sacrificed to their gods." Solomon mingled with and married the Gentiles. He learned to exert his efforts serving their false gods to such an extent that Solomon even built idolatrous high places of worship in the very place from which the glory of the Lord was supposed to come.[255] And this was *after* the Bible tells us that Solomon's "God was with him and exalted him exceedingly" (2 Chron. 11:1). If the wisest man to ever exist on earth could fall into the trap of idolatry, what makes us think we can't?

Biblically, God's attitude toward godly and wicked kings largely depended upon their attitude and action toward the high places, for He knows that we become what we behold. "From the earliest of times men have tended to choose high places for their worship, whether of God or of false gods which men have invented."[256]

The roots of the high places Solomon built for Chemosh and Molech still existed in Jeremiah's day.

> Thus says the Lord of hosts, the God of Israel: "Amend your ways and your doings, and I will cause you to dwell in this place . . . Obey My voice, and I will be your God, and you shall be My people. And walk in all the ways that I have commanded you, that it may be well with you. Yet they did not obey or incline their ear, but followed the counsels and dictates of their evil hearts, and went backward and not forward. . . . For the children of Judah have done evil in My sight," says the Lord. "They have set their abominations in

the house which is called by My name, to pollute it. And they have built the high places of Tophet, which is in the valley of the son of Hinnom to burn their sons and their daughters in the fire, which I did not command, nor did it come into My heart."

—Jeremiah 7:3, 23-24, 30-31 NKJV

Although Tophet is a different high place than Solomon's Mount Olivet, they both were places where idols were exalted and God's children were sacrificed to the same bloodthirsty gods east of Jerusalem.

Do you think that it's a mere coincidence that enthroned Chemosh (worshiped by the Moabites), Mithra (from Persia, worshiped in Rome), and Tammuz (of Babylon fame) wore the same Phrygian[257] cap as Santa Claus? In Michael Rood's enlightening book *The Pagan-Christian Connection Exposed, Truth vs. Tradition*, he expounds that Chemosh was the pagan god of prosperity that was the same cast iron, pot-bellied god of their kin, the Ammonites, who was worshiped by the name of Molech or Moloch. At the time of the winter solstice on the ancient calendar, they had a public child mass. "Mass" literally means sacrifice in this context. "The priests stoked the iron image of the enthroned Chemosh with wood and burning pitch, which turned the idol into a cherry red furnace. Moabite people made long lists of their desires, and recited them to the god of prosperity just before they put their infant children into the red-hot lap of their god with his Phrygian cap. As the babies were incinerated during the December 25th child mass, the people were assured that their sacrifices would be rewarded in the coming year."[258] Michael Rood has an interesting perspective: "A month before the birthday of Tammuz (December 25th) we have our children make endless lists to a cherry-red pot-bellied god of prosperity, and then we place our terrified children in the lap of this god who wears his Phrygian cap and sits on his throne in the shopping malls."[259] Minimally, I believe that each Christmas we currently sacrifice our children's well-being to gods of prosperity, creating the unrighteous dispositions of being demanding and spoiled. Am I the only parent to experience my child's ungrateful complaint, "Is that it?" when he had just opened a boatload of gifts?

Baal or Moloch or Chemosh—the name may change, but their bloodthirsty appetite for the most acceptable offering of infants does not. "We have ample and melancholy evidence on this subject from the records of antiquity."[260] It was believed that human sacrifice to Baal held the key to prosperity. Therefore, selfish people desiring to live in ease brought their firstborn child to the high priest, where scholars say the child would be offered as a burnt offering to the deity. Recently, archaeologists unearthed a baal cemetery containing the remains of more than twenty thousand children.[261] "I will cut off from this place every remnant of Baal . . . those who bow down and swear by the LORD and who also swear by Molech" (Zeph. 1:4-5). The late Reverend Hislop's extensive research led him to conclude: "Moloch and Roman Saturn have the same bloody character."[262] This fact is important in our analysis of Christmas being the golden calf of America. As you will discover later in this chapter, the church of Rome was unable to eradicate the heathen celebration of Saturnalia, so they slightly modified it and designated a Feast of the Nativity to be observed.[263]

CONSTANTINE COMPROMISES

The city is Nicaea. The year is AD 325. The Roman emperor Constantine assured the unity of the church by quickly exerting efforts to centralize authority.[264] The pressured bishops, at the Council of Nicaea, played their part in helping to forge the church in the crucible of politics. The Roman Catholic Church, with the help of Constantine's policies and practices, had pagans join Christianity as if it were some sort of club. The people jostled for favor and funds from the generous Constantine, as the sole Roman Emperor sought to "Christianize" his empire; thus, making "efforts to obtain unity in the Church so that it might better subserve the needs of the empire."[265] The truth is that Christ's church politically merged with Rome. The church compromised in many ways in its quest for power and sole supremacy over people's souls, as they sought to separate themselves from the church's original Jewish flavor, and even, from Jewish believers themselves.[266] After the Council of Nicaea declared: "our worship follows a more legitimate and convenient course"[267] and "we desire . . . to separate ourselves from the detestable company of the Jews,"[268] Jewish and Gentile believers drifted apart. My primary concern stems from how the Christian church could say, "the Saviour has shown them another way,"[269] when the appointed feasts of the Lord listed in Leviticus 23 and practiced by His people are called feasts forever and the Lord expressly says, "these are My feasts" (Lev. 23:2, 14, 21, 31, 41). Understandably, some scholars suggest that Constantine's primary motivation at Nicaea was to make sure the church was cut off from Judaism. "The consequences of this council included the establishment of Christian holidays, which were to take place at least one week before or after the Jewish holidays. *Shabbat* (the Sabbath) had already been moved from Saturday to Sunday (named after *Sol Invictus*, the sun god) in 321 A.D. Again, the idea was to obscure any connection between the Church and Judaism."[270]

No one knows for sure the extent of Constantine's influence on the Council of Nicaea, but we do know of his larger-than-life presence and of his approval of the proceedings. James Carroll tells us that "Constantine had demonstrated his authority over bishops by convening the Council of Nicaea. The empire was unified under Constantine as supreme head, with the leaders of the Church subservient to him."[271]

One may question the validity of the work brought forth at Nicaea, especially since the emperor himself was the first to admit that the articles of faith proposed were perfectly correct and he entertained the sentiments contained in them[272] at a time when he could not participate in communion (i.e., the Eucharist), because he wasn't baptized.[273] Also of note is that corruption, as we would think of it, was not so much a disease of Roman administration, as an integral part of it.[274] However, since the approved canon of Scripture and articles of faith (for example: "The Apostle's Creed") lined up with their original context in the first-century church, I for one believe that the Lord steered the course of imperfect man. We just need to re-examine what was agreed upon, according to the plumb line of Scripture and the Spirit of the living God, for the pure and spotless

Bride of Christ to become manifest. For one thing, our timetable is off, due to the calendar being switched to accommodate the sun and pagan holidays, instead of being solely based on the Word of God and the Lord's religious festivals, new moon celebrations, and Sabbath days, which regulates a biblical year, month, and week. According to T.G. Elliott, "Constantine particularly wished, as did all churchmen, that all Christians should celebrate Easter on the same day, but he also wanted them freed from the Jewish lunisolar calendar, which might produce two Easters in the same solar year, or no Easter at all."[275] How significant that God's biblical calendar would not support a pagan holiday.

Christ's church is being asked to revisit the very areas where biblical compromises have been made. Our compromises have allowed controversies to arise, which have brought confusion both to those who are Christian and to those who are not.

In 2005, a Wisconsin elementary school secularized the lyrics to "Silent Night" and added *La Befana*, the Christmas Witch, to their classroom decorations.[276] Christians may like to believe that the Christmas Witch rides her broom delivering toys to bad little boys and girls, like some sort of Anti-Santa; but then again her name means "the epiphany."[277] In Italy, the Christmas Witch is said to make perfect sense because she used to deliver presents in Italian children's stockings on the day of Epiphany, January 6, which is the day that the Catholic church speciously instituted as the celebration of the arrival of the wise men in Bethlehem. Just think, anyone can purchase an old world ornament of a Christmas witch with a cauldron from the *Noel Christmas Store's* website.[278] If that doesn't strike your fancy, how about a black bat, an evil eye, or a devil's head decoration for your tree?

The Christian controversy over Christmas rages on. What about Christmas trees versus holiday trees? What about "Merry Christmas" versus "Happy Holidays"? What about colored lights versus white? Christmas music being banned from a school bus? Christmas carols being forbidden? Christmas cards with Jesus barred? Christmas CD expelled for mentioning Jesus? Some Christians are becoming aggravated and offended. We should note that offense is the bait of Satan according to John Bevere, and anyone who remains in umbrage is in sin. The archaic definition of the word *offense* means "a cause or occasion of sin—a stumbling block."[279]

Dan Brown's blockbuster 2006 book *The DaVinci Code* is just one of the installments of a confusing controversy for the church. Granted, the book is a work of fiction, so one may question the vehemence of Christian opposition and the plethora of Christian books written to refute its claims. The Christian church must realize that Brown's assertion that Constantine merged paganism with Christianity for political gain is an accurate historical fact; and I quote:

> Historians still marvel at the brilliance with which Constantine converted the sun-worshiping pagans to Christianity. By fusing pagan symbols, dates and rituals into the growing Christian tradition, he created a kind of hybrid religion that was acceptable to both parties.[280]

> Christianity honored the Jewish Sabbath of Saturday, but Constantine shifted it to coincide with the pagan's veneration day of the sun.[281]

> Constantine took advantage of Christ's substantial influence and importance. And in doing so he shaped the face of Christianity as we know it today.[282]

All these statements I've cited from *The DaVinci Code* are accurate; but when misconstrued, unfortunately, leave room for people to falsely claim "that almost every thing our fathers taught us about Christ is false."[283] It fuels people's belief that Christianity is a man-made religion like all the rest. "They spoke about the God of Jerusalem as they did about the gods of the other peoples of the world—the work of men's hands" (2 Chron. 32:19). If Christians were completely honest, we would refute the claim of Jesus' marriage to Mary Magdalene and other heresies proclaimed by Dan Brown; but we would also admit that the Christian church made concessions to the truth in Constantine's day. Confessing the Constantine compromises and coming out of agreement with their besmirched practices, which contradict the Lord's eternal truth, will set the church free to operate in the reality of the kingdom of Christ and our God. Any compromise to the truthfulness articulated in God's Word lays it and us (i.e., the people of the Book) open to suspicion, disrepute, et cetera.

In AD 312, Constantine was said to have a "conversion" experience through a battle-eve vision of the cross at the Milvian Bridge,[284] which was not reliably recounted until 325 in Constantine's own words.[285] Recall that after his professed conversion until the day he died, "Constantine could not even take part in the Eucharist, because he was not baptized."[286] "Constantine himself for years after A.D. 312, continued to pay his public honors to the Sun. They were paid in the coin of the realm—rather, on coins, in the form of images of the emperor shown jointly with Sol,"[287] which was a concrete demonstration of the condition of his heart. On one side of Constantine's coin was embossed a virtuous image of the emperor himself. The other side displayed the image of a man with the whole world in his hands and sunbeams radiating from his face. One inscription encircling this "glorious" image was *Sol Invict to Commite,* which means committed to the invisible sun; the other inscription proclaimed *Sol Invictus Mithra,* which identified Constantine's invisible sun as Mithra.[288] Constantine was a worshiper of the sun god *Sol Invictus Mithra,* following in the footsteps of his supposedly Christian father, who had ruled under the protection of Sol Invictus or Apollo in Gaul and Britain.[289] "Sol, the pagan sun god, continued to be honored on Constantine's coins until 321,"[290] which was the same year the Christian Sabbath was moved from the seventh day to the first day of the week.

Not unlike marginal Christians of today, Constantine's actions didn't always indicate that he was a Christian, so one is left to wonder whether Constantine truly was a Christian or not. I think that Dan Brown may be correct in saying that "He [Constantine] was a life-long pagan who was baptized on his deathbed . . . In Constantine's day, Rome's official religion was sun worship—the cult of Sol Invictus—and Constantine was its head priest."[291] On the other hand, history also reveals that Constantine was officially baptized on May 22, 337—the day he died. The story goes that when his generals came to him in tears, Constantine declared that he was now in possession of true life, and in a hurry to go to God.[292] Only God and Constantine know if his deathbed baptism was a true profession of faith in Jesus, or if the Roman Emperor was merely covering all his bases. The Lord our God is full of grace for Constantine and for every other soul; and it is up to Him to determine Constantine's heart condition and, thus, his eternal destiny. However, I believe that it's important to note that although Constantine greatly enriched the church on earth physically and was instrumental in stopping Christian persecution, I believe that he did not show many signs of a born-again disposition.

Historically, we know that Constantine had his wife and his eldest son murdered in 326—a year after the Council of Nicaea convened (definitely not a fruit of the Spirit),[293] and beheaded confidant Sopater also would testify to Constantine's violation of the sixth commandment (i.e., thou shall not murder). Constantine's family is a picture of the true state of the empire he created. In the name of unity, violence was justified. After Constantine died, his surviving sons[294] immediately were embroiled in a secession struggle, which led to a Constantinople bloodbath. At the end, less than half of Constantine's male household was left alive (including his three sons). For more than two decades after Constantine's death, a pathological culture of "holy" violence reigned. There was ample precedence, but this brutality went by the name of Christianity. Various rivals claimed pious motives for political machinations.[295] The church still experiences its share of splits, with each side claiming to have more pious motives than the other. Constantine turned the cross of Christ into a sword. "But Jesus said to him, 'Put your sword in its place, for all who take the sword will perish by the sword'" (Matt. 26:52 NKJV). The fact that Christian piety included pagan practice and superstition lent a broad appeal to the "gospel" among the least educated masses. That the cross of Christ, as a standard to march behind, evoked the ancestral totem of the sacred tree familiar to the majority of Constantine's initial army[296] points more to Constantine's pragmatic tolerance as a modus operandi than to devout faith.

Christian scholars have exercised much in trying to explain Constantine's attempt to immortalize himself as the reincarnation of the god Apollo or Sol with an image wearing the rayed crown of the sun god after his supposed conversion.[297] "Constantine placed a statue of himself on a pillar high above all the other gods in Constantinople. Lightning struck the image, and the burnt column is still standing today—but without Constantine's charred image."[298] Many have questioned the genuineness of Constantine's conversion. He accommodated the old Byzantine cults of Rhea and Helios in a portico near the Basilica, and imported statuary from all over the Roman Empire to grace his new city Constantinople.[299] Another monument to Constantine's sun worship practices exists in that in "many Roman churches, including the Church of San Clemente in Rome most notably, still contain well-preserved mithraeums (underground temples where Mithras were worshiped) in their vaulted burial crypts."[300] Never mind the fact that Constantine had the Vatican built atop the hill where the Mithras cult worshiped the sun.[301]

The fruits of murder and idolatry plainly exhibit the less-than-godly character of Constantine; therefore, we need to examine what entered the church at this time, due to Constantine's powerful influence and him being a less-than-virtuous spearhead for the Christianization of Western Civilization. When Constantine and the Roman Christian Church mixed pagan solar customs with "The Way," they both had the ultimate aim to consolidate power under their own particular political agenda. Their goal was to build a kingdom—their own kingdom(s)—not fully realizing that their concessions moved them outside the veracity of God's eternal kingdom. Trying to appease the masses, together they promised to give the people the "best" of both worlds. But in fact God says: "They wouldn't listen; they kept on doing whatever they wanted to, following their own stubborn, evil thoughts. They went backward instead of forward. For the people of Judah have sinned before my very eyes, says the Lord. They have set up their idols right in My own Temple, polluting it" (Jer. 7:23-24, 30 TLB).

Christmas is an idol set up right in God's own temple. The immediate predecessors of our modern Christmas come from two sources:

- Today's Christmas season was formerly the mid-December to January first pagan celebration of Saturnalia in Rome.
- Today's Christmas day was originally Mithra's Winter Festival celebrated on December twenty-fifth.

The amount of supporting evidence is so extensive in this information age that a thick book could be written on Christmas's origins and its flow through almost every culture to date. As mentioned earlier, the pagan Romans supposedly became Christian, but the Saturnalia remained. Over the next thousand years, Christmas followed the ever-expanding community of Christianity. "By the end of the sixth century, Christianity had taken the holiday far northward and into England. During the next two hundred years in Scandinavia, it became fused with the pagan Norse feast season known as Yule — the time of year also known as the Teutonic Midwinter. Sometime around the Norman incursion in 1050, the Old English word *Christes maesse* . . . entered the English language."[302]

If you're interested in researching this more thoroughly, check out the late Reverend Alexander Hislop's book: *The Two Babylons*. It's helpful for us to note that Hislop records: The original name of Rome was "Saturnalia," the city of Saturn, the city on seven hills where the Roman god Saturn formerly reigned. The whole of Italy was long after called by his name being commonly called "The Saturnian Land." On the Capitoline hill, the image of Saturn, the formerly great Chaldean god, had been erected as a great high place of Roman worship when the Pagan Roman Emperors laid claim to the title *pontifex maximus*. The *pontifex maximus* existed in Rome from the earliest of times, and was modeled after the head Pontiff at Babylon.[303] By the way, Constantine never renounced his *pontifex maximus* title.[304]

There is no clean break between the sacred roots and fruits of Christmas versus the pagan. It's like everything else in life. Each person must decide for themselves what to reject, accept, and/or compromise. I personally cannot find a line that I can draw in the sand when it comes to celebrating Christmas. Believe me I have tried! But when my Beloved revealed His heart: "The mixture of Christmas grieves My heart. Come out of Babylon and lay down

Christmas, for I *will* have a pure and spotless Bride," I had no choice but to lay it and other Roman holidays down. I was included in the category of well-meaning Christians giving out Christmas cards, candy canes, and Christmas gifts every year as a witness that Jesus is the reason for the season. But if we come to grips with the fact that there is a God in heaven and He does have an opinion on everything; then we must evaluate our well-intended reminders and evangelistic tools according to the plumb line of Scripture.

That Christmas was originally a pagan festival is beyond all doubt. The time of year and the ceremonies still celebrated proves its origin, as does the documented testimony of the Roman Catholic Church. Jeremiah tells us that in the last days Israel would return to her own land, and the Gentiles (believers and unbelievers alike) would come to the sons of Israel and cry out in repentance: "Surely our fathers have inherited lies, vanity, and things wherein there is no profit" (Jer. 16:19 NKJV). God also says that one day we would ask why so much evil has come upon us and the answer will be: "It's because your fathers have followed after the ways of the heathen—worshiping their gods—and they say they were doing it for Me. Your fathers forsook my instruction and developed their own religion by following their own imaginations." Many of our Christmas traditions follow after heathen ways, and we Christians truly believe that Jesus is the reason for our Christmas season. I know I believed this; but Tertullian says, "By us who are strangers to Sabbaths, new moons, and festivals once acceptable to God, the Saturnalia, the feasts of January . . . are now frequented; gifts are carried to and fro, new year's day presents are made with din, and sports and banquets are celebrated with uproar; oh, how much more faithful are the heathen to their religion."[305]

Saturnalia itself developed from the older rituals of midwinter into a riotous assemblage of fun, laughter, and gift giving. It is, indeed, from this festival that we receive the idea of giving gifts at Christmas and not from the gifts of the Magi as commonly supposed. As its name suggests, the celebration was in honor of Saturn, the Roman god of agriculture and time [changing of time to be exact] . . . during which time the normal patterns of social behavior were abandoned . . . the law courts and schools were closed, and the whole community gave itself up to feasting, gambling, and drinking. The festival began with the *sacrificum publicum* in which a young pig was sacrificed in the temple of Saturn in the Forum. Senators put aside their togas . . . and gifts were exchanged, among them . . . terracotta dolls known as *signillaria*, which may well refer back to a time when human sacrifices were offered to the gods of midwinter.[306]

In the eastern provinces of the Roman Empire, during Saturnalia, a Mock King was crowned to rule over chaos. This Mock King, *Saturnalicus Princeps*, assumed the role of Saturn throughout the raucous winter festival. His task was to behave as foolishly as possible.[307] "The festival of Saturnalia continued to be celebrated every year right up until the end of the fourth century."[308]

ANCIENT IDOLATRY MADE MODERN

The process of assimilation has been characteristic of the Roman church throughout the centuries. Instead of having pagans give up their former idolatrous ways, the church replaced their pagan superstitions and practices with similar ecclesiastical institutions.[309] Its methodology was, and still is, conquest through assimilation. Within Roman Catholicism there is no policy designed to eradicate heathen practices. Pope Gregory wrote in AD 606: "The temples of the idols among the people should on no account be destroyed. . . . And since they have a custom of sacrificing many oxen to demons, let some other solemnity be substituted in its place."[310] The Roman Catholic Church was encouraged to give pagans church relics, rites, ceremonies, and festivals as substitutes for their heathen ones. My Bible tells me that God commands His children to cut down sacred groves, destroy the remnants of idolatry, and even burn heathen books in order to make a clean break with their formerly pagan ways (Exod. 34:12; Acts 19:19). It is the duty of God's people to remove all traces of idolatry from among them.[311]

Christmas, Easter, and other Roman holidays are idolatrous high places of worship for the Christian church, which have been carried over from its Babylonian root and have flowed through Greece, Rome, and every other empire/nation in the world. Christians have conveniently lost track of the fact that throughout the ancient world

December twenty-fifth was known as the birthday of the sun gods,[312] but pagans and historians have not. By the way, Dan Brown reveals that sun gods were born on December twenty-fifth too.[313] The church's amnesia does not negate the fact that December twenty-fifth was the birth date of Tammuz, the Babylonian sun god said to be reincarnated Nimrod.[314] As we have observed, the sun was a favorite object of worship in Babylon and elsewhere. It was an essential principle of the Babylonian system that the Sun or Baal or Tammuz was the one and only god. Egypt has infamously constructed its life and lifestyles around the sun and its deities. An Egyptian tree custom was performed on Ra's birthday—December twenty-fifth.[315] In 168 BC, the Syrian-Greek General Antiochus Epiphanes IV occupied Jerusalem. He set up a statue of Zeus and sacrificed a pig on the altar in God's temple on Zeus's birthday—December twenty-fifth. When Rome conquered Persia, many Romans liked merging their "modern" Western culture with the more ancient practices of the Orient, so they adopted the worship of the sun god Mithra (the Persian version of Babylonian Tammuz) with Roman Emperor Constantine, being the most famous worshiper of Mithraism in the Roman Empire. Do you remember what day the sun god Mithra was said to have been born? That's right. December twenty-fifth. Prior to the Roman Catholic Church adopting this date on her liturgical calendar, the ancient sun gods had their birthdays celebrated on the twenty-fifth day of December, for that day marked the returning of the sun (i.e., the winter solstice). Despite the fact that the twenty-fifth is no longer midwinter in a given year, due to the Roman shift to our calendar, the world continues to celebrate the successful amalgamation of the old pagan festivals dedicated to the sun with the newer, albeit inaccurate, birthday for Jesus. Have our partially remembered facts and our misremembered past turned truth on its head? Has the church enshrined a falsehood through its institutionalization of Christmas?

What should be our reaction to the earliest Christian's view that birthday celebrations were heathen? For now, I personally believe that celebrating people's birthdays is just fine. But I believe that we all should be concerned that by assigning Jesus the human quality of a birthday, the "official" church compromised with a heretical

Arianism philosophy, which regarded Jesus solely as a human agent, while still proclaiming that Jesus sustained His place in the Holy Trinity.[316] The Babylonian fingerprints of mixture and confusion are all over Jesus' birthday celebration.

The *Catholic Encyclopedia* tells us that Sol was the name of the sun god of the largest pagan religious cult of the time, which spanned both the Greek and Roman empires. Church father Tertullian asserted that Sol was not the Christians' God, and Augustine denounced the heretical identification of Christ with Sol.[317] There had been a cult of Sol in Rome before 10 BC. At this time, Roman Emperor Augustus outmoded Sol with celebratory games in honor of Greek Apollo. In time, another figure superseded Apollo—Mithras—who dates back to the sixth century BC. The cultic mysteries of Mithras were imported into Rome around the second century AD by legionaries, who served in the eastern portion of the Roman Empire. Being an important aspect of Roman spiritual life until as late as the fifth century, Mithraism's feast day was Sun-Day and declared to be on December twenty-fifth by Emperor Aurelian, who declared that day not only to be the birthday of Sol, but Mithras as well.[318] The pagan sun worship of Mithraism, with its god Mithra, had a winter festival called "The Nativity" or "The Nativity of the Sun" or "The Nativity of the Unconquered Sun."[319] The *Catholic Encyclopedia* itself admits that: "The Nativity of the Unconquered Sun, celebrated on 25 December, has a strong claim on the responsibility for our December date."[320] Clearly, Constantine's original piety was associated with the sun; and pagans would have recognized their own solar cults in the church's practice of orienting their cathedrals to the east, worshiping on "Sun Day," and celebrating the birth of the deity at the winter solstice.[321] It had become common practice in the fifth century for worshipers entering St. Peter's Basilica in Rome to turn at the door, put their backs to God's altar, and bow down to worship the rising sun.[322] Please refer to Ezekiel 8:16 for God's opinion of this practice. The first recorded evidence of Christmas actually taking place on December twenty-fifth isn't found until the time of Constantine in AD 336.[323]

For the first three hundred years, nothing resembling Christmas existed in the Christian church's ecclesiastical calendar. The church followed the pattern established by the apostles. They experienced a life and a power the world could not comprehend.[324] Both Irenaeus and Tertullian[325] omit Christmas from their list of feasts.[326] We will go into further detail in chapter 7 about how Christ's church, in its primal form, celebrated the Lord's feasts. One reason was that the church was entirely Jewish until salvation came to Cornelius and his house as well as the fact that Christianity began as a movement within the Jewish community. It continued to operate within a Jewish framework for several decades into the second century.[327] During the pre-Constantine period of the church, several major events in the life of Jesus had no corresponding festival, including His birth; because these events did not synchronize with any biblical festival, which is a solid testimony to the Jewish character of early Christian worship, due to their practices being based upon God's Word.[328] Even in the fourth century, only the birth of Jesus acquired a separate festival, being fixed on the basis of the Roman or Julian calendar on December twenty-fifth. Christianity's first move in the direction away from the biblical calendar happened in the second century. It began with a slight compromise to Passover, where the nearest Sunday was chosen to mark the day of Christ's resurrection,[329] rather than starting with the beginning of the Passover season on the fourteenth of *Nisan*, then counting three days to the Feast of First Fruits. By the way, the Feast of First Fruits (i.e., *Bikkurim*) is the actual day that Jesus Christ rose from the dead.

Long before the fourth century's Christian Christmas "holy" day was set and long before the Christian era itself, a festival was celebrated among the heathen at that precise time of the year. It was in honor of the birth of the son of the Babylonian Queen of Heaven. His name was Tammuz.[330] The earliest Christians were not interested in Jesus' birthday until the fourth century church began to regard Mary, the mother of Jesus, in a new light and cast her into an image of the earth. This idolatrous image was the supposedly "Christianized" QUEEN OF HEAVEN. Mary had long been revered with the saints and apostles, but only along with them, not exalted above them. The Roman church put Mary in heaven, not merely among the great cloud of witnesses cheering us on, but as a queen—the Queen of Heaven. This was not just any old Queen of Heaven position. Mary was exalted into the exact status as the Babylonian mother goddess, who had been positioned by pagans as the first counterfeit Queen of Heaven. Ironically, I believe that Jesus' mother is part of the authentic corporate queen of heaven, which will ultimately be the Bride of Christ. But Mary is only a part of the Bride of Christ, as you and I can be a part. The same fourth century that Christmas began to be celebrated by the Roman Catholic Church was the exact same timeframe that the Babylonian infant son and his adored Queen of Heaven mum both began to be worshiped too, and religious Babylon has been entangled in the church ever since. "They have set their abominations in the house which is called by My name, to pollute it" (Jer. 7:30 NKJV). "I have laid a snare for you; you have indeed been trapped, O Babylon, and you were not aware; you have been found and also caught, because you have contended against the Lord" (Jer. 50:24 NKJV).

I will give you a hint about the counterfeit truth that flows from the well of ancient Babylon: People were led to believe that a real spiritual change of heart was unnecessary, and as far as needful change, they could regenerate themselves by mere external means. The chief good for mankind promoted by Babylon was sensual enjoyment and the pleasures of sin without any fear from the wrath of God. A pagan, according to my *Webster's Collegiate Dictionary*, is one who has little or no religion and who delights in sensual pleasures and material goods—a hedonistic person. Personally, I'd replace the word "religion" with the concept of a personal relationship with God because I believe that not too many people are interested in merely religion.

AN IDOL IN THE FORM OF

"Even while these people were worshiping the LORD, they were serving their idols. To this day their children and grandchildren continue to do as their fathers did" (2 Kings 17:41). We need to lay aside our own preconceived notions and ask ourselves: How does Jesus view Himself being depicted as a statue in crèches during Christmas? It may surprise many Christians that some of the crèche fixtures aren't described in the Bible: the donkey, cows, sheep, and the wise men. Scripture articulates that the Magi came to a house not a manger (Matt. 2:11). If one considers that, historically, the Babylonian statues depicting a Madonna and child were used to facilitate worship to pagan gods, one must ask, what does Jesus really think of those statues of Him lying in a manger? And do my beliefs violate Scripture? "It is a snare for a man to devote rashly something as holy, and afterwards to reconsider his vows" (Prov. 20:25 NKJV).

To accurately answer these important questions, we have to look into the first two commandments of the Ten Commandments with the same viewpoint of Jesus and His first disciples. The first commandment to a Hebrew is to have faith in God's existence: "I am the LORD your God, who brought you out of Egypt, out of the land of slavery" (Exod. 20:2). This first commandment appears to be more of a statement than a commandment. Maybe that's why these words in Hebrew are called the Ten Statements instead of the Ten Commandments.[331] There have been considerable controversies among Jewish scholars over whether the first statement commands belief in God or belief can't be commanded. Most Jewish authorities agree with the great Jewish philosopher Maimonides[332] that belief in God is not only desirable, but is indeed commanded.[333]

God's people were taught that if they violated one of the first five commandments, they had sinned against God and they had to reject their belief in God at the outset. "Without faith it is impossible to please Him, for he who comes to God must believe that He is, and that He is a rewarder of those who seek Him" (Heb. 11:6 NASB). "I am the LORD your God, who brought you out of the land of Egypt, out of the house of slavery" (Exod. 20:2 NASB) is both a positive command and a simple statement of fact. "I am the LORD your God" announced that He is Israel's deity and sovereign. Laws are not official until the authority of the One in charge is established and acknowledged. Just think about the first commandment as an opening statement in a treaty between God and His people.

For years, I was confused over the church saying that the first commandment is: "You shall have no other gods before Me" (Exod. 20:3), and the second is: "You shall not make for yourself a carved image . . ." (Exod. 20:4-5). To me they seemed redundant. Why?

Probably because the Hebraic view of our Bible tells us that they are different sections of the same commandment.

Exodus 20:3-6 delineates the second commandment: "You shall have no other gods before me. You shall not make for yourself an idol in the form of anything in heaven above or on the earth beneath or in the waters below. You shall not bow down to them or worship them; for I, the LORD your God, am a jealous God, punishing the children for the sin of the fathers to the third and fourth generation of those who hate me, but showing love to a thousand [generations] of those who love me and keep my commandments." **The Second Commandment has four separate negative injunctions against idolatry where:**

1) **A person is forbidden to believe in idols.** We are told every Christmas season to believe in the spirit of Christmas, and as Christians we try to personalize this spirit as the Holy Spirit. But it's not. It's make-believe. The pagans inform us: "Take the spirit of Christmas himself—Santa Claus, Father Christmas, Saint Nicholas, Old St. Nick, Syre Christemas, Sinter Class—his names are legion and his true origins almost as old as history."[334]

   I have noticed over the past several years that whenever anyone mentions believing in the spirit of Christmas, Santa Claus is referenced. *The Polar Express* movie swept the country during the 2004 Christmas season. All the train tickets that the kids in the movie received spelled out two letters of the word "believe." The boy who held the only winning "BE" ticket had to first say "I believe" three times before he could receive the first gift of Christmas—a bell from one of Santa's reindeer. Kids who believe in Santa can hear the bell; but their parents can't, due to their unbelief. For several years, the annual Fort Collins Symphony Guild's Christmas concert's theme has been "Truly Believe," with its focus on Santa. I know of one family in my son's grade school who are atheists. They try to fill their spiritual void with at least one belief besides being the best in everything, which is perpetuating the Santa Claus myth so their fifth grade child can still accept it as true. A Christian should question anything that is based on lies and deceptions, for these vices are not of God's kingdom.

2) **A person is forbidden to make or process idols**. "Of what value is . . . an image that teaches lies? For he who makes it trusts in his own creation; he makes idols that cannot speak" (Hab. 2:18).

3) **A person is forbidden to worship idols** through any of the four forms of divine service, which are:
   - prostration,
   - animal slaughter,
   - bringing offerings, or
   - bringing libations of wine or other liquids to pour upon an altar/item.

4) **A person is forbidden to worship an idol by means that is unique to it**. For example, the believers of Mercury worshiped it by throwing stones at its statue.[335] What about all of our Christmas traditions? What about our stockings that are hung by the chimney with care? What about our Christmas trees, which are an extension of an ancient Babylonian practice?

THE COSMIC CHRISTMAS TREE

Every year most people in America take a tree (usually from the fir family) and bring it into their home. They decorate it with lights and sparkling ornaments with some sort of figure on top. It becomes the center of the house for a season. Gifts are laid beneath the evergreen, and eventually, family and friends sit around it. Yet, few remember, or even care to know, the pagan symbolism that gave rise to its place in our lives. Recall that the evergreen, displayed at the turn of the winter solstice, links ancient and modern traditions. Just look in your own hometown to see what an essential part of Christmas the decorated tree truly is.

Babylon marked the beginning of tree or creation worship. Emerging from Babylon was Egypt's worship of the pagan messiah Baal-Tamar, which was symbolized as a palm tree. Among the ancient baals, he was also known as Baal-Bereth, the "Lord of the fir tree." Baal-Bereth evolved into Baal-Berith, the "Lord of the Covenant," which apostate Israel worshiped in place of Jehovah—the only true God of the covenant. Ancient tree/creation worship, symbolized by the fir tree, extended into the pre-Christian Roman Empire; pagan-Romans referred to their god as Baal-Berith. Furthermore, early Romans marked the winter solstice with a feast in honor of Saturn and decorated their homes and temples with evergreen boughs.[336]

The Christmas tree, as we know it, dates back only a few centuries, but the idea of sacred trees is very ancient. "An old Babylonian tale told of an evergreen tree, which sprang out of a dead tree stump. The old stump symbolized the dead Nimrod, the new evergreen tree symbolized that Nimrod had come back to life again in Tammuz!"[337]

In at least ten biblical references, the green tree is associated with idolatry and false worship. Case in point: "Judah did evil in the sight of the LORD, and they provoked him to jealousy with their sins which they had committed, above all that their fathers had done. For they also built them high places, and images, and groves, on every high hill, and under every green tree" (1 Kings 14:22-23 KJV). Prior to pagan winter solstice traditions being adopted by Christianity, the Canaanite high places were embraced as sanctuaries in Israel. Biblical prophets and prophetic historians rightly regarded these Canaanite trappings (i.e., idols[338]) as profane. Generally speaking, Israel was rebuked for worshiping the baals and Astarte, gods of the land, alongside Jehovah. Significantly, it was a common opinion that the wooden Asherah pole, which ordinarily stood at Palestinian "holy" places, was a surrogate for the living tree.[339] The green tree or Asherah poles were artificial, man-made sanctuaries, which provoked the Lord's anger.

The people in Jeremiah's day were making an idol out of a tree. Throughout history, many would decorate their trees with elaborate ornaments and set them up as shrines, in their homes, to honor the pagan sun god of their particular culture. In addition, they named the day of his birth Sun Day, and gave each other gifts in celebration. These pagan tree idols and rituals surrounding the Yule log and Yule day seem to be referred to in Jeremiah 10:3-4, which is the most enlightening Scripture in my mind in regards to a Christmas tree: "For the customs of the peoples are worthless; they cut a tree out of the forest, and a craftsman shapes it with his chisel. They adorn it with silver and gold; they fasten it with hammer and nails so it will not totter." Even though this scripture is referring to a person actually making an idol, my spirit tells me that the pagan roots of the Christmas tree appear to be very ancient indeed. The Christmas tree recapitulates the idea of tree worship with gilded nuts and balls on a tree symbolizing the sun.

"The Christmas tree began life as the solstice evergreen, being adapted in medieval and Victorian times to the tinsel-decked image of today."[340] Decorating evergreen trees had always been a part of the German winter solstice tradition.[341] In the world where everything is welcomed,[342] the solstice evergreen is called the world tree, which a shaman is said to climb to get through the smoke hole of a skin tent into the "bright heavens," where the spirits (i.e., demons) wait to take him on a journey to find the gifts of the subtle spirit realm. Sun images were hung on a tree, which also formed the central pole of the tent, and represented for the shamans the axis of the world, which was said to lead to the heavens (by the way, a shaman can only reach the lowest level of the heavens). The carnal worshipers of this world recognize the Christmas tree as a cosmic tree connecting heaven to earth.[343]

In chapter 1, we discussed how Ezekiel 8 details four increasingly detestable things that drive the Lord from His sanctuary. The fourth and most detestable practice is seen in the inner court of the house of the Lord between the portico and altar. Remember how the portico is a place of traversing back and forth; it can be akin to a heaven to earth connection.[344] Also recall that the most detestable practice involved God's close companions grievously bowing down to the sun. You may ask yourself: How is it possible that God's friends and family could worship the sun after being very tight with Him? As the Bible says, "There is nothing new under the sun" (Eccles. 1:9b). Today, on the birthday of the sun gods, most Christians bow down in front of a tree hung with sun images to exchange gifts with one another in honor of the ancient commemoration of The Nativity of the Sun, without realizing its idolatrous origins.

On the early Christian calendar, December twenty-fourth was identified as Adam and Eve's Day.[345] During the time that the Christmas holiday was being forged in America, *Godey's* magazine tried to fashion a conventional image for the ancient fertility symbol that became a domestic talisman. This evergreen icon of family was clearly meant to be commemorated as Adam and Eve's Day. Americans were told that "an orthodox Christmas-tree will have the figures of our first parents at its foot, and the serpent twining himself round its stem."[346] A legend from the early sixteenth century tells that the people of Germany adopted the Paradise Tree custom (a fir tree decorated with apples), which is said to represent the Tree of Life.[347] Fortunately, its fruit identifies itself as the Tree of the Knowledge of Good and Evil, which was the tree that serpent wrapped himself around. Its link continues on into today. This same Germany is credited with starting the Christmas tree tradition, as we know it, in the same sixteenth century. In the place where America's freedom was born—Philadelphia—*The Freethought Society* exercised their first amendment rights in 2007. They erected a Tree of Knowledge as part of the multicultural Christmas display.[348] These atheists can make the Tree of Knowledge connection to Christmas, because it's there. In our next chapter, we will see how exact this correlation is. Now who tempted Eve to eat of the Tree of the Knowledge of Good and Evil? "The serpent" (Gen. 3:1), which is "the dragon, the serpent of old, who is the devil and Satan" (Rev. 20:2 NASB).

The Christmas tree legend that Protestants have handed down originated in the sixteenth century too. Notice, this is a legend, not a documented historical account. "Legend has it that Martin Luther began the tradition of decorating trees to celebrate Christmas. One crisp Christmas Eve, about the year 1500, he was walking through snow-covered woods and was struck by the beauty of a group of small evergreens. Their branches, dusted with snow, shimmered in the moonlight. When he got home, he set up a little fir tree indoors so he could share this story with his children. He decorated it with candles, which he lighted in honor of Christ's birth."[349] Martin Luther

(1483-1546), who was used by the Lord to initiate the Reformation within the church in the sixteenth century, is popularly believed to have started the Christmas tree tradition. Historically, this legend just doesn't hold up. As noted previously, the decorated tree had a more ancient beginning as a solstice evergreen in Germany and elsewhere.

REFORMATION HITS A HOLIDAY

Winston Churchill has said: "Those that fail to learn from history, are doomed to repeat it. "[350] Any authentic confrontation with history results in the opposite of self-exoneration. The primal idea Martin Luther brought to the world is *sola scriptura*—a Christian is to be guided by Scripture alone. In reaction to the abuses of church authority, Luther appealed to the ultimate authority of the Bible. I have also sought the Scriptures to back up the reason to believe "Christmas will be the golden calf of America," as evidenced in this book; and as you can tell, Scripture completely backs up this radical statement. In Luther's rejection to what appeared to him to be the church's idolatry of its own hierarchy, he replaced it with deference to the Word, which can easily slip into an idolatry of its own, if the entire counsel of Scripture is not consulted.

Protestants were the first to reject the Christmas celebration, but the break did not happen in sixteenth-century Saxony or with Martin Luther. Martin Luther celebrated Christmas.[351] We should note that Luther did not appraise many of the practices in the church according to the *sola scriptura* idea he started. The sixteenth-century Reformation did not initially go into the substance of the church's traditions. I have a feeling that Luther's initial stance, which enacted the Reformation, when he nailed his ninety-five theses to the door of the church at Wittenberg, was what the Lord required of him. It was a great precedent-setting stance, and I greatly admire it. But lest we consider all of Luther's practices flawless, we should remember his anti-Semitic, Holocaust-inciting ravings.[352] It's a deeply disturbing part of his legacy. A couple successors to the Protestant Reformation, who endeavored to fully enacted Luther's *sola scriptura* concept, were John Calvin and John Knox.

As you can imagine, a ban of Roman holidays[353] (which included Christmas) caused uproar in certain quarters, and John Calvin was reproached as the instigator of the action. Calvin wrote a correspondence that if he had been asked for advice, he would have not supported this decision.[354] John Calvin initially was uneasy about the edict to ban the Roman festivals, because he feared that the sudden change might provoke tumult, which could impede the course of the Reformation, even though Calvin's general views on worship were clearly stated and were subsequently called the *regulative principle of worship*—all modes of worship must be expressly sanctioned by God's Word if they are to be considered legitimate.[355]

Although church leaders, in the midst of a reformation, are most likely to be hesitant to touch anything greatly loved by the masses, the Lord is not. God's patience and kindness is meant to lead people to repentance, not lead us to justify His endorsement of our faults. The Church's failure in relation to idolatry, embodied via Roman feasts, was a symptom of man's change in the times. Thank God that His grace has been, and continues to be, great!

> Dear friends, if we deliberately continue sinning after we have received a full knowledge of the truth, there is no other sacrifice that will cover these sins. . . . Anyone who refused to obey the law of Moses was put to death without mercy on the testimony of two or three witnesses. Think how much more terrible the punishment will be for those who have trampled on the Son of God and have treated the blood of the covenant as if it were common and unholy. Such people have insulted and enraged the Holy Spirit who brings God's mercy to his people.
>
> —Hebrews 10:26-29 NLT

Calvin's lack of endorsement for celebrating Christmas, due to his application of *sola scriptura*, is echoed by another successor of the Reformation. John Knox and the Scottish Reformation repeatedly affirmed that true worship must be instituted by God—in His Word. In 1560, Knox asserted the sole authority of scripture as it relates to doctrine and worship.[356] In 1566, the position of the Scottish church was reaffirmed when the General Assembly in Scotland wrote: "concerning the "festival of our Lord's nativity, circumcision, . . . these festivals at the present time obtain no place among us; for we dare not religiously celebrate any other feast-day than what the divine oracles prescribed."[357] While King James of England sought to appeal to the masses by imposing various ceremonies (Christmas, Easter, Whitsuntide, and Ascension) upon the church to enhance his Anglican cause, Presbyterians maintained a strong stance against Christmas. These Scottish ministers persistently resisted, with David Calderwood (1575-1651) representing their firm opposition: "Indeed, the brazen serpent was originally constructed by God's express command; yet it was destroyed when it became a snare to the people of God (2 Kings 18:4). How much more, then, should we discard man-made observances, which are additionally contaminated with Roman superstition and idolatry?"[358] Please remember that my aim is not to criticize or uplift any particular Christian denomination, but to give the reader a very cursory glance at how Christmas has flowed through church history and the circumstances involved.

In reaction to the Protestant Reformation, a defensive Catholic Church adopted an attitude that the church was sinless in itself, and had no need of reformation.[359] I have encountered this same argument when discussing the laying down of Christmas with devout Christians. When I mentioned to a close friend that "this is a holiness issue," she defensively challenged me. "Are you saying I'm not holy?" I told her that only God can make that call. I am only responsible for myself and my family, as well as for the things God gives me to do. As I discussed in chapter 1, writing this book is a matter of obedience for me. I am as fallible as anyone. I am merely sharing what the Lord our God has shown me. I additionally hear Christians declare something similar to: "I am saved by grace, and accepted by God just as I am. Therefore, I have no need to change; and am holy." This first sentence is absolutely correct. Yes, our spirits are saved, and the Lord incredibly accepts us just the way we are. Thank God! But when we accept Jesus as our Lord and Savior, our souls are still full-of-the-dickens. Have you lied since you have become a born-again believer? Have you coveted? Have you sewn to the flesh instead of to the Spirit?

The process of sanctification cleanses our souls: "Work out your salvation with fear and trembling, for it is God who is at work in you, both to will and to work for His good pleasure" (Phil. 2:12-13 NASB). To reform something means that it is made better. Don't you and I have room for improvement? Isn't that the purpose of the sanctifying work of the Holy Spirit in our lives, as we partner with Him? Ongoing reformation is the road a believer travels to become more like Christ. Hopefully, our ultimate destination is our will being enthroned in Christ's love. This is the kingdom road revealed in Isaiah 35 as the "Highway of Holiness": "And a highway will be there, a roadway, and it will be called the Highway of Holiness. The unclean will not travel on it, but it will be for him who walks *that way*, and fools will not wander *on it*" (Isa. 35:8 NASB).

Is the church infallible? Are you? Here's a helpful hint—when trying to discern the truth about infallibility, ask those outside. Glance at any congregation to see that there is a continual need to review the church's imperfections. Mankind's answer must be that we all fall short of the glory of God, as we journey unto perfection.

Let's remember to look into history's mirror to regard the reflection of past errors to help us not repeat them. The first formal declaration of the doctrine of infallibility (papal)[360] came during a time when so much was tearing at the fabric of the church's traditions of faith and its institutional power.[361] The church is again in a tumultuous time when traditions and institutions are being challenged by the King of Kings Himself. When you are in service of the King, you have to do what the King tells you to do. The Lord our God is currently in the process of removing all things from His kingdom that can be shaken "so that only eternal things will be left. Since we are receiving a Kingdom that cannot be destroyed, let us be thankful and please God by worshiping him with holy fear and awe. For our God is a consuming fire" (Heb. 12:27-29 NLT). Catholicism was more attuned to what nineteenth century liberalism threatened than what it promised; therefore, the church leadership made itself the bulwark against the new idea. Will the Lord's church do the same in this kingdom day? Will we take up the task of reformation? Or will we set ourselves up against God's new thing? Will we examine our imperfections, as led of the Lord? Or will we deny our shortcomings, or our need to deal with our faults?

Idolatry is a fundamental sin for all of us, so there is no need to become defensive. Right before the Lord declares "new things I declare" in Isaiah 42, God proclaims that He will not give His glory or praise to idols. The church's heart solely belongs to Jesus. Paul was speaking to believers in Galatia about freedom in Christ when he wrote: "So I advise you to live according to your new life in the Holy Spirit. Then you won't be doing what your sinful nature craves. . . . These two forces are constantly fighting each other, and your choices are never free from this conflict" (Gal. 5:16-17 NLT). Believers who are free in Christ paradoxically have a conflict raging within them. It's our old sinful nature that loves to do evil versus our new life in Christ directed by the Holy Spirit.

I am not advocating keeping the Jewish law, as some have accused, but living a life pleasing to the Lord with holy, reverential fear. Does endeavoring to avoid the sins listed in Galatians 5:19-21 amount to keeping the law or living a life of love, as directed by the Holy Spirit? "But if you are led by the Spirit, you are not under the law" (Gal. 5:18 NKJV). I am advocating abiding by the essential commandments given to all believers, which are Holy Spirit-given directives. I am also advocating living a yielded life in Christ, so we may bring forth eternal fruit as a natural product of abiding in Him. After the fruits of the Spirit are listed, Galatians 5:24-25 tells us: "And those who are Christ's have crucified the flesh with its passions and desires. If we live in the Spirit, let us also walk in the Spirit."

Paul would not exhort believers to walk in the Spirit, if the opposite could not be true. Galatians 5:19-21 enumerates the sins exhibited in believers' lives when we follow the desires of our sinful nature: adultery, fornication, uncleanness, lewdness, idolatry, sorcery, hatred, contentions, jealousies, outbursts of wrath, selfish ambition, dissensions, heresies, envy, murders, drunkenness, revelries, and the like. Once again, notice idolatry is one of them. Additionally, notice that many of these sins exist in the church today. Show me a church congregation without selfish ambition, envy, or strife, and I will show you one that operates in the kingdom of God. Remember that anyone living a life that produces idolatry will not inherit the kingdom of God. Therefore, the church worshiping idols in any shape, form, or fashion, especially by means unique to it (e.g., sun images hanging on a tree), is an area that needs sincere examination in this kingdom day. By the way, this kingdom day will be marked by reformation upon reformation until we are "conformed into the image of the Son" (Rom. 8:29 NASB).

The Latin word for "reform" is *reformare*. It's means "to shape something according to its own essential being."[362] Aren't you and I supposed to be transformed from glory to glory into the very image of God by the Spirit of the living God? Authentic reformation looks to the message of love preached and lived by Jesus. We are to do as He did in *all* things.

In our rediscovering of truth through our discovery of history, we distinguish that history actually records that the first Christmas trees explicitly decorated and named after the "Christian" holiday appeared in Strasbourg in Alsace in the beginning of the seventeenth century.[363] An anonymous German citizen wrote in 1605: "At Christmas they set up fir trees in the parlors of Strasbourg and hang thereon roses cut out of many colored paper, apples, wafers, gold-foil, sweets, etc . . ."[364] Additionally, we hear that Christmas, as we know, is a Victorian invention of the 1860s.[365] In 1846, Queen Victoria and her German Prince Albert were sketched in the *Illustrated London Times* standing around a Christmas tree with their children.[366] Queen Victoria's husband played a large part in the transformation of Santa Claus into the icon that we recognize today as the "The Spirit of Christmas Rejoicing." He brought in a Teutonic[367] element to the Christmas mix. At this point Santa Claus began to ride a sleigh, descend chimneys, and fill stockings, just as Prince Albert had practiced in Germany during childhood.[368] Due to Queen Victoria's popularity, fashion-conscious Brits and East Coast American society followed suit. The Christmas tree, and its totem figure Santa Claus, had arrived in America with style; and by the 1890s, its popularity was on the rise around the United States.[369]

I know you say: "I don't worship my Christmas tree." Neither did I, but the Lord has shown me that Christians cannot redeem anything whose origins are evil in His sight. Revelation 18:2 states,

"Babylon . . . has become a dwelling place of demons." In the same chapter where the Bible mentions that we "cannot have a part in both the Lord's table and the table of demons," the Lord states through Paul: "Therefore, my dear friends, flee from idolatry" (1 Cor. 10:14). Notice that my "flee from idolatry" began with a feeble, but genuine heart cry, "Lord, I want to. Help me. Show me the way. My husband's not ready for this. Give me, give us a way out." But it's biblical: "But He gives a greater grace. . . . 'God opposes the proud but gives grace to the humble.' Submit yourselves then to God. Resist the devil, and he will flee from you. Come near to God and He will come near to you. Wash your hands, you sinners, and purify your hearts, you double-minded" (James 4:6-8).

ଔ

6

THE GOLDEN CALF

☙

> And Jeroboam said in his heart, "Now the kingdom may
> return to the house of David:
> If these people go up to offer sacrifices in the house of
> the Lord at Jerusalem, then the heart of this people
> will turn back to their lord . . ." Therefore the king asked advice,
> made two calves of gold, and said to the people,
> "It is too much for you to go up to Jerusalem. Here are your gods,
> O Israel, which brought you up from the land of Egypt!"
> And he set up one in Bethel, and the other he put in Dan.
> —1 Kings 12:26-29 NKJV

CONTENDING WITH GOD

Incredulously, King Jeroboam[370] repeated the sin of the golden calf, even doubling down by setting up two golden calves to Aaron's one. It's not like God's people didn't know about the incident of the golden calf at Mount Sinai. They yearly celebrated the Passover Feast commemorating their deliverance from Egypt; and their ancestors had actually had wandered in the wilderness for forty years after they had worshiped the golden calf.

Jeroboam's name foretold God's covenantal dispute against him. The primitive root of Jeroboam's name is *rib,* which means to contend or have a legal complaint.[371] It communicates the idea that Jeroboam struggled, argued, quarreled, or held a controversy with God. Jeroboam didn't have just any old complaint, because this word *rib* has great covenantal overtones. The Bible uses this term in the context of God having a *rib* (a divine lawsuit) against Israel for not keeping the covenant. One of the primary understandings of Jeroboam's name indicates striving in the sense of physical combat.[372] Jeroboam contended with the God of Israel when he proclaimed: "Here are your gods, O Israel, which brought you up from the land of Egypt!" (1 Kings 12:28 NKJV). Amazingly, God's nation fell for this idolatrous farce when they should have known better. They knew that after Aaron made a golden calf from Israel's earrings, the people had also said, "This is your god, O Israel, that brought you out of the land of Egypt!" (Exod. 32:4 NKJV).

If we delve into the meaning of the places where Jeroboam set up the two golden idols for Israel, we can see the areas where people who contend with God seek to be superior to Him. Bethel is defined as "the house of God,"[373] while Dan means "to judge."[374] The golden calf set up in Bethel represents that the people wanted to be their own lord and master over their house of God (i.e., themselves). The golden calf put up in Dan corresponds to the concept that the people did not want anyone else to judge them but themselves. Sounds a lot like America, doesn't it? Our "Christian" nation seems to be a kingdom devoted to self.

If you study the kings Joshua conquered on the west side of the Jordan and the places they were from (Josh. 12), you'll discover that the battle to enter the Promised Land is ultimately a contest between the kingdom of self and the kingdom of God. To enter the kingdom of God—the Promised Land to all who believe—we must first discern what is of the kingdom of God and what is of the kingdom of self in our lives. Then we must "choose life" (Deut. 30:19). We must choose to serve the Lord our God and His kingdom above our own desires. "Jesus said to the disciples, 'If anyone desires to come after Me, let him deny himself and take up his cross, and follow Me'" (Matt. 16:24 NKJV). Our carnal nature must die so we can be totally captivated by His love.

When Jeroboam calculated that his kingdom might return to the unified house of David and he set up a similar but idolatrous object of worship, it's a picture of someone in authority (i.e., a king) caught up in self-interest, who strove to keep people away from God's rightful scepter—His dominion. He enticed them to worship an image made in the form of a creature of the earth (Exod. 20:3) rather than going up to Jerusalem, which symbolically always represents ascending to the Lord to worship Him only. Jeroboam's worship practices paralleled the righteous real,[375] where he ordained a feast like that which was in Judah and offered sacrifices on his "new and improved" altar with his "new and improved" priesthood.[376] Ironically, Jeroboam was not that far off in designating a new priesthood. He had returned to God's original plan outside of God's direction and timing. For in the Lord's original plan at Sinai, there would have been no need for a tabernacle, for every Jew would have been a minister. They would have been a holy nation and royal priesthood beginning at Sinai. They would have been worthy of building their own sacred altar in their hearts; and they would have each been a resting place for the divine presence. God's original intent was replaced with the concept of a central tabernacle and a designated priestly family after Israel fell from its spiritual pinnacle because of the golden calf. Their apex was a consequence of worshiping the Apis, which was the form of idolatry most familiar to the Israelites in Egypt. It was ox or calf worship, which resulted in Israel no longer being a nation of individual priests and tabernacles.[377]

Just like Jeroboam put up golden calves in Bethel and Dan to cut the people's ties to Jerusalem, Roman holidays, like Easter and Christmas, were set up so the church could sever its ties with the house of David (i.e., the Jews and the biblical calendar they followed). Constantine despised the Jews; and the church, which became politically entangled with a worldly empire, adjusted accordingly.

What if this is (at least part of) the great apostasy (i.e., falling away) of the last days? Recall from chapter 2 that the character of the beast or the Antichrist can be likened to a completely selfish man. This concept of the Antichrist does not negate that an antichrist figure, similar to Antiochus Epiphanes IV or Hitler, may arise in the last days.

> Do not love the world, nor the things in the world. If anyone loves the world, the love of the Father is nor in him. For all that is in the world, the lust of the flesh and the lust of the eyes and the boastful pride of life, is not from the Father,

but is from the world. And the world is passing away, and also its lusts; but the one who does the will of God abides forever. Children, it is the last hour; and just as you heard that antichrist is coming, even now many antichrists have arisen; from this we know that it is the last hour. *They went out from us, but they were not really of us . . .*
—1 John 2:15-19a NASB, emphasis mine

The image of the Antichrist I am talking about is not any old completely selfish man. It's the one prophesied by Daniel as the abomination that causes devastation, who stands with pride in the Holy Place where God is supposed to dwell. God dwells in His people. Basically, this gives us a picture of a person, who has accepted Jesus as Lord and Savior, but they dethrone Him from their heart. It's where a believer in the Lord Jesus Christ unrepentantly still sins. He in fact demonstrates that he is still lord of his life.

So when you see the abomination that causes devastation spoken about through the prophet Dani'el standing in the Holy Place (let the reader understand the allusion) . . . For there will appear false Messiahs and false prophets performing miracles—amazing things!—so as to fool even the chosen, if possible.
—Matthew 24:15, 24 CJB

The NASB version says: "so as to mislead, if possible, even the elect." God does not make rhetorical statements. As history so aptly demonstrates, His chosen ones can be misled. Only through humble reliance upon the One in whom we can trust will we be protected from deception. Vigilance against the antichrist within will protect our hearts from the corrupting influence of the antichrists without, which minimally requires that we don't lean on our own understanding, but in all our ways acknowledge Him (Prov. 3:5-6).

. . . With regard to the coming of our Lord Jesus Christ, and our gathering together in Him . . . Let no one deceive you, for it will not come unless the apostasy comes first, and the

man of lawlessness is revealed, the son of destruction, who opposes and exalts himself above every so-called god or object of worship, so that he takes his seat in the temple of God, displaying himself as being God.
—2 Thessalonians 2:1b, 3-4 NASB

Why would Matthew 24 say that not a single stone of the temple will be left standing? Yes, it foretold the destruction of the temple in Jerusalem in AD 70; but there's something more that Jesus is telling us. Not one of His living stones, which makes up His new temple (i.e., believers) will be left standing, because we will all be humbled. Recall that the Hebrew word picture for "pride" tells us that pride is to lift up (ourselves in our own) strength,[378] while the pictograph for the Hebrew word "humble" tells us that humility comes when self-protection is done away with.[379]

THE ORIGINAL GOLDEN CALF

The question that this chapter endeavors to answer is: Why would Jesus tell us: "Christmas will be the golden calf of America?" This may seem obvious, but hang with me, for we need a little more background to understand this allusion to the golden calf fully. An excellent place to begin is to go back to the first occurrence of the phrase "golden calf" in Scripture:

> When the people saw that Moses was so long in coming down from the mountain, they gathered around Aaron and said, "Come, make us gods who will go before us. As for this fellow Moses who brought us up out of Egypt, we don't know what has happened to him." Aaron answered them, "Take off the gold earrings that your wives, your sons and your daughters are wearing, and bring them to me." So all the people took off their earrings and brought them to Aaron. He took what they handed him and made it into an idol cast in the shape of a calf,fashioning it with a tool. Then they said, "These are your gods, O Israel, who brought you up out of Egypt."
> —Exodus 32:1-4

The incident of the golden calf in Exodus 32 shortly followed the glorious revelation at Sinai. The arrival at Mount Sinai was the climax of the exodus. God had foretold Moses at the burning bush, "I will be with you, and this shall be the sign to you that it is I who have sent you: when you have brought the people out of Egypt, you shall worship God at this mountain" (Exo3:12 NASB). Creator God had chosen to identify Himself in time and history six full weeks after the Israelites left Egypt.[380] At Sinai, for the first and only time to date, God spoke to all of His people at once. The nation of Israel foreknew that its moment of fulfillment would be at the mountain of God. Indeed, God's people became a nation after they arrived there. Earlier encampments were tainted with grievances against Moses and God, but here at Sinai the people didn't complain—a miracle in itself. The people knew that they had arrived at the place of their corporate destiny. God's people finally had arrived at their place of promise. They had been filled with impatient anticipation for the day when they would finally reach Sinai.

But in their impatience, God's people tragically misinterpreted what was meant by "forty days" (Exod. 24:18; 34:28). When the people gathered around Aaron to pressure him to rise up and "make us gods that will go before us," they used the excuse that we don't know what became of Moses. They thought Moses had been delayed or something awful had happened to him. People have used any old excuse to justify sinful activity—the excuse of God delaying being just one of them. Remember how Saul grew impatient waiting for Samuel, but even before that God's nation was recklessly restless for Moses' return.

The people had their eyes more on man than God, even after the mind-blowing encounter with the Lord only thirty-nine days earlier at Mount Sinai (Exod. 19). Evidence is supplied by Israel's own words: "this fellow Moses who brought us up out of Egypt" (Exod. 32:1). Moses was merely a servant of the Most High God, and he knew that it would have been impossible for him to even pry the Israelites out of Pharaoh's hand, let alone bring His people out of Egypt. God's people impatiently wanted to get to their destination—the Promised Land. Not understanding that the Giver of the Promised Land was the ultimate fulfillment of the Promised Land.

The Lord Himself is the greatest promise of all, but His people wanted the benefits of the Giver, not necessarily the Giver Himself.

It was the thirty-ninth day of forty. All the people could still actually see the cloud of God's presence on the summit of Mount Sinai, and they had seen Moses ascend up into it. The cloud of His presence had miraculously remained on Sinai the entire time, but it seems that this incredible atmospheric sign of the Lord's manifest presence was not enough. The people wanted something more tangible, something familiar to their senses, something earthly that would feed their carnal nature.

THE CHRISTMAS CONNECTION

The golden calf Aaron fashioned was borrowed from the ordinary way in which the favorite Egyptian divinity Osiris was mystically represented.[381] As already mentioned, this sacrificial yearling calf, bull, or ox in Egypt was called the Apis. God's people invented their own representation of God, presuming that they were pleasing Him (Exod. 32:4). After all, didn't their leader Aaron build an altar to God as the Lord had instructed in Exodus 20:24? And didn't their leader proclaim: "Tomorrow is a feast to the Lord" (Exod. 32:5)? Maybe Aaron thought if He used God's name and parts of his instructions it somehow justified any wrong he might do. But no matter how much they tried to please the Lord by their own inventions and imaginations, as evidenced in the golden calf, God's people could not get around the fact that they had all heard the second commandment directly from God's own awe-inspiring voice.

What did these people hear exactly? The Hebrew sages say that Moses taught the people 611 of the 613 commandments. The first two commandments God's people heard directly and clearly from the Lord. The Jewish sages Rashi and Ramban explain that the nation heard all Ten Commandments simultaneously from God; but since the words were all uttered in a single instant, the people could not comprehend them. Then God began to repeat the Ten Commandments one by one, word for word, so His people could understand each facet of His simultaneous utterances.[382]

Christian disconnectedness from the Hebrews has had many ramifications. I feel that one of our most valuable missing links is Hebrew history. Our Bibles tell us that God's presence on Mount Sinai was heralded by an awesome display of thunder, lightning, smoke, trumpet (i.e., *shofar*) blasts, and fire (Exod. 19:16-25). *The Stone Edition of the Chumash* is one of the most incredible books I have ever studied. It elaborates on the day of revelation, when God came down to visit His people. Exodus 20:15 says: "The entire people saw the thunder and the flames . . ." Saw the thunder? Isn't thunder an invisible sound? *The Chumash* shares that Hebrew sage Rashi remarks that the nation was able to see the thunder because at the revelation millions of people transcended normal limitations of the body. Jews rose to a level where they had superhuman comprehension; and therefore, they could see what is normally heard.[383] God spoke to Moses from the midst of a thick cloud, so the entire nation could hear the divine voice (Exod. 19:9). As God's voice thundered, the Hebrew letters of the words He uttered were formed out of the smoke and flames. The people could literally see His words . . . see the thunder . . . as it manifested and traveled over His nation. The thunder became etched in the wind like some sort of smoky, flaming tickertape (without the paper). Can you image? Talk about earth shattering! "You shall not recognize the gods of others in My presence" (Exod. 20:3). Okay, God! Ahaaaaaaaaaaaaa! As you fall prostrate.

After God completed the first two commandments, we can understand why the nation could not tolerate God's intense holiness dispersed through His direct communication, so they pleaded with Moses to teach them the rest (Deut. 5:22-24). Thus, God's holy nation heard all Ten Commandments from God, but was taught eight of them by Moses. Deuteronomy 4:12 states that the people only heard "the sound of words"; however, Moses heard, understood, and then taught them to Israel.[384] Comparably, Paul had a Damascus Road experience where he heard God's voice and experience the blinding light of His presence while his companions only heard some sounds (Acts 9:7).

Aaron and the Israelites had been pre-programmed by their life experience in Egypt, just as the converted Roman believers in the fourth century AD had come out of celebrating the Saturnalia. Stephen tells us in Acts 7:38-40 that when the Jewish people said to Aaron, "Make us gods," they had turned their hearts back into Egypt (i.e., the world). Ezekiel 20:8 reiterates: "They did not forsake the idols of Egypt." Israel fell back into the form of idolatry most familiar to them—the ox worship of the Egyptians.

At the time of the exodus, we know that living bulls were worshiped in Memphis, Egypt. Reverend Hislop reveals that Apis is simply another name for Saturn, because that calf represented the divinity in the character of Saturn.[385] Aha! Apis was the image Aaron had in mind as he tried to epitomize God's divinity, when "Aaron took the gold, melted it down, and molded and tooled it into the shape of a calf" (Exod. 32:4 NLT). And this same Apis was just another name for Saturn, of Saturnalia fame. Recall that the Saturnalia is one of the founts of Christmas. This is our connection for Christmas being the golden calf of America! When Aaron fashioned the golden calf after the likeness of the Apis, there was an older and automatic connection to the great Chaldean/Babylonian god Saturn, too. Therefore, when Jesus declared, "Christmas will be the golden calf of America," the Lord is espousing that Christmas has a direct and ancient connection to the original golden calf made by Aaron. OUR MODERN-DAY CHRISTMAS CELEBRATION IS *LITERALLY* MADE IN THE SAME IMAGE AS THE ORIGINAL GOLDEN CALF FABRICATED AT SINAI.

The Bible declares: "And the LORD said to Moses, 'Whoever has sinned against Me, I will blot him out of My book. But go now, lead the people where I told you. Behold, My angel shall go before you; nevertheless in the day when I punish, I will punish them for their sin.' Then the Lord smote the people, because of what they did with the calf which Aaron had made" (Exod. 32:33-35 NASB, emphasis mine). How much more should God's people, bought by grace through faith via the blood of the Lamb, take notice, especially since a voice from heaven proclaims to end-time believers: "Come out of her [Babylon], my people, that you may not participate in her sins and that you may not receive her plagues" (Rev. 18:4 NASB). "How much severer punishment do you think he will deserve who has trampled under foot the Son of God, and has regarded as unclean the blood of the covenant by which he was sanctified, and insulted the Spirit of grace?" (Heb. 10:29 NASB).When God tells us "Christmas will be the golden calf of America," he means *every* word of it. When the Lord says it will be the golden calf of America, He is additionally saying that Christmas currently is a golden calf for His church in America.

THE FATHER OF CHRISTMAS

Alexander Hislop reveals: "The name of Saturn denotes 'the hidden one.'" In the Egyptian language, "Apis" also was called *Hepi* or *Hapi*, which is evidently from the Chaldee name *Hap,* meaning "to cover."[386] The Egyptian word for *Hap* signifies concealing, which is the very character of the Father of Lies himself. Throughout Hislop's book, he plainly points out that Saturn is another name for Satan. Are you kidding me?! Don't tell me that Dana Carvey's hilarious *Saturday Night Live* Church Lady skit could actually be based on truth! Most good humor is, by the way. Remember how Dana, complete in a conservative dress, sensible shoes, and a gray wig spelled out the word "Santa" with magnetic letters on a white board; then rearranged them to spell "Satan." Do you recall the Church Lady's byline? "Could it be Sssss . . . atan!?"

History Professor Jeffrey Burton Russell incredibly agrees with the tongue-in-cheek Santa-Satan assessment of the Church Lady. Russell wrote *The Prince of Darkness,* which draws attention to the historical dark links between Satan and Santa Claus. This is a link many Christians have sought to ignore or minimize. From a European folklore viewpoint, Russell notes: "The Devil lives in the far north and drives reindeer; he wears a suit of red fur; he goes down chimneys in the guise of Black Jack or the Black Man covered in soot; as Black Peter he carries a large sack into which he pops sins or sinners (including naughty children); he carries a stick or cane to thrash the guilty (now he merely brings candy canes); he flies through the air with the help of strange animals; food and wine are left out for him as a bribe to secure his favors. The Devil's nickname 'Old Nick' derives directly from Saint Nicholas. Nicholas was often associated with fertility cults, hence with fruit, nuts, and fruitcake, his characteristic gifts."[387]

If you ask most Christians who have the Santa Claus tradition included in their Christmas morning routine, they will most likely tell you that Santa Claus is based on a real saint. The history and legend of Saint Nicholas is so intertwined that the only things that we can say for sure about him is the general time he lived and where he was located. I base this assertion on the *Catholic Encyclopedia*: "Though he is one of the most popular saints in the Greek as well as the Latin Church, there is scarcely anything historically certain about him except that he was Bishop of Myra in the fourth century."[388] Saint Nicholas is said to be renowned for his generosity, miracles, and love of children. He supposedly dropped coins down the chimney to preserve his anonymity and the dignity of his recipients.[389] Bishop Nicholas of Myra may have become the first official Saint Nicholas, but this is not Santa's sole point of origin or his earliest.

The power that stands behind the jolly old man of Christmas goes *way* back—back to the beginning of recorded history and beyond. The worldly figure of Santa really derives from an even earlier set of figures—the shamans who were the first magicians of the human race. The very notion of a gift-giver descending from a high place bearing gifts can be traced back to the shaman's climbing up the world tree to reach the other-world, then returning with gifts for everyone.[390] These were not toys or iPods, but messages concerning the year to come and/or the fate of the world. Previously, I mentioned that Saturn was also known as the Roman god of time and agriculture. Other sun gods also were associated with the changing of time and vegetation, like Babylonian Tammuz and Phrygian Attis. The celebration of the returning of the sun, and its worldly blessing for the New Year, connects people to the controlling god of this world through his shamanistic priests (whether magicians or images of St. Nick).

The shamans, from whom we get some of our Christmas traditions, were all over the world; but for obvious reasons we will focus on those who originate in the North. Please note that the devil proclaimed: "I will raise my throne above the stars of God. And I will sit on the mount of assembly in the recesses of the north" (Isa.

14:13-14). Why does the devil want to sit enthroned in the recesses of the north? Psalm 48 says that Mount Zion, which is beautiful in elevation and the joy of the whole earth, is in the far north. George Otis, Jr., reveals that "the far north is well beyond the polluted atmosphere of imaginary gods and fallen angels Only on Mount Zion can the true God be found."[391] The northern shamans often wore bells on their ritual red robes trimmed in white and, as mentioned before, shinned up and down the central pole (i.e., tree) adorned with sun images in their skin tent to receive messages from the other-world. Remember that their central pole represented the axis of the world, which led to the shaman's final demonic destination. The father figure of Christmas (i.e., Santa Claus) and his shamanistic predecessors were first said to be the midwives of the sun.[392]

Prior to 1823, Santa Claus neither had reindeer nor the ability to fly or descend chimneys. "These elements arrived with the publication of Clement Clarke Moore's classic poem *A Visit from Saint Nicholas* (or *The Night Before Christmas*). Some have speculated that Moore, a professor of Oriental languages, drew his inspiration from the rituals of Siberia's Koryak, Kamchandal, and Chukchi peoples—rituals that, to this day, include the worship of the "great reindeer spirit."[393] "The only person who can communicate with the reindeer spirit, according to these traditional societies, is the tribal shaman, who does so by eating the fly agaric mushroom. Once entranced, he 'flies' to the spirit world, where he collects messages and 'gifts' in the shape of new songs, dances and stories for the tribe. Interestingly, the shaman enters the realm of the spirits through the smoke hole on the roof on his *yurt*, or hide tent."[394]

I happened to be watching CNN when they featured a special Christmas display in England called "Satan's Grotto," where kids get a "free" gift of an eyeball or severed finger, plus the additional chance to sign their life away.[395] CNN said it was all tongue-in-cheek, but the picture of the horned-one in a Santa suit was telling. There is more truth to this tongue-in-cheek caricature of Satan as Santa than many would care to admit. The devil is prideful and enjoys revealing what he's involved in; but you have to look very carefully because he continually masks as an angel of light, while his character is based solely on lies and deception. The devil playing Santa is reiterated in the Czech Republic on St. Nicholas Eve: "A devil prowls neighborhoods to interrogate children to find out whether they were naughty or nice. The devil carries a large switch with him for emphasis, and it's not unusual to find photos in Prague newspapers of 'frightened kids being menaced by the devil.'"[396] Thus Santa Claus's association with Christmas is not an accident or a coincidence. He is inextricably connected to the Saturn roots of Christmas whether Christians participate in his "Ho . . . ho . . . ho . . ." tradition or not. Just casually pay attention during the Christmas season, and you will see that Santa Claus is one of the most common and celebrated sights of the holiday. As Christians, we say that we don't worship Christmas like Secularists, Buddhists, Pagans, or Satanists; we only worship the "golden" type, saying that Jesus is the reason for our season. The reality is that Christians have brought Christmas out of the pagan world, just as the Jews brought the Apis out of Egypt. "Israel cries out to me, O our God, we acknowledge you! But Israel has rejected what is good . . . Throw out your calf-idol . . . My anger burns against them. How long will they be incapable of purity? . . . This calf—a craftman has made it; it is not God" (Hos. 8:2, 5-6).

When Jesus came to me with tears in His eyes telling me: "The mixture of Christmas grieves My heart," I had to come to grips with the thought that my Christian celebration of Christ's birth actually upset, and even opposed, Him. It did not exalt Him as I had been taught. "Those who oppose Him he [the Lord's servant] must gently instruct, in hope that God will grant them repentance leading them to a knowledge of the truth, and that they will come to their senses and escape from the trap of the devil, who has taken them captive to do his will" (2 Tim. 2:25-26). Believers can oppose Jesus Christ, and sometimes, regrettably, we do.

God's solid foundation is sealed with these trustworthy inscriptions: "The Lord knows those who are His," and "Everyone who confesses the name of the Lord must turn away from wickedness" (2 Tim. 2:19). I pray that we will not show contempt for God's kindness, tolerance, and patience toward us. Romans 2:4 declares that God's kindness leads us toward repentance. Actually coming out of Babylon and laying down Christmas fulfills turning away[397] from this celebratory practice that grieves our Savior's heart. We are exhorted to "make every effort to be found spotless, blameless, and at peace with Him" (2 Pet. 3:14). Our orders from headquarters are rules to live by, given to us in God's Word. They are our rules of engagement to the King of kings, where we receive the victor's crown because we serve the Lord according to His rules.[398] We are called to no longer live as the world or pagans do. Second Timothy 2:21 shows us that we are "made holy;" and thus, "useful to the Master," if we cleanse ourselves from perishable, earthly practices. Then we are "prepared to do any good work."

Purification is a two-way process, as is most every work of the Holy Spirit in people's lives. We are first made holy through Christ's atoning sacrifice, and then we must also choose to cleanse our lives. "Now that you have purified yourselves by obeying the truth so that you have sincere love . . ." (1 Pet. 1:22). But please remember that purification is ultimately wrought by Christ: "To purify for Himself a people that are His very own, eager to do what is good" (Titus 2:14). It's like we love Him, because He first loved us. Please notice that our love is proven by what we do. Let's not "claim to know God, but by their actions they deny Him" (Titus 1:6).

CRITICAL MASS—CHRISTMAS

Rather than discouraging the people's idolatrous hearts, Aaron's demand for the people's gold seemed to gratify their superstition. Their readiness to part with the wealth of their ears showed the extravagance with which they were willing to shower upon their affection for this form of worship. "With their silver and gold they make idols for themselves to their own destruction" (Hos. 8:4). The Israelites seemed more ready, willing, and able to invest in their own invented form of worship than abide by the worship God designed, and still desires. Does our own readiness to part with our hard-earned money in our extravagant indulgence of Christmas please God or not?

In this vein I'd like to share a profound, disquieting God-given dream. I actually had the dream twice, one repeating and being a continuation of the other. In these dreams I was casually out with another man. We were holding hands while walking and as we sat across from one another at the dinner table. It was a seemingly innocent thing, but when my husband found out about it, he was extremely hurt. I got upset trying to justify the encounter—after all many people are into porn or have an actual affair. I had only causally flirted. Evidence of the "innocent affair" was produced by a check written out to support a worthy cause that the other man had told me about. I didn't understand how this could be evidence against me. After mediating upon my God-given dreams to receive their interpretation, I understood that it was related to my writing this book. The other man represents a god other than the One True God. My husband, in this context, is Yeshua. The "innocent affair" is Christmas, where the church has casually held hands with another god in both walking with the god of this world and dining at his table. The evidence of my "innocent affair" was a check written to a worthy charitable cause. The church is to walk as Jesus walked. We are to have no other gods in preference/before Him. Obviously, the act of giving to charity was not bad in itself. In fact, my charitable giving seemed to justify my unfaithful, casual affair, for I had buried the incident in my subconscious until confronted. It was that the spirit of Christmas (not the Spirit of the living God) had presented me with the charitable opportunity; and it caused me to give of my finances according to Christmas, not my Beloved. Indeed, hindsight showed that I had mainly given to charitable causes when the other man (i.e., god) offered the opportunity. To my shame, I tried to deny the "innocent affair"; but when first confronted by my heavenly Husband, I had not only felt guilty, seeing merely a glimpse of my affair (before I tried to deny and justify myself), I also momentarily saw His hurt and withdrawal.

The fabulous, glorious bridal company will operate in the Lord's perfect will, not merely His permissive will. "These are the ones who follow the Lamb wherever He goes" (Rev. 14:4), which not only applies to the literal 144,000 Jewish servants of our God, but additionally to the overcomers redeemed among men, who make up the Lamb's wife (Rev. 21). We mustn't forget that the basic law of the temple is holiness, and the New Jerusalem is a holy city filled with His holy people, who are the tabernacle of God (Rev. 21:2-3,10).

Christian giving should be a daily practice instead of a yearly ritual. Ideally, great organizations, like the Salvation Army, should not have to wait until December to get the bulk of their support. In Fort Collins we have an "Adopt-A-Family" program, where churches endeavor to take care of those in need during the Christmas season. I have talked to the founder and organizer of this ministry about the possibility of expanding the "Adopt-A-Family" program to be a year-round ministry, which is his heart, too. He has told me that many people only want to give during the holiday season. The fact is that Christmas is the season when giving is most on the church's radar screen. We need to analyze whether our sacrificial giving with goodwill to all men makes the holiday associated with Five Golden Rings propitious.

Does Aaron's proclamation, "Tomorrow is a feast to the Lord," ring as our Christian proclamation for Christmas? Since the feast to honor Jesus' birth is just a re-adaptation of the age-old Babylonian worship of the mother and child, we need to examine this lamb of Christmas that we have been offering as worship to the King. Every feast to the Lord is meant to be dedicated to Him. To dedicate something means to set it apart for a definite use or to devote to the worship of a divine being.[399] Yet, this festival, which Aaron and God's people dedicated to Jehovah, was not only offensive to Him, but it also invoked His judgment. They set aside the golden calf for "sacred use" to commemorate their being brought out of Egypt. It was to serve as an intermediary, like Moses, in leading them to the Promised Land. Harmless it seemed. They believed they were genuinely devoting themselves to worshiping the God of Israel. But God is neither fooled nor mocked. The Lord saw into the heart of the matter: the people had corrupted themselves with crass idolatry. "If we had turned away from worshiping our God, and were worshiping idols, would God not know it? Yes, He knows the secrets of every heart" (Ps. 44:20-21 TLB). God's people believed that they were worshiping the big "E" Elohim (the Most High God), but the Lord saw the motives of their hearts and said that they had worshiped little "e" elohim (gods/demons) instead. They had turned aside quickly out of the way for which God commanded them. They have made themselves a molded calf, worshiped it, sacrificed to it, and said, "This is your god, O Israel that brought you out of the land of Egypt!" (Exod. 32:7-8).

Aaron and the people were so strongly and grossly sensual, they did not imagine that this image was itself a god nor did they plan to terminate their adoration. They made the golden calf a representation of the true God, whom they intended to worship in and through this image. Remember when you regard Christmas being the golden calf of America that His thoughts are not like ours, nor are His ways like ours (Isa. 55:8). The more I contemplate the manger scenes at Christmas time, the more I see that it is indeed a "golden" commemoration of Christ's birth. The truth and beauty that Christ came as a babe in a manger does not give us license for it to be set aside for a particular purpose with the literal graven image of Jesus wrapped in swaddling clothes, funneling worship. This concept also applied to the golden calf. The truth and beauty of God bringing His people out of Egypt and taking them to the Promised Land did not justify the creation and worship of the golden calf. It seemed that the Israelites forgot that the Lord already had instituted a festival for His family called Passover for these exact same purposes; and He set it as a permanent or eternal ordinance (Exod. 12:14). Will we follow history in choosing to party with the crowd and their golden calf, or will we choose to party at the wedding feast of the Lamb with the King of Kings?

Christians say Christmas only represents a truth in God's Word and that the baby Jesus is merely a representation of the Most High, whom we intend to worship in and through this image, not the image itself. As with the golden calf, it is not a sufficient plea that we do not worship the image, but God through the image. A feast said to be a feast to Jehovah is not necessarily as we say. God will be the Judge.

The Lord's people were eager to celebrate the feast of the golden calf, just as we have been with Christmas. "They rose early on the next day, offered burnt offerings, and brought peace offerings; and the people sat down to eat and drink, and rose up to play" (Exod. 32:6 NKJV). Had they offered these sacrifices to Jehovah without the intervention of an image, the sacrifices may have been accepted. "An altar of earth you shall make for Me, and you shall sacrifice on it your burnt offerings and your peace offerings, your sheep and your oxen, in every place where I record My name I will come to you, and I will bless you" (Exod. 20:24 NKJV). However, having set up an image before them as a symbol of God's presence, and in their emulation of the idolatrous worship of Egypt, they "exchanged the truth of God for a lie and worshiped and served the creature rather than the Creator" (Rom. 1:23 NASB).

According to the ancient rites of worship, the people offered sacrifice(s) to this new-made deity, and they feasted on the sacrifice."[400] Likewise, Christians make sacrifices to celebrate Christmas in style. We eagerly rise early on Christmas morning to celebrate this festival memorializing Christ's birth. We feast on the sacrifices we have made in giving gifts to one another in honor of Jesus' birth.

Having, at the expense of their gold earrings, made their god, God's people endeavored at the expense of their beasts to make their golden god propitious. The Israelites thought their God-ordained sacrifices would make the Lord favorably disposed toward their benevolent gestures. Christians believe that our generous giving to worthy charitable causes at Christmastime in fulfillment of God-given directives is evidence that Jesus is pleased, and favorably disposed, to our celebration of His birth. The propitious end the Israelites accomplished was neither advantageous, nor prosperous as they had hoped; but it did portend a future event whose sacrifices are also atrocities in His eyes. When the folly of the golden calf is spoken about in 1 Corinthians 10:7, it says, "they sat down to eat and drink." They consumed what was sacrificed, then "rose up to play." What do we do on Christmas morn? We consume the gifts given to us in the honor of our Savior, and we rise up to play with them, usually for the rest of the day. The Israelites rose up to play the fool—to play the wanton. Don't the believers in Jesus Christ of Nazareth do that too? The definition for *wanton* is: "hard to control; undisciplined; unruly; playfully mean and cruel; mischievous; lustful; sensual; having no foundation or provocation; being without check or limitation; and extravagant."[401]

"When Moses saw that the people were **out of control**," he called for "whoever is for the Lord, come to me!" (Exod. 32:25-26). Lacking self-control and extravagance were fruits of the celebrants of the golden calf, as it is evident today at Christmastime too. All of the definitions for the word "wanton" above fit perfectly with the fruits of the Christmas season. Let's take a glance at the above definition of wanton in regard to Christmas.

First, is there another time of the year when God's people are more extravagant? "Undisciplined, unruly and being without check or limitations" is evident in children and adults alike. The Roman practice of "The Feast of Fools" owes its nature to the Saturnalia. "The Feast of Fools" continued in its various forms well into the seventeenth century. A similar celebration existed in England since the Middle Ages called "The Lord of Misrule,"[402] where the master becomes the servant and the servant switches places with their master. In chapter 3, I told you how "The Lord of Misrule" practice originated in Babylon. It manifests today in the family giving their children rule of the house during the Christmas season. A good friend told me that she has to rectify her children's expectations and attitudes when school starts up again after New Year's Day. My family has had to make this correction as well. Only in 2004, six years after my family began to lay down Christmas, was the Lord of Misrule or lawlessness shown to me as the root of my child's rebellious conduct during the holiday season. Of course, we also gave over our authority as masters of the household too. In 2005, we saw no trace of lawlessness (rebellion or defiance) from mid-December to January 1. I believe that this switching of master-servant roles phenomenon is pervasive in America, being more the rule than the exception during the holiday season. We just haven't equated it to the ancient licentious practice of the Feast of Fools or the Lord of Misrule. The "sensual and lustful" connotations to Christmas are as ancient as this pagan holiday itself. Gluttony, sexual immorality, and greed need no explanation; they are as obvious during Christmas as Rudolf's red nose. The wanton definition of "mischievous" exemplifies Santa and his elves if one looks close enough beyond the spell of innocence. To teach that Santa Claus is all-seeing, all-knowing, all-powerful—he knows everyone who is naughty or nice—is actually a callous joke. To sow deceit and innocent white lies for the purpose of having fun is being "playfully mean and cruel" to our kids.

American Christians have not realized that we are sowing unbelief in the fabric of our children's souls instead of God's kingdom.

THE PROMISED LAND

Joshua led God's people into the Promised Land. Some of God's people remained strong in their faith. Others turned back to pagan practices. But there was a large group of Israelites without any clear perception of whom they were in relation with.

Spiritual restlessness still marked the lives of the people in Joshua's day. While they had experienced the Lord's supernatural and practical guidance throughout the times of their wanderings in the wilderness, they were now tempted to revert back to their days of pagan worship. But the catch was now that they had experienced Jehovah firsthand, they had to dress pagan worship up to look and feel like they were worshiping the One True God (like they did with the golden calf). This is also what happened in Christ's Christian church in the fourth century when they added Christmas to the church's ecclesiastical calendar. Mixing pagan worship into our Christian culture was, and is, more gratifying to our flesh and it helps us fit into the world a bit better. But the Word of the Lord says:

> Do not be deceived, God is not mocked; for whatever a man sows, that he will also reap. For he who sows to his flesh reap corruption, he who sows to the Spirit will of the Spirit reap everlasting life.
> —Galatians 6:7-8 NKJV

Who hindered you from obeying the truth? This persuasion does not come from Him who calls you. For you, brethren, have been called to liberty; do not use liberty as an opportunity for the flesh, but through love serve one another. For all the law is fulfilled in one word, even in this: "You shall love your neighbor as yourself" I say then: Walk in the Spirit, and you shall not fulfill the lust of the flesh. For the flesh lusts against the Spirit and the Spirit against the flesh; and these are contrary to one another, so that you do not do the things you wish. . . .Those who are Christ's have crucified the flesh with its passions and desires. If we live in the Spirit, let us also walk in the Spirit.

—Galatians 5:7-24 NKJV

Our Christian church in America, even worldwide, has reverted back in some ways to worshiping the Lord our God through pagan forms of worship. Grievously, we can legitimately be classified as carnal. It's time once again for the golden calf to be addressed in Christian lives. We must move beyond indecision, restlessness, and living two lives into a total commitment to the One True God. The demands of Yahweh and of other pagan gods are mutually exclusive. Compromise in this manner is not acceptable for God's people. We either serve the living God of history or the gods of this world.

Remember that we are not our own. We have been bought for a price. Our understanding of life's meaning and purpose partially depends on stories and traditions that remind us of our past and point us to our future. But those stories and traditions in God's family must line up with our heavenly Father's system articulated in His Word. We must come out of Egypt, Babylon, or any other worldly systems that will hold us back from becoming part of His special corporate one.

"Pagans project their consciousness of God into a visible image or associate Him with a phenomenon in nature with a thing of space. In the Ten Commandments, the Creator of the universe identifies Himself by an event in history, by an event in time, the liberation of the people from Egypt, and proclaims: 'Thou shalt not make unto thee any graven image or any likeness of any thing that is in heaven above, or that is in the earth, or that is in the water under the earth.'"[403] I believe that we are all guilty of wanting something more tangible to worship when it comes to the Lord our God. The Israelites did at Sinai, and so do Christians at Christmastime. "'To whom will you compare Me? Or who is My equal?' says the Holy One. To whom, then, will you compare God? What image will you compare Him to?" (Isa. 40:25; 18).

Unless we get into God's presence and get to really know Him and His desires, we will all feed on things contaminated by idols; because an "idol" is merely "a representation or symbol of an object of worship." It's an "impostor" or "a false god." It's "a form or appearance that's visible, but without substance." It's any "object of extreme devotion."[404] Any object. Anything other than the Lord.

If the worship of the golden calf was earthly vanity, we need to consider if the Lord considers Christmas empty and valueless eternally as well. The truth is that we can accept Jesus Christ as our Savior; and thus, live eternally with him. But our works in this life on earth will be tested by fire, and we will receive a reward accordingly. "For no man can lay a foundation other than the one which is laid, which is Jesus Christ. Now if any man builds upon the foundation with gold, silver, precious stones, wood, hay straw, each man's work will become evident; for the day will show it, because it is to be revealed with fire; and the fire itself will test the quality of each man's work. If any man's work which he has built upon it remains, he shall receive a reward. If any man's work is burned up, he shall suffer loss; but he himself shall be saved, yet so as through fire" (1 Cor. 3:11-15 NASB).

Yeshua's measurement of Christmas as a golden calf implies that He will count our good deeds done at Christmastime as wood, hay, or straw, burning up in the all-consuming fire (Heb. 12:29). Let's rectify the compromises that the church has made, which displease the Lord our God. What an incredible legacy to hand down to the next generation! Therefore, let's hear Jesus' heart. Let's let Him wash us by the water of His Word, with the pure river of water of life proceeding from the throne of God (Eph. 5:26; Rev. 22:1). Let's choose to lay down Christmas and come out of Babylon, so He might present us to Himself a glorious church, not having spot or wrinkle or any such thing. Let's be holy and without blemish, as we perfectly reflect Him (Eph. 5:27).

Our next section urges believers to act like the royal priesthood that God declares we are. Those who will be part of the Bride of Christ will act like the descendants of Zadok. They were Levites (i.e., priests), who remained faithful by doing the right things when the other Israelites got lost:

But the priests, who are Levites and descendants of Zadok and who faithfully carried out the duties of my sanctuary when the Israelites went astray from me, are to come near to minister before me. . . . They alone are to enter my sanctuary; and perform my service. When they enter the gates of the inner court, they are to wear linen [refer to Revelation 19:8] . . . They are to teach my people the difference between the holy and the common [i.e., the profane] and show them how to distinguish between the unclean and the clean. In any dispute, the priests are to serve as judges and decide it according to my ordinances. *They are to keep my laws and my decrees for all my appointed feasts*, and they are to keep my Sabbaths holy.
 —Ezekiel 44:15-17, 23-24, emphasis mine

ଔ

SECTION II

LAY DOWN CHRISTMAS

(Present)

7

THIS IS RADICAL!

☙

> I will make mention of . . . Babylon to those who know Me . . .
> —Psalm 87:4 NKJV

THE WORD OF MY TESTIMONY

"Here I am, Lord. Do what You will." I had actually quoted from the core of my being Isaiah 6:8: "Here am I. Send me!" Then I added, "Here I am Lord. Do what You will." Talk about life-changing words!

I had gotten to the place in my spiritual walk where I wanted Jesus to be more than my Savior. I wanted Him to reign in me sovereignly as Lord; thus paradoxically, but progressively, fully becoming what and who He made me to be. I have grown to know that to truly live I have to be crucified daily to my own ambitions and desires; but little did I expect the way the Lord has chosen for me. After Thanksgiving in 1998 and prior to Christmas Day, the Lord plopped several resources into my lap. I had some slight recollection of knowing that there was mixture in celebrating a Christian Christmas . . . obviously Santa and his reindeers weren't in the Bible, but I literally saw no harm in it. To me, it seemed like innocent fun. Besides, I considered that celebrating Christmas was celebrating Christ (both with Santa and without). I felt that the saying "Jesus is the reason for the season" was a reality in my life.

In 1998, I loved the beauty of the Christmas season. I enjoyed the Christmas plays with children dressed in their finest doing the "darnedest" things. I thought few things compared to the beauty of a lit Christmas tree with gorgeously wrapped packages strewn about. I looked forward to seeing family, for it seemed like the best time of the year to get together. It made me smile when children got so excited about Santa and the gifts he gave to good boys and girls. At the time, I could have been counted to be among the majority who loved Christmas. Yet way back (even when I was a small child), somewhere deep inside of me I sensed that something was amiss. Like Halloween, I shelved the "feeling," remembering it only when the Lord chose to unveil the reason for my uneasiness. Within a very short amount of time, not only had I divinely acquired resources about the pagan root and rituals of Christmas, but I also had the grace to read them all quickly, taking most of it to heart. I remember having an EXTREMELY strong spirit of conviction, which I knew only God could manufacture.

When I saw a vivid apparition of Jesus with tears in His eyes, it was the last straw. I inquired, "Why are you crying, Yeshua?" He replied, "The mixture of Christmas grieves My heart." As I reeled at this revelation, He then added, "Come out of Babylon and lay down Christmas, for I *will* have a pure and spotless Bride." Truly God's Word became manifest at that moment: "I will make mention of . . . Babylon to those who know Me . . ." (Ps. 87:4 NKJV).

I knew from a previous experience that to do anything less than what God had revealed to me was to choose myself and my own ways. This rough lesson taught me that choosing my own way was an act of unbelief; and unbelief was an open door for a deaf-and-dumb spirit to oppress my life. Another name for the deaf-and-dumb spirit is the spirit of stupor, where your eyes can't see, your ears can't hear, and your mind does not understand (Isa. 6:9-10). And believe me, I wanted no part of that spirit of stupor again! Before God led me through repentance, which cleansed my soul from unbelief and a hardened heart, He showed me some of the main ways a deaf-and-dumb spirit manifests in America today: learning disabilities (dyslexia, ADD, etc.), grinding (i.e., gnashing) teeth at night, and seizures—epileptic and otherwise.[405] The deaf-and-dumb spirit's influence was the reason I could hear the Word of God and felt I understood it; but then it was quickly lost in my own inability to communicate or even remember what I had heard and what it meant to me. Taking notes and struggling to brand God's truth on my mind was par for me at that time. By God's incredible grace, I grew . . . with much effort. Like my Dad, I also had ground my teeth when I slept, since I could remember.

Suffice it to say, I was totally cognizant that when the Lord said, "Come out of Babylon and lay down Christmas," my choice would either move me closer to Him or farther away. If I chose to not obey, I would begin an arduous journey on a road called unbelief, which would progressively lead me toward an ever-increasing compromised and useless Christian life. If I chose to hear God and seek understanding (so I could obey the dictates of the Lord's heart), I would begin to travel on the glorious road called the Highway of Holiness. Its way leads to an ever-increasing knowledge of Him and His ways. The only option for my sold-out heart was to respond: "Lord, I want to. Help me. Show me the way. My husband's not ready for this. Give me, give us a way out." "No temptation has seized you except what is common to man. And God is faithful; he will not let you be tempted beyond what you can bear. But when you are tempted, He will also provide a way out so that you can stand up under it. Therefore, my dear friends, flee from idolatry . . ." (1 Cor. 10:13-14).

A WAY OUT

When I prayed my feeble little heart cry, little did I expect God's response so soon. Within a couple hours, I saw something between my two crystal angel candleholders. It looked like pieces of artificially-spun snow. The problem being I had never used the substance. So . . . I curiously sauntered toward the mantle. Of course, I reached out to see what this spun stuff was. I drew my hand through the seemingly ethereal material up toward my face. Ahhhhhhhhhhhhhhhh! I screamed at the top of my lungs and danced some sort of a jig when I discovered that I was holding a web and several tiny spiders right before my eyes. My heart was racing and my eyes were wide. I frantically looked around our family room with adrenaline clarity only to realize that they had invaded. Invaded! Spiders were everywhere!

The Lord knew how to flush our Christmas tree[406] instantaneously. Spiders. As I previously told you, at the time I could have been diagnosed with arachnophobia. My husband just loves to tell the story of when we were dating in California, I discovered a *gigantic* spider directly over my bed. I instantly called John on the phone and exclaimed: "There's a spider on my ceiling right over my head! What should I do?!" He chuckled, which didn't make me feel any better, so I informed him: "I'm serious! It's a HUGE spider with eight GIANT legs, a humongous disgusting body and it's was directly over me!" He calmed me down slightly, with mirth still in his voice, and told me to get a broom. John stayed on the phone to allay some of my fears. He heard the broom going swish, swish, swish as I put an end to the crisis with his help. I would call on my husband to dispose of any and all spiders in our house after that. I have a rule. Insects are okay, and I usually leave them alone if they are outside. Inside, they are fair game . . . splat! My Mom has told me since then that I was bitten by a poisonous brown recluse spider when I was a toddler. My arm was wilting as I was rushed to the hospital. God miraculously healed and saved me as my mother's heartfelt prayers hit the Lord's heart.

The first thing I did, before getting rid of the spider-infested tree, was call my good friend Linda. She was a very wise and caring friend, who would understand my dilemma. You see, as the Holy Spirit was convicting me as I read the materials about Christmas, I would run some of it by my husband. John's a *really* smart guy and knew where the Lord was leading me; but he was not ready to be radical in throwing out Christmas, as symbolized by our tree. I would dare say that not many people are.

My conversation with Linda went something like: "Liiinnnnn-da!!! I just prayed a couple hours ago that the Lord would give me a way out of Christmas. Now my Christmas tree is infested with spiders, and they are all over the house! I can't *stand* this! What am I to do?! John is going to be upset if I throw out this Christmas tree! But I cannot live with spiders!" Linda, through the guidance of Spirit of the living God, got me calmed down enough to think fairly rationally. She also gave me some excellent advice: (1) Call John. Tell him what's happening. Your husband is kind and supportive. He will understand if you have to throw out your Christmas tree due to spiders. (2) I'll be right over to help you . . . a friend indeed.

After a couple phone calls, I found out that John was unavailable. He was in an all-day meeting.[407] I could interrupt for emergencies, but I reasoned that telling him now or when he got home wouldn't make that much of a difference . . . besides I could deter his focus . . . and I knew the outcome would be the same. Those spiders with "their" tree were *outta here!* I can still picture my poor husband driving up to the house seeing our formerly gorgeous tree stripped of all its glory and laying ceremony-less at the curb. You should have seen the dazed look on his face when he came through the door. When Linda got to my house, I informed her of my inability to get a hold of John. I showed her the infamous spiders. In hindsight, it was nice to have an eyewitness. Then, with supernatural glee, we started to dismantle the Christmas tree. I handed Linda some of the garland, ornaments, and the like to box up. I saved ornaments with special memories attached, like our first Christmas bride and groom ornament, my son's baby ornaments, et cetera. I've wondered if the Lord will have me throw them out too; but I have learned not to assume anything.

Some of the items the Lord told me to toss. I grabbed a large box, and with a childlike heart I listened to Him for directions—what to keep and what to toss. As each item came off the Christmas tree, I gave the keepers to Linda or threw them in the trash. As I tossed out a lot of beautiful possessions (not to mention the sentimental attachments), I kept thinking over and over again: "Man, this is radical! This is radical! This is radical!"

During the entire dismantling process, there was such an incredible spirit of joy where we both had no doubt that the Lord was pleased. I wished that this was one of the times that the Lord would have opened my spiritual eyes to be able to see the spiritual realm for I sensed both God and angels rejoicing. Linda and I thought how funny it was that the Lord would choose the one thing that I would not tolerate.

Update, December 30, 2005: Today was the perfect time to throw out the remnants of Christmas. It has been eight years and nine days since I dismantled our Christmas tree in 1998. The number "eight" in scripture refers to a new beginning, while the number "nine" refers to the fruits of the Spirit (Gal. 5:22-23), the gifts of the Spirit (1 Cor. 12:8-10), and the garden fruits of the bride (Song of Songs 4:12-14). E.W. Bullinger says that the number nine is the last of the digits and thus marks the end or the conclusion of a matter. It is the number of finality or judgment—the judgment of man and all his works.[408] It was more difficult than I thought. I cried. I hadn't thought about cleaning out the Christmas stuff at all. I suppose I was avoiding the subject. I already had prayed though: "I will get rid of anything you want me to, Lord . . . just lead me, guide me, and direct me. I side with You, even against myself, if need be." My husband was in his throwing-out mood, which he tends to get into if he's home for more than five days. John asked me in the spur of the moment if we could go downstairs and clean things out. I was game. We got rid of an old stereo, books, wall hangings, et cetera. I saw the Christmas box and just knew it was time. The most difficult item for me to throw out was my son's cross-stitched stocking. I had labored over it for weeks before Cody's first Christmas. I'm sure many of you can relate to the excessive exertion that went on to get the item ready for the big day. Cody's stocking had a kind-looking, holly-garnished Santa on the front that was cuddling a plump little teddy bear with his name caringly embroidered at the top. My handmade gift was a way I wanted to show my newborn son I loved him. Something as simple as Cody's stocking demonstrates the reality that love and worship are intimately woven into the fabric of any celebration. In fact, many of us have felt most loved during celebratory seasons. Celebrations set significant parts of the culture for both a pagan and a holy nation. The Bible tells us that ultimately *any* ungodly compromise will not be allowed in His dwelling place. Be assured that in this kingdom day, God's people will celebrate the Lord His way.

Today (December 30, 2005) is the fifth day of Chanukah. "Five" in Scripture is the number of grace. Favor shown to the unworthy we call *grace*. This is favor indeed: favor which is truly divine in its source and its character.[409] Grace, Grace to this mountain of human obstacles! (Zech. 4:7 AMP) I have to admit I *needed* grace today. Obedience to the Lord is not always easy, but it is good. "The fifth book of the Bible—Deuteronomy—magnifies the grace of God . . . it emphasizes the great fact that not for the sake of the people but for God's own Name's sake had He called, and chosen, and blessed them (Deuteronomy 4:7, 20, 32, 37)."[410] Remember that David chose five smooth stones when he went to meet the giant enemy of Israel (1 Sam. 17:40). The stones signified David's own perfect weakness supplemented by divine strength.[411] What a perfect analogy for my family throwing out Christmas. "But He said to me, 'My grace is sufficient for you, for my power is made perfect in weakness. Therefore I will boast all the more gladly about my weaknesses, so that Christ's power may rest on me. That is why, for Christ's sake, I delight in weaknesses, in insults, in hardships, in persecutions, in difficulties. For when I am weak, then I am strong" (2 Cor. 12:9-10).

IT'S GOOD ENOUGH FOR ME

Once the tree, which represented Christmas for us, was taken to the curb, I took a moment to fix a cup of soothing black tea (with cream and sugar, of course). I sat at my kitchen table staring at our presents, which had been placed in the bare corner of the family room where the tree used to reside. I took a sip of tea and stared. I took a sip and stared. This went on for some time. I still was in touch with the unspeakable spirit of joy and peace that started during the dismantling process, but I also felt a distinct void. It was like having a rug being pulled out from beneath you. I had lost my footing, so I sought the Lord. I said something similar to: "There's a big hole in our life now. What are we to do?" I clearly heard Yeshua say: "Do what I did. If Chanukah was good enough for Me, it's good enough for you." "What will you do on the day of your appointed feasts, on the festival days of the Lord?" (Hos. 9:5).

Wow! This was news to me. But of course, Jesus grew up and lived as a Jew while He was here on earth. I just never thought about Jesus celebrating the winter festival of Chanukah. There must be biblical proof of this, and there is: "Then came the Feast of

Dedication at Jerusalem. It was winter and Jesus was in the temple area walking in Solomon's Colonnade" (John 10:22-23). Chanukah is also called the Feast of Dedication, the Feast of Miracles, and the Feast of Lights.

Jesus walked in Solomon's Colonnade during the feast of Chanukah, declaring to the Jews that His miraculous works plainly revealed He was the Messiah. Israel's priests had previously concluded that when they heard the testimony of someone being healed of the incurable disease of leprosy, it would be an obvious sign of the Messiah . . . that He had come. And not only that, but the Messiah also would restore the sight of someone born blind. One born lame would walk.[412] When John the Baptist asked Jesus: Are you the One? Yeshua sent back the message: Tell John the blind see, the leper is cleansed, the lame walk and the captives are set free (Matt. 11:4-5). These, and even greater, works believers are called to do. How many of these miracles happen in America today? How many have you personally seen? The church, universally, was a supernatural community prior to the pagan feasts being integrated into the church's calendar. Daily, even several times a day, miracles occurred. Jesus set the precedence when He walked in Solomon's Colonnade during the Feast of Miracles declaring the miracles done by God's kingdom had come upon them.

All the passages that speak of Solomon's Colonnade tell us it's a place of miracles. Acts 5:12 informs us that all the believers met together at Solomon's Colonnade. It's the place where the apostles performed many miracles, signs, and wonders among the people. It is also the place where a beggar, who had been crippled from birth, held on to Peter and John and was healed (Acts 3:11).

Solomon's Colonnade is also called Solomon's Porch. It was built by Solomon on the east side of the temple. This is the side where the glory is supposed to fill God's temple. A porch or portico is a covered area adjoining an entrance to a building and usually has a separate roof. Spiritually speaking, it represents the place where a believer already has entered the temple (i.e., a relationship with God), but not the building (i.e., become a permanent dwelling place for God). I believe that the celebration of Chanukah holds several keys for end-time believers.

THE FEASTS OF THE LORD

Jerusalem is where the Lord set the church's foundation, not Rome, which it gravitated toward after the severance with Judaism was made.[413] "When the church was completely cut off from its Jewish roots, pagan rituals were substituted for those that really did speak of Christ, and the drift toward deep darkness ensued."[414] Even the most basic elements of the church were tweaked to such an extent that even time became a trigger for ancient idolatrous practices within the church where the "Christian" calendar revolves around the pagan feasts of Lent, Easter, Christmas, et cetera.[415]

Christian scholars have used Colossians 2:16-17 to rationalize why Christians should no longer exclusively celebrate the Lord's feasts:[416] "Therefore do not let anyone judge you by what you eat or drink, or with regard to a religious festival, a New Moon celebration or a Sabbath day. These are a shadow of the things that were to come; the reality, however, is found in Christ." Yeshua is the substance; but we must comprehend that a shadow always resembles its substance.[417] When the Bible says it's a shadow of things to come, it means that we will be answering to the Creator, who is casting the shadow. Believers are not told not to celebrate the Lord's feasts in Colossians 2:16-17, but not to let anyone judge us with regard to them. Meaning we are not to criticize, censure, condemn, or punish people on how they celebrate a biblical festival, a New Moon celebration, or a Sabbath day. If Christians used the same logic for the Ten Commandments as we have for religious festivals, where would the church be? There is an assumption in the statement "Don't let anyone judge you" that God's people are already eating, drinking, and celebrating religious, New Moon, and Sabbath day festivals. It's similar to when God states in Matthew 6: "So when you give to the needy" (v. 2), "when you pray" (v. 5), and "when you fast" (v. 16); the Lord is assuming that His people are already giving alms, praying, and fasting.

The whole nation of Israel is said to be God's example for us (1 Cor. 10:4-11). Don't you think Jesus would have confronted any corrupt thought or practice in Jewish society? Everyone knows Jesus overturned the moneychangers' tables. Jesus taught against the traditions of man upheld by the Pharisees. He also told people that just to look upon a woman in lust was to commit adultery. Have you ever wondered why Jesus never told the Jewish believers to cease celebrating the feasts that were a shadow of Him? Don't you think that if any biblical feast was idolatrous that Jesus would have come out against it, instead of being in the temple participating in the festivities? Jesus was not timid, and He would have come out against the Lord's feasts if they were or had a corrupting influence. Not only did Jesus NOT rebuke the Jews for celebrating His feasts, but He also actually used them as object lessons in teaching His people about the fulfillment in Himself of their biblical traditions.

The feasts of the Lord are God's occasions for celebrating, just as the Ten Commandments are God's ordained laws. They are "cheerful feasts" (Zech. 8:19 KJV). "You will sing as on the night you celebrate a holy festival; your heart will rejoice . . ." (Isa. 30:29). God created us to celebrate Him His glorious ways. Read the Gospels. Jesus loved a party! His first miracle was at the wedding feast of Cana where He turned 180 gallons of water into fine wine (John 2:6). The church has not flushed the Ten Commandments. Why should we throw away His feasts—parties celebrating Him? Just as the New Testament sums up the entirety of the Law (i.e., the Ten Commandments) in "a single command: 'Love your neighbor as yourself'" (Gal. 5:14), so the feasts of the Lord are fulfilled in the Messiah. I can't think of a better reason to celebrate the Lord's feasts than using it as an occasion to celebrate Jesus in spirit and in truth! I am not talking about Christians religiously observing every minute detail specified in the Law, but according to the Spirit of the Law. By the way, the minute details are packed with profound revelatory truths, so if you want some meat, you just might want to delve into minute details.

The spring feasts of the Lord speak of Jesus' first coming. The fall feasts speak of Jesus' second coming. I believe that the winter feasts of Chanukah and Purim tell the story of the church and her journey until the Messiah comes again. Chanukah is not a feast forever, like Passover, Pentecost, and Tabernacles, which are types and shadows of Jesus' ministry on earth. It's a feast that celebrates the temporal walk of His church becoming the Bride. You will have to wait until my next book comes out to get more details. In a nutshell, both Purim and Chanukah are celebrated in winter when things look asleep, just as all ten virgins in Matthew 25 were asleep because "the Bridegroom was a long time in coming" (Matt. 25:5). By the way, both the wise and foolish virgins are representative of believers. Purim is a celebration according to the book of Esther, where a portion of God's people were (and still are) in Babylon and the queen (i.e., symbolically the Bride of Christ) prepared to have favor before the king. Queen Esther had to expose who she really was and what she stood for at "such a time as this" — so she and her people would not be destroyed. Chanukah emphasizes God's people celebrating both a miraculous military victory over heathen oppressors, by a small, ragtag righteous remnant, and their miraculous provision of oil needed to light the temple so they could clean it out and rededicate it to the Lord. Could the miraculous provision of oil and cleansing of God's temple be associated with Matthew 25:1-13 (the parable with the five prepared virgins that have their lamps full when the Bridegroom comes)? Definitely.

Chanukah is not one of the seven feasts of the Lord specified in Leviticus 23, but it is one of the two winter feasts mentioned in the Bible — Chanukah (John 10:22-23) and Purim (Esther). If we operate on the premise that the entire Bible is inspired by God (2 Tim. 3:16-17), we must contemplate why these feasts are in God's Word. Are they mentioned positively or negatively? Positively. Does God discourage or encourage their celebration? Definitely not discouraged. In fact, Yeshua celebrated these feasts as a Jew when he walked here on this earth. I don't know about you, but I want to do what Jesus did, say what Jesus said, et cetera. Jesus celebrated Passover (*Pesach*), the Feast of Unleavened Bread (*Hag HaMatzah*), the Feast of First Fruits (*Bikkurim*), Pentecost (*Shavuot*), the Feast of Trumpets (*Rosh HaShana*), the Day of Atonement (*Yom Kippur*), the Feast of Tabernacles (*Sukkot*), the Feast of Lights (*Chanukah*), and the Feast of Lots (*Purim*). Jesus celebrated the Lord's feasts as a shadow of things to come because they are part of His Word — part of Him. The fulfillment of everything in God's Word, including the feasts of the Lord, is found in Christ. Jesus Christ of Nazareth — the Head and His body — gives definitive form to the Lord's feasts. He embodies them. Jesus brings the feasts of the Lord into an organized whole, as a prophetic picture of His ministry to His body and the redemption of all creation.

The truth is, we're all called to one grand, common purpose, and to one ministry: that is, to be like Jesus. We're called to grow in His likeness, to be changed into His express image. You simply can't be a Christian unless this is your calling, your single goal in life: "I want to become more and more Christlike. I want to be set free from all self, all human ambition, all jealousy, impatience, bad temper, thinking evil of others. I want to be all that Paul says I should be if I'm to walk in faith and love. Lord, my heart yearns to be like you" (David Wilkerson).[418]

Ezekiel 46:9 declares that when God's people come before the Lord on the appointed feast days to worship, they will not return the way they came. The celebrated sons of the living God, who revere and worship the Lord, will be changed into His image as they honor and get to know the Messiah in and through His biblically-prescribed feasts (Nah. 1:15).

In the first-century church, God sent Jewish believers to the Gentiles; thus, "presenting to you the word of God in its fullness—the mystery that has been kept hidden for ages and generations, but is now disclosed to the saints. To them God has chosen to make known among the Gentiles the glorious riches of this mystery, which is Christ in you, the hope of glory" (Col. 1:25-27). Our mostly Gentile church is now being sent by God to both Jews and Gentiles for "His purpose . . . to create in Himself one new man out of the two [Jew and Gentile] . . . and in this one body to reconcile both of them to God through the cross" (Eph. 2:15-16). The Lord loves diversity, and I am so glad He does! Just as a man does not become one with his wife by making her a man, so the Jewish and Gentile believers must learn to appreciate one another and their God-given differences.[419] The community called the kingdom of God will come into unity on earth as it is in heaven. Heaven is not a homogeneous blob. It's fresh, vibrant, lively, and diverse.

BEING BROUGHT TOGETHER

The audio-visual displays of the prophetic reality of Christ's first and second coming, portrayed in the Lord's feasts, can only serve to bring Christians into a deeper relationship with one another and with Jesus Christ of Nazareth. Aligning with God's calendar enables us to know and understand God's exact times for the world and His set appointments for mankind.

Mo-ed[420] is the Hebrew word translated as "feasts" in the King James Version of Leviticus 23:2: "Speak unto the children of Israel, and say unto them, *Concerning* the <u>feasts</u> of the LORD, which ye shall proclaim *to be* holy convocations, *even* these *are* my <u>feasts</u>." Technically, *mo-ed* is not the Hebrew word for feasts,[421] but it carries the concept of calling God's people together for His sacred assemblies, which celebrate the annual recurrence of particular dates marking notable events. To *mo-ed* is to have an appointment, a fixed time or season, a cycle or year, an assembly, an appointed time, a set time or exact time.[422] In chapter 4, we learned that: The Sabbath sets our weeks. The New Moon sets our months. The Lord's festivals set our years according to God's timetable.

Through the feasts of the Lord, God is telling us that He has ordained an exact, set, and appointed time when He will fulfill definite events in His plan of redemption. Jesus came to earth in the fullness of time, which was the exact time ordained by God (Gal. 4:2-4). The Lord also has set an exact time when He is appointed to judge the world (Acts 17:31). Technically, God's feasts represent the congregation where God's people are brought together or assembled together for worship as an organized body. "I urge you therefore, brethren, by the mercies of God, to present your bodies a living and holy sacrifice, acceptable to God, which is your spiritual service of worship" (Rom. 12:1 NASB).

In 2 Chronicles 8:13, the primitive root for *mo-ed* is the Hebrew word *ya-ad*,[423] which also is defined as fixing an appointment—like writing a critical meeting in your day-timer. But more importantly, this primitive root implies that the Lord is summoning His people to meet Him at His stated time, He is directing us into a certain position, and He is engaging us for marriage (i.e., to be betrothed[424]).

Just as *mo-ed* in space refers to the locality where mankind has their appointed place of assembly for an appointed purpose, so *mo-ed* in time is a point in time which summons God's people communally to an appointed activity. As it is written: "As You summon to a feast day . . ." (Lam. 2:22). "We give thanks to you, O God, we give thanks, for your Name is near . . . You say, 'I choose the appointed time'" (Ps. 75:1-2). "Look upon Zion, the city of our festivals" (Isa. 33:20). The question remains for Christians: If we aren't celebrating the feasts of the Lords, can we truly be betrothed to Him?

Leviticus 23, verses 2, 4, and 37, tells us "the feasts of the Lord" are "holy convocations." We know that the word *holy* means "a sacred place or thing." It's consecrated. It's dedicated. It's a hollowed thing. This signifies that the self-existent, eternal One (i.e., Jehovah)[425] proclaims that His feasts are most holy days, and the sanctuary in which they are celebrated is sacred. Sometimes I am slow on the uptake; but even I can understand that the self-existent, eternal One does not need anyone's help. When we combine the Hebrew word for convocation (*miqra*[426]) with the word *holy,* as in the phrase "holy convocations," we understand that the feasts of the Lord are times when God is playing host to His holy priesthood. They are divinely ordained events when the Lord's holy nation is being called out to publicly meet with their God. ". . . The people gathered themselves together as one man to Jerusalem . . . offered the continual burnt offering, both of the new moons, and of all the set feasts of the Lord that were consecrated" (Ezra 3:1-5 KJV).

Out of the seventy holy days in a year, eighteen are festivals[427] and fifty-two are Sabbaths. On these joyful holy days, God's people are supposed to devote themselves to sacred pursuits, not to the human concoctions dedicated chiefly to sensual and material pleasure. One doesn't need to look long, nor hard, to see that atheists, Satanists, and others (including Christians) exhibit that sensual gratification is Christmas's end unto itself. The feasts of the Lord include special food and other enjoyable activities, but they are subservient to the greater purpose of spiritual elevation—communing with God. The Lord solely desires festivals that pay tribute to the elevated spirit inherent in "these are My appointed festivals (Lev 23:2)."

As we have previously discovered, the Lord's spring feasts are reminders of Jesus' first coming, while the fall feasts are rehearsals for the time of Jesus' second coming. Christians need to quit using the term "Jewish feasts (or Jewish festivals)," because God says: "these are My feasts" (Lev. 23:2). If we serve and worship the God of Abraham, Isaac, and Jacob, then these feasts are for us too.

Am I saying that Gentile believers should celebrate the Lord's feasts just like the Jews? No. Not necessarily. Are we required to? Definitely not. But it would be wise for Christians to be teachable and let the Holy Spirit show us the reality of Christ[428] showcased in the Lord's feasts. The church celebrating the Lord's feasts is actually returning to her primordial state (i.e., first order). When the church was entirely Jewish, for approximately its first seven years, she understood and was an eyewitness to the reality of Christ's atoning sacrifice and the audiovisual aids for remembrance that God left behind—the Lord's feasts.

I am saying that Christian churches can learn about the Messiah through the lessons taught via the Lord's feasts and come up with fresh and new ways of understanding and celebrating Him. I have done this in my children's church class that I teach on Sunday mornings. Not only do the kids have fun in learning about Jesus Christ; but the entire Bible comes vibrantly alive for them, as well as giving them a more detailed, historically accurate perspective. I just love how the feasts pull together different biblical truths. I think it would be really wonderful if various cultures added their own unique flavor when celebrating the Lord's feasts.

I am also saying that Christian churches can graciously extend ourselves by asking local Jewish congregations if they could teach us and if we could mutually celebrate the feasts of the LORD. Hint: The Jews probably know more about the Lord's feasts than Christians. Some Christian churches have already partnered with Jewish congregations during Passover for a Seder meal. Don't stop there! Let's learn all there is to know about the God of Abraham, Isaac, and Jacob.

Romans 11:28 tells us, "From the standpoint of the gospel they are enemies for your sake." The partial hardening that God Himself put upon the Jewish people[429] was to make them the greatest challenge to our gospel message, for the purpose of strengthening the gospel[430] and purifying our message. The church always has been called to get so close to God that she would actually provoke the Jewish people to a godly jealousy so they would be saved (Rom. 11:11-12). The problem with much of the church is we have not gotten close enough to the "consuming fire" (Heb. 12:29) to have our message purified. God knows that if the church could reach the Jews with the gospel, then the church could reach the entire world. It was for this very reason that the church was exhorted to preach to "the Jew first" (Rom. 1:16).[431]

The Jews will not be provoked to a godly jealously by a cheap knockoff of a great treasure. The stubbornness that the church encounters with Jewish people today is the same tenaciousness that kept them on the right track (with God's help) so that the Lord our God could provide His Messiah for the redemption of mankind. Instead of resenting their tenacious faith, we should appreciate it and them.

We also should let the Holy Spirit guide our lives and, thus, our message. Then the church can become the tried and true manifestation of God's glory, which will make both Jews and Gentiles zealous, even jealous, for their Messiah. The Jewish people are the touchstone for a purified Christian message. A touchstone was formerly used to test the purity of gold and silver. It was a test or criterion for determining the quality or genuineness of a thing. According to *Webster*, "touchstone" also means the fundamental or quintessential part or feature. The Jewish people are the standard by which our gospel message will be measured. Additionally, when Leviticus 23:37 KJV says: "These are the feasts of the Lord, which ye shall proclaim to be holy convocations, to offer an offering made by fire unto the Lord," the word *offering*[432] means "a voluntary sacrificial offering." The sacrificial gifts made by fire at the Lord's feasts, which were burnt on God's altar, prophetically foreshadowed the Messiah Jesus giving up His life for the world (for our sakes). Let us remember that the Lord says He desires our obedience more than our sacrifice; therefore, let us not continue to taint or even minimize this greatest gift of all.

Jews know that the Christmas holiday is of pagan origin, and that their God—the God of Abraham, Isaac, and Jacob—would not allow His people to "go there." Aviad Cohen, better known as the musical group 50 Shekel, was asked by *Israel Today* magazine: "Do you feel equally comfortable in a church and a Messianic synagogue?" Cohen replied: "Yes, though I disagree with the paganism of the church with Santa, Christmas, Easter and all that. It's Babylonian. Come out of Babylon already!"[433] The fact that the majority of Christians currently celebrate Christmas must bring the Jewish people quite a bit of confusion. No wonder many Jewish minds reject the concept that Christians and Jews worship the same God. And the Jews should know—throughout their history—that when they mixed the precious with the vile, it always became a stumbling block for them, even crushing many under the weight of their own sins. "Now all these things happened to them as examples, and they were written for our admonition, upon whom the end of the ages have come" (1 Cor. 10:11).

ARDENT REFORMATION

It really wasn't that long ago that devout Christians acknowledged Christmas's paganism. We already discussed how "in Scotland, John Knox put an end to Christmas in 1562. In England, the observance of Christmas was forbidden by act of Parliament in 1644. The Puritans had brought to New England a Cromwellian detestation of Christmas."[434] From 1659 to 1681, Christmas was outlawed in Boston.[435] "Because of the Puritan influence, the festive aspects of Christmas, including the tree, were not accepted in New England until about 1875."[436] As late as the 1840s, Christmas trees were seen as pagan symbols and not accepted by most Americans.[437]

Puritans first got their name due to their attempt to purify the Church in England. Although many were Calvinists, Puritans were not associated with a single theology or with a single definition of the church; but they were extremely critical regarding religious compromises. The Bible was their sole authority. Puritans believed that access to Scripture was a fundamental necessity and the principles articulated in the Bible applied to every area of their life. They also encouraged direct personal religious experience (i.e., individual faith) and sincere moral conduit. On the grounds that Christmas was invented by man, not prescribed by the Bible, and the early church fathers had simply co-opted the midwinter celebration of several pagan societies, Puritans disapproved of their celebration.[438] As mentioned before, Puritans weren't the only ones to come out of Christmas, most English-speaking Protestant denominations—Quakers, Baptists, Presbyterians, and Methodists—who dissented from the Church of England did too.

Technically, the Pilgrims that came to America in 1620 were English Separatists that were more orthodox in their Puritan beliefs than Oliver Cromwell.[439] Both the Pilgrims and the Puritans were nonconformists in refusing to accept an authority beyond the revealed Word. With the Pilgrims this had translated to an egalitarian mode (removal of inequalities among people), while the Puritans were a scholarly society where education tended to translate into authoritarian positions. Just remember, both the Pilgrims and the Puritans were logical fruits of the Reformation, and the key to life for them was God's written instructions in the Bible.

When the term "Puritan" is referenced in this book, I am embracing the ardent reformation with which they sought to bring the church into a state of purity that matched, and even exceeded, Christianity as it had been in the time of Christ. I am embracing the humility exhibited by the Pilgrims, their seed of increasing liberating individualism, and their original mission of seeking after a more righteous society in the New World. Although I acknowledge Puritanism's faults in my own eyes, as typified by witch-hunts, elitism, killjoy attitudes, and a general sense of somberness and gloominess, I agree with their great hope of the gospel of the kingdom of Christ.[440]

Ironically, the proliferation of commerce (i.e., the accumulation of surplus capital) together with Christmas being transformed into a domestic celebration was a result of the prosperity and ideals propagated by a Puritan society[441] based on merit—ideals like deferral of gratification, nose-to-the-grindstone industriousness, perseverance, thrift, humility, responsibility, and self-control. It's amazing that our modern hedonistic Christmas emerged from the wave of religious reformation displayed by Puritanism.[442] It needs to be noted that the morphing of Christmas into the appearance of something more acceptable to Christians cannot hide its pronounced product of fleshly excess. The History Channel website explains that: "By the Middle Ages, Christianity had, for the most part, replaced pagan religion. On Christmas, believers attended church; then celebrated raucously in a drunken, carnival-like atmosphere similar to today's Mardi Gras."[443] In actuality, the family-centered domesticating of Christmas was merely an external change, being rooted in the Babylonian land of the merchants (Ezek. 16:29), that continues to demonstrate its rampant and inextricable fruit of commercialism, as testified by the retail industry's adoption of Christmas as its own. Although even pagans bemoan the commercialization of Christmas,[444] we would do well to remember that as a matter of American history, the strongest complaints and oppositions to celebrating Christmas has been lodged by devout Christians. "For a surprising number of Americans believers, the chief concern wasn't putting Christ back into Christmas. It was taking Christmas out of Christianity."[445]

After Puritanism waned, the religious piety concerning abstaining from Christmas was still in place throughout the 1800s, due to the fact that many religious leaders (i.e., clergy) remained steadfast in resistance.[446] In 1855 the *New York Times* report on Christmas services in the city noted that Methodist and Baptist churches were closed because they "do not accept the day as a holy one."[447] It might surprise Methodists to learn that their founder, John Wesley, gave no Christmas sermon.[448]

Then again we have another giant in the faith, Charles Finney, who stated in 1843: "Even among Protestants, how many regard it as a duty, to observe Christmas. I have been afraid our Methodist brethren were becoming entangled."[449] The famous Baptist preacher Charles H. Spurgeon opened a sermon on December 24, 1871, with the following words: "We have no superstitious regard for times and seasons. Certainly we do not believe in the present ecclesiastical arrangement of Christmas: . . . because we find no scriptural warrant whatever for observing any day as the birthday of the Savior; and, consequently, its observance is a superstition, because not of divine authority."[450] I personally like how the Quakers never translated their dismissal of Christmas into legislation; rather they urged their members to be "zealous in their testimony against the holding up of such days."[451] The Presbyterians maintained a strong stance against Christmas until about the turn of the twentieth century when various Christmas customs began appearing in Presbyterian churches, coming in through frivolities like St. Nicholas in the children's Sunday school, the use of Christmas trees, and other festive items.[452] Incredibly, Christmas and Easter did not appear on the official Southern Presbyterian calendar until the late 1940s and 1950s.[453] Historically, it seems like when any major move of God has hit His church, like the Reformation, Christmas and other pagan rites and rituals within the church are either questioned or rejected outright.

I encourage us all to be open to change. The ability to accept change is a characteristic of Christians who are seeking to be part of God's new wineskin. Even now, the Lord is preparing a wineskin that is perpetually flexible, like gold (Job 23:10). This perpetually flexible wineskin will allow the rivers of living water to be turned into golden new wine. The essence of the best saved for last (golden new wine) is genu-wine[454] — genuine believers flowing in the best God has to offer — His perfect love.

⊗

8

FULLNESS OF TIME

☙

> And when the fullness of the time came, God sent forth His Son,
> born of a woman, born under the Law,
> in order that He might receive the adoption of sons.
> —Galatians 4:4-5 NASB

THE KINGDOM

It's critical that we understand the unique time we are in. Time is one of those things where man has no control. No matter how hard man tries, he will never be able to stop the ticking away of the hours, minutes, seconds, days, months, and years. The clock is always advancing . . . propelling us toward a goal.

Is it just me or doesn't it feel like we have never been this way before? Is it possible to lose one's bearings while simply continuing to live day-to-day? The answer is yes, if there's a sovereign shift to the divine order of earthly things. And as amazing as it may seem, we are currently experiencing a global shift in the earth's administration. We have ended one macro season and begun a new one. I am using the term "macro" to designate a whopping two-thousand year cycle. The whole world has become engulfed in an atmospheric climate of change. Earthquakes, floods, tornadoes, hurricanes, volcanic activity, et cetera, are some of the signs accompanying the birth pains. We shouldn't be surprised. The Lord told us that the end days would be like this (please refer to Matt. 24). We are in a macro season described in Romans 8, where all creation groans for the manifestation of the sons of God. It's a time when the Lord is beginning to reveal many previously hidden truths regarding God's kingdom. The word *kingdom* is in the air. You can hear it in sermons or being touted by Hollywood. Pay attention, rent a movie, and choose from: *The Kingdom of Heaven* (2005), *The Kingdom* (2007), *The Forbidden Kingdom* (2008), or *Indiana Jones: The Kingdom of the Crystal Skull* (2008). The whole world, here specifically the secular world, is prophetically illustrating clashing kingdoms.

The mysteries of God's kingdom have always existed, but their vast reality has barely been delved into. The Lord is unveiling much more about a mystery, which He calls His pure and spotless Bride (sometimes called the Bride of Christ). Her code name or alias is the New Jerusalem (Rev. 3:12; 21:2) or the One New Man in Christ (Eph. 2:15). Please don't get hung up on gender-specific terms; both men and women are called to be sons of God, the Bride of Christ, and the One New Man. In this chapter, we will contemplate how the perfect resurrection of Christ's body will inaugurate the age of the Bride of Christ or the New Jerusalem or the One New Man in Christ—these three being one as diverse aspects of the same consummation. In Him and in fellowship with one another, we actually are being built according to His time and His way into an eternal dwelling place for the King of Kings.

The promises, which have regulated human affairs for the past two thousand years, are not going away, but shifting to prepare God's people for our coming King. Jews are receiving an exemption from their God-given spirit of stupor (Deut. 19:4; Rom. 11:8). "For if their rejection be the reconciliation of the world, what will their acceptance be but life from the dead?" (Rom. 11:15 NASB). Meanwhile Gentiles are being confronted with their false mind-set of "cheap grace" that whitewashes sin. Yes, we are justified by faith: "For by grace you have been saved through faith . . ." (Eph. 2:8a); but don't forget to consider other passages like: "And having been made perfect, He became to all those who obey Him the source of eternal salvation" (Heb. 5:9 NASB).

A very appropriate word for the season we just entered is the word *dispensation,* which simply put means an administrative system. It's an ordering of events under divine authority.[455] Any change of management can be disconcerting, whether one has worked for a company six months, two years, or twenty; because once we get to know all the ins and outs of our job, it can be difficult to adjust to changes in procedures, rules, and even the game plan. Sometimes new ownership accompanies new management. Obviously, there is no change in ownership in relation to our new dispensation: "The earth is the Lord's, and the fullness thereof; the world, and they that dwell therein" (Ps. 24:1 KJV). God is in charge of this and any shift in the divine order of earthly things. He has been, and will always be, large and in charge. He is simply administering things on earth a bit different than before, and it affects everything we do and who we are. That's the point. God is making adjustments so that His resurrected body of believers and bridal company can come into their fullness. If God can measure the waters of the earth in the hollow of His hand, and with the breadth of His hand mark off the heavens . . . If He has held the dust of the earth in a basket, and weighed the mountains on the scales (Isa. 40:12); then know that a small thing for the Lord, like a global shift in the earth's administration, will probably be massive, even revolutionary, to us.

The whole world has entered the latest season of administration where Christ Himself, together with His beloved, is managing the execution, use, and conduct of God's temple in a new-fangled way. Several keys to deciphering the purpose behind each macro season reside in the concepts of: a temple, its stones, the adoption of sons, and the Father heart of God.

TEMPLE OF SONS

Spiritually speaking, the people of God are "a royal priesthood" (1 Pet. 2:9), and at the same time we are being built into a spiritual house (i.e., temple; 1 Pet. 2:5). From heaven's point of view, God's people aren't *in* a temple; we *are* the temple, with each of us being a living stone. We *are* also its priests, but only the sons of a King can be considered royalty. When the term *temple* comes up throughout this book, keep in the back of your mind that the Bible says that those who believe in Jesus Christ's death, burial, and resurrection become sons of God. The adopted sons of the heavenly Father are the fundamental spiritual substance of His temple.

Currently, our individual bodies provide a house for our spirits and souls, which are temples of the Spirit of the living God (1 Cor. 3:16-17). Additionally, corporately, those of us who overcome (i.e., move onto perfection) will literally become the eternal dwelling place of God. After His resurrection approximately two thousand years ago, Jesus Christ was seen by his disciples in His glorified or resurrected body. Somehow this mystery is expanding into a new supernatural dimension in our day to include the Head, who is forever the Messiah, and His resurrected body of believers. We have entered the season where an elemental change is occurring so that a corporate body will be prepared for Him (Heb. 10:5). I know that I am simplifying all this, due to me catching a mere smidgen of the mind of Christ. I feel that this new way of life being ushered in is far above what we can even think or imagine.

IN THE DISPENSATION OF THE FULLNESS OF TIME

A radically new dispensation has arrived upon the scene of human history every two thousand years since the dawn of time. Around two thousand years have come and gone since the fullness of time had come for Yeshua being born so we might be reconciled to God:

> But when the fullness of time had come, God sent forth His Son, born of a woman, born under the law, that we might receive the adoption of sons.
> —Galatians 4:4-5

Two thousand years before that Abraham walked up Mount Moriah to worship God by offering up his son of promise—Isaac. Many experts agree that God's physical temple in Jerusalem—the city of our great king—was built upon the same Mount Moriah.[456]

The biblical pattern appears to be first an only son volunteers to become a worshipful, sacrificial burnt offering; then a stable dwelling place for God is gradually built. This seems to be some sort of divine building pattern. Please notice that on earth the Creator of our universe started with something wholly natural, but eventually His divine building pattern looks like it will culminate in something entirely spiritual. "The spiritual is not first, but the natural; then the spiritual. . . . Just as we have borne the image of the earthly, we will bear the image of the heavenly . . . flesh and blood cannot inherit the Kingdom of God" (1 Cor. 15:46, 49-50 NASB). Whether one considers a stone temple built in Jerusalem or the living stones built of human beings in the New Jerusalem, the fundamental building material for God's temple starts out as organic.

We must first understand what I have already stated: God has been, and currently is, building a lasting temple of living stones where "the tabernacle of God is among men, and He shall dwell among them, and they shall be His people, and God Himself shall be their God" (Rev. 21:3). Christendom has taught us that all who accept Jesus Christ as their Lord and Savior are automatically part of His Bride. You will see that I scripturally refute this teaching. Yes, we all have the glorious potential; but each bridal candidate must choose to journey beyond the gift of salvation toward the Spirit-led process of sanctification. In section III, you will see that the Bible shows us an additional third step is required. Yeshua was baptized three different ways: by water, by the Spirit, and by fire. The final and most arduous leg of our bridal quest is a baptism of fire, which will produce perfection in the sons of God who voluntarily and wholly offer themselves as a pleasing aroma. Stay tuned, for I believe that the Bible shows us that we can be part of God's household and the Bride of Christ; however, one does not necessarily guarantee the other.

Let's try to clarify this divine building pattern a little more by running through it chronologically. We begin with a man of flesh and blood who against hope believed God's promises. We have seen that this man was the first person to come out of Babylon. His name was Abraham. Our heavenly Father's heart responded to Abraham's obedience and sincerity by forging a unilateral covenant with him and his descendants. This covenant of faith was, and is, only dependent of God's faithfulness. God called out a people—Abraham's people—as His sons. This promise was extended first to his natural sons; and then, spiritually, to all who believe. Thus, Abraham became the father of many nations. After Abraham miraculously became God's son and father to his promise, we are told in Genesis 22 that both the father and the son ascended the mountain of God to worship. Of their own free will, they both obediently and sacrificially placed Isaac on God's altar. Full of faith, Abraham offered up his only begotten son. It was a Messianic foreshadow of an unprecedented event, literally fulfilled around two-thousand years later.

After Abraham was tested by God, his descendants grew. They prospered. Long story short, a portable temple was erected by Moses and company. The latter chapters of the book of Exodus discuss how the wilderness tabernacle was built and how it became a fitting resting place for the *Shekinah* (i.e., God's glory/presence).[457]

The book of Leviticus shows us the first revelation in the new tabernacle. God's people were made aware of their responsibility to maintain a high level of holiness. So significant was the wilderness tabernacle's earthly image that God warned Moses to make all things according to the pattern shown to him on another mountain of God—Sinai (Exod. 25:40; Heb. 8:5). We are told that the wilderness tabernacle served as a copy and shadow of heavenly things to come. This is the same pattern Solomon used around a thousand years after Abraham and Isaac's ascension up Mount Moriah. Note that the temples built by Moses, Solomon, and Herod still speak of eternal truths, which can help us understand the spiritual realties behind what God is fashioning in our day. This king's son, who was a king himself (i.e., royalty), built God's first quasi-permanent residence. It was made of stone. One stone was laid upon another. But when God's people rebelled and their time for change had come, the stones were dismantled here on earth to make room for the next temple and the next and the next.

About another thousand years pass after Solomon's reign, when another time of reformation came, the only begotten Son of our heavenly Father comes to earth as a priest forever according to the order of Melchizedek (Heb. 5:5-6). We all know the story. Both the Father and the Son voluntarily laid down Yeshua's life on the cross so that the world through Him might be saved. Hebrews 3:6 tells how "Christ was faithful as a Son over His house whose house we are, if we hold fast our confidence and the boast of our hope firm until the end." Check out the entire book of Hebrews for keys to the mysteries of the divine building pattern. It's loaded with gems. There was and is and is to come a perfect Son. Yeshua was true to all covenants that came before and after Him in our time-space continuum, through perfectly loving His Father with all His heart, all His soul, and all His strength. He told us that doing the will of the Father is His food and drink—His sustenance. The shift that Yeshua brought to the divine building pattern was a quantum leap in the spiritual direction. An entirely natural picture of solid stones was destroyed so a revised version of God's living stones could come forth. After Christ's resurrection, it was like the natural and supernatural realms overlapped even more. They became wedded in a profound new way. God's people have always been the living stones of His presence. They are His temple; but once the stone temple in Jerusalem was destroyed, a monumental global transformation ensued due to a change in God's administration of His temple.

Consider the Hebrew word for *stone:* אֶבֶן *(even).*[458] It has the appearance or is akin to two Hebrew words: אָב for *father* and בֵּן for *son,* which if placed together would be pronounced *av-ben* and carry the nuance of *Father and Son.* We should note that the word *even* is used to refer to God. "But his bow remained firm, and his arms were agile, from the hands of the Mighty One of Jacob (From there is the Shepherd, the Stone of Israel)" (Gen. 49:24 NAS). The Hebrew word for stone additionally has a Messianic touch: "Therefore thus says the Lord God, "Behold, I am laying in Zion a stone, a tested stone, a costly cornerstone *for* the foundation, firmly placed. He who believes *in it* will not be disturbed" (Isa. 28:16 NAS). Therefore, the Hebraic language shows us that a stone represents the concept that the Father and the Son are like a rock. They are inseparable. It communicates what Jesus declared: "I and the Father are one" (John 10:30). "He who has seen Me has seen the Father" (John 14:9b). Here's a mystery that will manifest in our newest dispensation: the heavenly Father, His Son the Messiah, and the sons of the living God will actually be made one . . . so will everything in heaven and on earth.

Note how those in the first century, who believed that Yeshua was the fulfillment of the atoning Messiah, didn't worry about the animal sacrifices still being performed in Jerusalem's temple. They had to trust that the Lord Himself would take care of this practice. They had to trust God, because the temple sacrifices were initially given by God, and they had become a deeply ingrained institution. And in 70 CE, the heavens and the earth moved. Literally no stone was left unturned. A great slide from the natural toward the supernatural began with Jesus' death, burial, and resurrection on earth; but God's grace allowed the temple's animal sacrifices to continue another thirty to forty years. It's funny how Herod's temple was finally finished in 62 CE, then eight years later it was destroyed. As we have seen, eight is the number in Scripture that symbolizes new beginnings. It's where we begin again. Even though a macro new beginning was inaugurated at the cross for the transformation of God's temple, historically, we also know that there was a comparatively gradual turning after Jesus' atonement, so God's people could transition into the new dispensation. Its promise was, and still is, the adoption of sons (Gal. 4:5). This promise is eternal; therefore, it will continue.

Now in our day we have a fresh dispensation dawning, which encompasses and expands upon everything that has gone before it. I predict that another quantum leap in the spiritual direction will take place. I anticipate that it will result in something completely enveloped by the heavenly realm. God's royal priesthood still has confidence to enter the holy place by the blood of Jesus, which was a new and living way, which He inaugurated for us through tearing the veil of His flesh (Heb. 10:19-20). According to the Bible, our new macro dispensation's hallmark will be the Messiah gathering all things together in Him:

> that in the dispensation of the fullness of time He might gather together in one all things in Christ, both which are in heaven and which are on earth—in Him.
> —Ephesians 1:10

Christ's body and His Bride will hold center stage, for all creation groans for the manifestation of the sons of the living God. A manifestation is more than professing faith. It's a walking, talking, many-member organism that's readily perceived by the senses. Not only will people know the genuineness of God's sons, but all of creation—the birds, the bees, the flowers, and the trees—will recognize this new and living phenomenon. Can I say that we aren't there yet? As individuals some of us may have entered into this reality already in part; but corporately, and I mean universally, there is still too much gunk. Please note that we began this journey two millennia ago, but somehow the metamorphosis is going to be kicked up a quark or two.

DRAW CLOSER AND GO UP

Let's more fully identify the traits of the sons of the living God. Please keep in mind our biblical building pattern: a son volunteers to become a burnt offering; then a stable dwelling place for God is progressively built.

Have you ever had Jesus whisper to your spirit something so profound and clear that it shook you way down deep? This happened to me in the month of November in the year 2003. Yeshua whispered: "The one to be sacrificed is called laughter." The first thought that popped into my mind was Abraham's sacrifice of Isaac, but I knew it went loads deeper.

Isaac's name means "laughter." When Abraham fell on his face and laughed at having a son at one hundred years old, God told him: "Sarah your wife shall bear you a son, and you shall call his name Isaac" (Gen. 17:19 NASB), which means "he laughs." After Abraham's son of promise was born, "God tested Abraham" (Gen. 22:1). The Lord told Abraham to take Isaac, whom he loved, go to Mount Moriah, and offer his son as a burnt offering on the mountain of God's choice. For those who may think that this was a barbaric request, please remember that God's ways are not our ways. The Bible doesn't condone human sacrifice.

The Word of God tells us of at least three virtues in our lives that have eternal substance: faith, hope, and love (1 Cor. 13:13). When

God tested Abraham, He was accessing Abraham's character to see if these and other eternal qualities abided in him. Just as Abraham's walk was tested to see if it matched his talk, so will ours.

To comprehend why God asked Abraham to offer Isaac as a burnt offering, we need to delve into the ancient Hebraic understanding of burnt offerings provided for us in the book of Leviticus. First, let's note that the only name of God used in connection with offerings is *Adonai*.[459] This name represents His attribute of mercy. The Hebraic root of the word *offering* means "coming near."[460] Any type of offering is meant to bring oneself closer to God. Additionally, the Hebrew word for "burnt" is *olah*,[461] which literally means going up.

Therefore, when one sincerely offers themselves or anything dear to themselves to the Lord for the purpose of drawing close, they spiritually go up to meet with the God of mercy personally. "This is what the LORD says: 'I will restore the fortunes of Jacob's tents and have compassion on his dwellings . . . I will bring him near and he will come close to me, for who is he who will devote himself to be close to me?'" (Jer. 30:18; 21).

The burnt offering is also called by another name—the elevation offering. As it's name suggests, it raises one's spiritual level. The elevation offering was *brought by everyone* who went up to Jerusalem for the three prescribed pilgrimage feasts of the Lord. The Hebrew prophets spoke that in the end times, all the nations will be coming to Jerusalem—going up physically and/or spiritually—and they will take part in building the temple. It's nice to know that we don't serve an unreasonable God: a person was only expected to serve God according to their ability; that's why an animal from the herd, flock, or birds were allowed.

The elevation (i.e., burnt) offering in Old Testament days was considered to be superior to all others, because it was a voluntary sacrifice and it was offered in its entirety.[462] The word *unblemished*[463] in Leviticus 1:3 symbolizes a person coming close to God with nothing missing. All one's faculties are wholly engaged. When a person brought his burnt offering to the priests (i.e., *Kohanim*[464]), he was required to lean his hand on the head of his sacrifice. Actually, one had to literally lay both hands on the animal's head and then confess his sin or shortcoming. Leaning both hands on one's sacrifice alluded to leaning on the Lord with your entire strength. In the "Here Comes the Bride" chapter, we will discover how loving God with all your strength is synonymous with loving God vehemently, wholly, exceedingly, diligently, utterly. It is the highest form of love.

The burnt offering was the first service performed by Aaron's descendants — the *Kohanim* — in God's wilderness tabernacle. Anyone could slaughter an animal; but it took the descendants of the high priest, who received abundant mercy, to receive the shed blood and transport it to the burnt altar. It's interesting that even though there was a heavenly fire always on the altar, the Kohanim were commanded to add an earthly fire. Once the Kohanim arranged all the cut up parts on the fire, they tended the fire until the sacrifice was consumed. The smoke that rises up to God from the burnt offering is a symbol of the owner's striving, and the Lord tells us that it pleases Him (Lev. 1:9).

In our day, God's people, who become a royal priesthood through their reception of the gift of the shed blood of the Lamb, receive forgiveness for their shortcomings once they sincerely confess their sin. We bypass animal sacrifices because Jesus Christ (*Yeshua ha Mashiach*) offered up the perfect sacrifice of His earthly body once for all. Yeshua became our burnt offering on the cross, and Yeshua's Bride will be like Him. The spiritual principle behind the burnt offering that remains true today is: "Behold, I have come to do thy will" (Ps. 40:7-8; Heb. 10:7). The fulfillment of the picture of the burnt offering in our fresh dispensation will be the baptism of fire that the Bride of Christ will come through to be the Lord's pure and spotless Bride. Bridal lovers of God must recognize what practices and beliefs please Adonai, and which do not; then adjust accordingly, come what may. The Word of God together with Holy Spirit will be our guide; this is at least a partial realization of the picture that the fire that consumes any burnt offering is first and foremost a heavenly fire. Our offering to give up earthly desires and practices will combine with heaven's fiery perfect will. Like the smoke that rises up from the burnt offering, our total surrender to the all-consuming Fire will be one of our most pleasing sacrifices, as well as one of our most satisfying services.

IN THE MIDST

When I heard the one-liner: "The one to be sacrificed is called laughter," I thoroughly researched the word laughter.[465] I discovered the Hebrew word *qereb*.[466] The inward part of the body is the seat of laughter. It is the center of a person, the bowels, the heart, the midst, or the nearest part. It is likened to a person's spirit.

In our assessment of the phrase: "The one to be sacrificed is called laughter," we need to remember that the man named laughter (i.e., Isaac) was a foreshadow of the One "for the joy that was set before Him endured the cross" (Hebrews 12:2 NASB). A phrase in the King James Version of the Bible that consistently appears in association with the word *bowels* (the seat of laughter) is "in the midst." Many times this phrase refers to Jesus (scriptural emphasis is mine):

> Where they crucified him, and two other with him, on either side, and *Jesus in the midst.*–
> —John 19:18 KJV

> *For the Lamb who is in the midst of the throne* will shepherd them and lead them to living fountains of water . . .
> —Revelation 7:17 NKJV

> And the sun was darkened, and *the veil of the temple was rent in the midst.*
> —Luke 23:45 KJV

Our previous dispensation initiated a shift in the concept of taking up one's cross and following Him. In our fresh dispensation, we will continue in this vein; but somehow, it will intensify. I have a feeling that that the baptism of fire, which the Bride of Christ will go through, has some relation to Colossians 1:24: "Now I rejoice in what was suffered for you, and I fill up in my flesh what is still lacking in regard to Christ's afflictions, for the sake of His body, which is the church." God's special corporate one (made up of ones) will demonstrate: "Do all things without grumbling or disputing: that you may prove yourselves to be blameless and innocent, children of God above reproach in the midst of a crooked and perverse generation, among whom you appear as lights in the world" (Phil. 2:14-15 NASB).

Qereb's primitive root *qarab*[467] alludes to the concept of offerings through its reference to the entrails of sacrificial animals.[468] To *qarab* is to approach or bring near for whatever purpose, to cause to come near, to be at hand, or to join. When we lay down Christmas or anything in preference to the Lord our God, *Adonai* invites us to boldly come to His throne of grace, that we may obtain mercy and find grace in time of need" (Heb. 4:16). We will need all the mercy and grace we can get, for Christmas will be one difficult sacred cow to get rid of. The Lord of Love is asking us to come closer, which amongst other things require us to walk in a greater measure of holiness.

FULLNESS OF HIM

The macro dispensation we just entered is the second time the phrase "fullness of time" is mentioned in the Bible. This fullness of time will result in the fullness of Him, and the fullness of the Gentiles is a door to it all. "For I do not desire, brethren, that you should be ignorant of this mystery, lest you should be wise in your own opinion, that blindness in part has happened to Israel until the fullness of the Gentiles has come in" (Rom. 11:25 NKJV).

I have heard consistently from others that the "fullness of the Gentiles" means that a certain number of people from the nations have become part of God's household.[469] While I agree with this explanation, I believe that it is the easiest and most minimal interpretation of the phrase. Missionologists are saying that we are within reach of fulfilling the Great Commission, having preached the gospel and made disciples of every tribe, tongue, and nation. The Greek word translated as "fullness" in the phrase "the fullness of the Gentiles" is *plaroma*,[470] which conveys a sense of completion. My *Webster's*

Collegiate Dictionary says that *completion* is "the act or process of completing." It is also the quality or state of being complete. The word *complete* carries the meaning of: "to make whole or perfect; to mark the end of; fully carried out; and having all parts, elements or steps." Therefore, the fullness of the Gentiles is a time when the Gentile outreach has reached God's predetermined state of completion, having all necessary elements to proceed to the next step.

As I have contemplated the meaning of the "fullness of time" for years now, I have seen where it is not just limited to a quantified number or to a fixed moment when something occurs. The fullness of time is also a measurable period during which a condition exists or continues. It is a season of time (a non-spacial continuum) measured in terms of events. For example, when Cornelius and his household were saved, I believe that the overarching season called the fullness of the Gentiles began;[471] and it will continue until the Lord says it has ended. "He has made everything appropriate in its time. He has also set eternity in their heart without which man will not find out the work which God has done from the beginning even to the end" (Eccles.3:11 NASB).

Let's recap. The fullness of the Gentiles appears to be a fixed event in time, a quantifiable stopping point determined by the Lord; but it also can be defined as the season in which an end to a determined fullness will come. I believe that in addition to marking the end of a season in terms of a quantifiable number of people, the fullness of the Gentiles is a season within a season. I personally believe that when the fullness of the Gentiles season ends, it does not mean that no more Gentiles will be saved, for that would contradict Scripture. Just as there were Jews saved through faith by grace during the Church Age (i.e., the time of the Gentiles), so will Gentiles receive salvation in the emerging age: "not wanting anyone to perish, but everyone to come to repentance" (1 Pet. 3:9).

SEISMIC SHIFT

I don't think anyone but God truly knows what we are in for. But I do know that we can look back about two thousand years ago to pull out some principles that can guide us in the coming days.

There's a new door opening to the age of God's kingdom; therefore, I think it behooves us to study the time when the door opened to the Gentiles. Shortly after Jesus' final ascension to the right hand of the Father, the Gentiles began to join the people of God in much greater numbers than before. Yet on this vital issue, Jesus remained silent while He still walked among us in flesh and blood. Only after divine revelation did divine intervention for the Gentiles and a new paradigm shift take place.

Acts chapter 10 marks a turn of something new and amazing. It's when the door of faith opened to all nations. Similarly, we are turning anew to the age-old foundation of the kingdom of God in our day. It is very telling how when the gospel was brought to the Gentiles (i.e., nations), it astounded the very ones who were personally taught by Yeshua. Note to self: The next move of God should be a surprise to *everyone*. The Gentiles speaking in tongues surprised them all, but the circumcised believers additionally had a feeling of uneasiness. What the Lord our God will require of those who are His in this kingdom day will probably surprise us, make us feel anxious, uncomfortable, and possibly even perturbed. Nevertheless, not our will, but thine be done. Had the Jews understood the Scriptures that pointed to the Spirit being poured out on all flesh, they probably would not have been so astonished by Cornelius's unprecedented encounter with the Holy Spirit. Had we Gentiles consistently practiced the Essential Commandments for All Believers, we probably would not be so astounded at what the Lord is requiring of us this day.

Jews understood and believed that the God of Israel was, and is, the God of the nations; and that Gentiles would be brought into God's household. These spiritual realities had always been spoken of in the Scriptures, but it took a supernatural vision from God to both a Jew—Peter—and a Gentile—Cornelius—to prepare both of them to go forward into God's new dispensation. "To everything there is a season, a time for every purpose under heaven" (Eccles. 3:1). When a new divine system of administration comes around, God seems to share things which no eye has seen, no ear has heard, and no mind has previously understood. It is a very unusual *kairos* (i.e., right) time that appears to come around every two thousand years.[472]

Peter's vision in Acts 10:9-16 was not as plain and to-the-point as Cornelius's vision, due to Peter's closer relationship to God. Recall that Peter fell into a supernatural trance, or some people call it an ecstasy of contemplation. He was caught up into the heavenly realm. I think that it's crucial that something very similar happened to me when Yeshua revealed: "Christmas will be the golden calf of America."

The Bible says Peter "saw heaven open"[473] (Acts 10:11), which signifies the opening of a mystery that had been previously hid or minimally understood (Rom. 16:25). The open heaven also indicated that Peter's authority to go to a Gentile was indeed from God. We need to grasp how significant this directive was. Before this time, the Jews were never allowed to associate with people from idolatrous nations. It had been an unlawful thing for Jews to keep company or come to one of another nation. Notice that this ceremonial law was made by a decree of their wise men, not by God, which was no less binding on a Jew.[474] God's Word had told them to not become corrupted by the sinful activities of other nations, and to remain separate and holy from these practices. Also, they were told not to intermarry. Jews were not forbidden to converse or traffic with Gentiles in the street or in shops, but they were forbidden to eat with them,[475] due to the fact that most pagan meals were dedicated to foreign gods before they were served. Peter articulated in Acts 10:28: "But God has shown me that I should not call any man common or unclean." This is ultimately the meaning behind Peter's vision of the sheet full of unclean creatures, not the repealing of the kosher laws. Please note that the kosher laws in regard to food are still part of God's eternal Word. These regulations were not abolished, but fulfilled in Christ (Matt. 5:17); and they are still valid for our Jewish brethren.

Peter totally changed his mind and religious practice by means of this divine revelation. God tore down Peter's wall of partition that kept a Jew from fully preaching the gospel to a Gentile. By the way, it's time for another wall of partition to come down. The disciples of Yeshua in the early first century had some concept of preaching the gospel to the Gentiles before Peter went to Cornelius, but in hindsight needed some divine adjustments. The Jews most probably imagined that they were to preach only to those Gentiles that came into their synagogues. Groups of Gentiles, who had been convinced that that the God of the Bible was the Only True God, tried to fulfill the ethical precepts of the Bible. They were called "God-fearers." They became attached to synagogues, mainly outside of Israel (i.e., Diaspora), with some even contemplating or following through on a full conversion to Judaism.[476]

History shows us that the God-fearers were attached to almost every Diaspora synagogue. When the gospel message was preached to the Jew first and then to the Gentiles by Paul and folks, the first Gentiles, who received the good news, were these God-fearers. The earliest spread of "The Way" (i.e., the earliest form of Christianity) followed the route populated by Diaspora synagogues in Asia Minor, Alexandria, Rome, Syria Greece, et cetera.[477] The book of Acts testifies to this truth, as well as the presence of Christian communities circa A.D. 100-300.[478] "Turning to the Gentiles" did not radically change the missionary procedure of believers, but it was earth-shattering in its focus and scope. Paul did not initially address an entirely new audience. He preached in Diaspora synagogues until the Jewish audience split into believing and unbelieving factions; then he began to focus more on the God-fearers when he established his apostolic headquarters somewhere other than the synagogue (Acts 18:5-11).[479] Jewish believers still followed Paul, and to the average person on the street and to the Roman authorities, Paul's mission to the Gentiles appeared to be essentially a Jewish affair.[480]

In the first century, the Jewish paradigm of preaching to all nations had to make a seismic shift to begin to accomplish the Great Commission. Today, another seismic shift on how Jew and Gentile relate to one another is about to, and is even already beginning to, take place. I believe that, like in the first century, we haven't even thought much about the adjustments necessary for accomplishing God's purposes in preparation for Christ's body and His Bride.

According to providence, the One New Man of Jew and Gentile in the Messiah will manifest. We will do the Lord our God a disservice if we think that His previous silence about a particular issue or practice means that He agrees with it 100 percent and He will never ask us to change. The cycle of life through many millennia flows. We are all called to live and move and have our being in the way, the truth, and the life.

God repealed a human tradition, a man-made ceremonial law in Acts 10, which enabled the revelation of a mystery: "Gentiles are heirs together with Israel, members together of one body, and sharers together in the promise in Christ Jesus" (Eph. 3:6). At the time, it was revolutionary that Jews and Gentiles were placed on the same level before God. The truth of the matter is that the Lord has never, and will never, reject/refuse any honest seeker (Rom. 10:12-13).

The first apostolic council in Jerusalem sought the Lord and the Scriptures on how Gentiles would be taking part in the temple service. Acts 15 lays out their conclusion. When they sought the Scriptures, they saw that the prophets spoke about the Gentiles' participation in end-time salvation. The saved Gentiles were described as "Gentiles" not Jews;[481] therefore, it seemed good to the Holy Spirit and to the Jerusalem Council to lay upon Gentiles no greater burden than the Essential Commandments for All Believers.

☙

9

THE ONE TO BE SACRIFICED

ଓଷ

> At the time of sacrifice, the prophet Elijah stepped forward and prayed:
> "O LORD, God of Abraham, Isaac and Israel,
> let it be known today that you are God in Israel
> And that I am your servant and have done all these things at your command."
> —1 Kings 18:36

THE SPIRIT OF ELIJAH

The "troubler of Israel" went before the nation, and challenged them: "How long will you waver between two opinions? If the LORD is God, follow him; but if Baal is God, follow him" (1 Kings 18:21). This is the same challenge that faces Christians today. How long will the church follow a sensual gospel with its Babylonian traits of materialism, idolatry, and egocentricity? How long will she sow to her flesh? We are coming to a Mount Carmel moment, which holds the potential for being one of the church's finest hours. We are at a crossover place where each one of us must challenge the compromises we have made or be caught in their consequences.

The Holy One of Israel had Elijah summon His people to Mount Carmel. Elijah is probably best known for challenging the prophets of Baal. He threw down the gauntlet: "The god who answers by fire—he is God" (1 Kings 18:24). Christians either make sacrifices to celebrate Christmas or they have sacrificed society's greatest feast—the majority currently being the former. I ask you: Which one of these worship stances would you like tested by fire? The fire of the Lord will once again fall and burn up the sacrifice (1 Kings 18:38)—your sacrifice. Will your sacrifice survive? "It will be revealed with fire, and the fire will test the quality of each man's work. If what he has built survives, he will receive his reward. If it is burned up, he will suffer loss; he himself will be saved, but only as one escaping through the flames" (1 Cor. 3:13-15).

God's Word tells us that surely the day is coming that will burn like a furnace (Mal. 4:1). But before that great and dreadful day of the Lord, God tells us that He will send His people Elijah the prophet (Mal. 4:5). While I do not exclude the 1 Kings Elijah actually returning in the flesh as one of the possible two witnesses of Revelation 11, that is not the focus of this book.

Our focus is a corporate spirit of Elijah that will challenge the prophets of Baal in our day. Recall that both Christmas and abortion are connected to the spirit of Baal. As we have seen, we can substitute other gods for Baal, like Saturn or Molech. "They built high places for Baal in the Valley of Ben Hinnom to sacrifice their sons and daughters to Molech, though I never commanded, nor did it enter my mind, that they should do such a detestable thing . . ." (Jer. 32:35). In order to simplify things for this chapter, we will hone in on the false god named baal.[482] Basically, *Baal* means a lord or master. It is a different lord that the King of Kings and the Lord of Lords. Baal is the name used throughout the Bible for the chief deity/deities of Canaan. Notably, Canaan was the name of Nimrod's uncle.

The prophets of Baal in the book of 1 Kings 18 received no response when they called on the name of Baal, cut themselves, and frantically prophesied. Theirs was not God with the big "G." The prophets of Baal in our day have been given their chance to show the god who answers by fire, but no one will answer. No one will pay attention (1 Kings 18:29). When the corporate spirit of Elijah rises up, they will repair the altar of the Lord, which lies in ruins (1 Kings 18:30); and the God of Elijah will answer them with fire that will burn up the people's sacrifice.

As previously discussed, I believe that the ultimate ungodly sacrifice is a firstborn child dedicated to Baal. It is no mere coincidence that the generation born in 1983 and 1984 faced the highest abortion rate in the history of the United States of America.[483] Why would the spirit of this world try to abort as many as these children as possible? Why has Satan especially targeted those born after 1980? Satan knows every generation's calling. This generation that has been marked for eXtinction has also been marked with the sign of Christ. They are radical worshipers of the Most High God, who will settle for nothing less. They are a prophetic corporate spirit of Elijah confronting religious Babylon. The youth of *The Call Nashville,* led by Lou Engle, are an example of what I am talking about. They are a type of firstfruits for America. They have a holy mission, and it has been foreseen. They have been called to repair the altar of the Lord by laying down everything for Him. They have been called to a holy fast. They have been called to divorce Baal and marry the God of Abraham, Isaac, and Jacob. Theirs is a holy call. It's a bridal call. Many of these children, who have not had godly earthly fathers, are turning their hearts to their glorious heavenly Father.

Malachi 4:6 declares that Elijah will "turn the hearts of the fathers to their children, and the hearts of the children to their fathers." The reality is that we are all called to be part of the corporate spirit of Elijah to one degree or another. We are all called to restore the altar of worship in our own lives.

CHRISTMAS I HAVE LOVED

The Lord of Love is asking us to come closer, which among other things requires us to walk in a greater measure of holiness. I believe that He is asking us to lay down Christmas willingly, which is a sacrifice very similar to the sacrifice of Isaac. Just as Abraham loved Isaac with all his heart, so has the majority of Christians loved Christmas. Just as Abraham went up the mountain of God to worship by offering up his most treasured possession to the Lord, so will we. "And foreigners who bind themselves to the LORD to serve him, to love the name of the LORD, and to worship him . . . these I will bring to my holy mountain and give them joy in my house of prayer. Their burnt offerings and sacrifices will be accepted on my altar; for my house will be called a house of prayer for all nations" (Isa.

56:6-7). The Lord our God is restoring the holy altar of worship in His Christian church.

Please remember that the One calling us to sacrifice Christmas is the God of mercy. He knows where we have been and the condition of our hearts. He alone is worthy to judge our deeds, thoughts, and attitudes. It is because of His great mercy and His love that endures forever that the Lord is revealing how He regards Christmas in this hour. In section III, we will go into much more detail about our bridal call in this season.

This section entitled "Lay Down Christmas (Present)" is meant to help Christians honestly assess our most celebrated holiday. If we move beyond all our defense mechanisms and emotional ties in our evaluation of Christmas, we come face-to-face with mixture being brought into a Christian celebration of Christmas from the beginning. Most Christmas customs and traditions were originally pagan and remain among its most attractive features. The Lord our God is not surprised by our behavior:

> They worshiped the LORD, but they also served their own gods in accordance with the customs of the nations from which they had been brought.
> —2 Kings 17:33

> Israel; cries out to me, "O our God, we acknowledge you!" But Israel has rejected what is good . . . With their silver and gold they make idols for themselves to their own destruction. Throw out your calf-idol, O Samaria! My anger burns against them. How long will they be incapable of purity? They are from Israel! This calf—a craftsman has made it; it is not God. It will be broken in pieces, that calf of Samaria.
> —Hosea 8:2-6

Biblical Samaria is notorious for being a place of mixed religion. The Word of God declares over and over again that they feared Jehovah and served their own gods. Luxury, vice, and paganism were general traditions of Samaria. Aren't luxury, vice, and secularism extensive traits in America, too?

When the Lord divided Israel, due to Solomon going after other gods, Jeroboam was divinely raised to the throne of the ten tribes. The prophet Ahijah of Shiloh told Jeroboam the conditions for his success—obedience to the Lord's commands. Significantly, King Solomon, who held fast in love to his foreign wives and their gods (1 Kings 11:2), learned too late that after all has been heard here is the conclusion of the matter: "Fear God and keep his commandments, for this is the whole duty of man. For God will bring every deed into judgment, including every hidden thing, whether it is good or evil" (Eccles. 12:13-14).

Shortly after Jeroboam's coronation, he departed from the Lord's counsel. The new king was concerned about how the annual pilgrimage feasts to Jerusalem would affect his subjects' loyalty. Recall that the Lord Himself prescribed the annual practice of going up to Jerusalem to worship at His feasts.

The first part of chapter 6 in this book talks about Jeroboam's establishment of his kingdom of self. Let's go into greater detail about how it happened. Jeroboam's fear of man resulted in his seeking man's counsel, when he had already been given God's perfect formula for success. Please note that the first fabricator of a golden calf, Aaron, also had succumbed to pleasing people. Before long, Jeroboam established his own worship centers at the extremities of his kingdom—Dan in the north and Bethel in the south.

Jeroboam's first variance with Scripture was in defiance to the second commandment, which forbids the worship of God by means of an image. Remember that he set up two golden calves and quoted the people's declaration after Aaron made their first golden calf. "Here are your gods, O Israel, which brought you up from the land of Egypt!" (Exod. 32:4; 1 Kings 12:28). Additionally, the Bible informs us that there be but one altar—one place to meet with God. Building an altar for each golden calf at his own separate place of worship was Jeroboam's second variance with the Word of God; but his disobedience went even further. Since the God-ordained priests refused to serve at the new altars and returned to Jerusalem, Jeroboam made it possible for anyone to be a priest (2 Chron. 11:15-16; 1 Kings 12:31). This was Jeroboam's third strike, for at that time only Levites were designated to serve as God's priests. Last but not least, Jeroboam's changes to God's laws coincided with the antichrist formula of changing His designated times. After Jeroboam made his own idolatrous houses of worship, he ordained that the Feast of Tabernacles be observed in the eighth month instead of the original seventh (1 Kings 12:32-34).

You will notice that two of these compromises coincide with the first two steps Antiochus Epiphanes IV enacted in his quest to eradiate the worship of the God of Abraham, Isaac, and Jacob. Remember that Antiochus first set up his own high priest, then tried to enforce the changing of God-ordained times. Prior to Constantine and Antiochus Epiphanes VI, Jeroboam led God's people into heathen practices in order to firmly establish *his own* kingdom. A mass of people conformed to the "new" man-made religious practices, which were sensual, earthly, and even demonic in nature. It fed the people's flesh. It felt good, and "even while these people were worshiping the LORD, they were serving their idols. To this day their children and grandchildren continue to do as their fathers did" (2 Kings 17:41). The truth is that Christians do the same today. We continue to do as our fathers did. We say that we worship the LORD, and we sincerely believe that we do; but in reality we also serve our own gods in accordance with the customs of the nations—even the United States of America.

In a sense, Christianity in America can be likened unto Samaria. Our golden calf is definitely Christmas. The house of God in America has become corrupted. To touch the tip of an iceberg, merely regard divorce statistics for Christians in America. Divorce is as high, and even higher, among Christians as those outside the church.

> The people who live in Samaria [America] fear for their calf-idol [Christmas] of Beth Aven [derogatory name for house of God—Bethel—which means the house of wickedness]. Its people will mourn over it, and so will its idolatrous priests [merchants of the world, Santa Clauses, and everyone who chooses to worship at the Christmas altar], those who rejoiced over its splendor, because it is taken from them into exile.
> —Hosea 10:5, additional comments mine

Revelation 18 tells us that Babylon will be thrown down with violence; and as you have seen, Christmas will take its part in being laid waste because it has inextricable Babylonian roots. All the nations have been deceived by the sorcery wrapped up in the festive trappings of Christmas cheer. It is a charming emotional cocktail that appears so innocent, so benign; but its roots are a beguiling, tricksterish concoction invented by man.

COLONIAL HISTORY OF THE FESTIVAL OF LAUGHTER

It behooves us to reach back into the season of America's birth to understand the origins of the American Christmas that has been exported throughout the entire world. Penne L. Restad's incredible book, *Christmas in America,* is a must-read for those interested in the colonial history of Christmas. The stark reality is that "Americans celebrated few holidays before independence and even fewer after."[484] The sparseness of the American calendars seems even more unusual when one considers the almost universal appearance and function of holidays in cultures throughout the world.[485] Just as the Lord our God marks His people's years according to festivals, so do the nations.

Social and economic upheavals mark the turbulent times when the English Christmas entered Virginia and New England. Remember that Cromwellian England had outlawed Christmas. After a decade of Puritan rule, parliament restored the Stuarts to England's throne in 1660. Once Charles II had the crown on his head, the previously forbidden holiday rituals were promoted with even a greater zeal than before. We need to note that this restorer of Christmas gave England "twenty-five years of jolly sexual intrigue, extravagant private entertainments, and baroque scandals."[486] Virtuous is not the word that would come to mind. His mistresses and illegitimate children would testify to this fact.

In support of the Revolution, patriots revoked all official British holidays on all thirteen colonial calendars, but they did nothing to replace them.[487] Consequently, the American calendars (no single calendar served all the colonists) looked more barren than they did in the early seventeenth century.[488] It was almost like the one nation under God had a blank celebratory canvas with two main placeholders: Thanksgiving and the Fourth of July. A smattering of colonists from various cultures celebrated Christmas and New Year's Day too.

Like modern America, Virginia tended to have a broadly permissive approach to Christmas, which contrasted sharply with the prevailing attitude in New England. Note the predominance of mixture in the way the *Virginia Gazette* recounted the history of Christmas in 1739: "Some Christians 'celebrate this Season in a Mixture of *Piety* and *Licentiousness*,' others 'in a *pious Way* only,' others 'behave themselves *profusely* and *extravagantly alone*.' The last category was comprised of the many who 'pass over the *Holy Time*, without paying any Regard to it at all.' The writer concluded that . . . 'the Little Liberties of the old Roman December, which are taken by the Multitude, ought to be overlooked and excused, for an Hundred Reasons . . .'"[489] Notice that this quote is talking about Christians. Two of the ways Christians celebrated Christmas were: (1) with a mixture of piety and licentiousness, and (2) behaving profusely and extravagantly alone. Also notice this author makes provision for the flesh—"the little Liberties of the old Roman December . . . ought to be overlooked and excused for an Hundred Reasons." If I had a dime for every time I have heard this excuse, I could almost buy Manhattan.

Drinking, fighting, revelry, and squandering money had become a fairly routine way to spend almost any holiday throughout the colonies.[490] These vices especially fit with Christmas. America's free-form holiday mayhem differed somewhat from Europe's ritualized revelry of mumming and masquerading, but they both can be described as a "temporary plunge into chaos."[491] This should not surprise us when we consider that its roots come from the first and supreme man to open the door to a massive and mighty spread of chaos. There has always been a general license of licentiousness to the season. The annual indulgence of excessive eating, drinking, gambling, revelry, et cetera (discouraged in and by the church the rest of the year) is overlooked as everyone, Christians and non-Christians alike, devote much of their holiday season to pagan pleasures.

Americans only began to celebrate Christmas widely in the late nineteenth century,[492] which corresponded with America's struggle to find her own identity. Christmas emerged through circumstances cast by the American Revolution, not to mention the worldwide revolution in commerce and industry. It was modeled in a time of titanic progress and change. There was a need for social harmony . . . something universal in nature. What briefly unites a dissimilar people more than a celebration? The answer is nothing. Christmas being the most important national holiday within America today testifies to this certainty. It was man's inventive way for binding American society together. In the 1820s, Christmas was meant to provide an antidote for the ills of modern life.[493] As evidenced by our increasingly depraved society, the cure is yet to be seen. I love this country. I love the opportunity and freedom it affords, but I am concerned when I listen to the nightly news. Madness seems to be in the air. Just after the Civil War, the American Christmas matured and began to take on a metastasizing life of its own. A knowledgeable glance at Christmas reveals that commerce is her veiled name, and trade is her resourceful game.

THE HOLIDAY THAT TRADE BUILT

The American Christmas we celebrate today was dreamed up in New York City—the city that trade built. New York is the city of moneymakers. It's the city of commerce. The city itself was founded as a trading post on the periphery of a Dutch mercantile empire.[494] The Dutch were a trading people; and their town will ever bear the imprint of its creators.[495] Since its inception, New York City has been a vital conduit of people, money, commodities, cultures, and information essential to the world's economy.[496] Even though it wasn't until the aftermath of World War I that New York began to vie with London as a hinge of the global economy, its "land of merchants" (Ezek. 16:29) roots were established from the city's beginning. Once the United States emerged as a superpower after World War II, New York became the capital of a new multinational economy. The arrival of the United Nations served to make it a global political capital as well. Sound a little like religious and political Babylon?

Especially when we consider that many people believe that, religiously, mammon, not God, rules, despite the formidable number of churches established in the city.[497] Personally, I am a fan of New York City. I enjoy visiting the city and everyone I have met who hails from there. I especially enjoy much of the culture the city promotes, but I do not want to be ignorant to any form of deception, especially if it defiles anything that the Lord considers holy.

New York City's origins are encapsulated in a myth that ratifies the popular conviction that deal driving, moneymaking, and real estate lie somewhere near core of New York's genetic makeup.[498] Washington Irving, the same inventor of Santa Claus myth, created a foundation story for New York City. He regretted that his town was bereft of imaginative associations "which live like charms and spells about the cities of the old world, binding the hearts of the native inhabitant to his home."[499] We need to be aware that the title of Washington Irving's book—*Knickerbocker's History of New York*—is a misnomer. Although Irving's account is interesting, and some say hilarious, it is not based solely on the evidence of history. It is actually a potpourri of fact and fiction that plays knowingly and ironically with make-believe events and bona fide history. Its fingerprint of confusion coincides with Babylon's name, and we already know that mixture is her game. *History's* invented narrator, the pompous Diedrich Knickerbocker, envies his predecessors for being able to summon up "waggish deities" to descend to earth and "play their pranks upon its wondering inhabitants." This "history" was simply some sort of knock-off of Virgil's *Aeneid,* where Irving tried to cast an image for New York City like Virgil had done for Rome.[500] With tongue in cheek, Knickerbocker/Irving explained the story of New York's origins.[501] The invented narrator, Diedrich Knickerbocker, told how an "adroit bargain" was struck with the local Indians, where they received just enough land as a man could cover with his under garments. Knickerbocker introduced Mynheer Ten Broeck (Mr. Ten Breeches), the man who would produce breeches after breeches until the land of the city was covered. Just as Irving's form of Santa Claus didn't take, so his pseudo-classical foundation story never passed into popular lore. Just as a simpler, kinder version of Santa Claus took, so did New York City's foundation story; and they both played to the notion of New York as a city of tricksters. Basically, the accepted form of the foundation myth asserts that the Dutch bought Manhattan from the Indians for twenty-four dollars.[502] Like all proper myths, this story has been passed down from generation to generation. Mere facts are beside the point for any myth.

One of America's most exported commodities is our image of the festival of laughter called Christmas. Of Americans, 97 to 98 percent celebrate it as well as 95 percent of the world. Remember that wealthy New Yorkers, called patricians, didn't invent the new cult of domesticity in the 1820s, but they did give it Christmas.[503]

Prior to the invention of the American Christmas, the favorite winter holiday of the city's propertied classes was New Year's Day. Families commonly exchanged gifts on New Year's Day, and gentlemen called on family and friends.[504] This contrasted dramatically from the previous eve's revelry and mischief. Let's not forget that both of these rituals have been brought over from Babylon.

In ancient Babylon, the greatest agricultural holiday was called the *Akiti* (in the Sumerian language). Get this! The *Akiti*[505] lasted for twelve days and it was called a New Year festival—albeit it was a springtime celebration. By the way, prior to England adopting the Gregorian calendar in the middle of the eighteenth century, they were still connected to the Babylonian New Year's marked in the spring, i.e., March 25.[506] Babylon's high priest had the king of Babylon bow before Marduk's firstborn son Nabu's "holy" image. Note that Marduk is synonymous to Nimrod and Nabu is synonymous with Tammuz. Prior to this the Nabu shrine was covered with a golden canopy in anticipation of Babylon's great god's (i.e., Marduk's) arrival. This appears to be a similar ancient golden canopy tradition that was mentioned in chapter 3 where the live Apis calf was transported to his sanctuary in a gold cabin, which gives us a little more insight about a golden calf that's an idol. Remember that the Apis bull was widely known as the incarnation of the sun god, so was Marduk (deified Nimrod) and Tammuz. Midway through this most ancient twelve-day festival, a great public banquet was held in the *Akiti* building after the Babylonian king took the image of Marduk by the hand and led him out of his temple into Nabu's sanctuary. Significantly, a couple of Sumerian documents speak of a symbolic ritual where the Babylonian king made love to the goddess Ishtar, which took place in his palace on New Year's Eve.[507] Ishtar is just another name for the Babylonian Queen of Heaven. She goes by hundreds of names, but most primordially her name is Semiramis. Please refer back to the "Semiramis" and "Yuletide Season" sections in chapter 3 if you get lost. Although there is quite a bit of confusion, the *Akiti* celebrated during Babylon's New Year and the birthday celebration for Tammuz on December 25 appears to have merged and morphed into our modern-day Christmas season via the Roman Saturnalia. It was jumbled together. Listen to how Jeremiah laments over this practice: "Do you not see what they are doing in the cities of Judah and in the streets of Jerusalem? The sons gather wood, and the fathers kindle the fire, and the women kneed dough to make cakes for the queen of heaven; and they pour out libations to other gods in order to spite Me" (Jer. 7:17-18 NASB).

Let us return to our fairly succinct study on how our American Christmas came to be. A prominent New York City merchant and civic leader named John Pintard saw that the city's expansion after 1800 rendered this "joyous older fashion" of New Year's so impractical that it was rapidly dying out. To Pintard's dissatisfaction, his family knew that New Year's Eve marked the peak of the carnival revels in New York. He preferred the quiet, daytime, domesticated winter holiday with the laughter of families drowning out the nocturnal hoodlum's merriment, debauchery, and folly.[508]

Although John Pintard appears to have been a near perfect gentleman, businessman, and reformer, his closet seems to have plenty of clattering bones. First of all, like many wealthy merchants of his day, he considered himself much better than the "swinish multitude."[509] Pintard helped the poor, but he admitted that this mass of humanity—immigrants, working poor, the aged and infirm, blacks, widows, orphans—seemed hardly worth the trouble.[510] Although his charitable actions lined up with the first half of the definition of pure and undefiled religion in James 1:27,[511] it seems that his heart did not. The second half of "keeping oneself unspotted from the world" appears to be a wash too, for most significantly, in regards to the origins of Christmas in America, Pintard was active in Freemasonry.[512] In fact, he was a master of New York City's Holland

Lodge.[513] The Holland Lodge website states that it is: "recognized as one of the country's foremost Masonic Lodges."[514] Significantly, they conferred honorary membership on our first President George Washington in 1789, when our nation's capital was in New York City.[515] In chapter 3, we went over a brief synopsis on how all "Mysteries" come from the idolatrous fountain of Babylon. The institution of Freemasonry is "like . . . all the Mysteries, [it] . . . CONCEALS its secrets from all except . . . the Elect, and uses false explanations and misinterpretations of its symbols to mislead those who deserve only to be mislead."[516]

Truth be told, Albert G. Mackey wrote in *An Encyclopedia of Freemasonry and Its Kindred Sciences:* "NIMROD. The legend of the craft in the old constitutions refer to Nimrod as one of the founders of Masonry."[517] Without going into detail, let's additionally note that the sun god Osiris is predominantly featured in Freemasonry. Recall that Osiris's birth date, along with all the other infamous sun gods, is celebrated on the ancient winter solstice of December 25. Pintard was in active agreement with the Masonic illumination that everyone's religion is universal. This means that a Mason worships at every shrine,[518] which is contrary to the biblical standard. This worldly universality is spoken of in Scripture:

> We know that anyone born of God does not continue to sin; the one who was born of God keeps him safe, and the evil one cannot harm him. We know that we are children of God, and that the whole world is under the control of the evil one . . . Dear children, keep yourself from idols.
> —1 John 5:18-19, 21

> The great dragon was hurled down—that ancient serpent called the devil, or Satan, who leads the whole world astray. He was hurled to the earth and his angels with him.
> —Revelation 12:9

> Again, the devil took him to a very high mountain and showed him all the kingdoms of the world and their splendor. "All this I will give you," he said, "if you will bow down

and worship me." Jesus said to him, "Away from me, Satan! For it is written: 'Worship the Lord your God and serve him only.'"

—Matthew 4:8-10

All faiths bow at the altar of Masonry, and like Christmas, the followers of Buddha, Mohammad, Zoroaster, Brahmin, Confucius, and even unfortunately Jesus assemble and unite in their homage. Christians need to examine how 97 to 98 percent of Americans and at least two billion people worldwide can celebrate Christmas if it truly is a Christian holiday, especially since many who celebrate Christmas are vehemently opposed to Jesus Christ. Christmas is a holiday where the world unites at its own table. For example: "Although India is primarily Hindu and Muslim, they nevertheless plunge into the Christmas season with the same fervor as their Western neighbors. In Delhi, Santa can be spotted in shopping areas, while in other areas, mango and banana trees are decked out in holiday ornaments."[519] Indonesia is the largest Muslim nation in the world, which currently decimates entire villages of Christians. Lily Yulianti reports, "In my home country, Indonesia, a country nearly 90 percent Muslim with a population of 220 million, Christian people are a minority. However, Christmas is always celebrated full of joy." In big cities such as Jakarta or Surabaya, shopping centers display Christmas ornaments such as Christmas trees, Santa Claus with his eight reindeers, and artificial snow made from cotton and foam. In Muslim "Beirut, Lebanon's tallest Christmas tree is adorned with shiny shooting stars and red and silver ornaments."[520] In predominantly Buddhist Japan, "Christmas is not a national holiday, but you'd never know it by looking at the retail stores, which are decked out with almost as many decorations as the average North American mall."[521] You get the world universality idea. Getting along is a good thing. Compromised faith is not.

John Pintard endeavored to cast the New Year's celebration into a new image. He proposed an alternative—St. Nicholas Day on December 6 as a home and hearth winter holiday for polite society.[522] His good friend, Washington Irving, was the first to brand Saint Nicholas as the patron saint of New Amsterdam in his book

Knickerbocker's History of New York, in spite of the fact that the earliest evidence of anyone celebrating St. Nicholas Day in Manhattan dated back only thirty-three-years to 1773.[523] Irving described Saint Nicholas as a jolly old Dutchman named Sancte Claus, who slid down chimneys giving gifts to sleeping children on his feast day. On December 6, 1810, one year after Irving published *Knickerbocker's History,* Pintard launched what he called a revival of St. Nicholas Day at city hall for members of the New York Historical Society.[524] Mr. Pintard did his research and tapped into the original man-made tradition of Saint Nicholas, which proclaimed his feast day as a kind of judgment day where good children got rewarded and bad ones got punished. His motive was to manipulate the spoilt dispositions of children. Unfortunately, being spoilt was, and still is, one of the fruits of our cozy, domesticated Christmas.

Pintard's St. Nicholas Day never caught on like he'd hoped, but Irving's Sancte Claus did, with the help of another friend, Clement Clarke Moore. For how our modern-day Santa Claus came to be, please refer back to chapter 6. In 1831, John Pintard forgot his earlier promotion of St. Nicholas Day. He asserted that the new rituals of Christmas were of "ancient usage," and "St. Claas is too firmly riveted in this city ever to be forgotten."[525]

Once well-bred New Yorkers of the early nineteenth century substituted Christmas for New Year's Day, they brought into their homes the pouring out of libations tradition newly renamed "Christmas logs."[526] The festive firewood, or as the ancients called it—the Yule Log—is a stark indication to the Babylonian roots of our America Christmas. The holiday that brings laughter, which is an idol in so many American's hearts, was, and still is, represented by its primordial pagan images: a mere log and an evergreen tree. As discussed in chapter 3, the Yule log is not so prevalent today; but its ancient calling card—the Yuletide Season—still sticks.

Just as New Year's Day shifted the focus from the problematic revelry associations of New Year's Eve, so Christmas Eve deftly shifts the focus away from the problematic religious associations of Christmas Day. Nineteenth century New York remembered that December 25 coincided with the ancient calendar's winter solstice. They knew that the Catholic Church mixed Christ's birthday celebration with the pagan sun gods, because the Protestant Reformation had brought these particulars to light. Additionally, some New England churches had tried to counteract the spread of gluttony, drunkenness, and misrule on December 25 with public worship services. Like the proverbial frog being slowly cooked in a kettle of water, the entire American Christian Church—Protestant and Catholic alike—has succeeded in bringing mixture into her religious celebrations. In particular, the golden snare of Christmas, which is America's golden calf, has become entrenched.

HIS WILL ENTIRELY

When I came across Ecclesiastes 10:19, "A feast is made for laughter," in my daily devotions, it hit me that the mysterious statement "the one to be sacrificed is called laughter" had a deeper context related to this book. I perceived that Adonai was telling me that a feast is to be sacrificed. Will you have the courage to examine this lamb of Christmas we yearly offer to God?

We have discussed how the Bible clearly outlines that a person cannot come nearer to God without maintaining a high level of holiness. For the Lord's presence to rest among His people, each one of us must voluntarily offer ourselves up to God in our entirety to do His will.

> Therefore, when He came into the world, He said, "Sacrifice and offering You did not desire, but a body You have prepared for Me. In burnt offerings and sacrifices for sin You had no pleasure." Then I said, "Behold, I have come—In the volume of the book it is written of Me—To do your will, O God."
> —Hebrews 10:5-7 NKJV

You and I make up the body of Christ; and according to Revelation 19:7-8, the righteous deeds of the saints prepares Yeshua's wife for the Lamb (we will go into greater depth about this in chapter 10). The question everyone must answer is: Do Christians come to do God's will or our own will when we celebrate Christmas? I believe that this kingdom hour demands a greater degree of holiness, because the Lord desires to come and dwell among His people. Our Beloved is asking us to come closer. The One who loves us is summoning His people to meet Him at His stated time. The Holy One of Israel is directing us into a certain position. Adonai is engaging us for marriage. He is asking His people (all people) to sacrifice a holiday they love for the One they love. For these precious ones, a feast is to be sacrificed, and it is called laughter. Ask anyone in the American church today when is the happiest time of year for you, and you will most likely hear Christmastime. As mentioned previously, Christmas has been a time when many of us have felt most loved.

Christmas is the time of year when there's much laughter and frivolity. You "feast on the abundance of your house" (Ps. 36:8). It is the holiday where Americans, including those in the church, currently spend most of our resources. In the next chapter we will see that loving God with all your strength in reality means to love Him with all your resources (time, talent, wealth, etc.). Now is the time to offer our strength completely to the King of Kings.

SACRIFICE OF LAUGHTER

The mysterious statement: "The one to be sacrificed is called laughter" has more than one facet to it. Remember how my first thought was of Abraham's sacrifice of Isaac. It also primarily refers to our heavenly Father's sacrifice of his only begotten Son—Jesus—on the same Mount Moriah. Additionally, it foreshadows an event for the sons of the living God. It's an occasion where you and I, sons of the living God, will lay down one of our most precious possessions and practices. A feast is to be sacrificed, and it is called laughter. ". . . Go and serve your idols, every one of you! But afterward you will surely listen to me and no longer profane my holy name with your gifts and idols. For on my holy mountain . . . There I will require your offerings and your choice gifts, along with all your holy sacrifices" (Ezek. 20:39-40).

I did not know that there is a passage in the Bible that prophetically speaks of the world's laying down of Christmas—America's golden calf—until I came across it in my daily devotions at just the right time. "Behold I am about to put a plumb line in the midst of

My people Israel. I will pass him by no longer. The high places of Isaac [i.e., laughter] will be desolated . . . Then shall I rise up against the house of Jeroboam [golden calves] with the sword" (Amos 7:8-9 NASB).

Christmas is a high place of worship in the American church in our day; it's undeniable that Christians, as well as the rest of the world, have built their altar to its glory. As we have seen, Christmas's mixture includes idols being set up right in God's temple. Amos 7:9 prophetically declares that the idolatrous worship of laughter will be destroyed, and my guess is that it will be annihilated by fire (Isa. 1:10-31). Christmas will be a work that will be tested. As a heavenly reward, it will burn up according to biblical standards. Christians who hold onto the Christmas celebration will suffer the loss of a heavenly reward; but 1 Corinthians 3:15 NKJV says that the believer himself "will be saved, yet so as through fire."

Moreover, Amos 7:9 tells us that the sword of the Lord will rise against the house of Jeroboam. The living and active two-edged sword of the Word of God will separate our fleshly practices from truly spiritual ones. Hebrews 4:12 NASB even says that the Word of God is "able to judge the thoughts and intentions of the heart." The house that Jeroboam built was filled with golden calves and sinful, self-appointed priests (1 Kings 12:28-31; 2 Chron. 11:15); furthermore, Jeroboam changed the time when the Lord's Feast of Tabernacles was to be celebrated among the ten tribes (1 Kings 12:32-34). This prophetically speaks of three things in our day:

- God's holy priesthood choosing to serve Him the way they choose.
- God's people fabricating a worshipful image made in the likeness of a golden calf.
- God's people choosing their own month to celebrate a feast, which was said to be dedicated to Jehovah.

God's holy priesthood in America has chosen our own way to serve Him. We say that we are worshiping Jehovah in and through the image of Christmas, and we have chosen our own time to celebrate—December. Of note, I particularly believe that Amos 7:9 foretells that the Holy One of Israel, the One with a two-edged sword in His mouth, is going to rise against the house with His name on it that worships the golden calf in order to cleanse it. "Her priests do violence to my law and profane my holy things; they do not distinguish between the holy and the common; they teach that there is no difference between the unclean and clean . . ." (Ezek. 22:26).

When the Bible speaks of the unfaithful kings of the divided kingdoms of Israel and Judah, most of the time the refrain goes so-and-so "did evil in the eyes of the LORD. He did not turn away from the sins of Jeroboam son of Nebat, which he caused Israel to commit" (1 Kings 16:19, 30; 2 Kings 13:2, 11; 14:24; 15:9, 18, 24, 28; etc.). Even Jehu, who destroyed baal worship and cut down Jezebel, was rebuked for not turning away from the sins of Jeroboam (2 Kings 10:28-29). The sin of Jeroboam that the Bible specifies most is the worship of golden calves. Like Aaron, who set up the first golden calf at Sinai, Jeroboam fashioned a golden image due to the fear of man and his own selfish ambition. He cast an image, set up an altar, and declared a festival for Jehovah. The church in America has done the same.

○3

SECTION III

PURE AND SPOTLESS BRIDE

(Future)

10

HERE COMES THE BRIDE

CR

> Let us rejoice and be glad and give the glory to Him,
> for the marriage of the Lamb has come and
> His bride has made herself ready.
> And it was given to her to cloth herself in fine linen,
> bright and clean; for the fine linen is the righteous acts of the saints.
> —Revelation 19:7-8 NASB

PASSIONATE LOVE

To love vehemently; wholly, speedily, especially when repeated; diligently, especially, exceedingly, greatly, louder and louder, mightily, utterly. Doesn't this Hebrew word for "strength"[527] sound like passionate bridal love? I discovered this description for carrying a torch for the Lord as I was beginning to dive deeper into what it *really* meant to love my God. What did He have to say about it? I was drawn to the scripture that Yeshua calls the first and greatest commandment: "Love the LORD your God with all your heart and with all your soul and with all your mind" (Matt. 22:37). I noticed that this was first articulated in Deuteronomy 6, which frankly held the strongest attraction for me: "Love the Lord your God with all your heart and with all your soul and with all your strength" (Deut. 6:5).[528] As my whole being cried, "Yes!" I was already asking questions. Strength? Why strength? I heard a Bible teacher on the radio say that in the Bible the Hebrews usually listed items from easiest to hardest. Now I was really confused. This didn't line up with the paradigm I had been taught. Isn't loving God with all one's heart the paramount demonstration of love? How could loving God with all my heart or soul be easier than loving Him with all my strength? I rolled up my sleeves and pulled out my concordance. This, coupled with some other resources I had on hand, gave me the understanding that I needed.

The easiest way to love the Lord your God = "with all your heart." The Hebrew word for heart is *lev*,[529] and its ancient word picture tells us that the heart is what controls the family or what controls the inside.[530] Your heart is known as the center of your being—the most interior organ.[531] Your emotions and desires can be ways of transporting your love. In the Bible, the heart is synonymous with the mind. Consider how our minds consist of our intellect, will, and emotions. When our brain processes information, many times our will is faced with a choice to make. Our decision results in an action, whether passive or active, and then that particular action[532] creates an emotional memory or pathway. We all have experienced how other people's decisions toward us affect our emotional memories too. Scientists tell us that the deepest imprints come from exceptionally painful or joyful moments. Christmas has definitely been a time of extremes. We center in on the "Joy to the World" and "Merry Christmas" part, but sorrow, stress, and distress are its partner, too. The mixture of Christmas is like an incessant ribbon that winds itself throughout our emotions, which causes us to be caught between two opinions. It's time for God's people to end mixture and become pure. We literally have been double-minded over the Christmas issue. To come into the mind of Christ, we must subjugate our mind-sets to the Spirit of the living God. "Now I exhort you, brethren, by the name of our Lord Jesus Christ, that you all agree . . . you be made complete in the same mind and in the same judgment" (1 Cor. 1:10 NASB). The "same mind" here speaks of being perfectly joined together in the mind of Christ. The "same judgment" equates to the appraisal that God puts on a situation. It's His evaluation, His process. Any veiled hostility in our mind toward the character of Christ must shift/change to form a new order for the future—eventually the restoration of all things in the Messiah. America's bastion of idolatry has a captivating façade of innocence; but in reality, Christmas has caused the American church to become ensconced in worldly ways. We should welcome all of the righteous boundaries set by God, so we can fully connect to express His glorious nature.

The next hardest way to love the Lord your God = "with all your soul." The Hebrew word for soul *nephesh* (neh'-fesh)[533] means a breathing creature. Its verb *naphash* (naw-fash) means to breathe or be refreshed.[534] Therefore, to love God with all your soul means to love Him with your very life's breath. One may think of the authentic gift of martyrdom: "And they overcame him because of the blood of the Lamb and because of the word of their testimony, and *they did not love their life even to death*" (Rev. 12:11 NASB, emphasis mine). Even though loving God with your very life's breath is an *extremely* admirable characteristic, this form of love stays at a soulish level; hence, it's description: "loving the Lord your God with all your soul." How can loving God with all your strength be harder than that? Let's take a peek.

The hardest way to love the Lord your God = "with all your strength." The word "strength" in Hebrew basically means your resources. Say what?! It's harder to love God with all your resources than the very breath you take? Think about it. The windows in the high-rise hotels in Las Vegas only open three inches. Why? Because the casino owners don't want their clientele jumping out the window when they lose all their money. That's just one example of people valuing money or resources more than life itself. "For where your treasure is, there your heart will be also" (Matt. 6:21).

When all is said and done, it's about being fully connected to the Father, the Son, and the Holy Spirit in love. You and I must love God with all our strength *in its fullness,* or our love will remain entangled with soulish shackles. The carnal cares of this world will weigh us down. I believe that God's people demonstrate a bridal love for Him when all three of these areas of our lives are submitted to His lordship, especially our resources. My *Webster's Collegiate Dictionary* defines the word *resource* as: "a source of supply or support; a natural source of wealth; a source of information or expertise; an ability to meet and handle a situation." The word "resource" comes from the word *resourdre,* which means to relieve. It more importantly literally means to rise again, and my dictionary refers me to the word "resurrection." I greatly value the cross of Jesus Christ, but sometimes I am grieved when the church stops at His death. We need to follow Yeshua in burying the dead and walking in resurrected life. Now is the time for the spiritual resurrection of His corporate body. When we think of resurrection resources, we should search for clues by examining *kingdom* in God's Word.

SPENDING OURSELVES

I believe that common sense shows us that the ultimate form of loving the Lord our God with all our strength is interchangeable with keeping the feasts of the Lord. Don't we expend a tremendous amount of resources to celebrate any feast? Abundance is practically the definition of any celebration. Bridal love for the Lord our God is verified by how we spend our resources. It's a godly submission of stewardship. It's putting our money where our mouth is, so to speak.

Loving God with all our strength is fulfilled by spending our resources in Christ—as He perfectly desires. Anything and everything will be expended as worshipful acts of submission to our King. In the kingdom of God, we will adore the King diligently, spending ourselves for His good pleasure, which will be our greatest pleasure, too. Every day with the King is a celebration! Literally, there is a holiday or celebration each day on earth's calendar somewhere in the world.[535] Celebrations set significant parts of the culture for both a pagan and a holy nation. The Bible shows us that *any* ungodly compromise will not be allowed in His dwelling place—the holy city called the New Jerusalem—or in His holy nation, consisting of the royal priesthood of believers. Mankind has been made in God's image, and we all enjoy a good celebration. The Lord put the drive to celebrate within us. Many of us will go to great lengths to break a fun barrier. But will we go the greatest length by celebrating the Lord His way? The feasts of the Lord are God's occasions for celebrating where we spend our resources His glorious ways. Remember that God's feasts are fixed by Him in His Word. At His biblical feasts, the Lord our God is summoning His people to meet with Him, so we can be directed by Him into a certain place, situation, or arrangement that is conducive for marriage. All people have been made to be spent on Him.

"For the joy of the Lord is your strength" (Neh. 8:10 NASB). Over and over again in the Bible, the Lord articulates one theme more than any other in regard to the feasts of the Lord, and that theme is joy: "They observed the Feast of the Unleavened Bread seven days with joy, for the LORD had caused them to rejoice" (Ezra 6:22 NASB). Yeshua *loves* to have a good time, especially with His queen!

YOU ARE CORDIALLY INVITED

Jesus sends out an invitation to the marriage of the Lamb whenever anyone hears the message of the gospel. It is a wedding proposal by God to accept Him and be part of His Bride. The ancient Jewish wedding ceremony teaches us that the wedding of the Messiah consists of twelve steps, with the twelfth and final step being the wedding supper for all the guests invited by the Father of the Bride.[536] "And the angel said, 'Write this: Blessed are those who are invited to the wedding feast of the Lamb.' And he added, 'These are true words that come from God'" (Rev. 19:9 NLT). Those who believe in their hearts that God raised Yeshua from the dead and confess with their mouths that Jesus is Lord (Rom. 10:9-10) have made their first step toward attending the marriage feast by becoming part of His family. Recently, I received a wedding invitation from a friend. In the vellum envelope were several items: a wedding announcement and invitation by the bride and groom's parents, a map to the wedding and reception, and an RSVP card. To attend my friend's daughter's wedding, it is essential that I do a number of things. First, I needed to reserve the time by checking my calendar to make sure that day is open. Manners require me to return the self-addressed, stamped RSVP with the number of people attending. And last, but not least, I get to find an exquisite card, a gorgeous gift, and elegant clothing suitable for such a joyous event.

Taking these real-life attendance prerequisites for a wedding and overlaying them over our spiritual lives, we can see some of the things that the Lord our God is requiring of us so we will be able to attend the wedding supper of the Lamb. Once you or I receive a wedding invitation, we must reserve that time. Of note: The king initially sends out His wedding invitations only to His friends, then to all who will come.

> The kingdom of heaven is like a king who gave a wedding banquet for his son and he sent his servants to summon those who had been invited to the wedding banquet, but they refused to come. Again he sent other servants . . . but they were not concerned and paid no attention [they ignored and made light of the summons, treating it with contempt] and they went away . . . Then he said to his servants, The wedding [feast] is prepared, but those invited were not worthy. So go to the thoroughfares where they leave the city [where the main roads and those from the country end] and invite to the wedding feast as many as you find. And those servants went out on the crossroads and got together as many as they found, both good and bad, so [the room in which] the wedding feast [was held] was filled with guests.
> —Matthew 22:2-10 AMP

Once we reserve the time, we must tell the One giving the wedding and reception that we are coming. At formal occasions it is most inconsiderate to not RSVP. I feel that the biblical proclamation of the Spirit and the Bride saying, "Come!" in Revelation 22:17 can be likened to a self-addressed and stamped RSVP. Will you say "I do" to the Messiah's proposal to you?

The excitement of receiving this awesome wedding invitation to the best event *ever,* and the pleasure of responding is just the beginning. Now attendees, including the Bride and Groom, must prepare themselves for such an august occasion. Have you ever considered that the marriage of the Lamb and the marriage feast is an incredible facet of the culmination of the ages? God has been preparing for this glorious moment since before the foundations of the world. He is readying a place for the Bride. The King's Son will be married to His helpmate, and the invitations have gone out throughout the entire earth.

According to Scripture, God clothes His people with proper wedding attire: "I delight greatly in the LORD; my soul rejoices in my God. For He has clothed me with the garments of salvation and arrayed me in a robe of righteousness, as a bridegroom adorns his head like a priest, and as a bride adorn herself with her jewels" (Isa. 61:10). The Lord provides us with garments of salvation and a robe of righteousness at the cross, but we must not forget that our lives are journeys.

RIGHTEOUS READINESS

In 2001, I was part of a corporate ascension experience. We came to the Lord as the Bride of Christ. In the Spirit, I saw an attic door open up and Yeshua peeked down. He asked if I'd like to come up early. I hesitated; then realized it was Him. Yeshua reached down. I reached up. When we touched, I was immediately with Him in the Spirit. He said, "Let's wait here for the rest of them. I looked around. We were on purple clouds and the stars above were bright. Yeshua sat cross-legged and invited me to do the same. Shortly, He exclaimed, "Come on!" as He took my hand and pulled me to my feet. We started to walk on the purple clouds. He at first held my hand as we walked side-by-side; then He stepped in front as I followed. We walked and walked and walked and walked and walked and walked.[537] We walked until the leader of the group declared, "The window is open!" I looked up, because a glaring brightness became visible in another layer of clouds above us. Yeshua led. I followed. As I climbed through the radiant opening, we were encompassed with light. Nothing else was visible. I remember knowing at the time that He and I had become one—the same essence.

As soon as I was aware of oneness, I saw myself plainly dressed in a dressing room looking into a mirror. The door opened, and in stepped Jesus. He presented me with a simple gold chain necklace. My Beloved said, "For purity," as He raised the necklace up. He then asked me to turn around. I spun around and lifted my hair. Yeshua hooked the golden necklace around my neck and promptly exited the dressing room. When I saw a simple white undergarment above my head, I raised my arms to receive it; then I waited for a little while longer. Something inside of me prompted me to get up and open the door. I started to walk clothed only in my white camisole and gold necklace. As I walked, different pieces of my wedding dress flung onto me: my upper left sleeve, lower right sleeve, et cetera. My wedding dress was simple, but very elegant. It was white and sparkled. Just as I reached out to grab the handle to this huge wooden door, the last piece, completing my ensemble, flung onto me. I was fully, properly, and gloriously clothed. I opened the door and immediately saw myself at the left side of Yeshua, just as my wedding ring sits on my left hand. We were sitting at a banqueting table. I knew that there must have been a most sumptuous feast, but I truly didn't care, for I only had eyes for Him. I was literally "lost" in His eyes. I had a vague recollection that there must be many people in attendance, but still I just could not take my eyes off of Him. Everything paled in comparison. After a little while, Love told me to stand. I did. Then He told me to take a bow. I replied: "You are the One that is supposed to bow. You do it all." My Love repeated kindly, yet unwaveringly: "Bow, My dear. I want to honor My Bride." I could not deny His easy request. As I simply bowed, the whole of heaven applauded. I was so humbled and overwhelmed. I remember that I looked at Him and He smiled. He was so magnificent and truly deserved all the glory and honor and praise. Yet, here He was sharing it all.

Please place yourself in my place if you have a bridal heart, for this vision represents you as well. I'd like to point out how the Bride's glorious wedding ensemble is pulled together as she walks (i.e., lives, moves, and has her being in Him). Revelation 19:7-8 tells us: "Let us rejoice and be glad and give Him glory! For the wedding of the Lamb has come, and His Bride has made herself ready. Fine linen, bright and clean, was given her to wear. (Fine linen stands for the righteous acts of the saints.)" Most other versions of the Bible say: "for the fine linen is the righteous acts of the saints." The Bible also makes it clear that "those who are prepared went in with Him to the marriage feast; and the door was shut" (Matt. 25:10 AMP). So much for preparation being optional. Obviously, God's people must make themselves ready for the marriage feast of the Lamb.

Therefore, to be invited to the Lamb's wedding through one's acceptance of the death, burial, and resurrection of Jesus Christ and *not* to RSVP will make one ineligible to attend THE EVENT OF ALL TIME. Likewise, to simply RSVP to the Lamb's marriage feast, but not to get ready by preparing in advance will be an insufficient effort as well. Know that it will not be enough to merely verbally ascent to Jesus being your Lord and Savior. We will have to do what He did and even greater works (John 14:12). In other words, we will have to walk the talk, demonstrating the reality of our close relationship to God's kingdom. "Someone may say, 'I am a Christian; I am on my way to heaven; I belong to Christ.' But if he doesn't do what Christ tells him to, he is a liar. But those who do what Christ tells them to will learn to love God more and more. That is the way to know whether or not you are a Christian. Anyone who says he is a Christian should live as Christ" (1 John 2:4-6 TLB).

UNFAITHFUL FRIEND

> The kingdom of heaven is like a king who gave a wedding banquet for his son . . . the wedding feast was filled with guests. But when the king came in to view the guests, he looked intently at a man there who had no wedding garment. And he said, Friend, how did you come in here without putting on the [appropriate] wedding garment? And he was speechless (muzzled, gagged). Then the king said to the attendants, Tie him hand and foot, and throw him into the darkness outside; there will be weeping and grinding of teeth. For many are called (invited and summoned), but few are chosen.
> —Matthew 22:1, 10-13 AMP

The first thing that I would like to point out is that the wedding guest, who was thrown out of the wedding banquet, was called "friend" by the king. When I search the Bible, I see that only believers are called friends:

> Abraham believed God . . . and was called the friend of God.
> —James 2:23 NKJV

> He who has the bride is the bridegroom; but the friend of the bridegroom, who stands and hears him, rejoices greatly because of the bridegroom's voice.
> —John 3:29 NKJV

According to these Scriptures, this friend of God believed Him and rejoiced greatly at the Jesus' voice. It can be likened to a person receiving God's invitation by believing on the Lord Jesus Christ; and they also probably RSVP'ed by rejoicing at the bridegroom's voice saying, "Come Lord Jesus! Come!" But they were not prepared. They did not make themselves ready. They were not appropriately clad in wedding clothes.

We can have faith that Jesus Christ is the Son of God. We can have hope in His coming, but unless we demonstrate our love for God and one another, the Bible says that it profits us nothing (1 Cor. 13:2). "But when that which is perfect has come, then that which is in part will be done away. For now we see in a mirror dimly, but then face to face. Now I know in part, but then I shall know just as I also am known. And now abide faith, hope, love, these three; but the greatest of these is love" (1 Cor. 13:10, 12-13 NKJV). Faith and hope are necessary components to our Christian walk, but they only get us two-thirds of the way down our bridal path. The final, and most challenging, leg of our bridal journey leads us unto perfection. The manifestation of perfection is love:

> "Teacher, which is the greatest commandment in the Law?" Jesus replied: "Love the Lord your God with all your heart and with all your soul and with all your mind. This is the first and greatest commandment. And the second is like it: Love your neighbor as yourself."
> —Matthew 22:36-39

Beyond all these things put on love, which is the perfect bond of peace.
—Colossians 3:14 NASB

By this we know that we have come to know Him, if we keep His commandments. The one who says, "I have come to know Him," and does not keep His commandments, is a liar, and the truth is not in him; but *whoever keeps His word, in him the love of God has truly been perfected.* By this we know that we are in Him: the one who says he abides in Him ought himself walk in the same manner as He walked.
—1 John 2:1-6 NASB, emphasis mine

This is My commandment that you *love one another as I have loved you.* Greater love has no one than this, than to lay down one's life for his friends. You are My friends if you do whatever I command you. No longer do I call you servants, for a servant does not know what his master is doing; but I have called you friends, for all things that I heard from My Father I have made known to you.–
—John 15:12-15 NKJV, emphasis mine

The friends, who do whatever the Lord commands, are being clothed with fine, clean, bright linen so they can attend the marriage and banquet of the Lamb. Remember it's the righteous acts of the saints, which creates the fine linen that attires the Bride and the wedding guests. These are not good deeds we initiate showing the Lord how much we love him. We have all been there, done that, even bought the T-shirt when it comes to acting as an immature believer. "When I was a child, I spoke as a child, I understood as a child, I thought as a child; but when I became a man, I put away childish things" (1 Cor. 13:11 NKJV). By the way, bridal attire is worn by those who choose to move unto perfection (i.e., maturity), manifesting His endless, unfailing love. Let me reiterate: "the righteous acts of the saints" are not acts, deeds, or works we have decided on our own to do. The Lord initiates them and they coincide with His Word. That means if the Bible says, "love your neighbor as yourself," live your life abiding by that standard. We are to live our lives by the principles expressed in the Word of God, but we are also supposed to ask Him if any particular action is of Him and should we do it. Once a person consistently makes submitting to the Lord of Love a habit, maturing believers begin to just flow in His will and His way, without the need of constantly asking Him. Communication is still necessary. It's like when a married couple knows one another so well that not only do they finish one another's sentences, they also know what actions will please or not please each other. The two have become one. Bridal love causes us to submit everything to Him. Yes, we are to clothe the naked, feed the hungry, look after widows and orphans; but we are finite and we can only be in one place at a time. If we are spending our time trying to please Him without asking the Lord what actually will please Him at that exact moment in time, we will probably miss the perfect mark of doing what He did. "I tell you the truth, the Son can do nothing by Himself; He can do only what He sees His Father doing, because whatever the Father does the Son also does" (John 5:19).

SURRENDERING ALL

Many words can describe bridal character, but there seems to be one word that is unusually fit or qualified to describe it. That word is yieldedness. When we yield to Love, it means we surrender and submit ourselves to another (i.e., our Beloved). We relinquish possession of ourselves. We give the Lord whatever He requires as rightfully owed, rendering it as is fitting to our good and benevolent King of Kings. We are willing to give up our life's breath. We literally hand over control to Him, so we can bear eternal fruit as a natural product of abiding in Him. Our yieldedness to the Lord of Love will actually determine the amount, quality, and return of our produce (i.e., fruit).

The inappropriately dressed friend of the king in Matthew 22:12 is a believer, who has hope that the Messiah will come again. This friend probably heard what the Father is doing, because this sentiment coincides with Scripture, which says the Lord calls those who believe and hear Him His friend. But the king's friend did not obey

His instructions. This friend of the bridegroom heard, but did not do what the Lord commanded.

Don't forget that Jesus called Judas Iscariot "friend" at His betrayal (Matt. 26:49-50). Judas believed that Yeshua was the Messiah. He believed in His coming kingdom. But Judas leaned on his own understanding and tried to force the issue of Jesus becoming Israel's conquering king before His time. No one would argue that Judas didn't do things God's way.

"But be doers of the word, and not hearers only, deceiving yourselves" (James 1:22 NKJV). Please note that hearing comes before doing. Our relationship with the Lord comes before our responsibility, but equally our relationship does not negate our responsibilities. (If you don't know how to hear God's voice yet, take time to learn. He is faithful and will teach you. All you need to do is set your heart to the task of hearing the Lord's voice, spend time in His presence, and let Him guide you. I know I simplified the whole process of hearing God's voice. Whole books have been written to help you do just that. I know that hearing God's voice is a lot easier said than done, but the rewards are out-of-this world!) Let us remember that faith comes by hearing, and hearing by the Word of God; but it does not stop there. In the end, love will remain. Another way to say this is: living and active faith results in righteous acts. Deeds and actions are the true measure of anyone's substance.

> They claim to know God, but by their actions they deny him. They are detestable and unfit for doing anything good.–
> —Titus 2:16

> ... Their words and deeds are against the LORD, defying his glorious presence.
> —Isaiah 3:8

> Even a child is known for his actions, by whether his conduct is pure and right.
> —Proverbs 22:11

I believe that Christians in America need to become more balanced between our having faith in Jesus and obeying His commandments (Rev.14:12). It's obvious to the most casual observer that our pendulum needs to be corrected on the "doing" side. Please understand that legalistic behavior is not what I am promoting here. The "Do and do, do and do, rule on rule, rule on rule; a little here, a little there—so that they will go and fall backward, be injured and snared and captured" (Isa. 28:13). No! I repeat. I am promoting living our lives in love toward God and our fellow man.

I have been taught that all believers will be at the wedding feast of the Lamb. That may be true. All believers are part of God's family; but I don't want to be simply invited. I want to be a precious component of the bridal company that will ultimately be married to the King of Kings. Wouldn't you rather be in the thick of the festivities? It's going to be a *whole* lot of fun! I believe that the Matthew 22 passage may refute the idea of total inclusiveness for wedding participants: the Bride and guests, which may be one and the same (who knows). All believers need to reexamine the Scriptures and seek the Spirit of truth to see what God is saying. The one thing that I do know is that the Bridegroom and the King will have the last say on who attends the marriage supper of the Lamb, and I don't want to be left out! The only way I know of to be sure of being at the wedding banquet is to sell out completely. To love the Lord with all my heart, soul, mind, and strength; and my neighbor as myself.

Due to this lack of inclusiveness idea for the marriage feast being different than the church's previous paradigm, plus the possibility of controversy, I'd like to bring some additional scriptural evidence to the table. The famous Christian apologist, Josh McDowell, calls his supporting facts "evidence that demands a verdict."

First and foremost is the classic bridal passage of Matthew 25:1-13. Ten virgins are waiting for the Bridegroom, but only the five wise virgins with oil in their lamps went into the wedding banquet with the Bridegroom. "The virgins who were ready went in with Him to the wedding banquet. And the door was shut" (Matt. 25:10). Tragically, those five foolish bridal candidates (i.e., believers) never got into the wedding supper of the Lamb.

SANCTIFICATION—CLEAN HANDS AND PURE HEARTS

First Corinthians 10:11 tells us: "Now all these things happened to them as examples, and they were written for our admonition, upon whom the ends of the ages have come." What things? Passing through the Red Sea, eating manna, et cetera, et cetera, et cetera. It's what happened to the Israelites in the wilderness after they left Egypt, which is spoken of throughout the Old Testament, especially the first five books of the Bible. Jesus and His disciples taught from the Old Testament and so did Paul. If it's good enough for Jesus, Matthew, Mark, Luke, John, and Paul, it's good enough for Jesus' followers too.[538]

Notice that the wedding guest with an inappropriate wedding garment in Matthew 22:13 was tied hand and foot. This is our clue that leads us to the portable tabernacle in the wilderness. The priests washed their hands and feet in the temple laver before they entered the tent where they met God. "You shall also make a laver of bronze, with its base of bronze, for washing; and you shall put it between the tent of meeting and the altar, and you shall put water in it." (Exod. 30:18 NASB). Many Christian Bibles call the temple laver the bronze laver. This is a misnomer, for it was actually made of copper. The copper laver was an open circular basin that was set upon a copper base. The Hebrew sage Rashi[539] said it had two spouts at the bottom through which the water would flow,[540] keeping it from becoming stagnant. In the Hebrew language, the term "for washing" carries the idea that the laver was "for sanctification";[541] therefore the actual purpose for the priests washing their hands and feet was for holiness and sanctity rather than cleanliness (Exod. 30:17-21). The hands and feet represent the upper and lower extremities of the human body. By sanctifying their appendages, it was symbolic of the Lord's servants' total devotion to the service they were engaged in. It set apart their acts as righteous. A most literal picture of this is presented to us in Exodus 30:19. The Hebrew sage Or HaChaim said that the conjunction in the phrase "their hands together with their feet" (Exod. 30:19) indicated that the hands and feet must be washed at the same time.[542] Consequently, the right hand was placed on the priest's right foot and washed together at the same time, followed by his left hand together with his left foot. Concentration and balance were key to accomplishing this hand-foot sanctification feat. Try it some time in your bathtub. I had the kids in my children's church class try to do this by simply standing next to their chairs. It was a lot more difficult than they thought and funny too. It's quite the image that proper service to God requires all of a body's faculties, and those faculties must be directed toward the same goal.[543]

The laver was not made of copper from the regular contributions. The laver was made exclusively from the brightly polished sheets of copper that women used as mirrors in Egypt (Exod. 38:8).[544] When the call went out for freewill contributions, devout women, who used to come to Moses' tent to sit at his feet like Mary did with Jesus,[545] came with their copper mirrors and piled them up at Moses' dwelling, which was the God's dwelling place prior to the building of the tent of meeting (Exod. 33:7). Moses was said to be reluctant to accept such gifts for the tabernacle, due to his initial thinking that the mirrors had been used to incite lust. The story goes that God told Moses that he was wrong, because these very mirrors had been instrumental in saving the nation. In Egypt, when the men came home exhausted every night from heavy labors, their wives used these mirrors to get all dolled up to entice their husbands to continue normal marital relations. Thanks to these brightly, polished copper mirrors, legions of Jewish children were born. God not only told Moses to accept these precious mirrors, but they were to be used exclusively to fabricate the laver. The Hebrew sage Ibn Ezra tells us that the Bible doesn't give the specific size of the laver, due to that fact that every single mirror had to go into fashioning it, no matter how big it would become – so sacred were those mirrors.[546, 547] Of note, these devout women could no longer gaze upon themselves with any vanity, because they had to fix their eyes upon the laver to see themselves. The laver represents bridal lovers fixing their eyes upon the Author and Perfecter of their faith (Heb. 12:2).

The extreme reach of the body of Christ should be set apart for a sacred purpose. The farthest boundary of the One New Man in Christ should be free from sin due to our special tie (i.e., connected relationship) with Jesus. The word "tie" is from the Greek verb δέω *deo*, which means "to bind." It has many nuances. We can think of the concept of being restrained by authority, influence, agreement, or obligation. We can also think of a special tie that binds people together romantically. A marital tie binds two people together physically, mentally, and spiritually. If our lives yield to the Lord of Love and His sacred purposes, then we will not be tied hand and foot to be thrown out of the wedding feast. I sought the Lord about what it means that one of His friends would be cast outside for not having the proper clothing, and I believe that He told me: Once the friend saw the glory of the wedding feast, "outside" the feast would appear as darkness for he or she would weep at glimpsing, yet not being able to partake of the marriage feast. It is noteworthy that this place outside the wedding feast is also assigned to hypocrites—where people's actions don't line up with their words (Matt. 24:51).

A friend told me about a confirmation of this revelation. It's in Rick Joyner's book—*The Final Quest*:

> This great multitude are those whom the Lord called 'foolish virgins.' We knew the Lord, and trusted in His cross for salvation but we did not really live for Him, but for ourselves. . . . The grief that we experienced when we understood how we had so wasted our lives was beyond any grief possible on earth. . . . Such darkness is magnified when it is revealed next to the glory of the One we failed. . . . There is no greater folly than to know the great salvation of God, but to then go on living for yourself.[548]

Please don't forget that we are talking about unrepentant or willful sin. The Lord's awesome mercy, incredible grace, and humbling forgiveness is available to all of us, but one day, perhaps even today, each one of us will meet His Maker and we will be giving an account.

Psalms 24:3-4 tells us that only people with clean hands and a pure heart, who do not lift up their soul to an idol, can ascend to where God dwells. "These are the ones who are allowed to stand before the Lord and worship the God of Jacob" (Ps. 24:6 NLB). The Bible reiterates time and again that divine love is expressed through self-sacrificial service. All of God's people are called to show they really love God by loving our neighbors. If a person's hands and feet are immobilized, being tied together, it signifies the antithesis of being united in marriage, devotedly loving and serving your spouse.

For Yeshua's attendants (i.e., ones who performed pleasing service on the Lord's behalf) to be directed by Him to tie up the hands and feet of the friend with the unsuitable wedding clothing, that person had to have not served the Lord in an acceptable manner.

> Come, you blessed of My Father, inherit the kingdom prepared for you from the foundation of the world: for I was hungry and you gave Me food; I was thirsty and you gave Me drink; I was a stranger and you took Me in; I was naked and you clothed Me; I was sick and you visited Me; I was in prison and you came to Me. . . . Assuredly, I say to you, inasmuch as you did it to one of the least of these My brethren, you did it to Me.
> —Matthew 25:34-36, 40 NKJV

11

I THEE WED

> Now. For those who are married I have a command
> that comes not from me, but from the Lord.
> A wife must not leave her husband.
> A wife is bound as long as her husband lives.
> —1 Corinthians 7:10, 39 NLT

In 2000, I helped organize daily prayer for a citywide event. On the Tuesday before Resurrection Sunday, the Lord led a time of communion. Even though it was a group exercise of "doing this in remembrance of Me," I felt that God wanted each participant—as one—to look solely to Jesus and privately take the communion elements with Him. It was to be a corporate, but intimate time. I quieted myself as I slightly raised my bread. Immediately and clearly I heard a still, small voice say: "With this bread, I thee wed." Wow! What a surprise! I don't remember what I was thinking, but it certainly wasn't along that line. This was very revelatory for me. I raised my bread a little higher and solemnly whispered: "With this bread, I Thee wed." Then I took the bread and ate it. Next, I raised my cup. Again, I immediately and unmistakably heard inside my spirit: "With this wine, I thee wed." With total awe, I whispered: "With this wine, I Thee wed." I found out five years later that Tuesdays (i.e., the third day of the week) is the day when weddings took place in ancient Israel.[549] The Lord is coming to marry His pure and spotless Bride in this prophetic third day.

WITH THIS WINE AND BREAD, I THEE WED

The first time that bread and wine are mentioned in Scripture, we see a priest of the Most High—Melchizedek[550] King of Salem. He brought out bread and wine to Abram in Genesis 14:18. By this point, Abram had obeyed the Lord in leaving Babylon. He already had come to the land, which God had shown him (Gen. 12:1). He had continued on to Egypt for a short time due to a famine in the land (Gen. 12:10); and he had returned from Egypt to his promised land (Gen.13:1). This was a time that was just prior to Abram's name being changed to Abraham (Gen.17:5).

The kings of Babylon were making war with the kings of the Canaanites (Gen. 14:1). This war involved the major kingdoms of the region. It was a territorial or turf war. When Abram heard that his nephew Lot was taken captive by the kings of Babylon, he mustered 318 trained men from his own household (14:14) and pursued them as far as Dan—the place of judgment. Although Abram was hopelessly outnumbered, he went to battle to rescue his family. Miraculously, he triumphed. By refusing personal gain (the spoils of war he was entitled to by international law), Abram demonstrated that the kingdom of self had no part in him. He had acted only to save his nephew. Abram's actions revealed that he laid down his life for another. Abram's life was affected by violence, and he literally became a violent man to take back that which was near and dear to him.

Abraham's journey in Genesis 14 illustrates a kingdom truth in our day: In this kingdom day, God's people will come out of Babylon. We will temporarily go back into the world (i.e., Egypt), but then we will return to our Promised Land. There we must first conquer the rulership of the Babylonian practices/mind-sets in our own lives before we can receive the ministry of Melchizedek. We must dethrone the same Babylonian kings that Abram did. The Babylonian kings' names[551] indicate that we must overthrow: darkness, deception, savagery, mercilessness, false positions, and producing after the Tree of the Knowledge of Good and Evil.

The Midrash identifies the king of Elam as Shem's son. Although Chedorlaomer was the leader of the Babylonian alliance, the king of

Shinar—Amraphel—is mentioned first in the Bible, because he was the senior king of the four. Significantly, the Jewish sages identify Amraphel as Nimrod. The *Jewish Encyclopedia* shares: "Some say Amraphel was his real name, and he was called Nimrod—'the chief rebel,' as leader of the tower-builders, 'who led the world rebellion' against heaven's Ruler. Others say Nimrod was his real name, and he was called Amraphel as the one who commanded them to cast Abraham into the fire."[552] One of the etymologies[553] for the name Amraphel is explained as that of one whose "command brought darkness [destruction] on the world."[554] Abram was thrown into the furnace because he refused to accept the worship of idols.[555] Today, we are called to the same stance—refusing to accept idol worship and rising up to the challenge of the kingdom of heaven, suffering violence in our own lives and taking it back by force.

After Abram victoriously brought back the plundered goods and people, returning them to their rightful owners, the king of Sodom went out to meet him at the valley of Shaveh, which is notably called the King's Valley. The king of Sodom then escorted Abram to the city of Salem (i.e., Jerusalem) where they were met by its king—Melchizedek. The Jewish sages[556] identify Melchizedek as Shem, the righteous son of Noah. Initially, I dismissed the Shem being Melchizedek assertion outright, because I was taught that Melchizedek had some distinct qualities that I assumed Shem did not have. Most notably, Hebrews 7:3 tells us that Melchizedek had no mother, no father, no beginning of time, and no end of time; and I knew that Shem had all of these.

When the Holy Spirit prompted me to reexamine what I believed, I was amazed at what was revealed. First of all, the Hebrews probably would have kept the best track of their own history. Why would Jewish tradition say Shem is identified with Melchizedek?[557] I believe that he was. Just like Nimrod is identified with Amraphel. When people are associated with different names, each name signifies a different part of their nature.

Scripture is silent about many facts about Melchizedek, but we know that Melchizedek is mentioned twice in the Tanakh: Genesis 14:18 and Psalms 110:4. Melchizedek was called the king of Salem—king of peace—and king of righteousness (Gen.14:18;

Heb. 7:2). The basis of the priesthood of Melchizedek is everlasting life (Heb. 7:16). Jesus is the High Priest of the royal priesthood of Melchizedek (Heb. 7:15-17), who's the mediator of a new covenant (Heb. 8:6-12; 9:15) by putting away sin by the sacrifice of Himself once for all (Heb. 9:26-28). Jesus abides forever and holds the position of the High Priest permanently, according to the order of Melchizedek (Heb. 7:24) through which we all can draw near to God (Heb. 4:14-16; 7:19; 10:19-22). We could go on and on in an exhaustive study of Melchizedek, but that's not the purpose here.

The possibility of Shem being Melchizedek of Genesis 14 fame makes sense on several levels. Shem was known as the righteous son of Noah; therefore, it's not much of a stretch to believe he could have been called a king of righteousness. Just as the Messiah can sit on the throne of David, He can be the High Priest in the order of Melchizedek. Especially when we consider that Shem led the overthrow of the apostate world ruler of his time (Nimrod), we can extrapolate that Shem easily could have been exalted to such a status himself. Even though Shem was Abraham's great great great great great great great grandfather, I think that the priesthood of Melchizedek is earned, not inherited. Don't get me wrong, just as Abraham believed and was counted righteous, so did Melchizedek. In fact, Melchizedek must have epitomized a priesthood of believers, who draw near to God with a sincere heart in full assurance of faith (Heb. 10:22), else he would not have been considered righteous.

What if the author of the book of Hebrews was focusing on the most important particulars, relevant even today, for the royal priesthood of believers, encapsulated in the name and nature of Melchizedek? I believe that Melchizedek earned the right to be called the king of peace and righteousness, and the first example of the eternal, royal priesthood of believers. Even Jesus, "although He was a Son, He learned obedience from the things which He suffered. . . . being designated by God as a high priest according to the order of Melchizedek" (Heb. 5:8,10 NASB). Sincere obedience from the heart is a key that opens the door to being designated as a priest in the order of Melchizedek. It's significant that Hebrews 7:3 says Melchizedek is *"like* the Son of God," just as the term "Christian" is supposed to designate a person who is Christlike. I believe that

Melchizedek personified being a son, who was disciplined by God (Heb. 12:7). This discipline was for his good so he could share God's holiness (Heb. 12:10) and produce the peaceful fruit of righteousness (Heb. 12:11). Through abiding communion with God, genuine seekers occupy a governmental position in Christ to rule and reign with Him (Isa. 9:6-7). The mysteries of Christ and the eternity of His priesthood and His throne are deep subjects to tackle. Remember how in chapter 8 we discussed that the natural comes first, then the spiritual (1 Cor. 15:46). I hope that you will consider that Shem could have been the first physical manifestation of Melchizedek.

Minimally, we know that Melchizedek is a type of eternal priest within an eternal priesthood —Christ in you the hope of glory. Hebrews 5:9 says that Jesus Christ became THE SOURCE OF ETERNAL SALVATION TO ALL THOSE WHO OBEY HIM. The Lord's Christian church has emphasized the eternal salvation part of being saved through faith by grace, which is right and good; but to our detriment and degeneration, we have not emphasized enough the message that eternal salvation is to all those who obey Him. The apostle John wrote:

> My dear children, I write this to you so that you will not sin. But if anybody does sin, we have one who speaks to the Father in our defense—Jesus Christ, the Righteous One. He is the atoning sacrifice for our sins, and not only for ours but also for the sins of the whole world. We know that we have come to know him, if we obey his commands. The man who says, "I know him," and does not do what he commands is a liar, and the truth is not in him. But if anyone obeys His word, God's love is truly made complete in him. This is how we know we are in Him: Whoever claims to live in Him must walk as Jesus did.
> —1 John 1:1-6

The next place in Scripture that bread and wine are mentioned is in the book of Numbers, chapter 15. The offerings of Abel, Noah, and Abraham were all a "satisfying aroma to God." After the sin of the golden calf, the Lord commanded that wine libations be added to the continual daily offerings (Num. 15:1-16). Additionally, after the sin of the spies, this libation commandment was extended to certain other offerings too. Numbers 15:3 describes the offerings to which the wine libations applied:

- **Elevation-offerings**: "make an offering by fire to the Lord" are voluntary offerings burnt in their entirety on the altar.
- **Feast-offerings**: "a sacrifice to fulfill a special vow, or as a freewill offering or in your appointed times" are those offerings that were eaten and generally brought to celebrate happy occasions, where their "owners" invariably invite others to eat with them.

Both of the offerings cited in Numbers 15:3 relate directly to the golden calf. The Lord had elevated the entire nation at Sinai to be a dwelling place for Him, but their rejection in the form of a calf caused this reality to be postponed. Plus, the people called their feast to the golden calf a "feast to the Jehovah," which was offensive in His eyes. In both cases, only the shedding of blood could rectify these situations, which is why the bread and wine requirement was instituted after the sin of the golden calf.

> For this is what the Lord Himself said, and I pass it on to you just as I received it. On the night when He was betrayed, the Lord Jesus took a loaf of bread, and when He had given thanks, He broke it and said, "This is My body, which is given for you. Do this in remembrance of me." In the same way, He took the cup of wine after supper, saying, "This cup is the new covenant between God and you, sealed by the shedding of My blood. Do this in remembrance of Me as often as you drink it." For every time you eat this bread and drink this cup, you are announcing the Lord's death until He comes again.
> —1 Corinthians 11:23-26 NLT

SEASONED BRIDAL COMPANY

The two references in Genesis 14:18 and Numbers 15:1-21 to bread and wine have hidden treasure in their stories, which point to Jesus' baptism of fire. Recall that the king of Sodom came out to meet Abraham in Genesis 14:17. In Hebrew, the word "Sodom" means "burning," "conflagration," as being built on a bituminous soil, and being perhaps on this account liable to frequent fires.[558]

We can easily extrapolate the awe-inspiring image of an all-consuming fire burning up all that offends the Lord, which was starkly demonstrated in God's fiery judgment of Sodom and Gomorrah (Gen. 19:24-25 NASB). The place where the king of Sodom and the king of Salem met Abram was at the Valley of Shaveh,[559] which we already said refers to the King's Valley. The Hebrew word *shaveh* articulates several ideas: to be, to cause to be, to be like or alike, and to resemble. At the King's Valley, the Lord will adjust His body to yield to Him so we will not only be suitable for Him, but we will actually resemble Him. To be or not to be pure and spotless according to His standards. That is the question.

Mark 9:49 NKJV says: "For everyone will be seasoned with fire, and every sacrifice will be seasoned with salt." The reference in Numbers 15:3 to making "an offering by fire to the Lord" alludes to the Bride being elevated by offering her obedience over sacrifices. She also will become an elevation offering, where her carnal nature will be burnt entirely on the Lord's altar so she can be without spot or wrinkle. Taking refuge in an all- "consuming fire" (Heb. 12:29) can be quite exciting! If you are of the same substance, you will not be burnt.

> Who of us can dwell with the consuming fire? He who walks righteously and speaks what is right . . . Your eyes will see the king in his beauty . . . Look upon Zion, the city of our festivals . . . There the LORD will be our Mighty One.–
> —Isaiah 33:14-22

> . . . Fear not, for I have redeemed you; I have summoned you by name; you are mine. . . . When you walk through the fire,

you will not be burned; the flames will not set you ablaze. For I am the LORD, your God, the Holy One of Israel, your Savior . . ."

—Isaiah 43:1-3

We could say tongue-in-cheek that the Lord likes "crispy critters," where His heavenly brazier burns off all that offends. "The Son of Man will send out His angels and they will gather out of His Kingdom all things that offend" (Matt. 13:41 NKJV). "He will baptize you with the Holy Spirit and fire. . . . He will thoroughly clean out His threshing floor, and gather His wheat into the barn; but He will burn up the chaff with unquenchable fire" (Matt. 3:11-12 NKJV). Everyone who builds on the foundation of Jesus Christ will have their works revealed by fire where "the fire will test each one's work, of what sort it is" (1 Cor. 3:13 NKJV). First Corinthians 3:15 makes it clear that we can build with wood, hay, and straw upon the foundation of Jesus Christ; but if we build with these perishable materials, we "will suffer loss, but he himself will be saved as through fire." Saved, as through fire, is quite a vivid picture.

Mark 9:49 NKJV says: "For everyone will be seasoned with fire . . ." Everyone? Yes, everyone. The word *seasoned* in my handy-dandy *Webster's Collegiate Dictionary* means: "to add more flavor or zest by adding seasoning or savory ingredients." The Hebrew verb for "savor" is *ruach*, which is the same word for "Spirit," as in the tongues of fire, violent rushing wind being of Acts 2:2-4. Recall that it's the Spirit and the Bride that says, "Come!" (Rev. 22:17). *Seasoned* also is defined as: "to give a distinct quality to as if by seasoning, especially to make more agreeable; to treat so to prepare for use; to make fit by experience."[560] In our valleys, ordained by the King of Kings, we are becoming a seasoned bridal company. These searing experiences are preparing us for His personal use. They are making us fit to be His Bride, where we will have a distinct quality that makes us more agreeable to His taste. The Lord's bridal company will be perfectly delightful to Him and will have a more pleasing zest or flavor than we can even think or imagine.

Numbers 15:3 refers to the wine libation that must accompany voluntary offerings and offerings brought in celebration of the Lord's festivals. The wine libation was poured into a bowl-like vessel attached to the southwest corner of the Brazen Altar. In the wilderness tabernacle, the wine drained off to the ground. In the temple in Jerusalem, it flowed onto the top of the altar and into a pipe leading to a ditch located under Solomon's brazen sea.

Although the nations were allowed to bring peace offerings, only God's people could bring libations. This is a picture of how only believers can truly partake of the communion elements, as well as being the only ones that have a relationship where they can abide in the Vine (John 15). When a Jewish person worshiped the Lord by bringing an offering of a wine libation, it symbolized him or her dedicating their land to God—which could mean themselves, or their property, or more generally Israel in its entirety.

GENU-WINE

In 2002,[561] the Lord spoke to me gently about His "genu-wine,"[562] which is the new wine in these last days. He told me, "This is My blood of the covenant, which is poured out for many . . . I tell you the truth, I will not drink again of the fruit of the vine until that day when I drink it anew in the kingdom of God" (Mark 14:24-25). The Lord revelatorily showed me a vision of His side being pierced on the cross with a soldier's spear. I first saw blood then water. I understood when He comes again, a sign of His coming is first the water then the wine.

The water is being turned into wine on this third day (John 2:1). We must each be washed, cleansed, and filled to the brim with the living water, just as the ceremonial water jars were at the wedding feast at Cana in Galilee. As His servants, we are to do whatever the Lord tells us (John 2:5), then He will draw us out so we can be taken to the Master of the banquet and His people. The Master is calling the Bridegroom aside, for He has indeed saved the best for last. It says in John 2:11 that: "Thus He revealed His glory, and His disciples put their faith in him." "This is the new covenant in My blood; do this, whenever you drink it, in remembrance of Me" (1 Cor. 11:25). Remember Him. Re-member Him. Re-member His body. For "whoever . . . drinks the cup of the Lord in an unworthy manner will be guilty against the body and blood of the Lord" (1 Cor. 11:27).

"Wine depicts the inner qualities of the grape from which it comes. Buried within it was an essence that could be extracted, fermented and transformed into wine, a product that is greater than the grape from which it originated."[563] Wine reveals one's innermost self. The new wine in these last days is "genu-wine believers," who exhibit the incredibly perfect character of the Lord Jesus Christ. It's a golden new wine, where His most precious Bride will be perpetually flexible. There will be 14-karat, 18-karat, and 24-karat believers.[564] Twenty-four-karat believers will be the cluster of grapes from which the Lord's golden new wine will come. Buried within you is the beautiful essence that will be extracted, fermented, and transformed, so you can be poured out to a lost and dying world.

Numbers 15:17-21 speaks of the meal offering, *challah*[565] or bread given to the direct descendants of the High Priest Aaron—the *Kohanim*. A portion of *challah* was given to the *Kohanim* from every batch of dough made from the five species of cereal grains: wheat, barley, oats, rye, and spelt. God tied together the people who enjoyed the fruit of the land with those who devote themselves to matters of the Spirit. The servants of God were dependent on the gifts of the nation to survive, as well as His nation being obligated to provide for His anointed, appointed, and chosen servants.

The owner of the dough was forbidden to eat it before setting his *challah* portion aside. A priest (i.e., *Kohen*) was supposed to be given the choicest part of produce (Num. 18:29) and dough. The Jewish sages derived from the possessive form of "your dough" that the minimum amount of dough from which *challah* must be taken is the amount familiar to the people in the wilderness (the original addressees). They speculated that it was the volume of manna that fell daily for each Jew, which was equivalent to one *omer* or the volume of 43.2 eggs.[566] In actuality, verse 20 of Numbers 15 tells us, "as the offering of the threshing floor," which is called *terumah*.[567] Just as the Torah does not specify a minimum percentage of the crops or *terumah*, so is the minimum percentage not set for *challah* (bread). The *challah* portion speaks of remembering the Lord's body and keeping in mind the matter of the Spirit when concerned with the cares of this earth. Re-member—help put Christ's body together—"into a dwelling of God in the Spirit" (Eph. 2:22).

The Lord has saved the best for last. His genuine 24-karat believers are where "the Spirit is poured out upon us from a high" (Isa. 32:15). He knows the way that we take, when He has tried us, and we shall come forth as gold.[568] The Lord is re-membering His body (1 Cor. 11:24; Eph. 2:21-22; Eph. 4:15-16) by letting the peace of Christ be the arbiter in our hearts, to which indeed we are called in one body (Col. 3:15).

THE WAYWARD WIFE

What we lay down in this life will be nothing in comparison to what we will gain eternally. Those who wish to *be* must put aside the gilded confines of Christmas. There is so much more, spiritually speaking, beyond its sensual shackles and earthly clutter. And we get to choose—to be or not to be. If we don't endeavor to abide in the Messiah in every corner of our life, we will erect an idol to self. It's just how human nature operates. The Bible talks of jealousy when idolatry is referenced and when a suspicious husband justifiably claims that his wife has been unfaithful. These cases are one and the same. Idolatry deals with infidelity to God, while adultery deals with infidelity to one's spouse. Jealousy refers to an abuse of trust and someone's refusal to give up something that is rightfully his. In the context of idolatry, almighty God is entitled to the veneration of all human beings made in His image, and He will not accept our worship of any other thing or being.

Since idolatry and adultery are so integrally connected, let's examine the book of Numbers, chapter 5, verses 11-31. It describes the wayward wife and how the Lord wants mankind to handle the entire situation. It will give us unique discernment into how God deals with infidelity. "You also multiplied your harlotry with the land of merchants, Chaldea yet even with this you were not satisfied. You adulteress wife, who takes strangers instead of her husband!" (Ezek. 16:29,32 NASB).

The marital relationship between a husband and wife is a microcosm of the relationship between the Messiah and His Bride. Please feel free to insert the church when I speak of the woman/wife, and insert Jesus Christ—the Messiah—when I speak of the man/husband. The majority of the information in this section comes from an excellent resource called The Stone Edition of *The Chumash*. It's published by ArtScroll.[569] I highly recommend purchasing this book, because as you will see it contains profound history and background relevant to Scripture that has been generally lost when Gentile believers split from our Jewish counterparts. It seems to literally restore some of the church's ancient ruins. I also recommend buying this book to support the dedicated Bible scholars who worked so hard to bring the world this masterpiece.

Numbers 5:11-31 deals with a woman who behaved in an inappropriate manner, giving her husband good reason to suspect her of adultery, but there is no proof of either her guilt or innocence. This passage provides a miraculous process that will either prove she sinned and caused both her death and that of her illicit lover, or it will show conclusively that she was faithful and thereby restore trust and love to their marriage. Interestingly, this is the only legal procedure (i.e., *halachic*)[570] in the Torah that depends on supernatural intervention. If indeed the woman had been unfaithful, the process was designed to induce her confession through the terrifying prospect of her imminent death. If the wife confessed her infidelity, the marriage could end in divorce, but without any penalty to her, since there was no judicially acceptable evidence of her guilt.

In the course of this passage, Scripture uses two terms that emphasize the sanctity and purity of the marital relationship. Unfaithfulness is called "treachery" in Numbers 5:12, the same term used in the taking of tabernacle property—God's own possession—for one's personal use. The second term refers to the wife, who is guilty of the charge, has become "defiled" (verse 13). Defilement is the antithesis of the purity required for the presence of holiness.[571]

If a wife was wrongly accused, her innocence would be firmly established; but if found guilty, she would die a grotesque death. As mentioned before, this is the only legal procedure in the Bible that required God's supernatural intervention. This ordeal lost its effect and was discontinued by the Sanhedrin during the Second Temple Era.[572] During this time, Yeshua's death, burial, and resurrection perfectly fulfilled the requirement of the husband needing to bring the meal-offering for His wayward wife through the offering up of His body. "The Lord Jesus in the night in which He was betrayed took bread; and when He gave thanks, He broke it, and said, 'This is My body, which is for you; do this in remembrance of Me'" (1 Cor. 11:23-24 NASB).

The purpose of the ordeal, which tested a wayward wife, was twofold: (1) It was meant to punish adultery and help uproot immorality in God's people; and (2) it fostered trust between a man and wife. The psychological reality is that once a husband suspects his wife of infidelity, he will not trust her, even if a court rules that he is wrong. Legal discussions seldom, if ever, change emotions. Only God's own supernatural testimony would be convincing enough. This is why the Lord permits the erasure of His own sacred name and performs a miracle to set a suspicious husband's mind at ease (Num. 5:23, 28).[573]

A man and a married woman are described in Numbers 5:12-14 as having secluded themselves in such a way, for a sufficient amount of time, that they could have sinned. Prior to the seclusion, a spirit of jealousy, based on earlier improper activity, had seized her husband and he had become suspicious of his wife and another man. He had warned her not to seclude herself, but she ignored his warning. There had to be a pair of witnesses that testified the two were together and had the opportunity to commit adultery, but they did not see whether or not they had actually done so; thus: "she had . . . and she had not" (v. 14). By the way, the wife was required to not have been coerced into seclusion, for if she had been overpowered she would be innocent (v. 13).[574]

The phrase "but there was no witness against her" (Num. 5:13) is in the singular, implying that a single witness is sufficient to force an end to a marriage since there were strong grounds for suspicion. Ordinarily, a single witness had no credibility in such accusations—and even here no physical punishment could be imposed on the basis of one testimony—but in this case the husband's testimony is reenforced by the testimony of seclusion, which gives sufficient credence to merit a divorce.[575]

The distressed husband was required to bring "the meal-offering of jealousies" (Num. 5:15) on behalf of his wife. The "offering of jealousies" in Hebrew is plural, because she offended both her earthly husband and her Maker. Rather than the normal meal-offering, meant to bring mercy and forgiveness, this one was intended to serve as a reminder of the sin the wife was accused of committing.[576] "For this cause a man shall leave his father and his mother, and shall cleave to his wife; and they shall become one flesh" (Gen. 2:24 NASB). She was accused of committing sin against "one flesh." The husband brings this meal-offering, for it wouldn't be proper to require a woman to bring an offering that could invoke God's anger and judgment against her.

The meal-offering was composed of coarse barley flour (i.e., *bikkurim*).[577] The coarseness of the barley flour is symbolic of the wife acting coarsely. Also, barley is usually used as animal feed and is symbolic of her degrading herself and behaving like an animal. Other meal-offerings were beautifully anointed with oil and frankincense (refer to Lev. 2), while this one was not.[578]

Interestingly, the word *bikkurim* in Hebrew means "First Fruits." In Deuteronomy 26:2, God said to the children of Israel, ". . . you shall take some of the first fruit of all the produce of the ground . . . and put it in a basket and go to the place where the Lord your God chooses to make His name abide."[579] Yeshua resurrected conquering death forever on *Bikkurim* being the first fruit of many brethren (Rom. 8:29); and ". . . we ourselves, having the fruits of the Spirit, even we ourselves groan within ourselves, waiting eagerly for our adoption as sons, the redemption of our body" (Rom. 8:23).

On this same day of *Bikkurim*, Noah's ark came up out of the waters and rested securely on Mount Ararat.[580] On First Fruits, God parted the Red Sea so His people could pass through the waters and come up safely on the other side.[581] Also, on First Fruits, God's people were saved from certain death in Persia, because Queen Esther stood firmly for her people and God made a way on this day to have Haman hung on his own gallows.[582] The Jewish people knew the history of salvation that happened on this day when Yeshua rose from the dead. His resurrection made it possible for His body to be redeemed. Yeshua brought His body to the cross as the meal-offering for His disloyal wife. "For the husband is the head of the wife, as Christ also is the head of the church, He Himself being the Savior of the body. But as the church is subject to Christ, so also the wives ought to be to their husbands in everything. Husbands love your wives, just as Christ also loved the church and gave Himself up for her" (Eph.5:23-25 NASB).

The death of Jesus is/was of utmost importance, and I don't want to minimize it; but even greater still is Christ's resurrection. As the Son of Man, Jesus embraced the human condition. He experienced death. Let's just remember that the crucifixion was a moment in time, not the purpose. It was a part of Yeshua's earthly life story, not the entire meaning of it. God is not cruel. There is nothing evil in Him. The mark of Christianity is supposed to be love, which is a position constant with the religion of Israel.[583] Love yourself; love your neighbor; and, above all, love your God. The story of the prodigal son describes a father, whose attitude toward his incorrigible son is one of constant love. The father never changed. The son returned home once he recalled his father's provision and his stable place to dwell. The father's heart revealed that home was where the prodigal's heart had been planted (Luke 15:11-32). Recognition of the cross awakens prodigals, like you and me, to the compassion the Lord has placed within us. It awakens us to the one whose name means salvation—Yeshua.

EXTREME TRIBULATION

Let's return to our wayward wife analogy. Attempts were made to induce a confession from the accused wife, beginning with having "her stand before the LORD" (Num. 5:16). Although the woman would not be punished due to lack of evidence, in view of the gravity of the accusation and the bitter end it could bring if she were guilty, it would be best if the accused woman confessed her sin. The following verses (Num. 5:17-31) show us the pressure that was brought to bear to achieve this end. If the wife were indeed innocent, she would choose to undergo this extreme ordeal so she could be vindicated.[584] If she were guilty, hopefully she would confess. Remember that Paul preached the gospel as "strengthening the souls of the disciples, encouraging them to continue in the faith, and saying, 'Through many tribulations we must enter the kingdom of God" (Acts 14:22 NASB). Also remember that the great multitude from every nation, tribes, peoples, and tongues standing before the throne and before the Lamb in Revelation 7:9 were "the ones who come out of the great tribulation, and they have washed their robes and made them white in the blood of the Lamb" (Rev. 7:14 NASB).

Numbers 5:17 tells us how a priest drew sacred water from the temple laver. Remember that the laver was a very large copper basin in the tabernacle courtyard, from which the priest sanctified his hands and feet before performing acceptable service. It was not made of copper from the regular contributions, but from the brightly polished sheets of copper that devout women used as mirrors in Egypt. Thanks to these mirrors, a multitude of Jewish children had been born. The Lord foresaw that the implements that brought husbands and wives together in Egypt would be used to end suspicion and animosity in marriages, caused by the accusations of adultery. Don't forget that these devout women, who served at the doorway of the tent of meeting, could no longer gaze upon themselves vainly in their own mirrors; they had to fix their eyes upon the sanctifying source of the laver—their Messiah.

The temple laver, by its very essence, recalled the purity of Jewish women and their devotion to their husbands. Therefore, such water was a fitting agent with which to punish an unfaithful wife. The "earthenware vessel" (Num. 5:17) speaks of the flesh or the earthly sinful nature. Its reference to the earth was intended to force the wife to consider that she would die and return to the earth if she were guilty. In the wilderness, the floor of the tabernacle was the sand of the desert; but Solomon's temple in Jerusalem had a floor of marble. In order to fulfill this commandment, one of the marble floor tiles had to be fitted so it could be lifted to expose the earth underneath.[585]

"The priest shall then have the woman stand before the LORD and let the hair of the woman go loose, and place the grain offering of memorial in her hands, which is the grain offering of jealousy, and in the hand of the priest is to be the water of bitterness that brings a curse" (Num. 5:18 NASB). The *kohen* made the wife move from place to place in the doorway of the courtyard. This was the exact same place where the women, who contributed the polished copper mirrors for the fabrication of the laver, served at the doorway of the tent of meeting. The doorway can represent being in or out in their marriage or with God. The priest then uncovers the wife's hair (i.e., her glory) and places the meal-offering on her outstretched palms to humiliate and tire her, in hopes of eliciting a confession.[586] The bitter waters were not literally pungent, but rather its effect, when guilty, was bitter, for it caused an adulteress wife to die in a very bizarre, excessively expanding manner.[587] As a side note, the Hebrew sages derive that the ordeal of the bitter waters is only effective if the husband is free from sin himself.[588] Yeshua, the Word of God, is the Judge (2 Tim. 4:1), "able to judge the thoughts and intentions of the heart" (Heb. 4:12), and will always be justified in His judgment of a person's or the church's sin of idolatry and/or adultery.

Numbers 5:21-22 goes into detail about the gruesome death the wife will suffer if she is guilty of adultery. "These waters that cause curse shall enter your innards to cause your stomach to distend and thigh to collapse!" (Num. 5:22). The stomach distending means that it would stretch out and become swollen, while her thigh collapsing or wasting away refers to the womb, which would be destroyed in retribution for its sinful activity.[589] The stomach also is referred as one's innermost being or one's belly. "He who believes in Me, as the Scripture said, From his innermost being shall flow rivers of living water" (John 7:38 NASB). The Jewish sage Rashi tells us that this was such a horrible death that when the people of Israel would curse their enemies, they would say that the fate of an adulterous wife should happen to them.[590] It was also a way some people strengthened an oath by saying: "If I am lying, may I suffer the adulteress fate." In case you thought as I did, that this punishment was unfair—for what about the man who committed adultery with the wife, the repetition of the punishment in verse 22 means that this same penalty would befall the man with whom she committed adultery[591]—a swelling, bloated gut that could have exploded. Yuck. Disgusting. By the way, the concept for a stomach distending is the same idea behind Christmas stockings being stuffed to their limits.

The priest wrote the oaths contained in Numbers 5:19-22 on a parchment scroll, omitting the two narrative phrases: "The kohen shall adjure . . ." (vs. 21) and "the woman shall respond 'Amen, amen'" (v. 22). God's unspeakable, sacred name is then written on the scroll in its entirety. Ordinarily, it was forbidden to erase the sacred name. If one did erase the sacred name, the sage Rambam tells us they were liable to lashes. But here God Himself commanded that His name be erased in order to bring peace between man and wife.[592] The eraser of the sacred name speaks of God temporary removal of His name through the giving His only begotten Son as a sacrifice to bridge the gap between God and man, Christ and His church.

Verse 28 tells us about the woman who had not become defiled, which also speaks of God's redemption through the Messiah's gift of atonement. The wayward wife was found pure after she went through this arduous, humiliating process. I believe that Christ's Bride needs not only to accept the incredible gift of salvation, but she must also go through the strenuous process of sanctification, where she works out her salvation with fear and trembling (Phil. 2:12). Sanctification is a work of the Holy Spirit in a believer's life, where God labors with us to lead us through a process of confessing, repenting, and practically being changed, so we become more and more like Jesus. Believers also should consider a thorough concept of humiliation. Sanctification requires persistence, humility, and a teachable heart. I believe that a bridal commitment to the Lord of Lords and the King of Kings requires an additional Spirit-led step of purification, which is an entirely humiliating, all-consuming fire process, where no flesh should remain. Sounds awful, doesn't it? We'd like to forget that the word *awesome,* as in the "awesome, reverential fear of the Lord," comes from the concept of *awful.*

BAPTISM OF FIRE

When Jesus spoke in Luke 12, He already had been baptized by water and the Holy Spirit (Matt. 3-4). What remained was His baptism of fire. Yeshua's crucifixion experience was an entirely humiliating, all-consuming event. Jesus said in Luke 12:49-50 NKJV: "I came to send fire on the earth and how I wish it were already kindled! But I have a baptism to be baptized with, and how I am distressed till it is accomplished!" The Lamb of God was sacrificed (i.e., burnt) in His entirety as an elevation offering.

> For Christ also suffered once for sins, the just for the unjust, that He might bring us to God, being put to death in the flesh but made alive by the Spirit . . . Therefore since Christ suffered in the flesh, arm yourselves also with the same mind, for he who has suffered in the flesh has ceased from sin, that he no longer should live the rest of his time in the flesh for the lusts of men, but for the will of God.–
> —1 Peter 3:18; 4:1-2 NKJV

> Beloved, do not think it strange concerning the fiery trials which try you, as though some strange thing happened to you; but rejoice to the extent that you partake of Christ's sufferings . . .
> —1 Peter 4:12-13 NKJV

> Indeed, I . . . count all things loss for the excellence of the knowledge of Christ Jesus my Lord, for whom I have suffered the loss of all things, and count them as rubbish that I may gain Christ and be found in Him, not having my own righteousness, which is from the law, but that which is through faith in Christ, the righteousness which is from God by faith; that I may know Him and the power of His resurrection, and the fellowship of His sufferings, being conformed to His death . . .
> —Philippians 3:8-10 NKJV

If "He who sanctifies and those who are being sanctified are all one" (Heb. 2:11), be assured that if Jesus "learned obedience by the things which He suffered" (Heb. 5:8), so will His people. Peter says, "You have purified your souls in obeying the truth through the Spirit in sincere love . . . with a pure heart" (1 Pet. 1:22 NKJV).

The Lord clearly purifies His people through the fiery trials of our earthly existence. We all have choices to make during our grievous fiery trials, which tests the genuineness of our faith (1 Pet. 1:7). We will either choose God's will and His kingdom, or ourselves and the kingdom of self. Once we have knowledge of our sin, we must turn to the Lord to flee from our wicked ways. "For if we sin willfully after we have received the knowledge of the truth, there no longer remains a sacrifice for sins, but a certain fearful expectation of judgment, and fiery indignation which will devour the adversaries" (Heb.10:26-27 NKJV). We must not make the grievous mistake of thinking that people of faith can willfully sin without disastrous ramifications! Hebrews 10 says that anyone who rejected Moses' law died without mercy, and "of how much worse punishment, do you suppose will be thought worthy who has trampled the Son of God underfoot, counted the blood of the covenant by which he was sanctified a common thing, and insulted the Spirit of grace? It is a fearful thing to fall into the hands of the living God" (Heb. 10:29, 31 NKJV).

BRIDAL MYSTERIES

On this earth I became more and more intimate with my fiancé, and I only married him whom I vowed: "I do . . . to love and cherish . . . 'til death do us part." Jesus marries those who have taken the time to get to know Him personally and who say, "I do," completely to Him and His ways. The Bride subjects herself to Him fully and will not consider anything sacred, except Him. Calling sold-out hearts everywhere! Won't you forsake all for Jesus, our precious Jesus?

In actuality, the symbolism of a bride among Christmas traditions portrays the very opposite of the biblical concept of the Bride of Christ. It is a twisted counterfeit connecting the precious people made in God's image to Old Nick (a synonym for Lucifer, the Devil, and Satan[593]), not to the Messiah. Ironically, the feast day held on the anniversary of St. Nicholas's death December 6—the "saintly" icon of Christmas—has been traditionally considered a lucky day to get married.[594] "When we believe in luck, we turn to something outside the human realm,"[595] and it's not God. "Satan . . . gets empowerment in our lives through our beliefs."[596] Yearly, our Christmas celebrations wed us to the world. The annual December wedding rehearsal to the world unites people with a feeling of kinship. We seem to become one, and sensuality is excused.

There is a famous bridal picture in Scandinavian countries where most people honor St. Lucia on December 13, which is considered the beginning of the Christmas season for them. The oldest daughter of each family rises early on that day and wakes her family members as she wears a long, white gown with a red sash. The Lucy (i.e., Lucia) Bride dons a crown made of twigs with nine lighted candles.[597] No matter how physically gorgeous and charming this custom may appear, it will never truly represent the Bride of Christ, for the custom marks the beginning of the golden calf celebration of Christmas. Please don't forget that the Bible tells us that the devil is the god of this world, who disguises himself as an angel of light with a facade that appears good and right. The devil's original name, Lucifer, means "light-bearer,"[598] while Lucia's or Lucy's name means "light"[599] (as in the Lucy Bride). I believe that this book proves beyond all doubt that the Bride of Christ will not be associated with Christmas in any form. The Bible tells us how to become part of the pure and spotless Bride of Christ and the Spirit of the living God will guide us to this truth. It is an eternal, spiritual reality, not a fleshly one.

Ephesians 5:25-27 concentrates on what the Messiah did for the church: loving her, giving Himself up for her, sanctifying her, and cleansing her by the water of His Word. The process, which leads to a person becoming part of Christ's Bride, is full of grace and truth as He is; but once a person becomes part of Christ's Bride, fidelity is required.

There are bridal mysteries encoded in Ephesians 5:25-27 that can be better revealed when combined with the truths of Numbers 5:11-31—a most ancient path for an accused wife to show herself pure. The oath that the priest (one who presents man to God) writes on the parchment scroll says, "If no man has gone to bed with you, if you have not gone astray to make yourself unclean while under your husband's authority, then be free from this water of embitterment and cursing. But if you have in fact gone astray while under your husband's authority and become unclean, because some man other than your husband has gone to bed with you... may *Adonai* make you an object of cursing and condemnation among your people by making you private parts shrivel and your abdomen swell up!" (Num. 5:19-21 CJB). The Lord's Bride will not stray and be intimate with other beings or other "truths" without dire consequences. "Let marriage, be held in honor among all, and let the marriage bed be undefiled; for fornicators and adulterers God will judge" (Heb.13:4 NASB). Please remember the promise of 1 John 1:9, too: "If we confess our sins, He is faithful and righteous to forgive us our sins and to cleanse us from all unrighteousness."

Christ's Bride is one of His most valued possessions. That the commitment of being married to the King of Kings and the Lord of Lords is not to be taken lightly is almost an understatement. His queen will most excellently represent the King. The Lord our God will only come to us with a wedding ring after we begin to come out of Babylon and lay down Christmas. Our walk will certainly be shown as less than perfect. But if you ask our Beloved to keep you and protect you and clearly show you when you stray, your transparently honest disposition will keep you on His straight and narrow way.

ಌ

12

EPILOGUE

> O people, the LORD has already told you what is good,
> and this is what he requires:
> to do what is right, to love mercy,
> and to walk humbly with your God.
> —Micah 6:8 NLT

When the Bible tells us to deny ourselves, take up our cross, and follow Him, the Lord doesn't want us to be in denial of what we are denying. To truly deny oneself, one must be cognizant of what one is sacrificing. How can we give up something that we haven't grasped (physically, mentally, or spiritually)? Denying ourselves is a conscience decision, just as taking up one's cross is a conscience act.

Commitment to self-sacrifice is an essential quality for every believer. The caveat here is that Christians must understand that we don't crucify ourselves. Crucifying ourselves will result in some form of self-righteousness, which is actually one of the basest forms of pride. Beware if your attention is captured on how well you're doing or how you are in comparison to others. If your attention is focused on yourself rather than on the glory of God, then your confidence is in your own self-discipline and personal sacrifice.

The trouble with sacrifices happens when we put more faith in our own sacrifices than in the Lord's sacrifice. When we sacrifice anything for the Lord, the best motivation is always based in love.

Yeshua has told us the principal, most important, and first commandment is completely loving God—with all our heart, soul, mind, and strength (Matt. 22:37-38 AMP). Loving God vehemently; wholly; speedily, especially when repeated; diligently, especially, exceedingly; greatly; louder and louder; mightily; and utterly will keep us within the excellent curbs of God's kingdom.

If we give up anything simply for the sake of righteousness, purity, or maturity, it may appear virtuous and wise. We probably also will feel good about our spiritual condition; but if pride is involved, we will find ourselves being self-centered and self-seeking rather than seeking first His kingdom and His righteousness (Matt. 6:33).

Living a crucified life is different from crucifying ourselves. Living a crucified life requires a person to focus on their love for God and His glory. Jesus declares in Luke 9:23: "If anyone wishes to come after Me, let him deny himself, and take up his cross daily, and follow Me." First, we knowingly deny ourselves; then we are supposed to purposefully take up our cross. The cross is merely an object where our carnal stuff can be nailed so we can ultimately be free. Peter exhorts "aliens . . . [who are] chosen . . . that you may obey Jesus Christ and be sprinkled with His blood" (1 Pet. 1:1-2 NASB) to "act as free men, and do not use your freedom as a covering for evil, but *use it* as bondslaves of God" (2 Pet. 2:16 NASB).

Readers should be able to perceive by now that Christmas is self-centered and Babylonian to its core. The Lord our God is asking His people to come out of her:

> "Fallen, fallen is Babylon the great! And she has become a dwelling place of demons and a prison of every unclean spirit, and a prison of every unclean and hateful bird. For all the nations have drunk of the wine of the passion of her immorality, and the kings of the earth have committed *acts of* immorality with her, and the merchants of the earth have become rich by the wealth of her sensuality." And I heard another voice from heaven saying, "Come out of her my people, that you may not participate in her sins and that you

may not receive of her plagues; for her sins have piled up as high as heaven, and God had remembered her iniquities."
—Revelation 18:2-5 NASB

Remember how I held my Beloved's hand for a year in coming out of Babylon before the Lord delivered His next whopper: "Christmas will be the golden calf of America." Then He asked me three times, "Will you tell them?" Similar to Ruth, this was a way to test the genuineness of my commitment. Will I tell bridal hearts everywhere that Christmas will be the golden calf of America? Yes. I am telling them through obediently writing this love letter. May God our Father and Christ Jesus our Lord give you grace, mercy, and peace" (1 Tim. 1:2b NLT); and may God's people be full of truth and grace . . . as He is.

Rick Joyner tells us: "Babylon is not just a physical reality; Babylon is in the heart. Fleeing from physical Babylon . . . is the removal of all barriers that separate us from the Lord and our brothers that we might freely love and freely serve."[600]

. . . The Babylonians, that ruthless and impetuous people, who sweep across the whole earth . . . They are a law to themselves . . . whose own strength is their god.
—Habakkuk 1:6-7, 11

"I am the LORD; that is My Name! I will not give My glory to another or My praise to idols. *See, the former things have taken place, and new things I declare."*
—*Isaiah 42:8-9, emphasis mine*

"The mixture of Christmas grieves My heart. Come out of Babylon and lay down Christmas, for I *will* have a pure and spotless Bride."

—Yeshua

INDEX

A

Aaron 39, 137, 138, 141, 142, 143, 144, 145, 150, 152, 153, 193, 205, 219, 250
abortion 202, 203
Abraham 25, 48, 59, 60, 74, 95, 96, 177, 179, 186, 187, 188, 191, 192, 203, 206, 217, 232, 242, 243, 244, 245, 247
abstain 80, 81, 85, 86, 87, 181
abstinence 79, 80, 88, 89
Accad. 52
action 12, 56, 91, 108, 114, 131, 150, 212, 224, 234, 235, 239, 242
Acts 15 .... 75, 77, 78, 79, 80, 81, 89, 95, 200
addiction 38
administration 74, 111, 183, 185, 189, 197
Adonai 192, 193, 195, 216, 217, 261
Adonis 64
adoption 23, 181, 183, 185, 186, 190, 254
adultery 76, 134, 172, 251, 252, 253, 256, 257
Akiti 83, 211, 212
Alexander the Great 93, 94
Alexandria 86, 98, 99, 199
altar 24, 25, 27, 87, 94, 95, 120, 121, 126, 128, 139, 143, 153, 178, 188, 193, 202, 203, 204, 205, 206, 214, 218, 219, 237, 246, 247, 249
America 19, 20, 25, 27, 31, 32, 33, 39, 46, 47, 56, 58, 69, 71, 79, 83, 99, 106, 107, 110, 126, 129, 130, 135, 138,

141, 145, 146, 153, 155, 157, 164, 170, 180, 198, 203, 204, 206, 207, 208, 209, 211, 212, 215, 216, 217, 218, 219, 224, 236, 265
American.... 21, 32, 38, 39, 56, 80, 83, 85, 88, 101, 106, 108, 135, 156, 181, 207, 209, 211, 212, 214, 215, 216, 217, 218, 225
Americans 11, 12, 31, 34, 38, 52, 106, 129, 179, 181, 207, 209, 211, 214, 217
Ammonites 109
Ancient of Days 73, 101
Anno Domini 92, 93
antichrist 93, 95, 96, 98, 139, 140, 206
Antichrist 36, 50, 93, 139, 140
Antiochus (Epiphanes IV) 93, 94, 95, 96, 98, 120, 139, 206
antiquity 52, 58, 65, 66, 101, 110
Apis 53, 54, 55, 61, 139, 143, 145, 146, 149, 211
Apollo 114, 116, 121
apostasy 49, 64, 139, 140
Apostles 73, 80, 122, 170
Apostolic Decree 75, 78, 79, 80, 89, 95
apparition 13, 17, 164
appointed 57, 63, 93, 98, 111, 159, 169, 174, 175, 176, 218, 246, 250
Asherah 127
Assyrian 43, 52
Astarte 127
attendants 231, 240

B

Baal 54, 107, 110, 120, 127, 201, 202, 203, 219
Babel 45, 46, 47, 48, 50, 52, 53, 59, 63, 65, 68
Babylon 13, 15, 18, 20, 24, 25, 32, 33, 35, 37, 38, 39, 43, 45, 46, 47, 48, 49, 50, 51, 52, 53, 54, 57, 58, 59, 60, 61, 64, 66, 67, 69, 70, 72, 79, 80, 81, 83, 101, 109, 117, 120, 123, 127, 136, 145, 149, 155, 157, 158, 163, 164, 165, 173, 179, 187, 203, 207, 209, 210, 211, 212, 213, 242, 262, 264, 265
Babylonia 52, 55, 63
Babylonian(s) 24, 35, 43, 44, 48, 52, 55, 60, 63, 64, 65, 66, 67, 83, 101, 119, 120, 121, 122, 123, 124, 126, 127, 145, 147, 152, 179, 181, 201, 207, 211, 212, 215, 242, 264, 265

balance 14, 26, 34, 236, 238
baptism 115, 259
baptism of fire 59, 187, 193, 194, 247, 258
Baptist(s) 106, 180, 181
Battle for Christmas 34, 56
Beloved 17, 18, 19, 51, 80, 88, 117, 151, 217, 229, 234, 262, 265
Berean 13
Bethel 137, 138, 139, 205, 206
biblical feasts 226
biblical time-keeping 73, 90, 93, 95
Bikkurim (i.e. Feast of First Fruits) 122, 173, 254
bi-polar 12, 38
birth 12, 38, 46, 52, 58, 66, 71, 82, 92, 120, 121, 122, 128, 129, 149, 152, 153, 154, 170, 183, 207, 213
birthday 24, 52, 58, 101, 109, 120, 121, 122, 128, 181, 212, 215
blood 11, 38, 76, 77, 78, 80, 81, 86, 87, 110, 131, 145, 146, 187, 190, 193, 197, 225, 246, 249, 250, 256, 260, 264
body 37, 55, 60, 62, 65, 74, 85, 96, 104, 105, 106, 144, 166, 173, 174, 175, 184, 185, 186, 191, 193, 194, 195, 199, 200, 216, 226, 237, 238, 246, 247, 249, 250, 251, 253, 254, 255
Boston 179
boughs 33, 127
bowing down to the sun 25, 128
bread 91, 97, 173, 227, 241, 242, 245, 246, 247, 250, 253
bridal company 51, 151, 185, 236, 247, 248
Bride (of Christ) 13, 18, 20, 21, 27, 28, 29, 37, 39, 45, 59, 74, 79, 112, 118, 123, 158, 164, 172, 173, 184, 187, 191, 193, 194, 199, 223, 227, 228, 229, 230, 232, 233, 236, 241, 247, 248, 250, 251, 259, 260, 261, 262, 265
Bridegroom 18, 59, 79, 80, 173, 232, 235, 236, 249
Brown, Dan 113, 114, 120
Buche de Noel 68
Buddhist 149, 215
bull 53, 54, 55, 61, 64, 143, 145, 211
Bullinger, E.W. 36, 79, 168
burnt offering 110, 153, 154, 176, 186, 191, 192, 193, 203, 216

C

calendar.. 16, 32, 52, 66, 67, 90, 92, 93, 96, 98, 99, 100, 109, 112, 120, 121, 122, 129, 139, 156, 170, 171, 175, 182, 207, 211, 215, 226, 227

calf...... 19, 20, 25, 27, 39, 43, 46, 53, 54, 55, 61, 79, 91, 107, 110, 130, 137, 138, 139, 141, 142, 143, 145, 146, 149, 152, 153, 154, 155, 156, 157, 158, 198, 204, 205, 206, 211, 216, 217, 218, 219, 245, 246, 261, 265

Calvin, John 130, 131
Calvinists 179
Canaan 63, 127, 202, 242
capitalism 34
carnal 34, 48, 101, 128, 138, 143, 157, 225, 247, 264
carnival 56, 57, 69, 181, 212
Catholic 28, 67, 99, 100, 110, 112, 118, 119, 120, 123, 132, 215, 216
Catholic Encyclopedia 121, 147
Catholicism 119, 133

celebration(s)...... 12, 14, 16, 34, 38, 53, 56, 57, 58, 66, 67, 69, 71, 75, 82, 84, 94, 99, 101, 104, 110, 112, 117, 118, 120, 121, 128, 130, 145, 147, 149, 154, 155, 168, 170, 171, 173, 180, 204, 209, 211, 212, 214, 216, 218, 226, 260, 261

Chaldea 31, 32, 48, 52, 55, 60, 66, 251
Chaldean(s) 55, 65, 117, 145
challah 250
Chanukah (See Hanukkah) 16, 17, 168, 169, 170, 172, 173
chaos 45, 49, 53, 68, 119, 208
charitable 11, 38, 151, 154, 212
chaste 80
Chemosh 108, 109, 110
childhood 46, 47, 135

children 16, 46, 47, 57, 58, 78, 87, 90, 108, 109, 110, 112, 119, 123, 125, 129, 135, 140, 146, 147, 149, 155, 156, 164, 175, 177, 182, 195, 203, 206, 207, 213, 215, 238, 245, 254, 256

Christian church 23, 73, 75, 78, 91, 92, 105, 111, 113, 119, 121, 156, 157, 177, 204, 216, 245

Christianity 20, 38, 66, 71, 74, 78, 84, 93, 97, 110, 113, 115, 117, 122, 127, 180, 181, 199, 206, 255

Christmas cards 14, 112, 118
Christmas Day 53, 84, 117, 163, 215

Christmas dinner 84, 94
Christmas Eve 47, 68, 69, 129, 215
Christmas in America 20, 207, 212
Christmas King 57
Christmas logs 68, 215
Christmas season 14, 32, 47, 56, 58, 69, 72, 82, 83, 101, 117, 118, 125, 149, 152, 155, 164, 212, 214, 261
Christmas traditions 39, 68, 105, 118, 126, 147, 204, 260
Christmas tree 14, 15, 19, 47, 56, 58, 112, 126, 127, 128, 129, 130, 135, 164, 166, 167, 168, 179, 182, 214
Christmas witch 112
Christmas time 25, 45, 46, 58, 71, 100, 101, 154, 155, 157, 158, 217
Chrysostom 70, 75
Chumash 144, 252
church father(s) 27, 79, 84, 121, 180
clean or cleanse 27, 28, 37, 59, 117, 119, 133, 150, 159, 164, 168, 170, 173, 219, 223, 230, 233, 237, 239, 248, 249, 261, 262
cleanliness 237
colonial 106, 207
commercial 31, 34, 58, 181
communion 111, 241, 245, 249
complete 79, 80, 146, 196, 224, 245
compromise 15, 29, 58, 84, 107, 110, 112, 113, 114, 117, 120, 122, 157, 158, 165, 168, 179, 201, 206, 214, 226
confess 21, 88, 92, 113, 149, 193, 227, 252, 255, 257, 258, 262
consecrate 105, 106, 176
Constantine 75, 97, 98, 110, 111, 112, 113, 114, 115, 116, 117, 120, 121, 122, 139, 206
Constantinople 75, 115, 116
consumerism 57
consuming fire 133, 158, 178, 194, 247, 258
consummation 21, 184
consumption 31
contaminated 80, 81, 132, 158
controversy or controversies 112, 113, 124, 137, 236
copper 237, 238, 256, 257
counterfeit 50, 123, 260

Creator 14, 44, 48, 49, 142, 154, 157, 171, 187
crèche 123
Cornelius 122, 196, 197, 198, 199
Cromwell, Oliver 180
Cromwellian England 106, 179, 207
Crowley, Aleister 35
crucify 37, 263, 264
Cush 61
custom(s) 25, 62, 69, 71, 79, 81, 82, 86, 87, 93, 101, 116, 119, 120, 128, 129, 182, 204, 206, 261
Czech Republic 149

D

Dan 50, 137, 138, 139, 205, 242
Daniel 81, 140
darkness 49, 61, 78, 146, 171, 231, 239, 242, 243
David 88, 108, 132, 137, 138, 139, 169, 174, 244
DaVinci Code, The 113
death 11, 24, 33, 50, 51, 55, 59, 61, 62, 64, 65, 66, 68, 70, 71, 72, 86, 91, 95, 105, 114, 115, 131, 185, 190, 225, 226, 231, 246, 252, 254, 255, 257, 259, 260
deceive 44, 55, 59, 86, 107, 140, 156, 207
December twenty-fifth 24, 52, 66, 75, 117, 120, 121, 122
December twenty-fourth 66, 67, 129
deception 33, 49, 50, 107, 126, 140, 148, 210, 242
defiance 44, 155, 205
delusion 27
demonic 45, 148, 206
demons 50, 68, 86, 89, 119, 128, 136, 152, 264
desecrate 44
devil or Devil 36, 90, 112, 129, 136, 146, 147, 148, 149, 213, 260, 261
Diaspora 199
Dio Chrysostom 70
Dionysis Exiguus 92
disorder 57, 87, 98, 99, 100

dispensation 74, 184, 185, 186, 189, 190, 193, 194, 195, 197
divination 55, 76
divine.... 17, 18, 23, 74, 79, 80, 126, 132, 138, 139, 144, 152, 164, 168, 169, 176,
    181, 183, 184, 185, 187, 189, 197, 198, 199, 205, 239
domestic or domestication 57, 58, 69, 129, 180, 181, 211, 212, 215
dream 55, 150, 151, 209
dwelling place 21, 136, 168, 170, 184, 186, 191, 226, 238, 246, 264

E

Easter 32, 92, 97, 98, 99, 100, 112, 119, 132, 139, 171, 179, 182
economic 35, 64, 72, 207
Egypt 53, 54, 55, 44, 61, 62, 63, 98, 120, 124, 127, 137, 138, 139, 141,
    142, 143, 144, 145, 149, 152, 153, 154, 157, 205, 237, 238, 242, 256
elevation 51, 148, 176
elevation offering 192, 246, 247, 259
Elijah 201, 202, 203
emotional 46, 57, 79, 204, 207, 224
emotions 224, 253
end-time 27, 145, 170, 200
England 27, 94, 106, 117, 132, 148, 155, 179, 180, 207, 211
Epiphany 67, 112
Essential Commandments for All Believers 73, 75, 77, 78, 79, 80, 88, 92, 93,
    197, 200
Esther 173, 254
eternal 17, 19, 34, 51, 88, 92, 97, 107, 114, 115, 116, 133, 134, 153, 158, 176,
    184, 186, 188, 190, 191, 192, 198, 234, 244, 245, 251, 261
Eusebius 78
evergreen 12, 14, 33, 58, 66, 71, 83, 126, 127, 128, 129, 130, 215
everlasting life 156, 244
evil spirits 67, 68
exact times 175
extravagant 14, 27, 150, 154, 155, 207, 208
Ezekiel (the Book of) 23, 24, 25, 31, 32, 69, 145, 159, 174
Ezekiel 8 .... 24, 121, 128

F

faith 21, 23, 26, 48, 50, 77, 84, 91, 92, 96, 106, 111, 115, 124, 133, 145, 156, 174, 178, 180, 181, 184, 187, 188, 191, 196, 197, 214, 232, 235, 236, 238, 244, 245, 249, 256, 259, 260, 263
fall feasts 172, 177
Father Christmas 125
feast 91, 94, 117, 121, 132, 137, 139, 143, 152, 153, 154, 170, 172, 174, 176, 215, 216, 217, 218, 226, 227, 228, 230, 231, 236, 239, 246, 249, 260
Feast of Dedication 16, 170
Feast of First Fruits 97, 122, 173
Feast of Fools 57, 155
Feast of the Nativity 82, 110
Feast of Saturn 82, 84, 127
feasts 90, 91, 97, 111, 118, 122, 131, 159, 169, 170, 171, 172, 173, 174, 175, 176, 177, 178, 201, 205, 226
Feasts of the Lord................ 90, 91, 111, 171, 172, 173, 174, 175, 176, 177, 178, 192, 226, 227
fertility.. 129, 147
festival....... 31, 32, 53, 67, 69, 70, 71, 75, 82, 83, 84, 92, 100, 117, 118, 119, 121, 122, 152, 153, 154, 169, 171, 172, 211, 219
Festival of Laughter 207, 211
festivals 75, 82, 94, 96, 97, 112, 118, 119, 120, 131, 132, 171, 175, 176, 177, 207, 247, 249
fire 59, 60, 65, 67, 68, 109, 144, 158, 178, 187, 193, 194, 201, 202, 212, 218, 243, 246, 247, 248, 258
first fruits................................... 74, 97, 122, 173, 254
first-century 97, 111, 174
flesh 26, 38, 48, 50, 63, 74, 76, 101, 132, 134, 139, 156, 157, 181, 187, 190, 194, 197, 201, 202, 206, 208, 218, 254, 256, 258, 259, 261
flood 43, 45, 48, 60, 61, 63, 64, 183
fool 49, 57, 133, 140, 152, 154, 155
foolish 18, 49, 119, 173, 236, 239
forbidden.............. 67, 78, 112, 125, 126, 179, 184, 198, 207, 250, 258
forever................ 22, 23, 49, 91, 92, 93, 111, 140, 172, 186, 188, 204, 244, 254
forgiveness 86, 91, 92, 104, 193, 239, 254

foundation 12, 73, 75, 76, 90, 93, 149, 154, 158, 171, 189, 197, 210, 211, 228, 240, 248
Freemasonry 212, 213
friend(s) 12, 14, 15, 17, 32, 38, 59, 83, 89, 126, 128, 131, 132, 136, 155, 165, 166, 167, 211, 214, 215, 227, 228, 231, 232, 233, 234, 235, 239, 240
fruit(s) 28, 34, 57, 72, 74, 106, 107, 115, 116, 117, 129, 134, 147, 154, 155, 168, 180, 181, 203, 215, 234, 245, 249, 250, 254
fullness 26, 174, 185, 195, 196, 225
fullness of the Gentiles 195, 196
fullness of time 74, 175, 183, 186, 190, 195, 196
fun 14, 38, 57, 118, 155, 163, 177, 226, 236
fundamental 20, 55, 134, 178, 179, 186, 187
funeral(s) 33, 34, 71, 72

G

Gentile 51, 74, 75, 76, 78, 80, 91, 98, 111, 174, 177, 196, 198, 199, 252
Gentile church 20, 174
Gentiles 27, 74, 77, 78, 80, 81, 98, 103, 108, 118, 174, 178, 184, 195, 196, 197, 198, 199, 200
genuine 15, 21, 92, 136, 152, 178, 182, 191, 245, 251, 260, 265
genu-wine 182, 249, 250
Germany 129, 130, 135
giving 11, 12, 15, 32, 38, 45, 46, 56, 83, 118, 151, 152, 154, 155, 171, 177, 178, 215, 228, 239, 252, 258, 261
gladiator 71, 72
glory 22, 23, 25, 28, 52, 90, 108, 133, 134, 135, 167, 170, 174, 178, 188, 218, 223, 230, 239, 245, 249, 257, 263, 264, 265
gluttony 155, 216
God-fearers 78, 199
gold 34, 55, 70, 128, 135, 137, 145, 149, 158, 178, 182, 204, 211, 229, 230, 251
gold earrings 141, 154
golden calf 25, 27, 39, 53, 54, 55, 61, 91, 137, 138, 139, 141, 142, 143, 145, 146, 152, 153, 154, 155, 156, 157, 158, 205, 206, 211, 216, 217, 218, 219, 245, 246, 261

golden calf of America.................. 19, 20, 25, 39, 46, 79, 107, 110, 130, 141, 145, 153, 198, 265
gospel 70, 78, 106, 115, 172, 177, 178, 180, 195, 197, 198, 199, 201, 227, 255
grace... 14, 20, 21, 29, 36, 47, 49, 84, 88, 107, 115, 116, 131, 132, 136, 145, 146, 164, 165, 168, 169, 184, 190, 195, 196, 239, 245, 260, 261, 265
Greco-Roman 92, 97, 100
Greece 119, 199
Greek.......................... 64, 68, 70, 85, 93, 94, 95, 96, 97, 120, 121, 147, 195, 238
Greek mind-sets 101
Gregorian 100, 211
grieves... 13, 37, 39, 45, 59, 73, 117, 149, 150, 164, 265

H

Halloween 15, 56, 68, 164
ham... 84, 94
Ham 43, 48, 53, 63
Haman 254
Hanukkah 16
Happy Holidays 39, 112
Haran 59, 60
harlot 31, 103
harlotry 31, 32, 33, 83, 251
Harry Potter.. 56
Hasmoneans 94
heart(s) 11, 13, 15, 16, 17, 18, 19, 20, 21, 23, 26, 27, 29, 31, 33, 37, 39, 45, 49, 51, 59, 72, 73, 80, 84, 85, 87, 88, 89, 91, 96, 104, 107, 108, 109, 114, 115, 117, 123, 134, 136, 137, 139, 140, 145, 149, 150, 152, 158, 164, 165, 166, 167, 172, 174, 185, 187, 189, 194, 196, 203, 204, 210, 212, 215, 218, 223, 224, 225, 227, 230, 232, 235, 236, 237, 239, 244, 251, 255, 257, 258, 259, 260, 264, 265
heathen 84, 85, 94, 110, 118, 119, 120, 122, 173, 206
Hebrew 12, 22, 35, 44, 48, 49, 50, 59, 69, 91, 124, 141, 143, 144, 175, 176, 189, 192, 194, 223, 224, 225, 237, 238, 243, 247, 254, 257
Hebrews (The Book of) 85, 87, 131, 188, 189, 194, 216, 218, 243, 244, 245, 260

Hellenism 93, 94
Hercules 61, 64
high priest 35, 61, 95, 96, 110, 193, 206, 211, 244
High Priest 96, 244, 250
Highway of Holiness 133, 165
Hindu 214
Hislop, Rev. Alexander 46, 60, 69, 110, 117, 145, 146
history .... 20, 21 , 34, 44, 53, 60, 63, 74, 78, 83,
    93, 94, 114, 125, 127, 130, 132, 133, 135, 140, 142, 144, 146, 147, 153, 157,
    179, 181, 186, 199, 203, 207, 208, 210, 215, 243, 252, 254
holiday 12, 16, 23, 32, 34, 39, 47, 57, 66, 68, 72, 80, 84,
    97, 99, 111, 112, 117, 118, 119, 129, 130, 131, 135, 139, 149, 152, 155, 179,
    204, 207, 208, 209, 211, 212, 214, 215, 217, 226
holiness 21, 22, 23, 27, 37, 38, 50, 51, 60, 77, 79, 80, 89, 132, 133, 144, 151,
    165, 188, 195, 203, 216, 237, 245, 252
holy 21, 22, 23, 27, 28, 44, 46, 48, 50, 51, 79, 80, 85, 90, 96, 97, 101,
    104, 105, 106, 115, 122, 124, 127, 132, 133, 134, 139, 144, 150, 151, 158,
    159, 168, 172, 175, 176, 178, 181, 198, 203, 204, 208, 210, 211, 217, 218,
    219, 226
holy city 151, 226
holy day 31, 57, 66, 103, 176
Holy One (of Israel) 37, 157, 201, 217, 219, 248
Holy Place 140, 190
Holy Spirit 21, 23, 29, 38, 46, 62, 64, 80, 81, 125, 131,
    133, 134, 150, 166, 177, 178, 193, 197, 200, 225, 226, 243, 248, 258
Horus 53
humble 12, 13, 104, 136, 140, 141, 230
humility 12, 35, 141, 180, 258
hypocrisy 58
hypocrites 44, 239

I

idol(s) 22, 23, 24, 25, 27, 28, 33, 43, 48, 49, 50, 58, 59, 67, 69, 76, 80, 81, 84,
    89, 101, 103, 107, 109, 116, 123, 125, 126, 127, 128, 134, 135, 138, 141, 145,
    149, 150, 152, 158, 204, 206, 211, 213, 215, 217, 218, 239, 243, 251, 265

idolatrous............ 24, 25, 38, 48, 54, 55, 58, 59, 62, 63, 68, 74, 79, 82, 84, 87, 97, 100, 101, 103, 108, 119, 122, 129, 138, 150, 154, 171, 172, 206, 213, 218

idolatry............ 25, 33, 39, 44, 45, 50, 63, 64, 76, 78, 79, 81, 92, 107, 108, 116, 119, 125, 127, 130, 131, 132, 134, 135, 136, 139, 145, 152, 165, 201, 224, 251, 257

ignorance............ 88, 107

illusion............ 33, 49

immaculate conception 65

impure 86, 105

in the midst............ 22, 23, 131, 194, 195, 217

innocent............ 56, 95, 151, 155, 163, 195, 207, 253, 255

Irving, Washington............ 32, 210, 214, 215

Isaac............ 95, 177, 179, 186, 188, 191, 194, 201, 203, 206, 217, 218

Ishtar 44, 212

Israel..... 22, 23, 24, 27, 37, 43, 49, 77, 78, 95, 108, 118, 124, 127, 137, 138, 139, 141, 142, 144, 145, 149, 152, 153, 169, 170, 171, 175, 179, 189, 195, 197, 199, 200, 201, 204, 205, 217, 218, 219, 235, 241, 248, 249, 254, 255, 257

Israelites..... 22, 54, 55, 61, 87, 139, 142, 144, 150, 153, 154, 156, 157, 158, 159, 237

J

January 82, 83, 100, 112, 117, 118, 155

jealous or jealousy............ 24, 88, 125, 127, 134, 174, 178, 251, 253, 254, 256

Jehovah 91, 105, 127, 152, 153, 156, 176, 204, 218, 219, 246

Jeremiah 108, 109, 118, 127, 128, 212

Jeroboam 137, 138, 139, 205, 206, 218, 219

Jerusalem............ 16, 25, 78, 79, 96, 98, 108, 109, 113, 120, 137, 139, 141, 170, 171, 176, 186, 187, 189, 190, 192, 200, 205, 212, 243, 249, 256

Jerusalem Council 75, 77, 80, 81, 200

Jewish............ 44, 45, 48, 60, 74, 75, 77, 78, 84, 90, 92, 93, 95, 98, 99, 110, 111, 112, 113, 122, 124, 134, 143, 145, 151, 171, 172, 174, 177, 178, 179, 198, 199, 227, 238, 243, 249, 250, 252, 254, 256, 257

Jews............ 27, 48, 74, 75, 77, 78, 81, 93, 94, 95, 96, 111, 139, 144, 149, 170, 172, 174, 177, 178, 179, 184, 196, 197, 198, 199, 200

Joshua 138, 156
joy 11, 16, 51, 58, 148, 167, 169, 176, 194, 203, 214, 224, 227
Joyner, Rick 33, 37, 239, 265
Judaism 74, 78, 94, 95, 111, 171, 199
Judas Iscariot 235
Judea 93, 94
judge 50, 62, 63, 91, 108, 138, 153, 159, 171, 175, 204, 218, 257, 262
judgment 43, 80, 91, 152, 168, 205, 215, 224, 242, 247, 254, 257, 260
Julian 97, 99, 100, 122

K

Kalends 82, 83
kindness 21, 33, 84, 131, 149
King of Kings 17, 70, 133, 150, 153, 184, 202, 217, 234, 236, 248, 258, 262
King's valley 243, 247
Kingdom of God .. 36, 37, 38, 39, 82, 86, 101, 107, 134, 135, 138, 174, 187, 197, 226, 249, 256
kingdom of self 20, 24, 35, 36, 52, 101, 138, 205, 242, 260
Knickerbocker 210, 215
Kohanim 192, 193, 250
Kohen 250, 256, 258
kosher 86, 87, 94, 96, 198

L

La Befana (i.e. the Christmas witch) 112
Lamb 11, 26, 145, 151, 153, 193, 194, 216, 223, 225, 227, 228, 230, 231, 233, 236, 256, 259
last days 35, 36, 37, 79, 105, 118, 139, 249, 250
laughter 118, 191, 194, 207, 211, 212, 215, 216, 217, 218
laver 237, 238, 256, 257
lawlessness 56, 57, 141, 155
legalistic behavior 26, 88, 236
Levite 62, 158, 159, 205

liar 26, 33, 231, 233, 245
Libanius 82
libation(s) 67, 68, 84, 126, 212, 215, 245, 246, 248, 249
licentious 155, 208
lie(s) 23, 45, 48, 49, 56, 65, 71, 118, 126, 132, 146, 148, 154, 155, 202
living stones 79, 141, 187, 189
Lord of Misrule 56, 57, 69, 70, 155
love the Lord your God 26, 223, 224, 225, 232
love of money 33
love your neighbor 26, 89, 156, 172, 232, 233, 255
lovers of themselves 36, 105
Lucian 85
Lucifer 65, 260, 261
Lucy Bride 261
Luther, Martin 100, 129, 130

M

Maccabees 94, 95, 96
Magi 118, 124
magic 55, 56
magical 11, 31, 47, 68, 83
Maimonides 124
Manhattan 208, 211, 215
manger 71, 124, 153
manipulate or manipulation 35, 39, 50, 55, 56, 57, 58, 59, 215
Mardi Gras 56, 181
Marduk 44, 52, 53, 54, 211
mark 35, 36, 37, 54, 105, 122, 185, 196, 207, 234, 255
mark of the beast 35, 36, 37
marks 16, 31, 39, 65, 91, 92, 168, 197, 207, 261
marry 17, 203, 241
Masonry 213, 214
master 54, 57, 67, 69, 88, 138, 150, 155, 202, 212, 233, 249
materialism 33, 57, 101, 201
materialistic 34

matrimony 79, 80
mature 21, 26, 106
maturity 90, 233, 264
Mayflower 106
meal-offering 253, 254, 257
Melchizedek 188, 242, 243, 244, 245
Memphis 54, 55, 145
Merodach 44, 53
merriment 57, 212
Merry Christmas 39, 66, 112, 224
Mesopotamia 101
Mesopotamian 47
Messianic 179, 188, 189
Methodists 106, 180, 181
midwinter 12, 52, 66, 67, 69, 70, 101, 117, 118, 119, 120, 180
midwinter king 101
millennia 21, 191, 200
Milvian Bridge 114
mind of Christ 186, 224
mirrors 238, 256, 257
mischievous 17, 31, 32, 154, 155
Mithra 82, 109, 114, 120, 121
Mithra's Winter Festival 53, 117
mithraeums 116
Mithraism 82, 120, 121
Mithras 53, 116, 121
mix 12, 25, 38, 45, 61, 68, 93, 98, 116, 135, 156, 179, 204, 215
mixture ... 13, 27, 37, 39, 45, 46, 53, 71, 73, 83, 92, 105, 117, 121, 149, 163, 164, 204, 208, 210, 216, 218, 224, 265
Moab or Moabites 108, 109
Mock King 57, 69, 70, 119
Mohammad 214
Molech or Moloch 108, 109, 110, 202
money 31, 33, 34, 36, 99, 105, 150, 171, 208, 209, 210, 225, 226
Moses 22, 80, 95, 131, 141, 142, 143, 144, 145, 152, 154, 188, 238, 260
mumming 208
Muslim 214

Myra 147
mysteria 85
Mysteries 36, 38, 59, 62, 63, 64, 65, 121, 184, 189, 213, 260, 261
mystery 50, 53, 174, 184, 186, 189, 195, 198, 200
myth 32, 64, 95, 125, 210, 211

N

nativity 38, 132
Nativity 38, 82, 110, 121, 129
new beginning 16, 168, 190
New England 179, 207, 208, 216
New Jerusalem 51, 74, 151, 184, 187, 226
New Year's Day 32, 118, 155, 208, 211, 215
New Year's Eve 82, 212, 215
New York City 32, 57, 83, 209, 210, 212, 213
New York Historical Society 215
Nicaea 75, 97, 110, 111, 115
Nicene Council 75, 97
Nicholas 32, 125, 146, 147, 148, 149, 182, 214, 215, 260
Night Before Christmas 32, 148
Nightmare Before Christmas 68
Nimrod ... 24, 43, 44, 45, 46, 47, 48, 49, 52, 53, 54, 59, 60, 61, 62, 63, 64, 65, 66, 71, 72, 120, 127, 202, 211, 213, 243, 244
Nisan 97, 122
Nissenbaum, Stephen 34, 38, 58
Nordic 66
Norse 117
Norway 66
Noah 43, 45, 48, 59, 60, 63, 76, 243, 244, 245, 254
Noahiac commandments 75, 76
north 24, 50, 146, 147, 148, 205
North Pole 47
nostalgia 11, 46, 47

O

obey 15, 18, 23, 26, 37, 75, 88, 108, 131, 150, 156, 165, 184, 234, 236, 245, 259, 264
occult or occultic 55, 66, 67
offering(s) 38, 84, 85, 95, 110, 126, 152, 153, 154, 176, 178, 186, 191, 192, 193, 195, 203, 216, 217, 245, 246, 247, 248, 249, 250, 253, 254, 255, 256, 257, 259
oil 18, 67, 173, 236, 254
Old Saint Nick 57
One New Man 51, 73, 74, 75, 174, 184, 199, 238
Origen 86
ornaments 28, 126, 127, 167, 214
Osiris 54, 61, 62, 63, 64, 143, 213
Otis Jr., George 148

P

paganism 27, 65, 66, 71, 78, 81, 113, 179, 204
Pagan(s) 16, 28, 46, 61, 77, 89, 107, 110, 113, 119, 120, 121, 123, 125, 149, 150, 157, 164, 181
Paradise Tree 129
Passover 91, 96, 97, 99, 122, 137, 153, 172, 173, 177
patricians 57, 211
Paul 13, 37, 75, 78, 79, 82, 91, 97, 106, 134, 136, 144, 174, 199, 237, 255
peace 16, 20, 74, 95, 150, 153, 154, 169, 233, 243, 244, 249, 251, 258, 265
perfection 26, 46, 74, 80, 96, 106, 133, 186, 187, 232, 233
perpetual or perpetually 33, 97, 99, 182, 250
Peter 36, 121, 146, 170, 197, 198, 199, 259, 264
Pharisees 88, 172
Phrygian cap 109
pig 84, 86, 94, 96, 119, 120
Pilgrims 27, 106, 107, 180
Pintard, John 32, 212, 213, 214, 215
Plutarch 61
pollute 44, 50, 81, 95, 109, 123, 148

pontifex maximus 117
portico 24, 116, 128, 170
Presbyterians 106, 132, 180, 182
Presence 18, 22, 23, 24, 25, 48, 90, 139, 143, 144, 154, 158, 188, 189, 216, 235, 252
Price, Dr. Paula 44
pride 35, 48, 139, 140, 141, 263, 264
priesthood 95, 101, 106, 139, 158, 176, 185, 190, 193, 218, 226, 244, 245
primordial 12, 55, 66, 78, 83, 91, 177, 212, 215
profane 25, 38, 44, 45, 50, 127, 159, 217, 219
Promised Land 138, 142, 152, 153, 156, 242
Prophet's Dictionary, The 55
Protestant 27, 100, 129, 130, 132, 180, 181, 216
Ptah 54
pure 12, 13, 18, 20, 21, 23, 25, 27, 37, 39, 45, 88, 107, 111, 118, 158, 164, 184, 193, 212, 224, 235, 239, 241, 247, 258, 259, 261, 265
purification 150, 258
Puritans 27, 106, 107, 179, 180
purity 22, 23, 26, 77, 78, 88, 149, 178, 180, 204, 229, 252, 256, 264

Q

Quakers 206, 180, 181
Quartodeciman practice 97
queen 173, 227, 262
Queen of Heaven 64, 66, 68, 122, 123, 212
Queen Victoria 135

R

Ramban 45, 143
rash 105, 124
Rashi 59, 60, 143, 144, 237, 257
rebellion 44, 48, 59, 63, 64, 107, 155, 243

redemption 65, 174, 175, 178, 254, 258
reform.. 133, 135
Reformation 27, 31, 106, 107, 130, 131, 132, 133, 135,
    179, 180, 182, 188, 216
reindeer 56, 57, 125, 146, 148, 163, 214
repent... 24, 25, 92, 107, 258
repentance 92, 118, 131, 149, 164, 196
resources 28, 163, 164, 217, 224, 225, 226
Restad, Penne L. 207
resurrected body... 185, 186
resurrection 24, 99, 122, 184, 185, 186, 189, 190, 226,
    231, 241, 252, 254, 255, 259
revelation.. 142, 144, 164, 188, 197, 198, 200, 239
Revelation (The Book of) 11, 35, 64, 159, 194, 202, 213, 216, 223, 228, 230, 256
Revelation 18 .... 38, 59, 64, 135, 207, 265
Righteous Gentile... 75, 77
Roman holidays 80, 97, 106, 118, 119, 131, 139
Rome..... 71, 74, 80, 81, 82, 99, 109, 110, 114, 116, 117, 119, 120, 121, 171, 199,
    210
Rosh haShana.. 96, 173
royal 69, 70, 139, 158, 185, 190, 193, 226, 244
royalty 55, 70, 185, 188

S

Sabbath................................. 90, 96, 111, 112, 113, 114, 118, 159, 171, 175, 176
Sacaea 70
sacred 20, 25, 34, 38, 44, 45, 53, 54, 61, 62, 67, 87, 96, 104, 106, 115, 117,
    119, 127, 139, 152, 175, 176, 195, 238, 239, 253, 256, 258, 260
sacrifice 23, 43, 51, 65, 70, 71, 76, 77, 80, 81, 84, 87, 89, 91, 93,
    94, 96, 108, 109, 110, 119, 120, 131, 137, 139, 150, 152, 153, 154, 175, 177,
    178, 190, 191, 192, 193, 194, 201, 202, 203, 204, 216, 217, 244, 245, 246,
    247, 258, 259, 260, 263
salvation 88, 107, 122, 133, 184, 187, 196, 200, 229, 239, 245, 254, 255, 258
Samaria 204, 206
sanctification 133, 187, 237, 238, 258

sanctify 21, 27, 28, 38, 105, 106, 133, 237, 256, 261
sanctity 22, 79, 86, 96, 237, 252
sanctuary 24, 25, 55, 94, 128, 159, 176, 211
sanitize 37, 57
Santa Claus 31, 32, 47, 56, 57, 58, 83, 109, 125, 135, 146, 147, 148, 149, 155, 206, 210, 214, 215
Satan 35, 36, 45, 50, 67, 70, 71, 72, 112, 129, 146, 148, 203, 213, 214, 260
Satan's Grotto 148
Satanism 35
Satanists 149, 176
Saturn 70, 72, 82, 84, 101, 110, 117, 118, 119, 127, 145, 146, 147, 149, 202
Saturnalia ... 57, 69, 70, 71, 72, 82, 83, 84, 101, 110, 117, 118, 119, 145, 155, 212
Saturnus 70, 72
season 11, 12, 16, 17, 32, 34, 37, 38, 56, 57, 67, 71, 72, 74, 90, 117, 118, 126, 149, 152, 155, 163, 168, 175, 181, 183, 184, 185, 186, 196, 197, 204, 207, 208
seasoned 247, 248
second commandment 67, 125, 143, 205
secular 12, 25, 34, 38, 58, 81, 112, 184, 204
Seleucid 93, 94
self or selfish 20, 24, 35, 36, 52, 56, 57, 65, 97, 101, 110, 134, 138, 139, 140, 174, 197, 205, 219, 242, 250, 251, 260
self-deception 49
self-protection 12, 13, 35, 141
Semiramis 24, 64, 65, 71, 212
sensual 39, 45, 53, 57, 83, 101, 123, 153, 154, 155, 176, 201, 206, 251
serpent 36, 129, 132, 213
servant 25, 57, 69, 142, 149, 151, 155, 201, 228, 233, 237, 249, 250
sexual immorality 76, 85, 155
Shaman or shamanistic 57, 128, 147, 148
Shavuot (i.e. Pentecost) 96, 173
shekinah 22, 23, 24, 25, 188
Shem 48, 59, 60, 61, 63, 64, 242, 243, 244, 245
Shinar 46, 52, 60, 243
shopping 32, 83, 101, 109, 214
shrine 24, 31, 33, 34, 49, 83, 127, 211, 213
Siberia 148

Sinai 90, 105, 137, 139, 142, 143, 144, 145, 157, 188, 219, 246
sincere 16, 19, 21, 33, 59, 135, 150, 180, 244, 259
slaughter.. 44, 62, 126, 193
snare 100, 103, 104, 105, 123, 124, 132, 216
Sol 114, 116, 121
Sol Invictus 82, 111, 114
sola scriptura 130, 131
solar... 53, 54, 82, 97, 99, 112, 116, 121
Solomon 107, 109, 170, 188, 205, 249, 256
Solomon's Colonnade 16, 170
Solstice 15, 16, 58, 66, 71, 101, 109, 120, 121, 126, 127, 128, 130, 213, 215
sons of God 29, 184, 186, 187
sorcery.. 32, 55, 56, 59, 66, 134, 207
Sosigenes.. 99
spell 38, 55, 56, 155, 210
spending 33, 34, 83, 226, 234
spiders 15, 165, 166, 167
spirit of Christmas.. 34, 125, 135, 151
Spirit of the living God 21, 29, 46, 111, 135, 151, 166, 186, 224, 261
spiritual realm 72, 90, 167
spoilt.. 57, 215
spotless...... 13, 18, 20, 21, 27, 37, 39, 45, 111, 118, 150, 164, 184, 193, 241, 247,
    261, 265
spring feasts 172, 177
St. Nicholas Day 33, 214, 215
stockings 57, 112, 126, 135, 168, 257
stone 26, 56, 69, 126, 141, 158, 169, 185, 187, 188, 189, 190
strength............................. 27, 35, 44, 51, 88, 89, 141, 169, 189, 193,
    217, 223, 224, 225, 226, 227, 236, 264, 265
stubbornness.. 107, 178
submit.. 74, 88, 136, 225, 234
Sukkot (i.e. Tabernacles).. 96, 173
Sumeria 52, 211
sun god(s)........................... 24, 38, 52, 53, 54, 58, 82, 83, 111, 114, 116,
    120, 121, 127, 128, 147, 211, 213, 216
sun god worship 32, 52
Sunday.. 97, 99, 111, 122, 177, 182, 241

supernatural 14, 17, 48, 55, 56, 66, 74, 156, 167, 170, 186, 189, 190, 197, 198, 252, 253
superstition 66, 67, 84, 115, 119, 132, 150, 181
surrender 51, 193, 234
Sweden 66
swine 84, 95, 96

T

tabernacle 22, 43, 139, 151, 187, 188, 193, 237, 238, 249, 252, 256
Tabernacles (The Feast of) 172, 173, 206, 218
talisman 67, 83, 129
Talmud 25
Tammuz 24, 65, 71, 101, 109, 120, 122, 127, 147, 211, 212
Ten Commandments 89, 124, 143, 144, 157, 171, 172
Terah 48, 59, 60
Tertullian 84, 118, 121, 122
Teutonic 117, 135
Thanksgiving 32, 68, 94, 163, 208
third day 106, 241, 249
throne 22, 70, 109, 147, 158, 194, 195, 205, 207, 244, 245, 256
Torah 91, 96, 250, 252
totem 115, 135
touchstone 178
Tower of Babel 46, 48, 50, 53, 59
tradition(s) 11, 12, 25, 28, 38, 39, 47, 50, 56, 57, 58, 60, 61, 65, 67, 68, 69, 71, 79, 81, 82, 83, 97, 103, 104, 105, 106, 107, 109, 113, 118, 126, 127, 128, 129, 130, 133, 147, 149, 157, 172, 200, 204, 211, 215, 243, 260
Tree of Knowledge 129
Tree of Life 79, 129
trial(s) 259, 260
tribulation(s) 37, 255

U

unbelief 125, 156, 164, 165
unholy 20, 27, 106, 131
United States 20, 66, 69, 106, 135, 203, 206, 209
unruly 154, 155

V

virgin birth.. 71
Virgin Mother... 65
Virginia... 207, 208
virgins 173, 236, 239
vision(s)... 14, 114, 197, 198, 230, 249

W

wanton.. 154, 155
wassailing.. 69
Way, The 74, 77, 84, 116, 199
wayward wife... 251, 258
wed 17, 189, 241, 242, 260
wedding................................ 17, 18, 28, 153, 172, 227, 228, 229, 230,
   231, 232, 233, 236, 237, 239, 240, 241, 249, 260, 262
white lies 56, 155
Wiccan 46, 66
wilderness 22, 43, 89, 137, 156, 188, 193, 237, 249, 250, 256
wine. 67, 81, 84, 126, 146, 172, 182, 241, 242, 245, 246, 247, 248, 249, 250, 264
wineskin 182
winter 12, 16, 31, 53, 57, 72, 117, 119, 121, 169, 170, 172, 173, 211, 212, 214
winter solstice 15, 16, 58, 66, 71, 101, 109, 120, 121, 126, 127, 128, 213, 215
witchcraft 56, 57, 63, 76, 107
women.. 24, 184, 212, 238, 256, 257
wreaths 33

Y

year 11, 13, 16, 17, 34, 48, 57, 66, 67, 68, 71, 72, 83, 90, 92, 94, 97, 98, 99, 100, 109, 110, 112, 114, 115, 118, 119, 122, 126, 147, 155, 164, 175, 176, 183, 191, 208, 215, 217, 265
yieldedness 234
Yule 65, 66, 117, 128
Yule log 65, 66, 67, 68, 71, 128, 215
Yuletide 11, 65
Yuletide season 32, 65, 83, 212, 215

Z

Zadok 158, 159
Zeus 94, 95, 120
ziggurats 24
Zion 51, 148, 176, 189, 247
Zoroaster 214

Not Your Typical
GLOSSARY
ೞ

Akiti—the greatest agricultural holiday in ancient Babylon as well as Mesopotamia's most elaborate religious holiday. It reaffirmed the supremacy of Babylon's great god, Marduk, and offered thanksgiving for the fertility of the lands he ruled. The *Akiti* (in the Sumerian language) lasted for twelve days, and it was called a new year festival. Significantly, a couple of Sumerian documents speak of a symbolic ritual where the Babylonian king made love to the goddess Ishtar, which took place in his palace on New Year's Eve. Ishtar is just another name for the Babylonian Queen of Heaven. She goes by hundreds of names, but primarily her name is Semiramis. See ISHTAR, NIMROD, and SEMIRAMIS.

Antichrist—**a:** one who denies or opposes Christ; **b:** specifically, a great antagonist expected to fill the world with wickedness but to be conquered forever by Christ at His second coming. A false Christ, i.e., Messiah (Dan. 7:25; 1 John 2:18-22, 2 John 1:7).

Antiochus Epiphanes IV—Seleucid general and king (i.e., emperor) in charge of the Holy Land during the Maccabaean revolt. History infamously classifies him as an antichrist as prophesied by Daniel. The world-impacting movement he promoted originated with Alexander the Great. It was called Hellenism. In 168 BC, Antiochus Epiphanes sacrificed a pig on God's altar in Jerusalem and put a statue of Zeus in the sanctuary, which dedicated God's temple to the worship of Zeus in honor of Zeus' birthday—the ancient winter solstice December twenty-fifth. Antiochus then forced God's people to bow before the false Greek god under penalty of death. Many innocent people were massacred. The survivors were heavily taxed. This type of religious persecution was unknown up to its time. See ANTICHRIST.

Apis—The oldest and most popular object of worship in Egypt was probably the sacred bull called the Apis. Mankind has not been able to trace why Apis attained such an honor. It appears that the sacred bull was primordially an incarnation of Nimrod as Marduk. The ancients believed that the powerful bull represented the personality of the king. It is recorded that the first early king (Nimrod) wore bull's horns, which is the predecessor of our modern-day crowns. Also, note that the first idolatrous "Bel" or "Baal," which means owner or lord, was originally identified as the sun. Marduk was given the epithet Bel (i.e., Baal). In Egypt, the first Apis bull was considered to be an incarnation of the sun god Ptah, symbolizing the creator of the universe and a master of destiny. Thus, it was believed that in Apis dwelt the soul of Ptah. Later the Apis became widely known as the incarnation of the sun god Osiris. Alive, an Apis bull was conveyed to its sanctuary in Memphis on a boat housed in a specially built golden cabin; in death, his head was coated with gold. It is most likely that Aaron fashioned his golden calf after the likeness of the Apis, which has a more ancient and automatic connection to the great Chaldean god Saturn, too. See GOLDEN CALF, MARDUK, NIMROD, and OSIRIS.

Apparition—At this level of supernatural vision, a person sees a being that literally appears to him or her seemingly "out of thin air." This appearance may be observed with the natural eyes either open or closed, and may even be a tangible experience. In some cases, it may be perceived physically—the being's presence may be felt—without being obviously seen. It is an appearing, a visiting, but not necessarily a sighting. An appearance or apparition is different from a pictorial vision in that it is an actual—perhaps tangible and audible—visitation occurring outside of the person. These appearances can be "interactive" as well (Gen. 32:24-31; Josh. 5:13-15; Acts 1:3).

Attendants—ones who perform pleasing service on the Lord's behalf, i.e., servants (Matt. 22:13).

Baal—the first idolatrous "Bel" or "Baal," which means owner or lord, was originally identified as the sun. It was an essential principle of the Babylonian system that the Sun or Baal or Tammuz was the one and only god. Marduk was given the epithet Bel (i.e., Baal). It was believed that human sacrifice to Baal held the key to prosperity. Therefore, selfish people desiring to live in ease brought their firstborn child to the high priest, where scholars say the child would be offered as a burnt offering to the deity. Recently, archaeologists unearthed a baal cemetery containing the remains of more than twenty thousand children. "I will cut off from this place every remnant of Baal . . . those who bow down and swear by the LORD and who also swear by Molech" (Zeph. 1:4-5). Since the biblical writers did not intend to teach the Canaanite religion, we know more about Baal's roles, consorts, and cult from the extra-biblical literature than from the OT; but the picture of Baal presented in the OT comports well with the extra-biblical sources. He also was called Haddu (Hadad). He is above all the storm god who gives the sweet rain that revives vegetation. Dry years were attributed to his temporary captivity or even death. But at his revivification, fields, flocks, and families became productive. In addition, he is a war god and fertility deity, who consorts with Anat (is later equated with Astarte). Both by reciting the myth of his role in reviving life at the autumn new year festival and by magical ritual of sacred marriage represented in the cult by the king, the queen, and a priestess, the West Semites hoped to ensure the earth's fertility. (This ritual is witnessed to in Babylon but not clearly in Canaan.) Archaeological cultic objects with exaggerated sexual features, as well as the myths themselves, support the OT notices about the degraded moral features associated with the cult. Throughout the period of the judges, Israel succumbed to this infectious cult (Judg. 2:11; 6:25) and had to be rescued from its tragic consequences by Yahweh's judges. During the period of the Omrides, baal worship became the official state religion of the northern kingdom (1 Kings 16:31). Israel's miracles by Elijah and Elisha served as a polemic for God against the very powers attributed to this pagan nature deity, namely, fire (1 Kings 18:17.; 2 Kings 1:9–16), rain (1 Kings 17:1; 18:41–46), food (1 Kings 17:1–6, 8–16; 2 Kings 4:1); children (2 Kings 4:14–17); revivification (1 Kings 17:17–23; 2 Kings 4:18–37; 13:20–22). But their miracles did not rid the land of this degraded cult, and it brought about the captivity of the northern kingdom (Hosea). It also infiltrated the southern kingdom (2 Kings 11:18; 21:2); and in spite of Josiah's reform (2 Kings 23:4), brought the nation into exile (Ezek. 16; 23, etc.). The Hosea discourse describes how Israel, who received gifts of grain and oil from YHWH, used these for the worship of Baal (Hos. 2:8). The chapter fairly turns on the term *ba-al*, not only in the mention of the Canaanite god(s) (e.g., Hos. 2:8, 3, 17), but in the imagery throughout of God as Israel's husband. Israel will call the Lord her husband (*ish*, Hos. 2:16; cf. 2:2, 7) and no longer call him, apparently along with the list of other gods, my Baal (*ba-al*). God's supremacy over Baal is constantly affirmed. However, man's preoccupation from then and until this day is rather with sex and technology than with devotion to the almighty God of history, who is also the covenant God. See BEL, MOLECH, and SUN GODS.

Babel—is the term synonymous with a confusion of sounds or voices. Babel is the ancient city where the Lord confused words' meanings, and seventy nations with differing languages were forged, because the people of Babel tried to build a tower of their own design that would get them into heaven (Gen. 11:1-9). Archaeological evidence indicates that this was a spectacular pyramid-shaped structure (i.e., ziggurat). The Tower of Babel was built on a plain in Shinar. Their leader was Nimrod. The primitive Hebraic root for the word "Babel" means to overflow or to mix. As the people scattered from Babel with their different languages, they used different names for Nimrod (Tammuz, Osiris, etc) and Semiramis (Ishtar, Isis, etc). See ZIGGURAT.

Babylon—The ancient city in the southern region of Babylonia, which came to be considered Babylon, was called Chaldea. It was the place where sorcery and idolatry were institutionalized. Nimrod duplicated Satan's heavenly rebellion on earth by informing the assembly of gods, as well as the then-known world, that the center of the cosmos was Babylon. The essence of Babylon is mixture and confusion. It's the place where a group of people, spearheaded by Nimrod and Semiramis, began to mix the sacred with the profane indiscriminately, which brought confusion. Babylon can be equated to the kingdom of self or to the kingdom of this world (Rev. 14:8; 18). See BABEL, CHALDEA, NIMROD, and SEMIRAMIS.

Bel—meaning lord or master in the Akkadian language. This name signified the god Marduk. It is the biblical equivalent of Baal—the name given to the chief god of the Canaanites. See BAAL or MARDUK.

Biblical Feasts—These are the seven feasts of the Lord (recognized by the Jews), plus Purim and Chanukah, because both of these feasts are in the Christian Bible. Purim is detailed in the book of Esther. Chanukah is in John 10:22-23, and tells how Jesus walked in Solomon's Colonnade speaking about miracles during the Feast of Dedication (another name for Chanukah). Traditionally, Purim and Chanukah are not considered to be feasts of the Lord, because they are not in the Torah. Also, the main focus of these two Biblical feasts isn't the Messiah, but the journey God's people take to become the bride of Christ, i.e., coming out of Babylon, resisting the antichrist, cleansing our temples, etc. See BRIDE OF CHRIST, CHANUKAH, and FEASTS OF THE LORD.

Bikkurim—means "First Fruits" in Hebrew. The Feast of First Fruits is a feast of the Lord celebrated on the seventeenth of *Nisan/Aviv* (Lev. 23:9-14). It is literally the day that Jesus rose from the dead. Yeshua died as the Passover Lamb of God on the fourteenth of *Nisan/Aviv*. He was hidden in the ground on *Hag ha Matzah* (i.e., the Feast of Unleavened Bread) on the fifteenth as the broken bread without sin. Yeshua said in Matthew 12:40 that He had to be in the ground three days and three nights; therefore, he rose on the seventeenth. "Now the Messiah has been raised from the dead, the First Fruits of those who sleep" (1 Cor. 15:20). On First Fruits, Noah's ark came up out of the waters and rested safely on Mount Ararat. On First Fruits, the Jews passed through the parted waters of the Red Sea, and came up safely on the other side. On First Fruits, the Jews were saved from certain death in Persia when Haman was hung on his own gallows. On First Fruits, Yeshua resurrected conquering death forever.

Bowing down to the sun—is the most detestable practice in God's eyes that drives the Lord's glory from His temple (Ezek.8:6, 16). It was performed by the people intimate with God, as represented by about twenty-five men who were between the porch and the altar, with their backs to the temple of the Lord and their faces towards the east. They prostrated themselves toward the sun. Here God's close and personal friends were unmoved by their idolatry, because they didn't see sin as God does. See CHRISTMAS and CHRISTMAS TREE.

Bride of Christ—the wife of the Messiah (i.e., the heavenly Bridegroom), who makes herself ready (i.e., clothed) for the marriage supper of the Lamb through her righteous deeds done according to the King's directives (Rev. 19:6-7). The bride of Christ is a pure and spotless body of believers made up of many members. She is also referred to as the city called the New Jerusalem (Rev. 21:1-10). See BIBLICAL FEASTS and NEW JERUSALEM.

Chaldea—arose from Sumeria and Biblical Accad. It's an ancient city in the southern region of the Persian Gulf's Babylonia that came to be considered Babylon. Chaldea was not only the seat of earliest sun worship, but it was also the primordial center of sorcery. For clarity's sake, one can substitute "Chaldea" for "Babylonia" when we read Scripture, but when the Bible designates "Chaldea," it is more precisely pointing out the place of sorcery and the place where sun god worship and its associated "land of merchants" status originated (Jer. 50:10; 51:24; Ezek. 16:29; 23:15). See BABYLON and LAND OF MERCHANTS.

Chaldean—Babylonian experts in divination and magic. They were the highest priestly caste of the ancient pagan world. Their superior occultic powers and mysterious knowledge were famous throughout the ancient world. Renowned for sophisticated systems of divination; they used various manipulative means of accessing supernatural knowledge, like: omens, augury, dream interpretation, spell binding and casting, horoscopy, and sorcery. Magic was their main divinatory tool. Magic includes sorcery, witchcraft, incantations, enchantments, wizardry, spells and spell casting, and demonism of all kinds. The Chaldean mind-set was set toward nature worship. How it operated and its times and seasons of operation were essential to the success of their magic formulae. See DIVINATION and MAGIC.

Chanukah—is considered a rabbinical feast by Jews. It is a biblical feast for Christians, because Jesus celebrated it (John 10:22-23). The theme of Chanukah is: "... Not by might, nor by power, but by My spirit, says the Lord of hosts" (Zech. 4:6). Judah the Maccabee and his band of faithful men overcame overwhelming odds when they fought the first guerilla war in history to preserve their culture and religion from annihilation. Had this small, righteous remnant not taken their courageous stand against the Antichrist (i.e., Antiochus Epiphanes IV of the world-dominating Seleucid Empire), both Judaism and Christianity most likely would not exist today. Chanukah is an annual eight-day winter festival that honors the restoration of divine worship in Jerusalem's temple after it was defiled by heathens. When the Jewish people cleansed the temple from idols, they found only enough oil to light the temple's seven-branch menorah for one day. In faith, the Maccabees lit the little they had. Miraculously, the Temple Menorah (i.e., Golden Candlestick) burned for eight days until perfectly purified oil was available. Chanukah also can be spelled Hanukkah. It has several other names, including: the Feast of Dedication, the Feast of Lights and the Feast of Miracles.

Chemosh—pagan god of prosperity worshipped by the Moabites that was the same cast-iron, pot-bellied god of their kin, the Ammonites, who was worshipped by the name of Molech. At the time of the winter solstice on the ancient calendar, the Moabites had a public child mass. Their priests stoked the iron image of the enthroned Chemosh with wood and burning pitch, which turned the idol into a cherry-red furnace. Moabite people made long lists of their desires, and recited them to the god of prosperity just before they put their infant children into the red-hot lap of their god with his Phrygian cap. As the babies were incinerated during the December twenty-fifth child mass, the people were assured that their sacrifices would be rewarded in the coming year. Solomon built an idolatrous high place for Chemosh on the hill east of Jerusalem (1 Kings 11:7). See MOLECH and PHRYGIAN CAP.

Christmas—Bi-polar term Americans use to discuss a: (1) religious nativity—the events surrounding Jesus' birth (2) secular celebration—annual traditions that pre-date Christ's birth as characteristics of midwinter celebrations: the lights, the evergreen decorations, the gift giving, the music, the food, the chance to get together with family and friends, and the special feeling of warmth that comes with the season. From the very beginning, Christmas was formed by mixing preexisting winter celebrations with Christian themes; therefore, it can never be a pure spiritual holiday.

Christmas Day—Winter holiday celebrated by ninety-seven to ninety-eight percent of America, as well as ninety-five percent of the world. Its most immediate predecessor, Mithra's Winter Festival, was assimilated into the ecclesiastical calendar when political factions in Christ's church fixed it as a "holy" day (i.e., holiday) in AD 379. The first recorded evidence of Christmas actually taking place on December twenty-fifth isn't found until the time of Constantine in AD 336. Christmas became the traditional celebration of Jesus' birth after the fourth century church assigned Jesus the human quality of a birthday, but *Catholic Encyclopedia* admits that: The Nativity of the Unconquered Sun (i.e., Mithra's Winter Festival) has a strong claim on the responsibility for our December date. Constantine's original piety was associated with the sun; and pagans would have recognized their own solar cults in the church's practice of orienting their cathedrals to the east, worshiping on "Sun Day," and celebrating the birth of the deity at the winter solstice. It had become common practice in the fifth century for worshipers entering St. Peter's Basilica in Rome to turn at the door, put their backs to God's altar, and bow down to worship the rising sun. (Refer to Ezek. 8). Even today, pagans still celebrate the Winter Solstice when they mark Christmas. Our modern Christmas day was forged in the city that has been known as the world's land of the merchants—New York City. Upper-class New Yorkers (e.g., John Pintard, Washington Irving, and Clement Clarke Moore) collectively invented the first traditions of Christmas that American society, and even the world, now goes by. In the 1820s to 1840s, they gave the new cult of domesticity its celebration of hearth and home. See MITHRA and MITHRISM.

Christmas season—Its most immediate predecessor is the Roman Saturnalia celebrated from mid-December to the first of January, which was assimilated into the Christian church in the fourth century. It's also called the Yuletide season. Today in America, people participate in the Christmas season by shopping; wrapping presents; baking cookies; having parties; attending musicals, pageants, and plays; decorating homes and Christmas trees; singing Christmas carols; sending Christmas cards; and giving to charitable causes; amongst other activities. See SATURNALIA and YULE.

Christmas tree—the evergreen element, which has been displayed at the turn of the winter solstice since ancient times, literally links ancient and modern traditions. In ages gone by, evergreen, fir, or palm trees have been used in conjunction with celebrating various pagan sun gods' birthdays. Babylon marked the beginning of tree or creation worship, and it has become commonplace among most pagan religions today (Rom. 1:21-32). An old Babylonian tale tells of an evergreen tree, which sprang out of a dead tree stump. The old stump symbolized the dead Nimrod, the new evergreen tree symbolized that Nimrod had come back to life again in Tammuz. The Christmas tree was equally common in pagan Egypt as in pagan Rome. The people in Jeremiah's day were making an idol out of a tree. Although Jeremiah 10:3-4 refers to making an actual statue, it's also the most enlightening scripture in regards to a Christmas tree: "For the customs of the peoples are worthless; they cut a tree out of the forest, and a craftsman shapes it with his chisel. They adorn it with silver and gold; they fasten it with hammer and nails so it will not totter." The Christmas tree recapitulates the idea of tree worship, with gilded nuts and balls on a tree symbolizing the sun. Today, on the birthday of the sun gods, most Christians bow down in front of a tree hung with sun images (i.e., ornaments) to exchange gifts with one another in honor of the ancient commemoration of the Nativity of the Sun, without realizing its idolatrous origins.

Clean—**a:** free from dirt or pollution; **b:** free from contamination or disease; **c:** unadulterated, pure; **d:** having no interior flaws visible; **e:** free from moral corruption or sinister connection of any kind; **f:** thorough, complete; **g:** unencumbered; **h:** characterized by clarity and precision; **i:** habitually neat (Ps. 24:3-4; 51:10; Heb. 10:22).

Combine—**a:** to bring into such close relationship as to obscure individual characters: MERGE; **b:** to cause to unite into a single expression: INTERMIX, BLEND; **c:** to become one; **d:** to act together *syn* join.

Commandments—There are 613 commandments of the Torah (i.e., first five books of the Bible). A person cannot keep every commandment, because there are different commandments applicable to men versus women versus children versus animals... For example, there are laws involving temple service (Levitical priests and sacrifices); animals (kosher); concerning the land; Sabbath, fasts, and worship; moral laws having to deal with relationships (how to act toward man); holiness laws (how to act toward God); etc. Yeshua says that the new covenant is the Torah commandments written on your heart (the same ones), which are the simplest things in your house and His. The common sense of right and wrong has been written in people's hearts. The Torah's name means "the teachings," and its object is to help people know God. Your attitude toward God determines what the term "commandments" means to you. Commandments will either be burdens to disobedient hearts or instructions to obedient hearts. The Torah never teaches that it can save you. Remember that it was Abraham's faith that was counted as righteousness.

Constantine—the sole Roman emperor in the fourth century, who sought to unify a divided empire by "Christianizing" it. He directed the Christian church leaders to convene the Council of Nicaea in AD 325, and forced the bishops to resolve the Asian church difference in Easter from the Roman-African church, by declaring the Quartodeciman practice of the Asian church heretical. In AD 312, Constantine was said to have a "conversion" experience through a battle-eve vision of the cross at the Milvian Bridge, which was not reliably recounted by Constantine until he convened the Nicaean Council. For years after his supposed conversion, Constantine continued to pay his public honors to the sun. In fact, he was a worshiper of the sun god *Sol Invictus Mithra*, which was honored on Constantine's coins until 321. Although Constantine greatly enriched the church on earth physically and was instrumental in stopping Christian persecution, he did not show many signs of a born-again disposition while alive. Christian scholars have exercised much in trying to explain Constantine's attempt to immortalize himself as the reincarnation of the god Apollo or Sol with an image wearing the rayed crown of the sun-god after his supposed conversion. Another monument to Constantine's sun worship practices exists in that in many Roman churches still contain well-preserved mithraeums in their vaulted burial crypts. Never mind the fact that Constantine had the Vatican built atop the hill where the Mithras cult worshiped the sun.

Divination—the art or practice that seeks to foresee or foretell future events or discover hidden knowledge, usually by the interpretation of omens or manipulative means of accessing supernatural knowledge, like: augury, dream interpretation, magic, spell binding and casting, horoscopy, and sorcery. See MAGIC and SORCERY.

Easter—is a spring festival, commemorating Christ's resurrection, which is named after the pagan goddess Ishtar. Most reference books say that the name "Easter" is derived from the Teutonic goddess of spring—Eastre. Although this relationship exists, the origin of the name and the goddess are far more ancient. It goes all the way back to Babylon. When the people scattered from the tower of Babel, they used different names for Semiramis, including Ishtar (originally pronounced "Easter"). In other lands, she was called Eostre, Astarte, Ostera, Eastre, the wife of Baal, Ashtoreth, Queen of Heaven, etc. In the pagan mystery cults, their "savior" Tammuz, was worshiped with various rites during the spring season. According to the legends, after Tammuz was killed by a wild boar, he went into the underworld. But through the weeping of his mother and those who joined her in lamenting for Tammuz, he mystically was revived (i.e., resurrected) each spring and brought forth vegetation. Easter has as much pagan-Christian mixture as all the Roman holidays. Refer to CONSTANTINE and QUARTODECIMAN PRACTICE to see that the exact date that God established His primary spring feast—Passover (as perpetual in Scripture)—was opposed by the official church. See ISHTAR, SEMIRAMIS, TAMMUZ and VIRGIN MOTHER.

Egypt—a metaphor for the world or slavery. Its land is named after the patriarch of Nimrod's clan—Ham. The "land of Ham" is actually a poetic name for Egypt in the Bible (Ps. 106:22). Mizraim also is the scriptural name for the land of Egypt, being derived from the name of Ham's son (Gen. 10:6). To the Egyptian there was no god of higher standing than the sun god. A revered animal in Egypt was considered to be an incarnation of that particular god; therefore, the sun god and the sacred bull were synonymous.

Essential Commandments for All Believers—are abstinence requirements that bind believers in holy matrimony to their heavenly Bridegroom (i.e., the Messiah). Observing these essentials actually demonstrates God's people's rejection of idolatry. The four things prohibited in the Apostolic Decree of Acts 15 (I call the Essential Commandments for All Believers) have connections with pagan customs and traditions. They are listed three times in Scripture: Acts 15:20; Acts 15:29; and Acts 21:25. Both Jewish and Gentile believers are called to abstain from: (1) things contaminated by idols, (2) blood, (3) what is strangled, and (4) fornication. These abstinence requirements for holiness for the Lord's living stones were the *only* burdens that the Holy Spirit led the Jerusalem Council to place on the nations (i.e., Gentiles) so that they could become part of God's household. In the end-times, the steadfastness of the saints is described as those: "who keep the commandments of God and the faith of Jesus" (Rev. 14:12). Also refer to Revelation 12:17.

Feasts of the Lord—are God's occasions for celebration described in Leviticus 23: Passover (*Pesach*), The Feast of Unleavened Bread (*Hag HaMatzah*), The Feast of First Fruits (*Bikkurim*), Pentecost (*Shavuot*), The Feast of Trumpets (*Rosh*

HaShana), The Day of Atonement (*Yom Kippur*), and The Feast of Tabernacles (*Sukkot*). Significantly, the Lord says: "They are My feasts" (Lev. 23:2). The feasts of the Lord are God's appointed or exact times that set the years for mankind. The Hebraic primitive root for the word "feast," *ya ad*, implies that the Lord is summoning His people to meet Him at His stated time, so He can direct us into a certain position to engage us for marriage (i.e., to be betrothed). The feasts of the Lord teach us about the Messiah, which they shadow; and they set forth the pattern of heavenly things on earth (Heb. 8:1-5; 9:8-23; Exod. 25:8-9, 40; Ezek. 43:1-6, 10-12). The spring festivals speak of the Messiah's first coming; the fall feasts are rehearsals for His second. The Zadok priesthood, who symbolizes those who remain faithful to the end, will teach God's people to keep the Lord's statutes in all His appointed feasts (Ezek. 44:15-31).

Genu-wine—is a prophetic term that's a playful combination of the words genuine and wine. To be genuine is to be sincere and honest; to be free from hypocrisy or pretense; to actually have the reputed qualities of the character of Christ. Wine is made from pressing the grapes that abides in the Vine (i.e., Jesus). Communion wine is representative of Jesus' blood shed for us. The acceptance of the cross allows Christ's atoning sacrifice to wash away our sins. "Blood" is also a term for family; therefore the beautiful fermented beverage poured out to a lost and dying world is His very essence—His own family. Genu-wine believers will manifest the incredibly loving and perfect character of our Lord Jesus Christ. Genu-wine is a golden new wine that flows like a river of living water.

Golden Calf—made from the golden earrings of the Israelites thirty-nine days after God visited His people at Mount Sinai. The Israelites turned their hearts back to Egypt (Acts 7:39) when Aaron fabricated this idolatrous image. They rejoiced in the work of their hands (Acts 7:41). It often has been held that the golden calf worshiped by the Israelites was an imitation of the worship of the Apis bull of Memphis, Egypt (Exod. 32; Deut. 9:8-21; Neh. 9:18; Ps. 106:19; Hos. 8:5-6; Acts 7:39-43). Jeroboam duplicated and doubled Aaron's golden calf. He set up his golden images, his altars, and his self-appointed priests at his own worship centers on the extremities of his kingdom—Dan in the north and Bethel in the south (1 Kings 12:25-33).

Hellenisation—(or **Hellenization**, *hellenismos* in Greek) The process of Hellenising non-Greeks began before the establishment of the Macedonian Greek empire. It was greatly accelerated by this important event. The first result of the conquests of Philip and Alexander was the incorporation of Macedonia and its hinterland into the sphere of Hellenic culture. There followed the superficial Hellenisation of the kingdoms of Asia and Egypt, especially of the existing cities and of the newly established colonial cities, which were under the supervision of Macedonian Greece and the populations of which were partly Hellenised with the adoption of the Greek language and customs. Through mixed marriages there very quickly arose a semi-Greek world. The development took different forms in the different territories. In the kingdom of the Ptolemies, the term "Greek" was reserved for the ruling caste, which maintained its traditional language, culture, and religion in the new land. In Asia, however, there was a wider acceptance of the culture of the Ἕλληνες by native non-Hellenes. Here the number of new cities was greater, and these became centers for the Hellenisation of the surrounding districts. There was an increasing integration of those born Hellenes with Hellenes of barbarian origin who had accepted ἑλληνισμός, i.e., the Greek language, culture, and religion. Almost as important as the Hellenisation of the East is the spread of Greek culture and language to the West.

Holiness—the quality or state of being holy: SANCTIFICATION (2 Chron. 31:18; Ps. 93:5; Eph. 4:24; Heb. 12:10).

Holy—**a:** devoted entirely to the deity or the work of the deity; **b:** having a divine quality (Lev. 11:44; 21:8; Ezek. 43:12; 44:23-24; Rom. 12:1; 1 Cor. 3:17; 1 Pet. 1:15; 2:5, 9; Rev. 21:2).

Idol—**a:** a representation or symbol of an object of worship; **b:** impostor or a false god; **c:** a form or appearance that's visible, but without substance; **d:** any object of extreme devotion.

Idolatry—Worship, devotion, or veneration of other gods—i.e., objects, symbols, people, accomplishments, or anything shown to be superior to the One True God and His desires in a person's life. Abraham Joshua Heschel articulates: "Pagans project their consciousness of God into a visible image or associate Him with a phenomenon in nature, with a thing of space. In the Ten Commandments, the Creator of the universe identifies Himself by an event in history, by an event in time, the liberation of the people from Egypt, and proclaims: 'Thou shalt not make unto thee any graven image or any likeness of any thing that is in heaven above, or that is in the earth, or that is in the water under the earth'" Anyone living a life that produces idolatry will not inherit the kingdom of God (1 Cor. 6:9-10). See ESSENTIAL COMMANDMENTS FOR ALL BELIEVERS and GOLDEN CALF.

Ishtar— (West Semitic **Astarte**). The most popular deity of ancient Mesopotamia (i.e., Babylon). Ishtar was considered to be a moon goddess and represented the power of sexual attraction and the carnal pleasure that proceeds from it. This goddess was focused only on immediate sensual gratification, so she was neither a goddess of marriage or childbirth. Her sexual appetite was inexhaustible and relationship with men short-term. Legion were her lovers. She had to have her own way at any cost. The priestesses, who served in her shrines, were considered to be sacred prostitutes. See EASTER, SEMIRAMIS, and VIRGIN MOTHER.

Land of Merchants, The—Title given to Babylon, specifically Chaldea in Ezekiel 16:29-31, where God's people multiply their harlotry against the Lord God, but they are not satisfied. It can be recognized by its shrines that are built at the beginning of every street and in the high place in every town square (think about the evergreen boughs, wreaths, and trees decorating your city at Christmas time). The harlotry associated with the land of merchants has a general societal disdain for frugally spending money when it comes to its worship. See CHALDEA and CHRISTMAS.

Laver—The name "Bronze Laver" is actually a misnomer, because the Hebrews record that it was made out of copper. The laver was an open circular copper basin that was set upon a copper base that had two spouts at the bottom through which the water would flow keeping it from becoming stagnant. The laver was made exclusively from the brightly polished sheets of copper that women used as mirrors in Egypt. When the call went out for freewill contributions, devout women, who used to come to Moses' tent to sit at his feet like Mary did with Jesus, came with their copper mirrors and piled them up at Moses' dwelling (which was God's dwelling place prior to the Tent of Meeting being built; Exod. 33:7). God not only told Moses to accept these precious mirrors, but they were also to be used exclusively to fabricate the laver. The Bible doesn't give the specific size of the laver, due to that fact that every single mirror had to go into fashioning it—no matter how big it would become. Notably, these devout women could no longer gaze upon themselves with any vanity, because they had to fix their eyes upon the laver to see themselves. The laver represents the devout women (i.e., the bride of Christ) exclusively fixing their eyes upon the Author and Perfecter of their faith (Heb. 12:2). Placed between the Brazen (i.e., copper) Altar and God's Sanctuary, the priests washed their hands and feet in the laver before ministering in the tabernacle. Its purpose was for holiness and sanctity rather than for actual cleanliness (Exod. 30:17-21; 38:8; 40:30-32).

Living Stones—The holy city, the New Jerusalem, that comes out of the spiritual realm is constructed with God's living stones. "As you come to Him, the living Stone—rejected of men but chosen by God and precious to Him—you also, like living stones, are built into a spiritual house to be a holy priesthood, offering spiritual sacrifices acceptable to God through Jesus Christ" (1 Pet. 2:4-5). Whether one considers a stone temple built in Jerusalem or the living stones built of human beings in the New Jerusalem, the fundamental building material for God's temple starts out as organic. God has been, and currently is, building a lasting temple of living stones where "the tabernacle of God is among men, and He shall dwell among them, and they shall be His people, and God Himself shall be their God" (Rev. 21:3). The Essential Commandments for All Believers were the *only* burden the Holy Spirit led the Jerusalem Council to place on the living stones in the nations. They are heavenly requirements for holy matrimony, which are the abstinence requirements to live a holy life in order to preserve the sanctity of holy matrimony to our heavenly Bridegroom. Not one of His living stones will be left standing (Matt. 24:2), because all will be humbled.

Lord of Misrule—was appointed on All Hallow's Eve (Oct. 31) for the Christmas to come. Known also as the "Master of Merry Disport," "Abbot of Unreason," and "Christmas King." The man acting as the Lord of Misrule was the personification of the spirit of disorder, fun, and merriment. This jester was the principle ingredient in the medieval celebration of Christmas. This servant-made-king was a re-creation of the purple robed Mock King from Babylon, which Roman society adopted in their Saturnalia and the Roman church parodied in their Feast of Fools. In England, leading noblemen had a Lord of Misrule elected from the lower orders of their house. This was the practice for sheriffs, lord mayors, Oxford colleges, and Inns of Court as well. In the Elizabethan era, the Lords of Misrule used to lead their "courts" into the church to disrupt the service, as they had done during the Feast of Fools. The seventeenth-century Puritans condemned the profoundly pagan revelries of the Lord of Misrule. Before the 1820s in America, Christmas was a time of heavy drinking and promiscuity, when the rules that governed people's behavior were temporally abandoned in favor of an unrestrained carnival. With the growth of American cities in the early nineteenth century, the December Mardi Gras behavior became more threatening when combined with urban gang violence and Christmas season riots. By 1820, Christmas misrule had become such an acute social threat that respectable citizens of New York City could no longer ignore it, so some wealthy New Yorkers fashioned Christmas into a domestic ritual. See CHRISTMAS SEASON and MOCK KING.

Magic—**a:** the use of charms and spells believed to have supernatural power over natural forces; **b:** magic rites or incantations; **c:** enchantment **d:** the art of producing illusions by sleight of hand. See DIVINATION and SORCERY.

Marduk— (another name for Marduk is **Merodach**). These names were synonymous with Nimrod (i.e., his deific names) and so designate the wild ruthless hunter as a deity himself. Marduk was known as the Assyrian and Babylonian sun god. This was the patron deity of Babylon. His original character was a solar deity. Some sources define Marduk's name to mean either the "bull calf of the sun" or "the "solar calf." The ruins of the ancient city of Babylon speak of fifty-five chapels dedicated to its patron deity. Consider that Marduk assumed fifty names when one thinks of the first and supreme man to open the door to a massive and mighty spread of chaos.

Marry—**a:** to join as husband [Jesus the Bridegroom] and wife [the holy city, Jerusalem, made up of devoted believers (living stones)] according to law or custom; **b:** to unite in close and usually permanent relation; **c:** combine, unite.

Mithra—the sun god, who's the Persian version of Babylonian Tammuz. When Rome conquered Persia, many Romans liked merging their "modern" Western culture with the more ancient practices of the Orient, so they adopted the worship of the sun god Mithra. Roman Emperor Constantine was the most famous worshiper of Mithraism in the Roman Empire. Notably, the sacred bull was associated with the late Hellenistic and Roman solar cult of Mithras. See CONSTANTINE and SUN OR SOLAR GODS.

Mithraeums—underground temples where Mithras were worshiped. Many Roman churches, including the Church of San Clemente in Rome most notably, still contain well-preserved mithraeums in their vaulted burial crypts.

Mithraism—The pagan sun worship of Mithraism, with its god Mithra, had a winter festival, which was called "The Nativity" or "The Nativity of the Sun" or "The Nativity of the Unconquered Sun." The *Catholic Encyclopedia* itself admits that: The Nativity of the Unconquered Sun, celebrated on the twenty-fifth of December, has a strong claim on the responsibility for our December date. See MITHRA.

Mock King—custom in Babylon for masters to be subject to their servants, and one of them ruled the house clothed in purple garments. This Mock King was dressed in royal robes, allowed to enjoy the real king's concubines, and after reigning for five days was stripped, scourged, and killed. The Mock King had the same powers as the Lord of Misrule, and its tradition continued down through the centuries without the human sacrifice element, by the way of the lower clergy's Feast of Fools, the Lord of Misrule, and the Twelfth Night King and Queen. See LORD OF MISRULE.

Molech—or **Moloch** was worshiped by the Ammonites. They passed their children through the fire. Moloch, Chemosh, Baal, and the Roman god Saturn have the same bloody character (Lev. 20:3). See also BAAL, CHEMOSH, and SATURN.

Mysteries— (μυστήριον **mustarion** in Greek or **mystery** in English) The etymology of the word is itself a mystery. Probable, though not certain, is derivation from μύειν "to close" (the mouth, lips) μυστήριον (predominantly plur.) is the term for the many ancient mystery cults whose intensive development can be studied from the seventh century.BC to the fourth century AD. In line with the command of silence typically imposed by them—a command strictly enjoined and in the main carefully observed—our knowledge of the Mysteries is so fragmentary that we can only approximately delineate the main features. For all the multiplicity of cults, we can descry common features which are constitutive of the μυστήρια. Mysteries are cultic rites in which the destinies of a god are portrayed by sacred actions before a circle of devotees in such a way as to give them a part in the fate of the god. Integral to the concept of the Mysteries is the fact that those who wish to take part in their celebration must undergo initiation; the uninitiated are denied both access to the sacred actions and knowledge of them. The ceremony which makes the candidate a devotee of the deity embraces many different offerings and purifications. It is so firm a part of the whole mystery ritual that it is often hard to fix any precise distinction between the initiatory actions and the true mystery celebrations. By entrance qualification and dedication, the candidate is separated from the host of the uninitiated and enters into the fellowship of initiates who know each other by confessional formulae or symbolical signs. This society-forming element is of the very nature of the Mysteries. All Mysteries promise their devotees salvation (σωτηρία) by the dispensing of cosmic life. Their deities are chthonic [i.e., underworld or infernal] gods (Dionysus, Cybele and Attis, Adonis, Isis and Osiris). Their myths and feasts are closely connected with the change of seasons, also with human life and death. Their πάθη, which are enacted in the cultic drama, embrace sorrow and joy, seeking and finding, conception and birth, death and life, end and beginning. These πάθη are not present equally in all the Mysteries, but it is true of all mystery gods that in their mythical-personal destiny, the living forces of periodically perishing and returning nature hold sway.

Nativity—**a:** the process or circumstances of being born: birth; **b:** the birth of Jesus **c:** a horoscope at or of the time of one's birth **d:** assigns the human quality of a birthday **e:** the term "The Nativity" or "The Nativity of the Sun" or "The Nativity of the Unconquered Sun" was originally assigned to the pagan sun god Mithra, and is given credit by the *Catholic Encyclopedia* for responsibility of December twenty-fifth being chosen to celebrate Jesus' birth, even though God chose to hide this date (year, month, and day).

New Jerusalem—The holy city that comes out of the spiritual realm (i.e., heaven) that's constructed with God's living stones (1 Pet. 2:5). It is the pure and spotless individuals who make up the wife of the Lamb. This city is made ready like a bride adorned for her husband. The Messiah will reside with His bride, and thus, the New Jerusalem is also a metaphor for the tabernacle of God among men where the Lord permanently dwells with His people. See BRIDE OF CHRIST and LIVING STONES.

Nimrod—was the first earthly king, who was the grandson of Ham and great-grandson of Noah. Nimrod was the first and supreme man to open the door to a massive and mighty spread of chaos. Called "the mighty hunter" in Genesis 10:9, it appears that he controlled and conquered everything around him. Nimrod led the rebellion against Adonai at Babel, the place where God confused people's languages and dispersed them throughout the earth. Nimrod founded the four oldest cities of the world: Babel (Babylonia), Erech (Uruk), Accad (Akkad), and Calneh (Nippur). Corporately, they all made up the land of Shinar (Gen. 10:10), which is an ancient code name for Babylonia. Nimrod's ruling territories also extended into Assyria. When Nimrod created a new world order, he informed the assembly of gods and the then-known world that the center of the cosmos was Babylon.

Noahiac Commandments—First detailed in the Tosefta (late second or third century CE). The Seven Laws of Noah (Hebrew: חנ ינב תווצמ עבש, Sheva mitzvot B'nei Noach), often referred to as the Noahide Laws, are a set of seven moral imperatives that, according to the Talmud, were given by God to Noah as a binding set of laws for all mankind. According to Judaism, any non-Jew who lives according to these laws is regarded as a Righteous Gentile and is assured of a place in the world to come (Olam Haba), the Jewish concept of heaven. Adherents are often called "*B'nei Noah*" (Children of Noah) or "Noahides" and often networked in Jewish synagogues. The Noahide Laws were predated by six laws given to Adam in the Garden of Eden. The Talmud states that the instruction to not eat "flesh with the life" was given to Noah, and that Adam and Eve had already received six other commandments. Adam and Eve were not enjoined from eating a living animal since they were forbidden to eat any animal. The remaining six are exegetically derived from a seemingly unnecessary sentence in Gen 2:16. Later at the revelation at Sinai, the Seven Laws of Noah were re-given to humanity and embedded in the 613 laws given to the children of Israel along with the Ten Commandments, which are part of, not separate from, the 613 *mitzvot* (commandments). The Noahide Laws are regarded as the way through which non-Jews can have a direct and meaningful relationship with God, or at least comply with the minimal requisites of civilization and of divine law. One should also keep in mind that these laws are only the minimal basis for a Righteous Gentile's service to God, since there are many Jewish *mitzvos* that non-Jews are encouraged to adopt to accomplish more. Through these laws, a Gentile refines himself and the creation as a whole, fulfilling his purpose for existence.

One New Man—the term taken from Ephesians 2:15-16 for Jews and Gentiles being united in the Messiah.

Osiris—Egyptian god of the underworld. Much attention was given to train pharaohs in how to serve and please Osiris in the afterlife. The legend of Osiris tells how he was cut up into pieces and his body parts were scattered as a warning to others. His wife, Isis, re-gathered all his body parts, except one: his reproductive organ. She immortalized it through the creation of obelisks (sacred pillars). Osiris is prominently featured in Freemasonry. His worldly counterparts are Nimrod, Tammuz, Adonis, Zeus, etc.

Pagan—**a:** one who has little or no religion and who delights in sensual pleasures and material goods; **b:** a hedonistic person.

Perfect—**a:** being entirely without fault or defect: flawless; **b:** satisfying all requirements: accurate; **c:** corresponding to an ideal standard or abstract concept;

d: faithfully reproducing the original; **e:** complete; **f:** mature; **g:** legally valid (Gen. 6:9; 17:1; John 17:23; Rom. 12:2; Col. 1:28; Heb. 10:14; 12:23; James 1:4, 17, 25; 3:2; 1 John 4:15-18).

Perfection—the quality or state of being perfect as: **a:** freedom from fault or defect: flawlessness, **b:** maturity, **c:** the quality or state of being saintly; **d:** an exemplification of supreme excellence; **e:** an unsurpassing degree of accuracy or excellence; **f:** seamless or unlimited love (1 Cor. 13:11-13; 1 John 2:5).

Phrygian cap—A conical cap with top turned forward. It is often red to signify circumcision and is the origin of the bishop's mitre and the Rosicrucians' hat. Phrygia was an ancient country of Asia Minor, in what is now Turkey. The religion of the Phrygians was an ecstatic nature worship, in which the Great Mother of the Gods, Rhea, or Cybele, and a male deity, Sabazius, played a prominent part. The orgiastic rites of this religion influenced both the Greeks and the Romans. Croesus, king of Lydia, conquered all that was left of Phrygia in the sixth century BC, which passed successively under the rule of Persia, Macedonia, Pergamum, and Rome. The Phrygian cap was adopted by freed slaves in Roman times, and thus this cap also became a symbol of liberty. See CHEMOSH.

Pilgrims—came to America in 1620 on the Mayflower. Technically, the Pilgrims (our focus is on the saints not the strangers) were English Separatists that were more orthodox in their Puritan beliefs than Oliver Cromwell. Both the Pilgrims and the Puritans were nonconformists in refusing to accept an authority beyond the revealed Word. With the Pilgrims this had translated to an egalitarian mode, i.e., removal of inequalities among people, whereas the Puritans were a scholarly society where education tended to translate into authoritarian positions. Just remember, both the Pilgrims and the Puritans were logical fruits of the Reformation, and the key to life for them was God's written instructions in the Bible. See also PURITANS.

Profane—**a:** to treat (something sacred) with abuse, irreverence, or contempt; **b:** to desecrate; **c:** to debase by a wrong, unworthy, or vulgar use; **d:** not holy because unconsecrated, impure, or defiled; **e:** unsanctified (Lev. 20:3; 22:32; Heb. 12:14-17).

Pure—**a:** unmixed with other matter; free from dust, dirt, or taint: spotless; **b:** containing nothing that does not properly belong; **c:** marked by chastity: chaste (Eph. 5:27).

Puritans—first got their name due to their attempt to purify the church in England. Although many were Calvinists, Puritans were not associated with a single theology or with a single definition of the church; but they were extremely critical regarding religious compromises. The Bible was their sole authority. Puritans believed that access to Scripture was a fundamental necessity and the principles articulated in the Bible applied to every area of their life. They also encouraged direct personal religious experience (i.e., individual faith) and sincere moral conduit. On the grounds that Christmas was invented by man, not prescribed by the Bible, and the early church fathers had simply co-opted the midwinter celebration of several pagan societies, Puritans disapproved of its celebration. Being a fruit of the Reformation, Puritans were in charge of Cromwellian England. They brought to New England a Cromwellian detestation of Christmas. Because of the Puritan influence, the festive aspects of Christmas, including the tree, were not accepted in New England until about 1875. As late as the 1840s, Christmas trees were seen as pagan symbols and not accepted by most Americans.

Purity—the quality or state of being pure (Prov. 22:11; 1 Tim. 4:12; Titus 2:7).

Quartodeciman practice—Quartodeciman means the "fourteenth day." The Asian church in Constantine's day lived by the Quartodeciman practice. They did as Jesus and His first-century believers did, as defined in the Bible. They celebrated God's perpetual, holy feast called Passover (*Pesach*) on the fourteenth day of *Nisan*. Then they celebrated the Feast of First Fruits (*Bikkurim*) on seventeenth day of *Nisan*, which was the actual day Jesus rose from the dead.

Rhema—an utterance (individually or collectively or specifically); by implication a *matter* or *topic* (especially a narration, command, or dispute); pouring forth . . . to utter, i.e., speak or say. A rhema word from the Lord is not part of God's written Word (i.e., the Bible). It's an utterance or spoken word from God's heart that flows like a stream of living water and manifests in various ways: dreams, visions, apparitions, prophetic word spoken by another person, etc.

Sacaea—Persian midwinter festival, which was a counterpart to the Roman Saturnalia. Greek historian Dio Chrysostom records the following about a Mock King during the Sacaea: They take one of the prisoners condemned to death and make him sit on a royal throne; they dress him in royal robes . . . but in the end they undress him and hang (i.e., crucify) him.

Saint Nicholas—The history and legend of Saint Nicholas is so intertwined that the only things that we can say for sure about him is the general time he lived and where he was located. The *Catholic Encyclopedia* says: "Though he is one of the most popular saints in the Greek as well as the Latin Church, there is scarcely anything historically certain about him except that he was Bishop of Myra in the fourth century." He is renowned for his generosity, miracles, and love of children. He was said to drop coins down the chimney to preserve his anonymity and the dignity of his recipients. After the Protestant Reformation, there was considerably less emphasis on the worship of saints. To reduce Nicholas's saint-like qualities, his personage gradually merged with the pagan, red-faced, holly-crowned Father

Christmas. Bishop Nicholas of Myra became known as the first official Saint Nicholas, but this is not Santa's sole point of origin or his earliest. See SAINT NICK and SANTA CLAUS.

Saint Nick—nickname for the devil that was derived from Saint Nicholas. Nicholas often was associated with fertility cults, hence with fruit, nuts, and fruitcake, his characteristic gifts.

Sanctification—the state of growing in divine grace as a result of Christian commitment after baptism or conversion; working out our salvation with the help of the Holy Spirit (1 Cor. 1:30; Phil. 2:12; 1 Thess. 4:2-5; 2 Thess. 2:13). See SANCTIFY.

Sanctify—**a:** to set apart to a sacred purpose: consecrate; **b:** to free from sin: purify; **c:** to impart or impute sacredness; **d:** to give moral or social sanction to; **e:** to make productive of holiness or piety (Lev. 22:32-33; John 17:17; Rom. 15:16; Heb. 10:14).

Sanctity—**a:** holiness of life and character: goodness; **b:** the quality or state of being holy or sacred; **c:** sacred objects, obligations, or rights.

Santa Claus—the mischievous, magical, and generous red-suited father figure of Christmas. Santa Claus is the cultural deity in American's capitalistic, consumer-based society said to be the bringer of gifts. He is a compelling figure who commands our attention during the grand festival of consumption. His other names include: Chris Kringle, Father Christmas, Saint Nicholas, Old St. Nick, Syre Christemas, Sinter Klaas, Saint Basil, and Pere Noel. The image of Santa Claus celebrated today has been cast by many Americans, including: John Pintard (introduction of Saint Nicholas to New York City in an effort to create a domestic holiday to replace the revels of Christmas and New Year's Eve), Washington Irving (popularized St. Nicholas, but declassified him into the first image of a jolly, plebian elf), Clement Clarke Moore (wrote *The Night Before Christmas* introducing the joys of a domestic Christmas), Thomas Nast (his famous cartoons were responsible for much of the change into a jolly fat uncle), and so on infinitum. First recorded in the fifteenth century, Father Christmas predated Santa Claus and was associated with merrymaking and drunkenness, but the worldly figure of Santa derives from an even earlier set of figures—the shamans who were the first magicians of the human race (i.e., Chaldeans). We know that the northern shamans, said to be the midwives of the sun, often wore bells on their ritual red robes trimmed in white and, shinned up and down the central pole (i.e., tree representing the axis of the world) adorned with sun images in their skin tent to receive messages from the other-world for the next year. Just as Saturn was the central figure for Saturnalia, so is Santa Claus for Christmas. Throughout Hislop's book, he plainly points out that Saturn is another name for Satan. See CHRISTMAS DAY, CHRISTMAS SEASON, SATAN, and SATURN.

Satan—technically this word comes from the Hebrew *ha Satan*, which means the entire kingdom of darkness: the devil, his demons, and all who are in agreement with this kingdom. The first commandment of *The Satanic Bible* could be boiled down to: Do unto thy self. Although this commandment is not listed in their little black book, the high priest of the Church of Satan and author of *The Satanic Bible*, Anton LaVey, promoted a doctrine of self-indulgence, self-satisfaction, self-gratification, and self-rule. LaVey's predecessor, Aleister Crowley, is "often referred to as the father of modern Satanism." In Crowley's *Book of the Law* he proclaims: "In this new age, the only moral commandment will be, 'Do what thou wilt shall be the whole of the law.'" Therefore, the Satanic kingdom can be equated to the kingdom of self. The term "Satan" in this book means the devil—"the serpent" (Gen. 3:1), which is "the dragon, the serpent of old, who is the Devil and Satan" (Rev.20:2). Satan leads the whole world astray (Rev. 12:9); the whole world is under his control (1 John 5:19). The number "666" was the secret symbol of the ancient pagan mysteries connected with the worship of the devil. See BABYLON.

Saturn—ancient Roman god of seed (agriculture) and time called *Saturnus*; descendant of the great Chaldean god. The name of Saturn denotes "the hidden one." Reverend Alexander Hislop reveals that Apis is simply another name for Saturn, because that calf represented the divinity in the character of Saturn. Hislop also declares that Saturn is simply another name for Satan. See SATAN.

¹Saturnalia—the festival of Saturn in ancient Rome from mid-December to the first of January; an unrestrained often licentious celebration: ORGY; EXCESS; EXTRAVAGANCE. Saturnalia itself developed from the older rituals of the winter solstice into a riotous assemblage of fun, laughter, and gift giving. During this season, Romans decorated their homes with evergreen. This season also celebrated death: (1) the Mock King chosen by lot was sacrificed to Saturn at the conclusion of the festival, and (2) gladiators fought to the death in Saturnalia funeral games. Saturnalia was said to be a re-enactment of the golden age when Saturn reigned the earth as its first king. The Saturnalia was a direct descendant of the merged Egyptian and Persian mother-child/sun traditions, which both came from Babylon where the midwinter king's (initially Tammuz) birthday was celebrated on December 25. See MOCK KING, NIMROD, SATURN, TAMMUZ, VIRGIN MOTHER, and WINTER SOLSTICE.

²Saturnalia—was the original name of Rome, the city of Saturn, the city on seven hills where the Roman god Saturn formerly reigned. The whole of Italy was long after called by his name, being commonly called "The Saturnian Land." On the Capitoline hill, the image of Saturn, the formerly great Chaldean god, had been erected as a great high place of Roman worship when the pagan Roman emperors laid claim to the title *pontifex maximus*. The *pontifex maximus* existed in Rome from the earliest of times, and was modeled after the head pontiff at Babylon. See SATURN.

Semiramis— (*Sammuramat* in Sumerian) Nimrod's wife and the first Babylonian (i.e., idolatrous) Queen of Heaven. She was also the first one called the Virgin Mother. Semiramis told the world that Nimrod had been reincarnated in her son Tammuz through her own immaculate conception. The mother-child cult grew up out of Semiramis' immaculate conception lie. The pagan mother-child cult has been consistently represented as a woman holding a baby son in her arms—the Madonna and child. This Babylonian queen was not merely in character coincident with the Aphrodite of Greece and the Venus of Rome, but was, in point of fact, the historical original of that goddess, who by the ancient world was regarded as the very embodiment of everything attractive in female form, and the perfection of female beauty. Sanchuniathon assures us that Aphrodite or Venus was identical with Astarte, and Astarte being interpreted as none other than "The woman that made towers or encompassing walls"—i.e., Semiramis. After Semiramis installed herself as "The Queen of Heaven," she became the model for all subsequent goddesses. How extraordinary, yea, frantic, was the devotion to this goddess queen in the minds of the Babylonians is sufficiently proved by the statement of Herodotus, as to the way in which she required to be propitiated. That a whole people should ever have consented to such a custom as is there described shows the amazing hold her worship must have gained over them. Nonnus, speaking of the same goddess, calls her "The hope of the whole world." (DIONUSIACA in BRYANT) It was the same goddess, who was worshiped at Ephesus, whom Demetrius the silversmith characterized as the goddess "whom all Asia and the world worshipped" (Acts 19:27). So great was the devotion to this goddess queen, not of the Babylonians only, but of the ancient world in general, that the fame of the exploits of Semiramis has, in history, cast the exploits of her husband Ninus or Nimrod, entirely into the shade. See NIMROD, ISHTAR, and VIRGIN MOTHER.

Shekinah— (**Shechinah, Shekina, Shechina, Schechinah**, or **Shadanah**) When people spend quality time communing with God, a by-product is produced in and through our lives—His *shekinah* glory. This is the same *shekinah* that used to arise as a cloud of glory over the ark of the covenant in the wilderness tabernacle. It is also the same *shekinah* that used to radiate from Moses' face after he had spent time in the midst of God's presence. God's *shekinah* glory and His holiness are so closely related that the Bible tells us that His *shekinah* literally requires holiness. As a noun it's not used in Hebrew Scripture, although it is used in the Talmud. This noun has its etymology in the Hebrew verb שׁכן (*shacan*) meaning "to dwell." This verb, however, is used in many places. The idea of this noun is to describe the presence of the Lord. The ancient Hebrews were very descriptive and would used

כבוד׳ *(cavod)* meaning "heavy" to later mean "glory," because "heavy" is a good description of this presence. Thus the idea of shekinah is "dwelling presence."

Shinar—Although the origin of the word "Shinar" is said to be unknown, the late Reverend Alexander Hislop extrapolates that *Shinar* implies the idea of repeating childhood. *Shinar* is the OT designation for southern Mesopotamia, the alluvial plain between the rivers Euphrates and Tigris. The area was known by the Sumerians as Sumer and Akkad. It later became known as Babylonia. In two of the eight passages Shinar is called Babylonia in the LXX (Isa. 11:11 and Zech. 5:11). In Gen. 10:10, we are told that the great tyrant and empire builder Nimrod founded his kingdom in Babel, Erech (Sumerian Uruk), Akkad (Agade), and Calneh in the land of Shinar. From here he pushed north into Assyria. It was here also, in *Shinar,* that rebellious man built the well-known Tower of Babel in direct defiance of God (Gen. 11:2). In Dan. 1:2 it is the land of *Shinar* to which Nebuchadnezzar removes the vessels of the temple of God, and in Isa. 11:11 we are told that *Shinar* is one of the lands from which regathered Israel will return when the Millenial age is established. In Zech. 5:11, the woman in the ephah, representing a concentration of evil (v. 8), is removed to the land of *Shinar* where a temple is built for her. All of this points to a sinister significance for *Shinar* as being the major center for the development of a culture and civilization built on counterfeit religion, rebelliousness against the true God, and His revealed Word, the cradle of imperial tyranny, and the enemy of God's people, in short, the epitome of wickedness.

Snare—**a:** something by which one is entangled, involved in difficulties or impeded; **b:** something deceptively attractive; **c:** makes something complicated; **d:** a position or situation from which it is difficult or impossible to escape; **e:** caught as if in a trap or lured into a compromising statement or act.

Sorcery—**a:** the practice of manipulating creation, humans, or events to provoke manifestations of what is desired by the occultist; **b:** the use of power gained from the assistance or control of evil spirits especially for divining; c: necromancy; d: magic. See DIVINATION and MAGIC.

Spotless—**a:** having no spot; **b:** free from impurity: immaculate; **c:** pure, unblemished (Eph. 5:27).

Sun or solar gods—gods that supposedly rule or ruled with the sun and its power. They are usually male deities. Egypt is a major civilization that constructed its life and lifestyles around the sun and its deities: Horus, Re/Ra, etc. The worship of the sun and the sacred bull were the most widespread cults throughout the ancient world. A revered animal in Egypt was considered to be an incarnation of that particular god; therefore, the sun god and the sacred bull were synonymous. Anciently, there was an Egyptian tree custom performed on Ra's birthday—

December twenty-fifth. December twenty-fifth is known as the birthday of the sun gods, e.g., Babylonian Tammuz (reincarnated Nimrod), Egyptian Ra, Persian Mithra, and Grecian Zeus to name a few. The *Catholic Encyclopedia* tells us that Sol was the name of the sun god of the largest pagan religious cult, spanning both the Greek and Roman empires. Tertullian—a father of the church—asserted that Sol was not the Christian's God. The pagan sun worship of Mithraism, with its god Mithra, had a winter festival called "The Nativity" or "The Nativity of the Sun" or "The Nativity of the Unconquered Sun." The *Catholic Encyclopedia* admits that the Nativity of the Unconquered Sun had a strong claim for the responsibility of the date of Christmas. The Roman Emperor Constantine mixed pagan solar customs with "The Way," in order to appease the culture at the time. Historical evidence shows that Constantine was a devout Mithra worshiper. The *Encyclopedia Americana* says that by the fifth century, the Roman Catholic Church ordered that the birth of Christ be forever observed on December twenty-fifth, even though this was the day that the old Roman feast commemorated the birth of Sol (Mithra). See CHRISTMAS, MITHRA, MITHRISM, and NIMROD.

Talisman—**a:** an object held to act as a charm [i.e., practice or expression believed to have magic power; a trait that fascinates, allures, or delights; a physical grace or attraction] **b:** something producing apparently magical effects **c:** homing device.

Tammuz— (**Damu** in Sumerian or **Dammuz** in later Chaldean) Semiramis's son said to be reincarnated Nimrod. He held the title of sun god and was born on the winter solstice. Tammuz was not only Semiramis's (i.e., Ishtar's) son, but the Mysteries say also her husband, furthering the reincarnation myth and more confusion. He was originally a Sumerian or Babylonian sun-god, called Dumuzu. The Babylonian myth represents Dumuzu, or Tammuz, as a beautiful shepherd slain by a wild boar—the symbol of winter. Ishtar long mourned for him and descended into the underworld to deliver him from the embrace of death. The resurrection of Tammuz (Nimrod) through Ishtar's grief (Semiramis) was dramatically represented annually, in order to ensure the success of the crops and the fertility of the people. Each year men and women had to grieve with Ishtar over the death of Tammuz and celebrate the god's return, in order to win anew her favor and her benefits. This mourning for Tammuz was celebrated in Babylonia by women on the second day of the fourth month, which thus acquired the name of Tammuz. In Scripture, the women are in the temple lamenting Tammuz (Ezek. 8:14) while the men worship the sun in the east (Ezek. 8:16). Ezekiel 8 explains that both practices cause His glory to depart.

Tradition—English word derived from the Latin word *tradiere*, which means to lay into the hands of another (Matt. 15:3; Mark 7:8-9).

Winter Solstice (Midwinter)—The word solstice comes from the word "sun," and it means to "stand still," as it appears to do on the shortest day of the year as the sun gets nearest to the southern horizon. The theme of death flows through the various customs associated with the ancient winter solstice festival. See CHRISTMAS TREE, MOCK KING, SATURNALIA, or YULE LOG for further details. The day of the winter solstice was known as the birthday of the sun gods in antiquity. In the North, the months we know as December and January have long been called Freyja's Nights of Darkness. The year's longest night is the Mother Night, and in darkness the Lady labors to bring the Light to birth once more. The Young Sun is born at the Winter Solstice: Mithras, the Unconquered Sun of Persia, is born. Isis, Queen of Heaven, gives birth to Horus on the Solstice. Rhea gives birth to Saturn. See also SUN OR SOLAR GODS.

Unclean—**a:** morally or spiritually impure; **b:** infected with a harmful supernatural contagion; also: prohibited by ritual law for use or contact **c:** dirty, filthy **d:** lacking in clarity and precision of conception or execution (2 Cor. 6:17; Eph. 5:5; Rev. 18:2). See PROFANE.

Unite—**a:** to put together to form a single unit; **b:** to cause to adhere; **c:** to link by a legal or moral bond; **d:** to become one or as if one; **e:** to act in concert.

Virgin Mother—**a:** name of the mother of Jesus (Luke 1 and Isa. 7:14), who is one part of the true Queen of Heaven—the bride of Christ—as you and I can be one part. **b:** also, the slightly-twisted counterfeit "Christianized" Queen of Heaven, who became a deified woman elevated to goddess status by the Roman Catholic Church as an exact counterpart of the first Babylonian Queen of Heaven. **c:** primordially the title given to the Babylonian Queen of Heaven—Semiramis, which was part of the pagan mother-child cult. When the people scattered from the Tower of Babel, they used different names for Semiramis, including Ishtar (originally pronounced "Easter"). In other lands, she was called by other names: Mother of God, Artemis, Asherah, Isis, Istar, Diana, Rhea, Cybele, and Venus, to mention a few of her over five hundred names. See ISHTAR and SEMIRAMIS.

Yeshua—is the Hebrew/Aramaic name that Jesus went by when He walked the earth. It is a shortened form of *Yehoshua*, which means the Lord saves or salvation.

Yule—In the ancient Chaldean language of Babylon, the word "Yule" is the name for an infant or little child. Therefore, the very name by which Christmas is also known—Yule-day or the Yuletide season—is literally linked to its Babylonian origin. The date of December twenty-fifth was designated the highest holy day of the pagan year, because it was originally associated with the mother-child cult. Still today, one of the eight Wiccan/Pagan holidays is called Yule, and it celebrates the shortest day of the year.

Yule Log—The ceremony of the Yule log, like many of the oldest Christmas traditions, is thoroughly pagan in origin. Primordially, it was part of the birth celebration of the Babylonian Queen of Heaven's son. The Yule log symbolized Nimrod, cut down in the prime of his life and in the height of his power, then cut into pieces and burned. The Yule log ceremony celebrated the sun during the winter solstice. As recently as the nineteenth century, bringing in the Yule log was as much a part of Christmas as putting up an evergreen tree is today. On December twenty-fourth, an enormous freshly cut log would be brought from outside into the house with great ceremony. Everything to do with Yule logs was fraught with pagan rituals and superstitions, like one's Yule log should never be bought. Lucky ones were obtained from one's own land or from a neighbor. The master of the house placed the Yule log in the hearth, followed by making libations by sprinkling the wood with oil, salt, and mulled wine, accompanied by suitable prayers (in violation of the second commandment of the Big Ten—Exod. 20:3-6). Today, the Yule log has transformed itself into something sweet, just like other Christmas traditions. It's a pastry called the French Christmas cake or *Buche de Noel*. The idolatrous mother-child worship consisted of the burning of logs, the pouring out of libations, and the making of cakes for the Queen of Heaven (Jer. 7:17-18).

Ziggurat—an ancient Mesopotamian temple tower (e.g. the Tower of Babel dedicated to Marduk) consisting of a lofty pyramidal structure built in successive stages with outside staircases and a shrine at the top. Although the shrine was accessible by three stairways, the primary access was from the north. When a priest climbed this great stairway on the northern side, they entered a place called the "Gate of the Gods." The biblical root word for north means "an envelope of darkness." In *The Twilight Labyrinth*, George Otis, Jr., details that the hosts of darkness are linked to the north. The OT makes repeated idiomatic use of the term *tsaphon* for north, including using it as a synonym for Babylon. Otis tells us that *tsaphon* means hidden, dark, or gloomy. *Tsaphon* is derived from the word *tsaphan*, meaning unknown, to hide (by covering over), or to lurk. Ziggurats were brick mountains, which were precursors to re-enforced concrete. They were not public places of worship, but believed to be the actual dwelling places for the gods. The Mesopotamian and Canaanite gods lived on northern heights enveloped in precious stones, like the gem-encrusted Lucifer of Ezek. 28. The ziggurat's purpose was to connect heaven to earth. Of note, the entrance to Jerusalem's temple was on the opposite side—south. See BABEL.

BIBLIOGRAPHY

NOTE: I highly recommend those sources distinguished by an "*"

Achtemeier, Paul J. *Harper's Bible Dictionary*. San Francisco: Harper & Row, 1985.

Baddeley, Gavin. *Lucifer Rising: A Book of Sin, Devil-Worship and Rock-'N'-Roll*. Plexis, Medford, NJ: 1999.

Bede, Leo Sherley-Price. *A History of the English Church and People*. New York: Penguin Books, 1965.

Bertman, Stephen. *Handbook to Life in Ancient Mesopotamia:* New York, Oxford University Press, 2003.

Bottero, Jean. *Religion in Ancient Mesopotamia*. Translated by Teresa Lavender Fagan. Chicago: The University of Chicago Press, Ltd., 2001.

Bowler, Gerry. *World Encyclopedia of Christmas*. Toronto: McClelland & Steward, 2000.

Bradford, William. *Of Plymouth Plantation*. Mineola, NY: Dover Publications, 2006.

Brown, Dan. *The DaVinci Code*. New York: Anchor Books, A Division of Random House, 2003.

* Brown, Michael L. *Our Hands Are Stained With Blood*: *The Tragic Story of the "Church" and the Jewish People*. Shippensburg, PA: Destiny Image Publishers, 1992.

* Bullinger, E.W. *Number in Scripture: Its Supernatural Design and Spiritual Significance*. Grand Rapids: Kregel Publications, 1967.

* Burrows, Edwin G. and Mike Wallace. *Gotham: A History of New York City to 1898*. New York: Oxford University Press, 2000.

Calderwood, David. *Perth Assembly (1619)*. Edinburg, IN: Puritan Reprints, 2007.

* Carroll, James. *Constantine's Sword*: *The Church and The Jews: A History*. New York: A Mariner Book, Houghton Mifflin Company, 2001.

Cheyne, Thomas Kelly and John Sutherland Black. *Encyclopædia Biblica: A Critical Dictionary of the Literary, Political and Religious History, the Archæology, Geography, and Natural History of the Bible*. New York: Macmillan Company, 1902.

* Chumney, Edward. *The Seven Festivals of the Messiah*. Shippensburg, PA: Treasure House, An Imprint of DestinyImage Publishers, Inc., 1994.

Connelly, Mark. *Christmas: A Social History*. I.B. Tauris: London, 1999.

Cotterell, Arthur Flagg. *A Dictionary of World Mythology*. New York: Oxford University Press, 1986.

Davies, W.D., and Louis Finkelstein. *Cambridge History of Judaism*. New York: Cambridge University Press, 2006.

* DeChant, Dell. *The Sacred Santa: The Religious Dimensions of Consumer Culture*. Cleveland, OH: Pilgrim Press, 2002.

Deetz, Scott and Patricia Scott Deetz. *The Times of their Lives: Life, Love, and Death in Plymouth Colony*. New York: Anchor Press, 2001.

DeGreef, Wulfert. *The Writings Of John Calvin: An Introductory Guide.* Translated by Lyle D. Bierma. Louisville, KY: Westminster John Knox Press, 2008.

Durant, Will. *The Age of Faith: A History of Medieval Civilization—Christian, Islamic, and Judaic—From Constantine to Dante: A.D. 325-1300.* New York: Simon & Schuster, 1986.

Elliott, T.G. *The Christianity of Constantine the Great.* Bronx, NY: Fordham University Press, 1996.

Erman, Adolf. *A Handbook of Egyptian Religion.* London: Constable, 1907.

Eusebius. *Life of Constantine.* Translated by Averil Cameron and Stuart George Hall. Gloucestershire, England: Clarendon Press, 1999.

Eusebius, Roy Joseph Deferrari. *Ecclesiastical History: Books 1-5.* Berkeley: University of California, 1955.

Flynn, Tom. *The Trouble with Christmas.* Buffalo, NY: Prometheus Books, 1993.

Forbes, Bruce David. *Christmas: A Candid History.* Berkeley, University of California Press, Berkeley, 2007.

Frazer, James George. *The Golden Bough.* New York: Simon & Schuster, 1950.

Freedman, David Noel. *The Anchor Bible Dictionary.* New York: Bantam Dell Publishing Group, 1992.

Gesenius, Wilhelm, Samuel Prideaux Tregelles. *Gesenius' Hebrew and Chaldee Lexicon to the Old Testament Scriptures.* Bellingham, WA: Logos Research Systems, Inc, 2003.

Golby, J.M., A.W. Purdue. *The Making of the Modern Christmas.* Athens, GA: The University of Georgia Press, 1986.

* Goll, Jim W. *The Seer: The Prophetic Power of Visions, Dreams, and Open Heavens.* Shippensburg, PA: Destiny Image Publishers, Inc., 2004.

Harris, R. Laird, Gleason Leonard Archer, and Bruce K. Waltke. Theological Word Book of the Old Testament. CD-ROM. Moody Press, 1999.

* Heilbron, J.L. *The Sun in the Church: Cathedrals as Solar Observatories.* Boston, MA: Harvard University Press, 1999.

* Heidler, Dr. Robert D. *The Messianic Church Arising! Restoring the Church to Our Covenant Roots!* Denton, TX: Glory of Zion International Ministries, Inc., 2006.

Henry, Matthew. *Matthew Henry's Commentary on the Whole Bible, Complete and Unabridged.* Peabody, MA: Hendrickson Publishers, Inc., 1996.

* Heschel Abraham Joshua. *The Sabbath.* New York: Farrar, Straus and Giroux, 2005.

* Hislop, Rev. Alexander (of East Free Church Arbroath). *The Two Babylons.* James Wood: Edinburgh, Scotland: 1862.

Hullquist, C. Gary. *Sabbath Diagnosis: A Diagnostic History and Physical Examination of the Biblical Day of Rest.* Brushton, NY: TEACH Services, Inc., 2004.

* Jacobs, Cindy. *Deliver Us From Evil.* Ventura, CA: Regal Books 2001.

Johnson, Paul. *A History of Christianity.* New York: Simon & Schuster, 1976.

Jones, Arnold Hugh Martin. *Constantine and the Conversion of Europe.* Toronto: University of Toronto Press, 1978.

Kittel, Gerhard, Gerhard Friedrich, and Geoffrey W. Bromiley. *Theological Dictionary of the New Testament.* Translated by Geoffrey W. Bromiley. Grand Rapids: Wm. B. Eerdmans Publishing, 1969.

* Joyner, Rick. *Overcoming Poverty*. Charlotte, NC: MorningStar Publications, 1996.

* Joyner, Rick. *The Apostolic Ministry*. Charlotte, NC: MorningStar Publications, 2004.

* Joyner, Rick. *The Final Quest*. Charlotte, NC: MorningStar Publications, 1996.

Labuschagne, C. *The Incomparability of Yahweh in the Old Testament*. Leiden: Brill, 1966.

Mackey, Albert Gallatin, Edward L. Hawkins, and William James Hughan. *An Encyclopedia of Freemasonry and Its Kindred Sciences, Comprising the Whole Range of Arts, Sciences and Literature as Connected with the Institution*. New York: Masonic History Company, 1912.

MacMullen, Ramsay. *Christianity & Paganism in the Fourth to Eighth Centuries*. New Haven: Yale University Press, 1997.

MacMullen, Ramsay. *Christianizing the Roman Empire A.D. 100-400*. New Haven: Yale University Press, 1984.

MacMullen, Ramsay. *Paganism in the Roman Empire*. New Haven: Yale University Press, 1981.

Maier, Paul L. *Josephus: The Essential Works*. Grand Rapids: Kregel Publications, 1994.

Maier, Paul L. *In the Fullness of Time: A Historian Looks as Christmas, Easter, and the Early Church*. Grand Rapids: Kregel Publications, 1991.

Matthews, John. *The Winter Solstice: The Sacred Traditions of Christmas*. Philippines: Theosophical Publishing House, 2003.

Meijer, Fik. *The Gladiators: History's Most Deadly Sport*. Translated by Liz Waters. New York: Thomas Dunne Books, St. Martin's Press, 2004.

Miles, Clement A. *Christmas Customs and Traditions: Their History and Significance*. New York: Dover Publications, Inc., 1976.

Muir, Frank. *Christmas Customs & Traditions*. New York: Taplinger Publishing Company, 1977.

Munk, Rabbi Michael L. *The Wisdom in the Hebrew Alphabet*. Brooklyn, NY: Mesorah Publications, Ltd, 1983.

* Nanos, Mark D. *The Mystery of Romans: The Jewish Context of Paul's Letter*. Minneapolis: Fortress Press, 1996.

Nave, Orville J. *The Nave's Topical Bible*. Grand Rapids: Zondervan Publishing House, 1969.

Neal, Daniel. *The History of the Puritans, Or Protestant Nonconformists: From the Reformation in 1517, to the Revolution in 1688; Comprising an Account of Their Principles; Their Attempts for a Farther Reformation in the Church; Their Sufferings; and the Lives and Characters of Their Most Considerable Divines*. New York: Harper & brothers, 1843.

Nickelsburg, George W.E. *Ancient Judaism and Christian Origins: Diversity, Continuity, and Transformation*. Minneapolis: Fortress Press, 2003.

* Nissenbaum, Stephen. *The Battle for Christmas*. New York: Vintage Books, A Division of Random House, Inc., 1996.

Novak, David. *The Image of the Non-Jew in Judaism: An Historical and Constructive Study of the Noahide Laws*. Lewiston, NY: E. Mellen Press, 1983.

Oppenheim, A. Leo. *Ancient Mesopotamia: Portrait of a Dead Civilization*. Chicago: The University of Chicago Press, 1977.

* Otis, George, Jr., *The Twilight Labyrinth: Why Does Spiritual Darkness Linger Where It Does?* Ada MI: Chosen Books, A Division of Baker Book House Company, 1997.

* Packer, J.I. *Knowing God.* Downers Grove, IL: InterVarsity Press, 1973.

Pentecost, J. Dwight. *Things to Come: A Study in Biblical Eschatology.* Grand Rapids: Zondervan, 1958.

Petrie, W.M. Flinders. *Memphis I: British School of Archaeology in Egypt and Egyptian Research Account.* London: School of Archeology in Egypt, 1908.

* Price, Dr. Paula A. *The Prophet's Dictionary: The Ultimate Guide to Supernatural Wisdom.* Tulsa, OK: Flaming Vision Publications, 2002.

* Restad, Penne L. *Christmas in America: A History.* New York: Oxford University Press, 1995.

* Rood, Michael J. *The Pagan-Christian Connection Exposed: Truth vs Tradition: The Heavyweight Battle of the Ages.* Gainesville, FL: Bridge-Logos, 2004.

Russell, Jeffrey Burton. *The Prince of Darkness: Radical Evil and the Power of Good in History.* Ithica, NY: Cornell University Press, 1988.

* Scarlata, Robin, and Linda Pierce. *A Family Guide to the Biblical Holidays With Activities for all Ages.* Madison, TN: Family Christian Press, 1997.

* Scherman, Rabbi Nosson and Rabbi Meir Zlotowitz, general eds. *The Chumash: The Stone Edition.* Brooklyn, NY: Mesorah Publications, Ltd., 2000.

* Schmidt, Leigh Eric. *Consumer Rites: The Buying & Selling of American Holidays.* Princeton: Princeton University Press, 1995.

Seekins, Frank T. *Hebrew Word Pictures: How Does the Hebrew Alphabet Reveal Prophetic Truths?* Phoenix, AZ: Living Word Pictures Inc., 1994.

* Skarsaune, Oskar. *In the Shadow of the Temple: Jewish Influences on Early Christianity.* Downers Grove, IL: InterVarsity Press, 2002.

Smith, Morton H. *How is the Gold Become Dim (Lamentations 4: 1): the Decline of the Presbyterian Church, U.S., as Reflected in Its Assembly Actions.* Birmingham, AL: Steering Committee for a Continuing Presbyterian Church, Faithful to the Scriptures and the Reformed Faith, 1973.

Strong, James. *The New Strong's Exhaustive Concordance of the Bible.* Nashville, TN: Thomas Nelson Publishers, 1996.

Telushkin, Rabbi Joseph. *Jewish Literacy: The Most Important Things to Know About the Jewish Religion, Its People, and Its History* New York: William Morrow and Company, Inc., 1991.

Thomas, Robert L. *New American Standard Exhaustive Concordance of the Bible: Including Hebrew-Aramaic and Greek Dictionaries.* Philadelphia: A. J. Holman, 1981.

Thompson, Ernest Trice. *Presbyterians in the South.* Louisville, KY: John Knox Press, 1963.

* Tozer, A.W. *The Knowledge of the Holy: The Attributes of God: Their Meaning in the Christian Life.* New York: Harpercollins, 1992.

Walsh, William Shepard. *Curiosities of Popular Customs and of Rites, Ceremonies, Observances, and Miscellaneous Antiquities.* Philadelphia: J.B. Lippincott Co., 1897.

Woodrow, Ralph Edward. *Babylon Mystery Religion: Ancient and Modern.* Palm Springs, CA: Ralph Woodrow Evangelistic Association, 1966.

NOTES

CHAPTER 1
Supernatural Encounters

[1] Forbes, *Christmas: A Candid History*, 5.
[2] Seekins, *Hebrew Word Pictures*, 1, 94. Please note that although pictographs (aka, ideograms) do not have a standardized interpretation, Seekins taps into an ancient concept—Hebrew used to be an ideogramic language (i.e., many pictures are used to describe a word). "There are dozens of Christian and Jewish resources that speak of the pictures within the Hebrew alphabet. There are some slight differences in some of the letters, but they all agree on the majority" (ibid., 3). "As a picture language, Hebrew can be studied in ways that do not work with other languages (although there are parallels in studying the etymology of words). Hebrew has not been studied as an eastern picture language, but as a western phonetic language. The picture part of Hebrew does not negate, nor diminish the other studies that have gone before. In fact, to study the pictures, it is important to turn to the scholars to understand the meanings, the relationships and the usage of Hebrew. As a unique language that is both eastern and western, Hebrew fulfills a role that no other language can" (ibid., 101). Seekins goes by five precepts when studying Hebrew as an ideogramic language: "**1) The Bottom Line:** Sola Scriptura: Nothing can ever take the place of Scripture. **2) Find the clear picture:** This applies to word pictures that are so clear there is no question about its meaning. **3) Let the Hebrew language teach the foundations:** This means that you look to the language and the experts to understand key concepts. **4) Find the key word:** A key word is a simple word picture inside a more complex word picture. When you know the key word, the picture of the word becomes clear. **5) Find the clear pattern:** There are patterns in the Hebrew word pictures that are so consistent they confirm the meaning of a word picture. Learning a few patterns, and always looking for a pattern for confirmation is crucial" (ibid., 102).
[3] Liddell, *A Lexicon*, 717: "[ῥῆμα, ατος, τό, (ῥέω, ἐρῶ) *that which is said* or *spoken, a word, saying,* Theogn., Hdt., etc.; κατὰ ῥῆμα *word for word,* Aeschin. **2.** *a phrase,* opp. to ὄνομα (a single word), Plat. **3.** *the subject of speech, a thing,*

N.T. **II.** in Gramm., *a verb*, opp. to ὄνομα (a noun), ῥήματα καὶ ὀνόματα Plat." A rhema word from the Lord is not part of God's written Word (i.e., the Bible). It's an utterance or spoken word from God's heart that flows like a stream of living water and manifests in various ways: dreams, visions, apparitions, prophetic word spoken by another person, etc.

⁴ Goll, *The Seer*, 120. "Apparition: At this level of supernatural vision, a person sees a being that literally appears to him or her seemingly 'out of thin air.' This appearance may be observed with the natural eyes either open or closed, and may even be a tangible experience. In some cases, it may be perceived physically—the being's presence may be felt—without being obviously seen. It is an appearing, a visiting, but not necessarily a sighting. An appearance or apparition is different from a pictorial vision in that it is an actual—perhaps tangible and audible—visitation occurring outside of the person. These appearances can be 'interactive' as well (Genesis 32:24-31; Joshua 5:13-15; Acts 1:3)."

⁵ Strong, *The New Strong's Exhaustive Concordance*, NT:1461.

⁶ Please refer to the Glossary for my definition of biblical feasts and the Feasts of the Lord.

⁷ *Webster's Collegiate Dictionary*, 713, 1293, and 228: "Marry—to join as husband [Jesus the Bridegroom] and wife [the holy city, Jerusalem made up of devoted believers (living stones)] according to law or custom: to unite in close and usually permanent relation: COMBINE, UNITE. . . . Unite—to put together to form a single unit: to cause to adhere: to link by a legal or moral bond: to become one or as if one: to act in concert. . . Combine—to bring into such close relationship as to obscure individual characters: MERGE: to cause to unite into a single expression: INTERMIX, BLEND: to become one: to act together *syn* JOIN."

⁸ While Jesus has asked me to call Him Yeshua, I don't believe others are required to do the same. Just know that when I articulate the name Yeshua, I am referring to Jesus. It's Jesus' Aramaic/Hebrew (יֵשׁוּעַ) name, which He was called when He walked on the earth. It's a shortened form of *Yehoshua*, which means "salvation" or "the Lord saves."

⁹ Munk, *The Wisdom in the Hebrew Alphabet*, "Kuf," 194.

¹⁰ Ibid., 195.

¹¹ Please note that Shekinah, Shechinah, Shekina, Shechina, Schechinah, or Shadanah as a noun is not used in Hebrew Scripture, although it is used in the Talmud. This noun has its etymology in the Hebrew verb שָׁכַן (shacan) meaning "to dwell." This verb, however, is used in many places. The idea of this noun is to describe the presence of the Lord. The ancient Hebrews were very descriptive and would have used כָּבוֹד (cavod) meaning "heavy" to later mean "glory" because "heavy" is a good description of this presence. Thus the idea of *shekinah* is "dwelling presence."

¹² *Webster's Collegiate Dictionary*, 1376: "Ziggurat—an ancient Mesopotamian temple tower [e.g., the Tower of Babel dedicated to Marduk] consisting of a lofty pyramidal structure built in successive stages with outside staircases and a shrine at the top." Although the shrine was accessible by three stairways, the

primary access was from the north. When a priest climbed this great stairway on the northern side, they entered a place called the "Gate of the Gods." The biblical root word for north means "an envelope of darkness." In *The Twilight Labyrinth*, George Otis, Jr., details that the hosts of darkness are linked to the north. The Old Testament makes repeated idiomatic use of the term *tsaphon* for north, including using it as a synonym for Babylon. Otis tells us that *tsaphon* means hidden, dark, or gloomy. *Tsaphon* is derived from the word *tsaphan*, meaning unknown, to hide (by covering over), or to lurk. Ziggurats were brick mountains, which were precursors to reinforced concrete. They were not public places of worship, but believed to be the actual dwelling places for the gods. The Mesopotamian and Canaanite gods lived on northern heights enveloped in precious stones, like the gem-encrusted Lucifer in Ezekiel 28. The ziggurat's purpose was to connect heaven to earth. Of note, the entrance to Jerusalem's temple was on the opposite side—south.

[13] Price, *The Prophet's Dictionary*, "Altar," 35-36.
[14] Skarsaune, *In the Shadow of the Temple*, 233.
[15] Ludwig Schneider, "The Bar Mitzvah Ceremony," *Israel Today* Magazine, February 2007, no. 97, 13.

CHAPTER 2
The Land of the Merchants

[16] deChant, *The Sacred Santa*, 195.
[17] Matt Crenson, "Christmas Gone Wild: Take cheer: Holiday has been out of control for centuries," *The Coloradoan*, December 24, 2006, C1-C2.
[18] Here the KJV actually translates the Hebrew more accurately with **"**Thou hast moreover multiplied thy fornication in **the land of Canaan** unto Chaldea; and yet thou wast not satisfied herewith" (Ezek. 16:29). The AMP states: "Moreover, you multiplied your harlotry with the land of trade, with Chaldea, and yet even with this you were not satisfied" (Ezek. 16:29). The CJB says: "You multiplied your acts of fornication with the land of traders, the Kasdim, and still weren't satisfied." The NASB declares: "You also multiplied your harlotry with the land of the merchants, Chaldea, yet even with this you were not satisfied." The NIV translates the Hebrew phrase אֶל־אֶרֶץ כְּנַעַן as "a land of merchants." Although there is no direct Hebrew word for "merchants" in this phrase, there is justification for the NIV translation. The Hebrew word כְּנַעַן or "Canaan" is used in this phrase. The land of Canaan was inhabited in ancient times by the Phoenicians, who traded along the Mediterranean Sea, holding centers of trade in Canaan and Carthage in North Africa. Translating the phrase to describe Babylon as a land of "merchants-traders of goods" would not do injustice to the text and may fit the context. Also see Rev. 17 and 18, where the fall of Babylon is equivalent to the "fall of merchants."

[19] Sorcery, sun god worship, and trade (i.e., merchandising) are common themes that are associated with a specific Babylonian name—Chaldea—when one studies Babylon through historical accounts or the Bible.

[20] See note #18 for the reason the NIV phrase "the land of the merchants" was used.

[21] Ezek. 16:29; 1 Tim. 6:12.

[22] Joyner, *Overcoming the Spirit of Poverty*, 14.

[23] Peggy Noonan, "A Life's Lesson: Declarations by Peggy Noonan," Opinion, *The Wall Street Journal*, June 21-22, 2008, A9.

[24] Nissenbaum, *The Battle for Christmas*, 144.

[25] deChant, *The Sacred Santa*, xiv.

[26] Shepherd Smith, FOX News television, November 19, 2007.

[27] "And he causes all, the small and the great, and the rich and the poor, and the free man and the slaves, to be given a mark on their right hand, or on their forehead, and *he provides* that no one should be able to buy or to sell, except the one who has the mark, *either* the name of the beast or the number of his name. Here is wisdom. Let him who has understanding calculate the number of the beast, for the number is that of a man; and his number is six hundred and sixty-six" (Rev. 13:16-18 NASB). Minimally, the mark of the beast on a person's right hand or forehead is symbolic of what one does (hand) and thinks (forehead).

[28] Baddeley, *Lucifer Rising*, 23: "Aleister Crowley (1875-1947) was born Edward Alexander Crowley in England to a moderately wealthy Warwickshire brewing family. His parents were members of the Plymouth Brethren. His mother took to calling Crowley 'the Great Beast 666' after the devilish monster of the Book of Revelation."

[29] Ibid.

[30] Ibid., 26.

[31] Seekins, *Hebrew Word Pictures*, "Pride," 22.

[32] Ibid., "Humble," 94.

[33] Bullinger, *Number in Scripture*, 283.

[34] Ruben benAbraham, "Illuminati-666," http://www.benabraham.com/html/illuminati - 1b.html (accessed 09-16-08): ". . . We can trace the origin of the number 666. And this number of doom is derived out of Astrology [which comes from Babylon]. . . . The learned doctors of paganism believed that all the other gods were but emanations of the one god, the Sun-god. . . . The number 666 was a summary number of the Sun-god, because it was his sacred number as the Ruler of the Zodiac."

[35] Keith Newman, "The 666 Syndrome," http://www.wordworx.co.nz/6syndrom.html (accessed 09-16-08): "(Originally written circa 1983 with updates.) . . . Six six six is the ultimate, sinful godless system or man. Six is the 'number of the beast' (animal nature) pursuing only self interest and gratification for the five senses. 666 is material activity rather than spiritual—it is works without faith. Six six six governs the lower universe under the name Lucifer, who disguising

himself as an angel of light, brings subtle erosion and deception pleasingly packaged. Triple six is tyranny and self willed government."

[36] Wikipedia, http://en.wikipedia.org/wiki/666_(number) (accessed 09-16-08): "Earnest references to 666 occur both among apocalypticist Christian groups and in explicitly anti-Christian subcultures such as that surrounding some heavy metal bands. An appearance of the number 666 in contemporary Western art or literature is more likely than not an intentional reference to this number of the Beast symbolism. Such popular references to 666 are too numerous to list here. . . . Some people take the satanic associations of 666 so seriously that they actively avoid things related to 666 or the digits 6-6-6. This is known as hexakosioihexekontahexaphobia—the fear of the number 666."

[37] Bullinger, *Number in Scripture*, 150.

[38] Joyner, *Overcoming the Spirit of Poverty*, 15.

[39] Nissenbaum, *The Battle for Christmas*, 140.

[40] When the word *pagan* is used, think of the *Webster's Collegiate Dictionary*, 10th ed. definition: "one who has little or no religion and who delights in sensual pleasures and material goods; a hedonistic person."

CHAPTER 3
Babylon and Beyond

[41] Scherman, *The Chumash*, "Nimrod," 47.

[42] The term "a mighty hunter"—צֵיד גִּבּוֹר (*gibbor stayith* or *stayid* in modern pronunciation)—is only used in this fashion in reference to Nimrod. A *gibbor* is a hero or great man or person, a warrior; and *stayith* is a noun for "hunting" or "game."

[43] Price, *The Prophet's Dictionary*, "Nimrod," 358-359.

[44] Ibid.

[45] Rav Alex Israel, *Parshat Noach: Nimrod the Mighty*, www.lind.org.il/feature/alexisrael/5766/rai-noach66_nimrod.htm: "Ibn Ezra interprets 'a mighty hunter before God' (Gen 10:9) literally as 'a mighty hunter in God's presence.' He infers that Nimrod was righteous in his straightforward (i.e. without context) interpretation of the phrase *Gibor Tzayid Lifnei Hashem*. However, I agree with the Jewish Sage Rashi's figurative explanation of this phrase—'the arch-persuader confronting God;' because Rashi takes into account the context surrounding this phrase. The Tower of Babel was constructed in Shinar (11:2)—the place where Nimrod begins his rule. It was also called Babel (11:9), which is once again the place of Nimrod's beginnings. Also, the Hebrew word *hechel* appears as a central verb in the story of Nimrod and the Tower of Babel, which can mean 'to begin' or 'to profane.' The double meaning of this verb speaks that a new beginning can go one of two ways. Even Nimrod probably began his kingdom with good intentions as a means to reach God. He intended good, but Nimrod and his society set their agenda to further themselves not God: 'Let us make a name for ourselves.'"

⁴⁶ Scherman, *The Chumash*, "Nimrod," 47.

⁴⁷ Price, *The Prophet's Dictionary*, "Nimrod," 358-359.

⁴⁸ Linguistically the name Nimrod is formed from the verb מָרַד *(marad)* meaning "to revolt or rebel against" and is used 25 times in the OT with this nuance. The verbal form that creates his name is parsed as a Qal Imperfect third masculine singular from this root, thus forming the word נִמְרֹד in Hebrew and is pronounced *nimrod* (with a long "o" vowel).

⁴⁹ Strong, *The New Strong's Exhaustive Concordance of the Bible*, 3259, and Seekins, *Hebrew Word Pictures*, "Noon," 64, "Mem," 60, "Reysh," 88, "Dalet," 29. Nimrod's name is constructed from four Hebrew consonants: Nun + Mim + Resh + Daleth. The ideograms are something like: Nun נ which is stated by many to mean "activity or life." The pre-Exilic form of this consonant carries the idea of "fish darting through water." Next is the Mim מ which is stated to mean "liquid, massive, chaos," and the pre-Exilic carries the idea of "water." Next is the Resh ר which is stated to mean "the person, the head, the highest," and the pre-Exilic form carries the idea of "head of a man or chief." Finally there is the Daleth/Dalet ד which has a stated meaning of "pathway" or "enter." The pre-Exilic form denotes a "door."

⁵⁰ Scherman, *The Chumash*, "Come, Let Us Descend," 50.

⁵¹ Strong, *The New Strong's Exhaustive Concordance*, "To overcome; to mix," OT:1101. The name בָּבֶל Babel is formed from the verb בלל *(balal,)* which means "to mix, mingle, confuse, or confound." This verb is used some 44 times with this same nuance. As such the name of the city Babel would have the idea of "confusion by mixing."

⁵² Babylon is the Greek spelling of the name which in Hebrew is uniformly "Babel." The word occurs some 290 times and refers to an ancient city on the eastern bank of the Euphrates about 20 miles south of Bagdad, near the modern village of Hilla in Iraq. Akkadian seems to derive the name from *babili(m)* or from another earlier Sumerian source. But in both cases it means "Gate of God." Gen. 11:9 gives the name as Babel (perhaps from *bālal* "to confuse") but probably intended as a parody, a word play referring to what happened when the languages were confused.

⁵³ Strong, *The New Strong's Exhaustive Concordance*, "Confusion," OT:894

⁵⁴ Schmidt, *Consumer Rites*, 3.

⁵⁵ Harris, *Theological Word Book of the Old Testament:* "Shinar is the OT designation for southern Mesopotamia, the alluvial plain between the rivers Euphrates and Tigris. The area was known by the Sumerians as Sumer and Akkad. It later became known as Babylonia. In two of the eight passages Shinar is called Babylonia in the LXX (Isa 11:11 and Zech 5:11). In Gen 10:10 we are told that the great tyrant and empire builder Nimrod founded his kingdom in Babel, Erech (Sumerian Uruk), Akkad (Agade) and Calneh in the land of Shinar. From here he pushed north into Assyria. It was here also, in Shinar, that rebellious man built the well-known tower of Babel in direct defiance of God (Gen 11:2). In Dan 1:2 it is the land of Shinar to which Nebuchadnezzar removes the vessels of the temple of

God, and in Isaiah 11:11 we are told that Shinar is one of the lands from which regathered Israel will return when the Millenial age is established. In Zech 5:11 the woman in the ephah, representing a concentration of evil (v. 8), is removed to the land of Shinar where a temple is built for her." All of this points to a sinister significance for Shinar, as being the major center for the development of a culture and civilization built on counterfeit religion, rebelliousness against the true God and His revealed Word, the cradle of imperial tyranny, and the enemy of God's people; in short, the epitome of wickedness (cf. as well the many biblical references to Babylon).

[56] Hislop, *The Two Babylons*, 199: "There have been considerable speculations about the meaning of the name Shinar, as applied to the region of which Babylon was the capital. Do not the facts above stated cast light on it? What so likely a derivation of this name as to derive it from 'shene,' 'to repeat,' and 'naar,' 'childhood.' The land of 'Shinar,' then, according to this view, is just the land of the 'Regenerator.'"

[57] Dr. Neil Chadwick, "Christmas Is the Children's Holiday," http://www.webedelic.com/church/chrisch.htm.

[58] BBC News, "Whose Christmas Is It Anyway?", December 20, 1997, http://news.bbc.co.uk/2/hi/special_report/for_christmas/_new_year/pagan_christmas/37276.stm.

[59] Rev. Yeshayahu Heilczer, "Christmas or Pagan-mass?" http://messianicfellowship.50webs.com/xmas.html.

[60] Natalie Constanza-Chavez, "If You Believe in Santa Claus, He Is Real," Grace Notes, *Coloradoan*, December 11, 2005, C2.

[61] Price, *The Prophet's Dictionary*, "Babel," 77.

[62] Scherman, *The Chumash*, "The Tower of Babel and the Dispersion," 48.

[63] Ibid.: "The year . . . is 1996 from Creation, 340 years after the Flood. Noah and his children were still alive at the time, and Abraham, 48 years old, had already recognized his Creator (*Seder Olam*)."

[64] Ibid., 48-49.

[65] I would add that Abraham is the father for all who believe.

[66] Price, *The Prophet's Dictionary*, 118, 259: "Chaldea—An ancient city in the southern region of the Persian Gulf's Babylonia that came to be considered Babylon, more at ancient Babylonia. Ancient Babylonia derives its name from the control of the region by the Kassites.a region of the biblical Shinar was properly Babylonia in later years. Its culture was especially known for extensive and ecstatic worship of fire and astral deities and a wide array of elaborate fertility rites. Abraham, the father of the Jews, came from Chaldea and was recognized by God as one of its highly trained prophets. He was initially groomed under the Babylonian's supernatural dominance. Chaldea, arising from Sumeria and Akkadia (biblical Accad) was the seat of early sun worship. One of its cities, Nippur, is the Bible's Calneh (see Genesis 10:10). The city, as many of its time, was saturated with temples devoted to many gods it worshipped and feared. All temples had priestly schools to maintain a supply of knowledgeable ministers to

serve at their altars and catechize converts. Genesis 15:7, 11:31, and 20:7. See also Jeremiah 50:10 and 51:24."

[67] Skarsaune, *In The Shadow of the Temple*, 233.

[68] Scherman, *The Chumash*, 51.

[69] Ibid., 48-49.

[70] Hislop, *The Two Babylons*, "The Child in Greece," 76.

[71] Seekins, *Hebrew Word Pictures*, "To deceive," 90.

[72] Bricks, because there were no stones in the plain of Shinar, whereas stones were cut from mountains.

[73] "Dan" דִּין (noun) literally means "judge." As a verb it is used often. See Gen. 15:14.

[74] Munk, *The Wisdom of the Hebrew Alphabet*, 198.

[75] 2 Thess. 2:7-12; Col. 3:1-11; Gal. 6:7-8; Isa. 65:11-12; 1 Cor. 10:21; Prov. 11:23-28; 1 Tim. 6:7-11; 1 John 3:10-16; Rom. 6:16-23; 1 John 3:4-8; Rom. 8:4-8; Gal. 5:16-21; Rom. 8:2-3; 1 Cor. 2:12-14.

[76] Eph. 2:14-18.

[77] Mary D. James, "All for Jesus," http://songsandhymns.org/hymns/detail/all-for-jesus (accessed 10-05-08).

[78] Rood, *The Pagan-Christian Connection EXPOSED*, 61-62.

[79] Price, *The Prophet's Dictionary*, "Chaldea," 118.

[80] Ibid., 358: 937: "Nimrod—The son of Cush and founder of the four oldest cities of the world. They were Babel (Babylonia), Erech (Uruk), Accad (Akkad), and Calneh (Nippur). These were all in the Bible described in Genesis 10:10 as the land of Shinar, a code name for ancient Babylonia. In addition to being Ham's grandson, Nimrod was also the great-grandson of Noah, which reveals that this antediluvian patriarch was also a Babylonian (more of this definition will be shared later in this chapter)."

[81] Ibid., "Chaldea," 118.

[82] Ibid., 359: 937: "Nimrod—[definition continued] Nimrod and his offspring progenies were insolent, violent, and proudly independent of the Maker. He took his skills, gifts, and talents much like his surrogate father, the devil, and used them to turn on the Most High Lord and make himself a god instead. The name Merodach (Marduk) is synonymous with Nimrod and so designates the wild ruthless hunter as a deity himself. The words for his history, as simply stated as the Bible presents them, refer to one who used violence to profane, pollute, and desecrate the holy and sacred. Nimrod did this by instituting Marduk and Ishtar worship, among many other deities of the Babylonian pantheon. He injected full-scale ritual sexuality and idolatry into the mainstream of human culture."

[83] Ibid., 328:826, 332:846: "Marduk—A) Name of an ancient Akkadian and Babylonian deity credited with creation by both peoples B) Also, Assyrian and Babylonian sun god. With Ishtar, Marduk was symbolized by leonine images. The association sprung from the belief that the two deities were feared as guardians among the gods. C) Also called Merodach, a deific name for Nimrod of ancient Babylon. . . . Merodach—Marduk, the name of the Akkadian god after

whom Nimrod patterned himself in the religions he pandered among the ancient Babylonians."

[84] Ludwig Schneider, "Alas, Babylon," *Israel Today* Magazine, June 2007, no. 101, 19. www.israeltoday.co.il.

[85] Arthur Cotterell, *A Dictionary of World Mythology,* "Marduk," http://www.encyclopedia.com/A+Dictionary+of+World+Mythology/publications.aspx (accessed 10-06-08).

[86] Erman, *A Handbook of Egyptian Religion,* 8-9.

[87] Ibid.

[88] Petrie, *Memphis I,* 2.

[89] Erman, *A Handbook of Egyptian Religion,* 22.

[90] Anita Stratos, "Divine Cults of the Sacred Bulls," www.touregypt.net/featurestories/bull.htm.

[91] Harris, *Theological Word Book of the Old Testament:* "לַעֲבְ (bāʿal) possess, own, rule over, many. (ASV and RSV usually similar. though RSV prefers 'rule' to ASV 'have dominion' [e.g. Isa. 26:13]). Derivatives 262a לַעֲבְ (baʿal) owner, husband, Baal. 262b הַלְעֲב (baʿălâ) female owner. 262c לֵבּ (bēl) Bel. [With a focus on] "Owner, possessor, husband, Baal. Ugaritic also has the double use of master and the name of a deity. The root in most Semitic languages means either 'lord' or, when followed by a genitive, 'owner.' In addition to *baʿal* as owner of things, the noun in the plural is used for citizens (*baʿalîm*) of a city (Josh. 24:11). In Judges 9 where the noun occurs sixteen times, ASV consistently translates 'men,' but RSV in addition to 'men' employs 'citizens' (Jud. 9:2) and 'people' (Jud. 9:46). *baʿal* can refer to partner or ally (Gen. 14:13). Idiomatically *baʿal* as master of something characterizes the person (e.g. *baʿal* of wrath, Prov. 22:24; of appetite, Prov. 23:2; of dreams, Gen. 37:19) or identifies occupation (e.g. officer, *baʿal* of the guard, Jer. 37:13). In addition to its appearance in compound names of people and places (e.g. Jerubbaal, Jud. 9:16; Baalzephon, Exod. 14:2), BAʿAL is the name of a great active god in the Canaanite pantheon and has other religious connotations. The god Baal met in the OT is the West Semitic storm god, *bʿl* (sing..) and *bʿlm* (pl.), encountered in Egyptian texts (from fourteenth century B.C. on), . . . Both within the Bible and outside it the name appears either absolutely or in construct with place names; e.g. Baal-peor (Num 25:3, 5), Baal-berith (Jud. 9:40), Baal-zebub (II Kings 1:2). (Baal-zebub, 'lord of flies,' is a parody on his name found elsewhere, *bʿl zbl*, 'Prince Baal.') These names do not denote various gods with the epithet 'lord,' but local venerations of the same West Semitic storm and fertility deity called simply Baal, 'Lord.' . . . Since the biblical writers did not intend to teach the Canaanite religion, we know more about Baal's roles, consorts, and cult from the extra-biblical literature than from the OT; but the picture of Baal presented in the OT comports well with the extra-biblical sources. He was also called Haddu (Hadad). He is above all the storm god who gives the sweet rain that revives vegetation. Dry years were attributed to his temporary captivity or even death. But at his revivification fields, flocks, and families became productive. In addition, he is a war god and fertility deity who consorts with Anat (is

later equated with Astarte). Both by reciting the myth of his role in reviving life at the autumn new year festival and by magical ritual of sacred marriage represented in the cult by the king, the queen and a priestess, the West Semites hoped to ensure the earth's fertility. [This ritual is witnessed, too, in Babylon but not clearly in Canaan (cf. H. Frankfort, *Kingship and the Gods*, also K.A. Kitchen, *Ancient Orient and the O. T.*, 104). It should be noted that the identification of Baal as an annually dying and rising god with the Babylonian Tammuz has lately suffered. New Sumerian tablets published by S. Kramer show that Tammuz died once for all and C. H. Gordon has argued that Baal too had no annual death and resurrection. See the whole discussion with refs. in E. M. Yamauchi, "Tammuz and the Bible" JBL 84:283–90. R.L.H.] Archaeological cultic objects with exaggerated sexual features, as well as the myths themselves, support the OT notices about the degraded moral features associated with the cult. Throughout the period of the judges, Israel succumbed to this infectious cult (Jud 2:11ff.; 6:25) and had to be rescued from its tragic consequences by Yahweh's judges. During the period of the Omrides, Baal worship became the official state religion of the northern kingdom (I Kings 16:31). Leah Bronner has presented convincing argument that Israel's miracles by Elijah and Elisha served as a polemic for God against the very powers attributed to this pagan nature deity, namely, fire (I Kings 18:17ff.; II Kings 1:9–16), rain (I Kings 17:1; 18:41–46), food (I Kings 17:1–6, 8–16; II Kings 4:1ff.); children (II Kings 4:14–17); revivification (I Kings 17:17–23; II Kings 4:18–37; 13:20–22, *The Stories of Elijah and Elisha as Polemics Against Baal Worship*, Leiden, 1968.) But their miracles did not rid the land of this degraded cult and it brought about the captivity of the northern kingdom (Hosea). It also infiltrated the southern kingdom (II Kings 11:18; 21:2ff.), and in spite of Josiah's reform (II Kings 23:4ff.), brought the nation into exile (Ezek. 16; 23, etc.). The Hosea discourse describes how Israel, who received gifts of grain and oil from YHWH, used these for the worship of Baal (Hos. 2:8 [H 10]). The chapter fairly turns on the term *baʿal*, not only in the mention of the Canaanite god(s) (e.g. Hos. 2:8 [H 10]; 2:13 [H 15]); and 2:17 [H 19]), but in the imagery throughout of God as Israel's husband. Israel will call the Lord her husband (אִישׁ, Hos. 2:16 [H 18]; cf. 2:2 [H 4]; 2:7 [H 9]) and no longer call him, apparently along with the list of other gods, my Baal (*baʿal*). God's supremacy over Baal is constantly affirmed. However man's preoccupation from then and until this day is rather with sex and technology, than with devotion to the Almighty God of history, who is also the covenant God."

[92] Cheyne, *Encyclopedia Biblica*, "Idolatry & Primitive Religions," 2154.

[93] Arthur Cotterell, *A Dictionary of World Mythology*, http://www.encyclopedia.com/A+Dictionary+of+World+Mythology/publications.aspx (accessed 10-06-08).

[94] *1911 Encyclopedia*, "Marduk," www.1911encyclopedia.org/Marduk.

[95] Arthur Cotterell, *A Dictionary of World Mythology*, http://www.encyclopedia.com/A+Dictionary+of+World+Mythology/publications.aspx (accessed 10-06-08).

[96] Ibid.
[97] Cheyne, *Encyclopaedia Biblica*, 631.
[98] Anita Stratos, "Divine Cults of the Sacred Bulls," www.touregypt.net/feature-stories/bull.htm.
[99] Ibid.
[100] Erman, *A Handbook of Egyptian Religion*, 24.
[101] Ibid.
[102] Erman, *A Handbook of Egyptian Religion*, 23-24.
[103] Anita Stratos, "Divine Cults of the Sacred Bulls," www.touregypt.net/feature-stories/bull.htm.
[104] Erman, *A Handbook of Egyptian Religion*, 207.
[105] Anita Stratos, "Divine Cults of the Sacred Bulls," www.touregypt.net/feature-stories/bull.htm.
[106] Erman, *A Handbook of Egyptian Religion*, 79.
[107] Ibid., 170.
[108] Anita Stratos, "Divine Cults of the Sacred Bulls," www.touregypt.net/feature-stories/bull.htm.
[109] Price, *The Prophet's Dictionary*, "Sorcery," 522.
[110] Ibid., 118-119.
[111] Ibid., 319.
[112] "ABC Family to Air 'Harry Potter Weekend' in December," http://www.the-leaky-cauldron.org/2007/11/18/abc-family-to-air-harry-potter-weekend-in-december.
[113] Price, *The Prophet's Dictionary*, "Manipulation," 325-326.
[114] Please refer to the Glossary.
[115] Muir, *Christmas Customs & Traditions*, 13.
[116] Nissenbaum, *The Battle for Christmas*, 134.
[117] Scherman, *The Chumash*, 28, 51.
[118] Dan. 3.
[119] Reworded in some instances due to what I felt was the cumbersome nature of language of the 1800s.
[120] Rood, *The Pagan-Christian Connection EXPOSED*, 62.
[121] Hislop, *The Two Babylons*, "The Child in Egypt," 60.
[122] Hislop, *The Two Babylons*, "The Deification of the Child," 62: "It is admitted by Wilkinson that the most ancient Hercules, and truly primitive one, was he who was known in Egypt as having, 'by the power of the gods' (i.e., by the SPIRIT) fought against and overcame the Giants.... Now, no doubt, the title and character of Hercules were afterwards given by the Pagans to him whom they worshipped as the grand deliverer or Messiah, just as the adversaries of the Pagan divinities came to be stigmatized as the 'Giants' who rebelled against Heaven. But let the reader only reflect who were the real Giants that rebelled against Heaven. They were Nimrod and his party; for the 'Giants' were just the 'Mighty ones,' of whom Nimrod was the leader. Who, then, was most likely to head the opposition to the apostasy from the primitive worship? If Shem was at that time alive, as beyond question he was, who so likely as he? In exact accordance with this deduction, we

find that one of the names of the primitive Hercules in Egypt was 'Sem.' If 'Sem,' then, was the primitive Hercules, who overcame the Giants, and that not by mere physical force, but by 'the power of God,' or the influence of the Holy Spirit, that entirely agrees with his character; and more than that, it remarkably agrees with the Egyptian account of the death of Osiris."

[123] Ibid.

[124] Kittel, *Theological Dictionary of the New Testament*, vol. 4, 803-806: "μυστήριον mustarion in Greek or mystery in English—The etymology of the word is itself a mystery. Probable, though not certain, is derivation from μύειν "to close" (the mouth, lips) . . . μυστήριον (predominantly plur.) is the term for the many ancient mystery cults whose intensive development can be studied from the seventh-century BC to the fourth AD In line with the command of silence typically imposed by them—a command strictly enjoined and in the main carefully observed—our knowledge of the mysteries is so fragmentary that we can only approximately delineate the main features. . . . For all the multiplicity of cults, we can descry common features which are constitutive of the μυστήρια. Mysteries are cultic rites in which the destinies of a god are portrayed by sacred actions before a circle of devotees in such a way as to give them a part in the fate of the god. Integral to the concept of the mysteries is the fact that those who wish to take part in their celebration must undergo initiation; the uninitiated are denied both access to the sacred actions and knowledge of them. The ceremony which makes the candidate a devotee of the deity embraces many different offerings and purifications. It is so firm a part of the whole mystery ritual that it is often hard to fix any precise distinction between the initiatory actions and the true mystery celebrations. By entrance qualification and dedication the candidate is separated from the host of the uninitiated and enters into the fellowship of initiates who know each other by confessional formulae or symbolical signs. This society-forming element is of the very nature of the mysteries. All mysteries promise their devotees salvation (σωτηρία) by the dispensing of cosmic life. Their deities are chthonic [i.e. underworld or infernal] gods (Dionysus, Cybele and Attis, Adonis, Isis and Osiris). Their myths and feasts are closely connected with the change of seasons, also with human life and death. . . . Their πάθη, which are enacted in the cultic drama, embrace sorrow and joy, seeking and finding, conception and birth, death and life, end and beginning. These πάθη are not present equally in all the mysteries, but it is true of all mystery gods that in their mythical-personal destiny the living forces of periodically perishing and returning nature hold sway."

[125] Ibid.: "Wilkinson admits that different individuals at different times bore this hated name in Egypt. One of the most noted names by which Typho, or the Evil One, was called, was Seth (EPIPHANIUS, Adv. Hoeres). Now Seth and Shem are synonymous, both alike signifying 'The appointed one.' As Shem was a younger son of Noah, being 'the brother of Japhet the elder' (Gen 10:21), and as the pre-eminence was divinely destined to him, the name Shem, 'the appointed one,' had doubtless been given him by Divine direction, either at his birth or afterwards, to mark him out as Seth had been previously marked out as the 'child of promise.'

Shem, however, seems to have been known in Egypt as Typho, not only under the name of Seth, but under his own name; for Wilkinson tells us that Typho was characterized by a name that signified 'to destroy and render desert.' (Egyptians) Now the name of Shem also in one of its meanings signifies 'to desolate' or lay waste." So Shem, the appointed one, was by his enemies made Shem, the Desolator or Destroyer—i.e., the Devil."

[126] Hislop, *The Two Babylons*, 93.

[127] Encyclopaedia of the Orient, "Babylonia," http://i-cias.com/e.o/babylon.htm.

[128] Hislop, *The Two Babylons*, 94.

[129] Ibid.: "Semiramis gained glory from her dead and deified husband [Nimrod]; and in the course of time both of them, under the names of Rhea and Nin, or 'Goddess-Mother and Son,' were worshipped with an enthusiasm that was incredible, and their images were everywhere set up and adored. [It would seem that no public idolatry was ventured upon till the reign of the grandson of Semiramis, Arioch or Arius. (Cedreni Compendium)]" Chapter II, section III, "The Mother of the Child": "Valerius Maximus does not mention anything about the representation of Semiramis with the child in her arms; but as Semiramis was deified as Rhea, whose distinguishing character was that of goddess Mother, and as we have evidence that the name, 'Seed of the Woman,' or Zoroaster, goes back to the earliest times—viz., her own day (CLERICUS, De Chaldoeis), this implies that if there was any image-worship in these times, that 'Seed of the Woman' must have occupied a prominent place in it. As over all the world the Mother and the child appear in some shape or other, and are found on the early Egyptian monuments that shows that this worship must have had its roots in the primeval ages of the world.... This Babylonian queen was not merely in character coincident with the Aphrodite of Greece and the Venus of Rome, but was, in point of fact, the historical original of that goddess that by the ancient world was regarded as the very embodiment of everything attractive in female form, and the perfection of female beauty; for Sanchuniathon assures us that Aphrodite or Venus was identical with Astarte, and Astarte being interpreted, is none other than 'The woman that made towers or encompassing walls'—i.e., Semiramis.... How extraordinary, yea, frantic, was the devotion in the minds of the Babylonians to this goddess queen, is sufficiently proved by the statement of Herodotus, as to the way in which she required to be propitiated. That a whole people should ever have consented to such a custom as is there described shows the amazing hold her worship must have gained over them. Nonnus, speaking of the same goddess, calls her 'The hope of the whole world.' (DIONUSIACA in BRYANT) It was the same goddess, as we have seen, who was worshipped at Ephesus, whom Demetrius the silversmith characterized as the goddess 'whom all Asia and the world worshipped' (Acts 19:27). So great was the devotion to this goddess queen, not of the Babylonians only, but of the ancient world in general, that the fame of the exploits of Semiramis has, in history, cast the exploits of her husband Ninus or Nimrod, entirely into the shade."

[130] Hullquist, *Sabbath Diagnosis*, 124-125: "... The legendary Semiramis enters the picture. Her name is the Hellenized form of the Sumerian 'Sammuramat,' or

'gift of the sea.' Various historical references to this mysterious woman of antiquity tend to collaborate a common theme: she was beautiful, shrewd, and powerful ruler of ancient Sumer. Both famed as the wife and mother of Nimrod by different sources . . . Semiramis was originally Nimrod's wife, Queen of Shinar and ruler of a vast religious hierarchy of priests and priestesses. . . . Semiramis . . . deified herself as the mother of the god Damu [or Dammuz (later Chaldean), also known as Tammuz in Hebrew] (since only a god can beget a god), and installed herself as 'The Queen of Heaven.' She became the model for all subsequent goddesses . . ."

[131] Coffin, *The Book Of Christmas Folklore*, 18.

[132] Harvard Divinity School, "Multifaith Calendar Glossary," http://www.hds.harvard.edu/spiritual/calendar_glossary.html: "Yule: Winter Solstice, celebrating the longest night and the blessings of darkness as well as the rebirth of the sun god. (Wicca/Paganism) (December 21*)*."

[133] Hislop, *The Two Babylons*, 134: "The very name by which Christmas is popularly known among ourselves—Yule-day—proves at once its Pagan and Babylonian origin. 'Yule' is the Chaldee name for an 'infant' or 'little child'; (From Eol, an 'infant.' In Scotland, at least in the Lowlands, the Yule-cakes are also called Nur-cakes. Now in Chaldee Nour signifies 'birth.' Therefore, Nur-cakes are 'birth-cakes.' The Scandinavian goddesses, called 'norns,' who appointed children their destinies at their birth, evidently derived their name from the cognate Chaldee word 'Nor,' a child.) and as the 25th of December was called by our Pagan Anglo-Saxon ancestors, 'Yule-day,' or the 'Child's day,' and the night that preceded it, 'Mother-night,' long before they came in contact with Christianity, that sufficiently proves its real character. Far and wide, in the realms of Paganism, was this birth-day observed."

[134] Yule is a time for commemorating births and infants. Its most primeval celebration is the birth of the sun god. Lark, "Heritage of Yule," http://www.webofoz.org/heritage/Yule.shtml: "This is the night of the Winter Solstice, the night of Yule, 'the Wheel.' [the Wiccan religion bases its Wheel on the dance of the sun . . . Our light and darkness and our seasonal changes are determined by Mother Earth and her dance around the Sun creating the Wheel of the Year. Mother Earth/Nature and the Wheel of the Year is what Paganism (known as the Goddess religion) is all about. http://www.hecatescauldron.org/Sabbats.htm] . . . In the North, the months we know as December and January have long been called Freyja's Nights of Darkness. The year's longest night is the Mother Night, and in darkness the Lady labors to bring the Light to birth once more. The Young Sun is born at the Winter Solstice . . . Horus of Egypt, whose sign is the winged Sun, is born. . . . Mithras, the Unconquered Sun of Persia, is born. . . . Juno Lucina, 'the little light,' Goddess of the Moon and of the Midwinter Sun, is born. . . . Isis, Queen of Heaven, gives birth to Horus on the Solstice. Rhea gives birth to Saturn. . . ."

[135] John Plunkett, "Pagan Origins of Christmas," http://bibletools.org/index.cfm/fuseaction/Topical.show/RTD/cgg/ID/1143/Christmas-Pagan-Origins-of.htm.

[136] Hislop, *The Two Babylons*, 134.

[137] Lake Erie Bible Church, "Doctrine of Holidays," http://www.lakeeriebiblechurch.org/Doctrine/html/HOLIDAYS.html.
[138] "The Yule Log: A Pagan Tradition," http://www.exposingsatanism.org/yulelog.htm.
[139] Lake Erie Bible Church, "Doctrine of Holidays," http://www.lakeeriebiblechurch.org/Doctrine/html/HOLIDAYS.html.
[140] Terri Paajanen, "Pagan Origins of Modern Christmas Traditions," http://groups.msn.com/SpellsandRecipesforEverything/yule.msnw?action=get_message&mview=0&ID_Message=3558&LastModified=4675602446795053361 (accessed 10-04-08).
[141] "The History of the Yule Log, Christmas Lore," http://www.christmaslore.com/the_history_of_the_yule_log.html (accessed 10-03-08).
[142] "How Christmas Works," http://www.howstuffworks.com/christmas.htm (accessed 10-03-08).
[143] Jacobs, *Deliver Us From Evil*, 24.
[144] Ibid., 25.
[145] "The Yule Log," http://www.culture.gouv.fr/culture/noel/angl/buche.htm.
[146] "Yule Log Superstitions," http://worldofchristmas.net/christmas-superstitions/yule-log.html.
[147] "Yule Log," http://www.snopes.com/holidays/christmas/yulelog.asp.
[148] "The Yule Log," http://www.culture.gouv.fr/culture/noel/angl/buche.htm.
[149] "Yule Log Superstitions," http://worldofchristmas.net/christmas-superstitions/yule-log.html.
[150] "Yule Log," http://www.snopes.com/holidays/christmas/yulelog.asp.
[151] "Yule Log Superstitions," http://worldofchristmas.net/christmas-superstitions/yule-log.html.
[152] Teresa Ruano, "Sacaea," http://www.candlegrove.com/sacaea.html.
[153] Ibid.
[154] "Yule Log," http://www.snopes.com/holidays/christmas/yulelog.asp.
[155] "The History of the Yule Log, Christmas Lore," http://www.christmaslore.com/the_history_of_the_yule_log.html (accessed 10-03-08).
[156] Καλλικαντζαροι.
[157] Teresa Ruano, "Sacaea," http://www.candlegrove.com/sacaea.html.
[158] "Yule Log," http://www.snopes.com/holidays/christmas/yulelog.asp.
[159] Hislop, *The Two Babylons*, 139.
[160] Frazier, *The Golden Bough*, vi.
[161] Hislop, *The Two Babylons*, 139.
[162] Livio C. Stecchini and Jan Sammer, "King and Mock-King," http://www.nazarenus.com/2-4-mocking.htm.
[163] Ibid.
[164] Dio Chrysostom, *Oration IV*, 66.
[165] Teresa Ruano, "Sacaea," http://www.candlegrove.com/sacaea.html.
[166] πραιτώριον, Mark 15:16 (Latin loanword: praetorium): *the praetorium, governor's official residence* (Matt. 27:27; Mark 15:16; John 18:28, 33; 19:9; Acts

23:35). This may also be the meaning in Phil. 1:13, but here *praetorian guard* is also probable.

[167] Meijer, *The Gladiators*, 34-35.
[168] Coming from Nimrod perhaps?
[169] Meijer, *The Gladiators*, 17.
[170] Ibid., 16.
[171] Ray O'Hanlon, "Christmas suicide shakes community," December 22-28, 2004, www.irishecho.com/newspaper (accessed 12-30-04).
[172] Merriott Terry, Consumer Counseling Service, "Unplug the Christmas Tree, Taking a Holiday Inventory," www.cccsintl.org.

CHAPTER 4
Age-Old Foundation

[173] Nanos, *The Mystery of Romans*, 68.
[174] Ibid., 71-72, footnote 105.
[175] Ibid., 75, footnote 120.
[176] Dr. Wayne Meeks, "Separation from Judaism," http://www.pbs.org/wgbh/pages/frontline/shows/religion/first/wrestling.html.
[177] Eusebius, *Life of Constantine*, 3.17-20, specifically 3.18 NPNF 2nd sermon 1:524.
[178] There are 613 commandments of the Torah (i.e., first five books of the Bible). A person cannot keep every commandment, because there are different commandments applicable to men versus women versus children versus animals . . . For example, there are laws involving temple service (Levitical priests and sacrifices); animals (kosher); concerning the land; Sabbath, fasts, and worship; moral laws having to deal with relationships (how to act toward man); holiness laws (how to act toward God); etc. Yeshua says that the new covenant is the Torah commandments written on your heart (the same ones), which are the simplest things in your house and His. The common sense of right and wrong has been written in people's hearts. The Torah's name means "the teachings," and its object is to help people know God. Your attitude toward God determines what the term "commandments" means to you. Commandments will either be burdens to disobedient hearts or instructions to obedient hearts. The Torah never teaches that it can save you. Remember that it was Abraham's faith that was counted as righteousness.
[179] *Tosefta Avodah Zarah 8.4,* dated circa 300, quoted in Talmud Sanhedrin 56. First detailed in the Tosefta (late second or third century C.E.). The Seven Laws of Noah (Hebrew: שבע מצוות בני חנ, *Sheva mitzvot B'nei Noach*), often referred to as the Noahide Laws, are a set of seven moral imperatives that, according to the Talmud, were given by God to Noah as a binding set of laws for all mankind. According to Judaism, any non-Jew who lives according to these laws is regarded as a Righteous Gentile and is assured of a place in the world to come (Olam Haba), the Jewish concept of heaven. Adherents are often called *"B'nei Noah"* (Children

of Noah) or "Noahides" and often networked in Jewish synagogues. The Noahide Laws were predated by six laws given to Adam in the Garden of Eden. The Talmud states that the instruction to not eat "flesh with the life" was given to Noah, and that Adam and Eve already had received six other commandments. Adam and Eve were not enjoined from eating a living animal since they were forbidden to eat any animal. The remaining six are exegetically derived from a seemingly unnecessary sentence in Gen. 2:16. Later at the Revelation at Sinai, the Seven Laws of Noah were re-given to humanity and embedded in the 613 laws given to the children of Israel along with the Ten Commandments, which are part of, not separate from, the 613 *mitzvot* (commandments). The Noahide laws are regarded as the way through which non-Jews can have a direct and meaningful relationship with God or at least comply with the minimal requisites of civilization and of divine law. One should also keep in mind that these laws are only the minimal basis for a Righteous Gentile's service to God, since there are many Jewish *mitzvos* that non-Jews are encouraged to adopt to accomplish more. Through these laws, a Gentile refines himself and the creation as a whole, fulfilling his purpose for existence.

[180] Nanos, *The Mystery of Romans*, 52.
[181] Novak, *The Image of the Non-Jew in Judaism*, 3-4.
[182] Nanos, *The Mystery of Romans*, 53-54.
[183] Skarsaune, *In the Shadow of the Temple*, 259.
[184] Eusebius, *Ecclesiastical History*, 5.1-4.
[185] Skarsaune, *In the Shadow Of The Temple*, 235-239.
[186] Bullinger, *Number in Scripture*, 107-108.
[187] Nanos, *The Mystery of Romans*, 57.
[188] MacMullen, *Paganism in the Roman Empire*, 40.
[189] Nanos, *The Mystery of Romans*, 81.
[190] The History Channel, "The Real Story of Christmas—Saturnalia," http://www.history.com: "In Rome . . . Saturnalia—a holiday in honor of Saturn, the god of agriculture—was celebrated. Beginning in the week leading up to the winter solstice and continuing for a full month, Saturnalia was a hedonistic time, when food and drink were plentiful and the normal Roman social order was turned upside down. In the early years of Christianity, Easter was the main holiday; the birth of Jesus was not celebrated. In the fourth century, church officials decided to institute the birth of Jesus as a holiday. Although some evidence suggests that his birth may have occurred in the spring, Pope Julius I chose December 25. It is commonly believed that the church chose this date in an effort to adopt and absorb the traditions of the pagan Saturnalia festival."
[191] Miles, *Christmas Customs and Traditions*, 168.
[192] *Webster's Collegiate Dictionary*, 10th ed. "talisman: 1: an object held to act as a charm [i.e. practice or expression believed to have magic power; a trait that fascinates, allures, or delights; a physical grace or attraction] 2: something producing apparently magical effects."
[193] Matthews, *The Winter Solstice*, 23.
[194] Hislop, *The Two Babylons*, 133.

195 Victoria Westlane, "Christmas Around the World," *Tidbits of Fort Collins,* December 21, 2005, p.1.
196 MacMullen, *Paganism in the Roman Empire,* 24.
197 MacMullen, *Paganism in the Roman Empire,* 152-153, footnote 28.
198 Kittel, *Theological Dictionary of the New Testament,* vol. 6, 455-458.
199 Origen, Father of the Church (c. 185-254), who was called the most influential theologian of the early church, was the first to promote the idea that the church had replaced Israel as God's chosen people.
200 Wilson, *Luke,* 96-97.
201 Ibid., 89-91.
202 MacMullen, *Paganism in the Roman Empire,* 41.
203 In Acts 15, the word for blood is αἱμά (pronounced as "haima"). Kittel, *Theological Dictionary of the New Testament,* vol. 1, 176: "Hellenistic blood mysticism is to be seen in the Dionysus-Zagreuscult, in which union with the god is achieved by eating the divine animal torn and consumed in a wild frenzy, and especially in the Attic mysteries, with their regeneration and divinization of the devotee through the blood of the sacred animal sprinkled over him."
204 Wilson, *Luke,* 97-98.
205 Skarsaune, *In the Shadow of the Temple,* 433.
206 Popularized by the church historian Saint Bede (c. 673-735).
207 John 1:1; Rev. 1:8.
208 Tozer, *The Knowledge of the Holy,* 39.
209 Ibid.
210 Dionysis Exiguus, i.e. Denis the Lowly, was a compiler of canon law and a good computer.
211 Heilbron, *The Sun in the Church,* 36.
212 Scarlata, *A Family Guide to the Biblical Holidays.*
213 Skarsaune, *In the Shadow of the Temple,* 27-28.
214 Kittel, *Theological Dictionary of the New Testament,* vol. 2, 505: "The process of Hellenising non-Greeks began before the establishment of the Macedonian Greek empire. It was greatly accelerated by this important event. The first result of the conquests of Philip and Alexander was the incorporation of Macedonia and its hinterland into the sphere of Hellenic culture. There followed the superficial Hellenisation of the kingdoms of Asia and Egypt, especially of the existing cities and of the newly established colonial cities, which were under the supervision of Macedonian Greece and the populations of which were partly Hellenised with the adoption of the Greek language and customs. Through mixed marriages there very quickly arose a semi-Greek world. The development took different forms in the different territories. In the kingdom of the Ptolemies the term "Greek" was reserved for the ruling caste which maintained its traditional language, culture and religion in the new land. In Asia, however, there was a wider acceptance of the culture of the Ἕλληνες by native non-Hellenes. Here the number of new cities was greater, and these became centers for the Hellenisation of the surrounding districts. There was an increasing integration of those born Hellenes with Hellenes

of barbarian origin who had accepted ἑλληνισμός, i.e., the Greek language, culture and religion. Almost as important as the Hellenisation of the East is the spread of Greek culture and language to the West."
[215] Ἰουδαϊσμός is the spelling in 2 Maccabees 2:21.
[216] Although First & Second Maccabees are extra-canonical books, they are considered to be accurate historical accounts of events surrounding Chanukah.
[217] Skarsaune, *In the Shadow of the Temple*, 40.
[218] Aish.com staff, "Historic Timeline, Selucid Syrian/Greek conquer Israel," www.aish.com/chanukahbasics.
[219] Maier, *Josephus—The Essential Works*, 211.
[220] Rabbi Ken Spiro, "Alexander and the Jews," www.aish.com/chanukahbasics.
[221] Rabbi Ken Spiro, "Crash Course in Jewish History Part 28—Greek Persecution," www.aish.com/literacy/jewishhistory.
[222] Revelation from a dream given to Stephanie Hillberry.
[223] Heilbron, *The Sun in the Church*, 28.
[224] In Hebrew, the Passover Feast is called *Pesach* and was initiated in Exod. 12:6-7–Lev. 23:5; 1 Cor. 5:7.
[225] In Hebrew, the Feast of First Fruits is called *Bikkurim*—Lev. 23:9-14; 1 Cor. 15:20-23, which is the actual date Jesus rose from the dead, being the first fruit of many brethren.
[226] In Hebrew, the Feast of Unleavened Bread is called *Hag Ha Mazhah*—Lev. 23:6-8; 1 Cor. 15:7-8.
[227] Lev. 23:1.
[228] Heilbron, *The Sun in the Church*, 13.
[229] Ibid., 28.
[230] Ibid., 26.
[231] Ibid., 26.
[232] Bullinger, *Number in Scripture*, 251.
[233] Heilbron, *The Sun in the Church*, 24.
[234] Ibid., 26.
[235] In chapter II, section I, of *The Two Babylons*, Alexander Hislop quotes Zonaras, who finds concurrent testimony from ancient authors that arithmetic, magic, and astronomy came from the Chaldees to the Egyptians, and thence, to the Greeks. Although I greatly appreciate the value of mathematics and astronomy, we need to be aware that their origins on earth did not begin with the Lord initiating their practices.
[236] Heilbron, *The Sun in the Church*, 3.
[237] Ibid., 36.
[238] Carroll, *Constantine's Sword*, 191.
[239] Heilbron, *The Sun in the Church*, 37.
[240] Ibid., 38.
[241] Ibid., 38-39.
[242] Ibid., 39.
[243] Ibid.

244 Ibid., 144.
245 Ibid., 145.
246 Matthews, *The Winter Solstice*, 23.
247 Refer to Gen. 4:1-7. Cain brought an offering to the Lord of the fruit of the ground, for which the Lord had no regard.

CHAPTER 5
The Golden Snare

248 I.e., yeast.
249 Rood, *The Pagan-Christian Connection EXPOSED*, 52.
250 Thomas, *New American Standard Hebrew-Aramaic and Greek Dictionaries*: "The Hebrew verb translated 'rashly' here is 'laa' [לעע] (534b); a prim. root; *to talk wildly*:— been rash (1), say rashly (1), which is used only one other time in Job 6:3 where the context would give a meaning of 'rash'." "For then it would be heavier than the sands of the seas, Therefore my words have been rash" (Job 6:3 NASB). A key to any word that is used only a few times is context. What does the context determine that this word must mean?
251 Bradford, *Of Plymouth Plantation*, 97.
252 Paul Harvey, "The Rest of the Story," KCOL 600 AM radio, December 17, 2004, 3:05 PM.
253 Neal, *The History of the Puritans*, 458.
254 *Uncle John's Bathroom Reader Plunges Into History*, 245, footnote.
255 The east.
256 Tenney, *The Zondervan Pictorial Bible Dictionary*, "High Places," 354.
257 Simon Sleightholm, http://website.lineone.net/%7Essleightholm/dict/glossary/pcap.htm: "Phrygia was an ancient country of Asia Minor, in what is now Turkey. The religion of the Phrygians was an ecstatic nature worship, in which the Great Mother of the Gods, Rhea, or Cybele, and a male deity, Sabazius, played a prominent part. The orgiastic rites of this religion influenced both the Greeks and the Romans. In the 6th century BC Croesus, king of Lydia, conquered all that was left of Phrygia, which passed successively under the rule of Persia, Macedonia, Pergamum, and Rome. The Phrygian cap was adopted by freed slaves in Roman times, and thus this cap became a symbol of liberty. A conical cap with top turned forward, it is often red to signify circumcision and is the origin of the bishop's mitre and the Rosicrucians' hat."
258 Rood, *The Pagan-Christian Connection EXPOSED*, 85-86.
259 Ibid., 87.
260 Hislop, *The Two Babylons*, 338.
261 Thomas Horn, http://www.worthynews.com/christian/abortion-baal-worship-and-breast-cancer.
262 Hislop, *The Two Babylons*, "The Name of the Beast, the Number of His Name," 397.

[263] *The New International Dictionary of the Christian Church*, Christmas, James Taylor, 223.
[264] Carroll, *Constantine's Sword*, 315.
[265] Elliott, *The Christianity of Constantine The Great*, vii.
[266] Ibid., "Legislation," p.113. Additionally, it is clear from documented evidence that Constantine deplored Judaism and Jews.
[267] Eusebius, *Life of Constantine*, 3.18.
[268] Ibid.
[269] Ibid.
[270] Ludwig Schneider, "Anti-Semitism," *Israel Today*, No. 94, November 2006, 15.
[271] Carroll, *Constantine's Sword*, 281.
[272] Elliott, *The Christianity of Constantine The Great*, "The Council of Nicaea," 197.
[273] Ibid., 214.
[274] Ibid., "Legislation," 101.
[275] Ibid., "The Council of Nicaea," 211.
[276] WorldNetDaily, "'Silent Night' secularized," December 7, 2005, www.WorldNetDaily.com
[277] "La Befana," www.zuzu.org/italy.html.
[278] www.noelchristmasstore.com.
[279] *Merriam Webster's Collegiate Dictionary*, 10th ed.
[280] Brown, *The DaVinci Code*, 232.
[281] Ibid., 232-233.
[282] Ibid., 234.
[283] Ibid., 235.
[284] Jones, *Constantine The Great and the Conversion of Europe*, 185-187.
[285] Carroll, *Constantine's Sword*, 192-193, 195.
[286] Elliott, *The Christianity of Constantine The Great*, 214.
[287] MacMullen, *Christianizing the Roman Empire*, 44.
[288] Adapted from the Babylonian Tammuz.
[289] Elliott, *The Christianity of Constantine The Great*, 9.
[290] Carroll, *Constantine's Sword*, 185.
[291] Brown, *The DaVinci Code*, 232.
[292] Elliott, *The Christianity of Constantine The Great*, 325.
[293] Ibid., "Constantine Executed Fausta and Crispus," 18, 68, 232.
[294] Constantine II, Constans, and Constantius.
[295] Carroll, *Constantine's Sword*, 204.
[296] Trier army, mainly made up of Teutons and Celts.
[297] Elliott, *The Christianity of Constantine The Great*, 258.
[298] Rood, *The Pagan-Christian Connection EXPOSED*, "The Heavyweight Battle of the Ages," 100.
[299] Elliott, *The Christianity of Constantine The Great*, "Gothic Wars; Buildings; Administration," 256-257, 259.

[300] James Sill, "The Virgin Birth and Childhood Mysteries of Jesus," www.infidels.org
[301] Restad, *Christmas in America*, 4.
[302] Ibid., 5-6.
[303] Hislop, *The Two Babylons*, 350.
[304] Elliott, *The Christianity of Constantine The Great*, "Last Years," 326. He was still *pontifex maximus* as his successors were until Gratian renounced the title in 382.
[305] Hislop, *The Two Babylons*, 133.
[306] Matthews, *The Winter Solstice*, "The Solstice Dream," 23.
[307] Ibid., 28.
[308] Ibid., 24.
[309] Kevin Reed, "Christmas: An Historical Survey Regarding Its Origins and Opposition to It," http://www.swrb.com/newslett/actualNLs/Xmas_ch2.htm.
[310] Bede, *A History of the English Church and People*, 86-87.
[311] Kevin Reed, "Christmas: An Historical Survey Regarding Its Origins and Opposition to It," http://www.swrb.com/newslett/actualNLs/Xmas_ch2.htm.
[312] Rood, *The Pagan-Christian Connection EXPOSED*, 61-62.
[313] Brown, *The DaVinci Code*, 232.
[314] Rood, *The Pagan-Christian Connection EXPOSED*, 164, and Hislop, *The Two Babylons*, 62.
[315] Rood, *The Pagan-Christian Connection EXPOSED*, 86-87.
[316] Restad, *Christmas in America*, 4.
[317] *The Catholic Encyclopedia*, vol. 3, 727.
[318] Matthews, *The Winter Solstice*, "Child of Wonder," 52-54.
[319] Frazer, *The Golden Bough*, 471.
[320] *The Catholic Encyclopedia*, vol. 3, 727.
[321] Carroll, *Constantine's Sword*, 183.
[322] Dowley, *Eerdman's Handbook to the History of Christianity*, 130.
[323] Skarsaune, *In the Shadow of the Temple*, 433.
[324] Heidler, *The Messianic Church Arising!*, 26.
[325] Recognized Fathers of the church.
[326] *The Catholic Encyclopedia*, vol. 3, 724.
[327] Skarsaune, *In the Shadow of the Temple*, 259.
[328] Ibid., 432-433.
[329] Ibid., 433.
[330] Hislop, *The Two Babylons*, 133.
[331] Telushkin, *Jewish Literacy*, "The Ten Commandments/Aseret Ha-Dibrot," 56.
[332] Maimonides (Moses ben Maimon c. 1135-1204).
[333] Telushkin, *Jewish Literacy*, "The Ten Commandments/Aseret Ha-Dibrot," 56.
[334] Matthews, *The Winter Solstice*, 7.
[335] Scherman, *The Chumash*, "Second Commandment: Prohibition of Idolatry," 408.

336 The History Channel, "Christmas Trees," www.historychannel.com/exhibits/holidays/christmas/trees.html.
337 Walsh, *Curiosities of Popular Customs*, 242, 2155.
338 Cheyne, *Encyclopedia Biblica*, "Asherah," 330, www.case.edu/univlib/preserve/Etana/encyl_biblica_a-d/arimathaea-asshyrim.pdf (accessed 10/4/08). For example: fire altars, green trees, and Asherah poles. Asherah, rendered as "groves" (Exod. 34:13, Deut. 12:3, Judg. 6:25), were placed, down to the seventh century, by the altars of Yahweh not only on the high places, but also in Jerusalem's temple.
339 Cheyne, *Encyclopaedia Biblica*, 2145.
340 Matthews, *The Winter Solstice*, 7.
341 The History Channel, "World Traditions," www.historychannel.com/exhibits/holidays/christmas/world.html.
342 Matthew, *The Winter Solstice*, 6.
343 Ibid., "Old Sir Christmas," 118-119.
344 Price, *The Prophet's Dictionary*, "Altar," 35-36.
345 Matthews, *The Winter Solstice*, "The Green Bough," 82-83.
346 Restad, *Christmas in America*, 63-64.
347 The History Channel, "Christmas Trees, Germany," www.historychannel.com/exhibits/holidays/christmas/trees.html.
348 Steven Wells, "Taking the Christ out of Christmas," *Philadelphia Weekly*, December 19, 2007, http://www.philadelphiaweekly.com/articles/16080.
349 Captain Jack's Christmas Tree Farm Network, http://www.christmas-tree.com/where.html.
350 Said What? http://www.saidwhat.co.uk/quotes/political/winston_churchill/those_that_fail_to_learn_from_2804 (accessed 10-05-08).
351 John L. Hoh, Jr., "Review—Martin Luther's Christmas Book," http://www.suite101.com/article.cfm/lutheranism/97283 (accessed 10/4/08).
352 Refer to *Concerning the Jews and Their Lies* by Martin Luther, "Disputation and Dialogue," 34-36. Please note that The World Lutheran Federation in 1984, which celebrated the 500th anniversary of Martin Luther's birth, made a statement: "We cannot accept or condone the violent verbal attacks that the Reformer made against the Jews. The sins of Luther's anti-Jewish remarks and the violence of his attacks on the Jews must be acknowledged with deep distress, and on all occasion for similar sin in the present or the future must be removed from our churches . . ."
353 *The Register of Ministers in Geneva* (1546) detailed a list of "faults which went against the Reformation."
354 de Greef, *The Writings of John Calvin: An Introductory Guide*, 57.
355 Calvin, *Tracts Relating to the Reformation*, vol. 1, 123-236.
356 Knox, *Knox's History*, vol. 2, 281.
357 Ibid., vol. 6, 547-548.
358 Calderwood, *Perth Assembly* (circa 1619), 83-84.
359 Carroll, *Constantine's Sword*, 555.

360 Defined on July 18,1870.
361 Carroll, *Constantine's Sword*, 439-440.
362 Carroll, *Constantine's Sword*, 555.
363 The History Channel, "World Traditions," www.historychannel.com/exhibits/holidays/christmas/world.html.
364 Matthews, *The Winter Solstice*, "The Green Bough," 81.
365 The History Channel, "World Traditions," www.historychannel.com/exhibits/holidays/christmas/world.html.
366 The History Channel, "Christmas Trees," www.historychannel.com/exhibits/holidays/christmas/trees.html.
367 *Webster's New World Dictionary*, "Northern European peoples, especially the Germans," 444.
368 Matthews, *The Winter Solstice*, "Old Sir Christmas," 125.
369 The History Channel, "Christmas Trees," www.historychannel.com/exhibits/holidays/christmas/trees.html.

CHAPTER 6
The Golden Calf

370 At Solomon's death in 928 BC, his kingdom was divided in two: the northern kingdom comprised of 10 tribes (came under the dominion of Jeroboam) and the southern kingdom comprised of only Judah and Benjamin.

371 *Personal note*: Jeroboam's name יָרְבְעָם is a combination of two words: רִיב, which is a verb (as well as a primitive root) and *rîb* that means "to contend or have a legal complaint." The LORD uses this verb through the prophets to "lay a charge" against Israel. רִיב: (legal) dispute, case, lawsuit, submit one's case to, leave one's case in the hands of (Jer. 11:20). עַם (a whole) people (emphasis on internal ethnic solidarity, Gen. 11:6). Harris, *Theological Word Book of the Old Testament*, 2159: "בִיר (*rîb*) strive, contend. 3. . . . Its near restriction in the OT to use of the divine action, when civil functions are designated, is hard to explain. It is worth noting that about a third of the appearances of *rîb* (vb.) are in the LXX rendered by *krinō*, a word with prevalently legal-judicial overtones. There has been much discussion in recent times of the *rîb* motif as referring to the divine lawsuit against Israel for having broken the covenant. 5. Three times *rîb* has the connotation of 'to complain' (BDB). . . . this sense 'complain' was understood to be one of the genuine, if rare, senses of *rîb* in ancient times. בִיר (*rîb*). **Strife, controversy, cause, etc**. This noun, whether cognate or derived, or if the verb is denominative, seems beyond our present knowledge. In poetic parallel it appears with words for justification, pleading a cause, chastisement, punishment. *Rîb* is one of the rather large number of Hebrew words which must be examined by anyone wishing to construct a biblical theology of government."

372 Harris, *Theological Word Book of the Old Testament*, 2159: "בִיר (*rîb*) *strive, contend*. 1. To strive in the sense of physical combat is apparently primary. It may

be of single combat between two men (Exod. 21:18) or of contending groups (Deut. 33:7; Jud. 11:25, though the figure is of single combat). It is not surprising therefore that LXX, in ten of the approximately seventy occurrences of *rîb*, renders by *machomai* (Hatch and Redpath, Concordance to the LXX) deponent middle and aorist pass., beginning at Gen 26:20, meaning 'to fight,' in physical combat between single men, men and beasts, or between armies."

[373] Strong, *The New Strong's Exhaustive Concordance*, OT:1008.
[374] Ibid., OT:1835.
[375] There are times when something wicked is a slight twist off of something righteous.
[376] Nave, *The Naves's Topical Bible*, "High Places," 430.
[377] Scherman, *The Chumash*, "Moses Receives the Tablets," 492.
[378] Seekins, *Hebrew Word Pictures*, "Pride," 22.
[379] Ibid., "Sheen," 94.
[380] Teleshkin, *Jewish Literacy*, "Mount Sinai and the Giving of the Torah," 53.
[381] Hislop, *The Two Babylons*, 64, 65.
[382] Scherman, *The Chumash*, "The Ten Commandments," 407.
[383] Ibid., 15. "Saw the Thunder," 413.
[384] Ibid., 20. "The Ten Commandments," 407.
[385] Hislop, *The Two Babylons*, "The Child in Egypt," 65.
[386] Ibid.
[387] Russell, *The Prince of Darkness*, 111-114.
[388] Michael Ott, "Catholic Encyclopedia, St. Nicholas of Myra," www.newadvent.org/cathen/11063b.htm.
[389] "Saint Nicholas," http://en.wikipedia.org/wiki/Saint_Nicholas (accessed 10/4/08).
[390] Matthews, *The Winter Solstice*, 7.
[391] Otis, *The Twilight Labyrinth*, 334, footnote 103.
[392] Matthews, *The Winter Solstice*, "Old Sir Christmas," 117-118.
[393] Otis, *The Twilight Labyrinth*, "Enchanting the Lie," 161.
[394] Ibid.
[395] CNN Television, December 12, 2004, 7:30 PM.
[396] Victoria Westlane, "Christmas Around the World," *Tidbits of Fort Collins*, December 21, 2005, 3.
[397] The Hebrew word for repentance (*teshuvah*) means to turn away.
[398] 2 Tim. 2:3-5.
[399] *Webster's Collegiate Dictionary*, 10th ed., 300-301.
[400] Henry, *Matthew Henry's Commentary on the Whole Bible*, Exodus 32:6, 139.
[401] *Webster's Collegiate Dictionary*, 10th ed., 1330.
[402] Matthews, *The Winter Solstice*, "The Solstice Dream," 31.
[403] Heschel, *The Sabbath*, "To Sanctify Time," 85.
[404] *Webster's Collegiate Dictionary*, 10th ed., 576.

CHAPTER 7
This Is Radical!

[405] Refer to Mark 9:14-29.

[406] Our Christmas tree and packages represented the Christmas holiday for my family. I don't remember exactly how Santa was phased out for us, but I believe that it was a Holy Spirit-guided decision before my son was 5-years old. When we celebrated Christmas in Montana with my extended family, it was much more difficult to remain Santa-less. All of my son's older cousins received gifts from Santa; it seemed almost cruel to not go along with this "harmless" family/cultural tradition. Even though my husband instinctively recognized the commercial hoax of Christmas, he was quick to question who was I to defy societal reality and what the church has taught and endorsed for centuries.

[407] December 21, 1998—The day of the winter solstice.

[408] Bullinger, *Number in Scripture*, 235.

[409] Ibid., 135-136.

[410] Ibid., 137.

[411] Ibid., 138.

[412] Matt. 11:1-5, Mark 1:40-44, Luke 5:14.

[413] Joyner, *The Apostolic Ministry*, 105.

[414] Ibid., 113.

[415] For more information on Easter, I recommend Ralph Woodrow's book *Babylon Mystery Religion*.

[416] *Matthew Henry's Commentary,* "Colossians 2:16-23," 2333: "Much of the ceremonies of the law of Moses consisted in the distinction of meats and days. It appears by Rom. 14 that there were those who were for keeping up those distinctions; but here the apostle shows that since Christ has come, and has cancelled the ceremonial law, we ought no to keep it up." As already discussed, the Bible says that Jesus did not abolish or cancel the Law or the Prophets, He fulfilled them (Matt. 5:17). When the Christian church tried not to have anything in common with the Jews and cast out the feasts of the Lord (which they rightly associated with the Jews), there was a big hole in their celebratory life. As we have been taught, the world abhors a vacuum; therefore, pagan feasts were co-opted and magically made "Christian" to replace the feasts of the Lord, which were originally designated by God as His appointed times, His holy convocations, and three of His feasts are designated as perpetual—continuing forever, i.e., eternal. (See Lev. 23.) Even though Matthew Henry is not necessarily considered a scholar in these times, his work is very good, albeit dated.

[417] Brown, *Our Hands Are Stained With Blood*, 82.

[418] David Wilkerson, *World Challenge Pulpit Series,* "I Have Labored in Vain," December 19, 2005, 3.

[419] Joyner, *The Apostolic Ministry,* 118.

[420] מוֹעֵד (*mo-ed*): 1. meeting-place (Josh. 8:14); 2. meeting, assembly (Hos. 9:5); 3. appointed time, fixed day (Exod. 9:5); 4. (time of) feast (Lam. 2:7).

[421] The Hebrew word for *feast* is חַג (*hag*), which carries the meanings: 1. procession, round dance, festival 2. comb. for specific festivals. "And on the fifteenth day of the same month *is* the feast of unleavened bread unto the LORD: seven days ye must eat unleavened bread" (Lev. 23:6 KJV). "Then on the fifteenth day of the same month there is the Feast of Unleavened Bread to the LORD; for seven days you shall eat unleavened bread" (Lev. 23:6 NAS). *Fausset's Bible Dictionary*, 1238: "Feasts 1238.01 *Hag* (from a root, to dance) is the Hebrew applied to the Passover, and still more to the feast of Tabernacles, as both were celebrated with rejoicings and participation of food (Exod. 12:14; Lev. 23:39; Num. 29:12; Deut. 16:39). But *mo'ed* is the general term for all sacred assemblies convoked on stated anniversaries; God's people by His appointment meeting before Him in brotherly fellowship for worship. Their communion was primarily with God, then with one another. These national feasts tended to join all in one brotherhood. Hence, arose Jeroboam's measures to counteract the effect on his people (1 Kings 12:26, 27). Hezekiah made the revival of the national Passover a primary step in his efforts for a reformation (2 Chr. 30:1). The Roman government felt the feast a time when especial danger of rebellion existed (Mt. 26:5; Luke 13:1). The 'congregations,' 'calling of assemblies,' 'solemn meetings' (Isa. 1:13; Ps. 81:3), both on the convocation days of the three great feasts, Passover, Pentecost, and Tabernacles, and also on the Sabbaths, imply assemblies for worship, the forerunners of the synagogue (compare 2 Kings 4:23)."

[422] Strong, *The New Strong's Exhaustive Concordance*, OT:4150.

[423] Ibid., OT:3259. The primitive root is יָעַד (*ya'ad*) and this carries the meanings of "to meet or assemble."

[424] *Webster's Collegiate Dictionary*, 10th ed. "betroth: 1: to promise to marry 2: to give in marriage."

[425] Strong, *The New Strong's Exhaustive Concordance*, OT:3068.

[426] Ibid., OT:4744: "And in the first day *there shall be* an holy convocation, and in the seventh day there shall be an holy convocation to you; no manner of work shall be done in them, save *that* which every man must eat, that only may be done of you" (Exod. 12:16 KJV). "And on the first day you shall have a holy assembly, and *another* holy assembly on the seventh day; no work at all shall be done on them, except what must be eaten by every person, that alone may be prepared by you" (Exod. 12:16 NAS). The word is מִקְרָא (*mikra*), which does have the nuance of "convocation." This word is used with מִקְרָא־קֹדֶשׁ (*kodesh*) to mean "holy assembly/convocation."

[427] Pesach (7 days) + Shavuot (1 day) + Rosh Hashanah (1 day) + Yom Kippur (1 day) + Sukkot (7 days) + Shimini Atzeres (1 day).

[428] Greek name for the Messiah.

[429] Rom. 11:8.

[430] Joyner, *The Apostolic Ministry*, 110.

[431] Ibid.

[432] Strong, *The New Strong's Exhaustive Concordance*, OT:4503.
[433] "Interview—Aviad Cohen," *Israel Today*, no. 82, November 2005, 23.
[434] Ruth Reichmann, "Christmas," Max Kade German-American Center, IUPUI, Data Realm, http://www.serve.com/shea/germusa/xmasintr.htm (accessed 12-27-05).
[435] John Roach, "War on Christmas Charge Echoes Past Debates, Expert Says," December 23, 2005, http://www.news.nationalgeographic.com/news/2005/12/1223_051223_christmas.html.
[436] Ruth Reichman, "Christmas," Max Kade German-American Center, IUPUI, Data Realm, http://www.serve.com/shea/germusa/xmasintr.htm (accessed 12-27-05).
[437] The History Channel, "Christmas Trees," www.historychannel.com/exhibits/holidays/christmas.trees.html.
[438] "English Puritanism and the Puritan Revolution," http://hymnsandcarolsofchristmas/History/The_Puritans.htm.
[439] The History Channel, "An Outlaw Christmas," http://www.history.com/minisite.do?content_type=Minisite_generic&content_type_id=1254&display_order=1&sub_display_order=3&mini_id+1290.
[440] Scott Atkins, "The American Sense of Puritan," http://xroads.virginia.edu/~CAP/puritan/purmain.html.
[441] Within the Victorian era.
[442] George Will, "Blame the Puritans," *Jewish World Review*, December 4, 2003, http://www.jewishworldreview.com/cols/will20403.asp.
[443] The History Channel, "Saturnalia, The Real Story of Christmas," http://www.history.com/minisite.do?content_type=Minisite_Generic&content_type_id=1253&display_order=1&sub_display_order=2&mini_id=1290.
[444] Matthews, *The Winter Solstice*, 8: "People everywhere seem less and less concerned with the celebration of anything other than the holiday itself and its ever more commercially strident accompaniment."
[445] Andrew Santella, "The War on Christmas, the Prequel, When the holiday was banned," December 21, 2005, http://www.slate.com/id/2132387.
[446] Adam Cohen, "Commercial Christmas, or else," http://www.iht.com/articles/2005/12/07/opinion/edcohen.php.
[447] Andrew Santella, "The War on Christmas, the Prequel, When the holiday was banned," December 21, 2005, http://www.slate.com/id/2132387.
[448] Forbes, *Christmas: A Candid History*, 58.
[449] Finney, *Holiness of Christians in the Present Life*, No. 13, "Gospel Liberty," August 16, 1843.
[450] Spurgeon, *Metropolitan Tabernacle Pulpit*, 697.
[451] Andrew Santella, "The War on Christmas, the Prequel, When the holiday was banned," December 21, 2005, http://www.slate.com/id/2132387.
[452] Thompson, *Presbyterians in the South*, 434-435.
[453] Smith, *How Is the Gold Become Dim*, 97-105.

⁴⁵⁴ "Genu-wine" is a prophetic term that's a playful combination of the words genuine and wine. To be genuine is to be sincere and honest; to be free from hypocrisy or pretense; to actually have the reputed qualities of the character of Christ. Wine is made from pressing the grapes that abides in the Vine (i.e., Jesus). Communion wine is representative of Jesus' blood shed for us. The acceptance of the cross allows Christ's atoning sacrifice to wash away our sins. "Blood" is also a term for family; therefore the beautiful fermented beverage poured out to a lost and dying world is His very essence—His own family. Genu-wine believers will manifest the incredibly loving and perfect character of our Lord Jesus Christ. Genu-wine is a golden new wine that flows like a river of living water.

CHAPTER 8
Fullness of Time

⁴⁵⁵ *Webster's New World Dictionary*, 10th ed.

⁴⁵⁶ The Dome of the Rock is on the exact spot. Herod's temple had the Holy of Holies on that exact spot. This is why Jews today pray at the Wailing Wall, as it is the closest point to the Holy of Holies (aka, the Mount). There are other exposed points of the Jerusalem Wall. Why don't they pray there? They are not the closest point.

⁴⁵⁷ The exact term *Shekinah* is not used in Hebrew Scripture. This is a noun created from the Hebrew verb *shakan,* which means "to dwell." The term *Skekinah/Shakinah* is a later Talmud term which describes God's "dwelling." "Moses was not able to enter into the tent of the congregation, because the cloud <u>abode</u> thereon, and the glory of the LORD filled the tabernacle" (Exod. 40:35 KJV). "And Moses was not able to enter the tent of meeting because the cloud had <u>settled</u> on it, and the glory of the LORD filled the tabernacle" (Exod. 40:35 NAS). "Abode and settled" are a translation of this Hebrew verb שָׁכַן *(shacan).* In both translations "glory" is כָּבוֹד *(kabod)* or "heaviness-honor-glory."

⁴⁵⁸ Harris, *Theological Word book of the Old Testament*: "אֶבֶן *(even).* **Stone.** The meaning of *even* is almost singularly 'stone,' and in the cognate Semitic languages both meaning and usage are the same. Stones are common in the Middle East, and the word occurs more than 275 times in the Hebrew and Aramaic of the Bible. In all but a few places, which are cited below, the meaning is simply 'stone.'"

⁴⁵⁹ Scherman, *The Chumash*, 545: "Throughout the Torah, only this Four Letter Name of God—the Name representing His Attribute of Mercy—is used in connection with offerings, never the Name *Elohim*, which represents His Attribute of Judgment (*Sifra*). Ancient idolaters believed that animal-offerings were needed to assuage the anger of a judgmental, bloodthirsty god. This is totally foreign to a Jewish belief. The Torah teaches us that offerings are a means to draw closer to HASHEM—the Merciful God (*R'Hirsch*)." *Adonai* is what is said when the tetra gram יהוה is used. This is the four letter name of God that is not spoken and later comes to us as *Hashem* (The Name).

460 Lev. 1:2: "Speak to the Children of Israel and say to them: When a man among you brings an offering to HASHEM: from animals—from the cattle or from the flock shall you bring your offering." Scherman, *The Chumash*, 545: "The root of the word קָרְבָּן *offering*, is קרב, *coming near*, because an offering is the means to bring ourselves closer to God and to elevate ourselves (R'Hirsch). For this reason, the common translation, *sacrifice*, does not capture the essence of the word."

461 The term "burnt offering" is really one Hebrew word, which is first used in Gen. 8:20 KJV: "And Noah builded an altar unto the LORD; and took of every clean beast, and of every clean fowl, and offered burnt offerings on the altar." The Hebrew word here is עֹלָה, transliterated as *olah*. This noun is formed from the verb עָלָה, "to go up," which is a good description of what happens to the offering . . . it goes up. God in His playfulness will use the verb and the constructed noun together to form a phrase like: he make go up (offered) that which goes up (an offering).

462 *Webster's Collegiate Dictionary*, 10th ed., 387: "entirety 1: the state of being entire or complete 2: SUM TOTAL, WHOLE; entire 1: having no element or part left out: WHOLE 2: complete in degree: TOTAL 3 a: consisting of one piece b: HOMOGENEOUS, UNMIXED."

463 Lev. 1:3 KJV: "If his offering *be* a burnt sacrifice of the herd, let him offer a male without blemish: he shall offer it of his own voluntary will at the door of the tabernacle of the congregation before the LORD." Leviticus 1:3 NAS: "If his offering is a burnt offering from the herd, he shall offer it, a male without defect; he shall offer it at the doorway of the tent of meeting, that he may be accepted before the LORD." תָּמִים *(tamim)* 1. whole, entire: day (Josh. 10:13), year (Lev. 25:30); — 2. intact: tree (Ezek. 15:5); — 3 unobjectionable: way (2 Sam. 22:31), free of blemish: sacrificial animals (Exod. 12:5)— 4. blameless (Gen. 6:9). Harris, *Theological Word Book*: "2522d תָּמִים *(tāmîm)* **complete. 2522e** מְתֹם *(mĕtōm)* **entirety.** With the verb's fundamental idea of completeness, Samuel inquired of Jesse, 'Are here all (Heb *hătammû*) thy children?' (I Sam 16:11). Cf. *tāmîm* (the root *tāmam*'s most common derivative), describing an entire day (Josh 10:13) or a whole, and therefore healthy, vine (Ezk 15:5). *mĕtōm* indicates soundness of flesh (Ps 38:3). *tāmîm* delimits Israel's sacrifices, which were to be without blemish, perfect in that respect, so as to be accepted (Lev 22:21–22) as types of Christ, the spotless Lamb of God (I Pet 1:19). Speech which is *tāmîm* (Amos 5:10) corresponds to 'what is complete, entirely in accord with truth and fact' (BDB, p. 1071). . . . *tāmam* moves naturally toward that which is ethically sound, upright (Ps 19:13 [H 14]). . . . *tāmam* is used with the commandments of God meaning to fulfill them (Josh 4:10)."

464 Plural for priest, כֹּהֲנִים—specifically the *kohanim* were and are direct descendants of Aaron.

465 In Gen. 17:17, Abram laughed at the idea of Sarah having a son. In verse 19 God said that there would be a son and his name would be Isaac. In English there is no connection, but in Hebrew there is a story to be told. Isaac's name is formed from the Hebrew word mentioned above צחק *(tsachak)*, as "to laugh."

The form is a verb in what is called the Qal Imperfect, which has the action of the verb to be future and continual. Thus Isaac's name means "he will laugh." Just think, every time Sarah would call her son to come in for dinner she would be calling "Laughing Boy," and would thus remember the faithfulness of God and His Covenant. Isaac (*Yitschak*) carried this prophetic name his entire life.

[466] Strong, *The New Strong's Exhaustive Concordance*, OT:7130: "קֶרֶב (*qerev/ qereb/kerev/kereb*)—the inward part of body, considered the seat of laughter Gn 18:12, 1K 17:21." "Therefore Sarah laughed within herself, saying, 'After I am waxed old shall I have pleasure, my lord being old also?'" (Gen. 18:12 KJV). "And Sarah laughed to herself, saying, 'After I have become old, shall I have pleasure, my lord being old also?'" (Gen. 18:12 NAS). The word קֶרֶב (*qereb*) is not the verb "laughed" in these verses. The verb צחק (*tsachak*) is used. How qereb is used here is in the phrase translated: "within herself" KJV and "to herself" NAS. Please note קֶרֶב (*qereb*) is a noun and not a verb.

[467] Strong, *The New Strong's Exhaustive Concordance*, OT:7126: "'*kaw-rab*'; a prim. root; *to approach* (caus. *bring near*) for whatever purpose:—(cause to) approach, (cause to) bring (forth, near), (cause to) come (near, nigh), (cause to) draw near (nigh), go (near), be at hand, join, be near, offer, present, produce, make ready, stand, take." OT 7130: "*keh'-reb* from 7126; prop. the *nearest* part, i.e. the *center*, whether lit, fig or adv (espec. with prep.):— x among, x before, bowels, x unto charge, + eat (up), x heart, x him, x in, inward (x –ly, part, -s, thought), midst, + out of, purtenance, x therein, x through, x within self."

[468] Strong, *The New Strong's Exhaustive Concordance,*: "קֶרֶב qereb (*keh'- reb*) 1) midst, among, inner part, middle 1a) inward part 1a1) physical sense 1a2) as seat of thought and emotion 1a3) as faculty of thought and emotion 1b) in the midst, among, from among (of a number of persons) 1c) entrails (of sacrificial animals)."

[469] *Biblos.com*, Parallel Bible, Romans 11, Wesley's Notes on the Bible, http://bible.cc/romans/11-25.htm (accessed on 10-03-08): "St. Paul calls any truth known but to a few, a mystery. Such had been the calling of the gentiles: such was now the conversion of the Jews. Lest ye should be wise in your own conceits—Puffed up with your present advantages; dreaming that ye are the only church; or that the church of Rome cannot fail. Hardness in part is happened to Israel, till—Israel therefore is neither totally nor finally rejected. The fullness of the gentiles be come in—Till there be a vast harvest amongst the heathens."

[470] πλήρωμα (*plaroma*)—the root idea of this word is "that which fills or fulfills" and in that way it is complete.

[471] There is no general eschatological agreement as to when "the fullness of the Gentiles" began. For example, J. Dwight Pentecost states in *Things To Come*, 303: "From the standpoint of eschatology, the important point is that the fullness of the Gentiles began at Pentecost and will continue only as long as the present age of grace." While I understand this stance, I believe the fullness of the Gentiles began earlier when the Holy Spirit's direction turned in a new way toward Gentiles after Peter received divine revelation on a rooftop in Joppa (Acts 10).

⁴⁷² Gingrich, *Gingrich's Greek Lexicon*, 98: "καιρός, οῦ, ὁ *time*, i.e. *point of time* as well as *period of time*—1. generally Lk 21:36; Ac 14:17; 2 Cor 6:2; Eph 6:38; 2 Ti 3:1; *present (time)* Ro 3:26; 13:11. κατὰ καιρόν *from time to time* J 5:4.—2. *the right, proper, favorable time* Mt 24:45; Mk 12:2; Lk 20:10; J 7:6, 8; Ac 24:25. *Opportunity* Gal 6:10; Col 4:5; Hb 11:15.—3. *definite, fixed time* Mt 13:30; 26:18; Mk 11:13; Lk 8:13; 19:44; Gal 4:10; 6:9; 2 Ti 4:6.—4. *the time of crisis, the last times* Mt 8:29; 16:3; Mk 10:30; 13:33; Lk 21:8; 1 Cor 7:29; Eph 1:10; Rv 1:3." What makes this word so important is that it has the meaning of a "season of time," an "appointed time," and a "prophetic time."
⁴⁷³ μυστήριον, *mustarion*.
⁴⁷⁴ Henry, *Matthew Henry's Commentary of the Whole Bible*, 2108.
⁴⁷⁵ Ibid.
⁴⁷⁶ Skarsaune, *In the Shadow of the Temple*, 82.
⁴⁷⁷ Ibid., 82-83.
⁴⁷⁸ Ibid., 80-83.
⁴⁷⁹ Ibid., 172.
⁴⁸⁰ Ibid., 173.
⁴⁸¹ Ibid., 177.

CHAPTER 9
The One to Be Sacrificed

⁴⁸² Please refer to the Glossary for more on *baal*.
⁴⁸³ Nancy Gibbs, "The Abortion Campaign You Never Hear About," *Time Magazine*, February 26, 2007, 26.
⁴⁸⁴ Restad, *Christmas in America*, 17.
⁴⁸⁵ Ibid., 18.
⁴⁸⁶ Burrows, *Gotham*, 71.
⁴⁸⁷ Restad, *Christmas in America*, 20.
⁴⁸⁸ Ibid., 21.
⁴⁸⁹ Ibid., 13.
⁴⁹⁰ Ibid., 19.
⁴⁹¹ Ibid., 38.
⁴⁹² Ibid., 19; Ibid., viii.
⁴⁹³ Ibid., 27.
⁴⁹⁴ Burrows, *Gotham*, xvii.
⁴⁹⁵ Ibid., xvi.
⁴⁹⁶ Ibid., xviii.
⁴⁹⁷ Ibid., xvi.
⁴⁹⁸ Ibid., xv.
⁴⁹⁹ Ibid., xii.
⁵⁰⁰ Ibid., xii.
⁵⁰¹ Ibid., 417.

502 Ibid., xiv.
503 Ibid., 462.
504 Ibid.
505 Achtemeier, Harper's Bible Dictionary. CD-ROM. Libronix Digital Library System 3.0e,,2008. "Akiti: Another issue concerns the relation of the biblical New Year Festival to the Babylonian New Year or *akitu* festival. This festival, held in the spring from the first to the eleventh of Nisan, emphasized the renewal of creation and kingship. The celebration featured a liturgical recitation and reenactment of the Babylonian creation epic in which Marduk, the city god of Babylon, defeated the chaos monster Tiamat and set the cosmos in order. The festivities also included a ritual procession around the city, a ritual humiliation of the king, and a ritual marriage of Marduk atop the ziggurat of Babylon. At the end of the festival, the king received the tablets of destiny that assured his rule for another year. Some scholars have attempted to argue that a similar New Year Festival was observed in Jerusalem during the monarchical period, but the evidence does not support such a claim. It is more likely that the biblical New Year Festival was a harvest celebration associated with the Day of Atonement (Lev. 23:26-32; Num. 29:7-11) and the Festival of Booths (Lev. 23:33-43; Num. 29:12-38; Deut. 16:13-15; cf. Exod. 23:16; 34:22). ***See also*** Babylon; Nisan; Tiamat; Time; Tishri. M.A.S."
506 Muir, *Christmas Customs & Traditions,* "Old Christmas Eve and Twelfth Night," 97.
507 Bertman, *Handbook of Life in Ancient Mesopotamia,* "Holy Days and Festivals," 130-132.
508 Nissenbaum, *The Battle for Christmas,* 50.
509 Burrows, *Gotham,* 418.
510 Ibid.,. 381.
511 ". . . to visit orphans and widows in their trouble, *and* to keep oneself unspotted from the world."
512 Burrows, *Gotham,* 379.
513 Ibid., 380.
514 http://www.hollandlodgeno8.org/index.html.
515 http://www.hollandlodgeno8.org/about.php.
516 Decker, *The Question of Freemasonry,* 8.
517 Mackey, *An Encyclopedia of Freemasonry and Its kindred Sciences,* vol. 2, 518.
518 Ibid., 9.
519 Victoria Westlane, "Christmas Around the World," *Tidbits of Fort Collins,* December 21, 2005, 4.
520 Ibid., 4.
521 Ibid., 2.
522 Burrows, *Gotham,* 462.
523 Ibid.
524 Ibid.
525 Ibid.
526 Ibid.

CHAPTER 10
Here Comes the Bride

[527] "Love the LORD your God with all your heart and all your soul and with all your strength" (Deut. 6:5). The Hebrew word for *strength* has the root idea of "very much." Strong, *The New Strong's Exhaustive Concordance*, OT:3966: "מְאֹד (me'od) [pronounced *meh-ode'* or ma-od or ma-ode too since the 'e' on the end in English makes for a long 'o' and in Hebrew this is a long 'o']; from the same as 181; properly *vehemence*, i.e. (with or without preposition) *vehemently*; by implication *wholly, speedily*, etc. (often with other words as an intensive or superlative; especially when repeated):—diligently, especially, exceeding (-ly), far, fast, good, great (-ly), x louder and louder, might (-ily, -y), (so) much, quickly, (so) sore, utterly, very (+much, sore), well."

[528] Commenting on Deut 6:5, J. McBride noted: "The three parts of Deuteronomy 6:5; *lēbāb* לֵבָב (heart), *nepheš* נֶפֶשׁ (soul or life), and *meʾōd* מְאֹד (muchness) rather than signifying different spheres of biblical psychology seem to be semantically concentric. They were chosen to reinforce the absolute singularity of personal devotion to God. Thus, *lēbāb* denotes the intention or will of the whole man; *nepeš* means the whole self, a unity of flesh, will and vitality; and *mĕʾōd* accents the superlative degree of total commitment to Yahweh." Briggs, C. A., "The Use of *npš* in the OT," JBL 16. 17–30. Becker, J. H., Het Begrip Nefesj in het Oude Testament, 1942. Buswell, J. O., *A Systematic Theology of the Christian Religion*, Zondervan, 1962, vol. II, pp. 237–41. Seligson, M., *The Meaning of npsh mt in the Old Testament*, 1951; cf. Widengren, G., VT 4:97–102. Murtonen, A., *The Living Soul*, 1958. Lys, D., *Nepesh*, 1959. Johnson, A. R., *The Vitality of the Individual in the Thought of Ancient Israel*, 1949. Wolff, H. W., Anthropology of the Old Testament. Westermann, C., "Naefaes" in THAT, II, pp. 71–95. Richardson, TWB, pp. 144–45. TDOT, IX, pp. 617–37." Please note that the idea of the "soul" of a person being one's mind/will/emotion is a Western idea. It's not an Eastern idea, ala foreign to the Hebrew mind.

[529] *Lev* or *leb* is the shorter form of *labab* or *lavav* which is the longer more preferred form for לֵבָב.

[530] Seekins, *Hebrew Word Pictures*, 18.

[531] Strong's, *The New Strong's Exhaustive Concordance*, OT:5315: "Nephesh [pronounced neh'-fesh]; from 5314; properly a *breathing* creature, i.e. animal of (abstract) *vitality*; used very widely in a literal, accommodated or figurative sense (bodily or mentally):—any, appetite, beast, body, breath, creature, x dead (-ly), desire, x [dis-] contented, x fish, ghost, + greedy, he, heart (-y), (hath, x jeopardy of) life (x in jeopardy), lust, man, me, mind, mortally, one, own, person, pleasure, (her-, him-, my-, thy-) self, then (your-)selves, +slay, soul, +tablet, they, thing, (x she) will, x would have it."

[532] Coupled with your previous experiences, genetic make-up, belief systems, etc.

533 *Nephesh* is a noun created from the root consonants: *n-p-sh*. *Nephesh* is a word that uses onomatopoeia. This is an ancient Akkadian or Babylonian word. When you inhale the sound is *"neph"* and when you exhale the sound is *"phesh."* The *"ph"* sound is the transition sound from inhaling and exhaling. Try it. The Ancients knew that there was a part of you that they could not see and without it you were dead. That would be your *"nephesh,"* which one could tell if you had or not. Thus when David states in Ps. 25:1 "Unto you oh LORD do I lift up my soul," he was using *nephesh*. Thus he was lifting that part of his being that if he did not have it he was dead. *Nephesh* is your very life!

534 Strong's, *The New Strong's Exhaustive Concordance*, OT:5314: "Naphash [pronounced naw-fash']; a primitive root; to *breathe*; passively, to be breathed upon, i.e. (figuratively) *refreshed* (as if by a current of air): — (be) refresh selves (-ed)."

535 www.earthcalendar.net.

536 Chumney, *The Seven Festivals of the Messiah*, 125-135.

537 "Whoever claims to live in Him must walk as Jesus did" (1 John 2:6).

538 I am just affirming the validity of the Old Testament, for it is as much the Word of God as the New Testament. Some Christians have sought to minimize or invalidate it, which is in actuality slicing and dicing (i.e., taking away from) the Word of God.

539 Rashi (Rabbi Shlomo Yitzhaki, c. 1040-1105).

540 Scherman, *The Chumash*, 486.

541 Harris, *Theological Word Book*, 2150: "יָחַר (*rāḥaṣ*) wash. With Times New Roman the transliteration might be more like: *rachats*. Derivatives 2150a יָחַר (*rahaṣ*) *washing* (Ps 60:10; 108:10). 2150b הָצְחַר (*rahṣâ*) *washing* (Song 4:2; 6:6). The initial occurrence is Gen 18:4, with over forty-eight occurrences in the Pentateuch, twenty-six in Lev. Among the parts of the body ritually rinsed were: the face (Gen 43:31); the hands (Ex 30:19, 21); the body (Lev 17:16); the feet (Gen 18:4ff). In the Levitical rituals the flesh of sacrificial animals was washed (Lev 1:9 et al.). This washing would normally take a great deal of water and perhaps suggests that Solomon's great brazen sea was used as a reservoir for such water as well as for other rituals. Several interesting uses of the term appear in Song of Solomon giving details on Israelite cosmetology. The root *rāḥaṣ* describes the ritual foot washing (5:3) and an eye washing with milk (5:12). A similar usage of washing for romantic appeal appears in Ruth 3:3. But the much more serious use of the root is reserved for the notion of its representing the cleansing from sin (Isa 1:16; 4:4). It is this meaning which is carried throughout Ezek. (16:4, 9; 23:40) and on into the NT in the baptism of John and of Jesus. The NT has a number of references to the OT practices (Jon 2:6; Mt 15:2; Heb 9:10 etc.)."

542 Scherman, *The Chumash*, 487: "*Together with their feet*. The conjunction אֶת indicates that the hands and feet must be washed at the same time (*Or HaChaim*). Consequently, the Kohen places his right hand on his right foot and washes them, and then follows the same procedure with his left hand and foot (*Rashi* from *Zevachim* 19b)."

543 Ibid.
544 Ibid., 527.
545 They prayed there and listened to the teachings of God.
546 Scherman, *The Chumash*, From the mirrors of legions. 527.
547 Exodus 38:30-31 lists the items made from copper from the regular freewill contribution: sockets of the entrance to the tent of meeting, the altar, the sockets of the courtyard all around, the sockets of the gate of the courtyard, all the pegs of the tabernacle, and all the pegs of the courtyard, all around. The laver is NOT included in this list; therefore it was not made with copper from the regular contributions but "from the mirrors of the women who served at the entrance to the Tent of Meeting" (Exod. 38:8).
548 Joyner, *The Final Quest*, 89.

CHAPTER 11
I Thee Wed

549 Dee Sadler, August 20, 2005.
550 An interesting thing about Melchizedek's מַלְכִּי־צֶדֶק name: his name is a combination of two words. "My king" מֶלֶךְ (*melek*) plus the personal pronoun for "my" which is a Yod "י" and צֶדֶק *(tsedek/zedek)* "righteousness." Thus his name means: "my king of righteousness," pronounced in Hebrew more like: *makchitsedek*.
551 Gen. 14:1—Amraphel king of Shinar, Arioch king of Ellasar, Chedorlaomer king of Elam, and Tidal king of Goiim.
552 "Amraphel," http://www.jewishencyclopedia.com.
553 *Webster's Collegiate Dictionary*, 10th ed., 399: "etymology—the history of a linguistic form (as a word) shown by tracing its development since its earliest recorded occurrence in the language where it is found, by tracing its transmission from one language to another."
554 "Amraphel," http://www.jewishencyclopedia.com.
555 Scherman, *The Chumash*, 61.
556 *Babylonian Talmud Nedarim* 32b; Genesis Rabbah 46:7; Genesis Rabbah 56:10; Leviticus Rabbah 25:6; Numbers Rabbah 4:8.
557 http://en.wikipedia.org/wiki/Melchizedek, "Classical Rabbinical interpretation: Shem's death took place thirteen years after the death of Sarah (1881 B.C.) and ten years after Rebekah and Isaac married (1878 B.C.); therefore, he was alive when Abram brought a tithe of *all* [nothing missing] to Melchizedek."
558 Gesenius, *Gesenius' Hebrew and Chaldee Lexicon to the Old Testament Scriptures:* "Comp. that part of Phrygia which was called κατακεκαυμένη, [This insinuation about the frequency of fires may be an attempt to account for the destruction by natural causes; no one who believes in the word of God can do this;]) pr.n. of a city in the valley of Siddim, which was destroyed, together with three others, in the time of Abraham, and submerged in the Dead Sea, Gen. 10:19; 13:10; 18:20; Isa. 1:9. *Vines of Sodom* (which appear to have been degenerate;

compare as to the apples of Sodom, Jos. Bell. Jud. IV. 8, § 4), Deu. 32:32, furnish an image of a degenerate condition; compare the opp. Jerem. 2:21; *judges of Sodom* mean unjust judges of corrupt morals, Isa. 1:10."

[559] Gen. 14:5 and Gen. 14:17 are where the word שָׁוֵה (*shaveh*) is used. Harris, *Theological Word Book:* "**2342a** שָׁוֶה (*šāwēh*) ***level plain*** (Gen. 14:5). This verb is to be distinguished from *šāwâ* II, 'to set, place' although the commentaries and lexicons are often in disagreement which of the two verbs is so intended in a particular passage. The suggestion has been made . . . that *šāwâ* is a Shapel form of the verb *hāyâ* 'to be' and means therefore 'to cause to be' and in comparisons 'to cause to be like.' Then developed the meanings 'to be like, alike,' i.e, 'to resemble.' In seven passages *šāwâ* is used in comparisons. These are: Prov. 3:15, 'Nothing you could desire "is like" her (wisdom)'; Prov. 8:11; 27:15; Lam. 2:13, 'To what can I compare you, daughter of Jerusalem?'; Est 7:4 (perhaps the hardest verse in this book to translate), 'For would not this affliction (liquidation of the Jews) "amount to/be comparable to" a loss to the king?' or 'for our affliction is not "to be compared" to the king?' Two verses, Isa. 40:25; 46:5, use *šāwâ* to express God's incomparability. With him no one can be compared. The verb occurs also in Est 3:8; 5:13 and Job 33:27 where the idea of comparison is latent but not expressible in English translation. Wieder has suggested a connection between *šāwâ* and Ugaritic *twy* 'to rule' especially for Ps 89:19 [H 20], 'a lad "I made king" over the mighty.' Cf. too Gen. 14:17 ('Valley of Shaveh/ the Ruler')."

[560] *Webster's Collegiate Dictionary,* 10th ed.

[561] November 1, 2002, in Joppa, Israel.

[562] Refer to the Glossary.

[563] Munk, *The Wisdom of the Hebrew Alphabet,* 176.

[564] Revelation from Jennifer Lynn Joy.

[565] Harris, *Theological Word Book:* "**660** לָלַח (*ḥālal*) I, *wound (fatally), bore through, pierce.* Survives in Arabic *ḥalla* 'pierce through.' Occurs ninety-six times, including derivatives. Derivatives 660a לָלָח (*ḥālāl*) *slain, fatally wounded.* 660b הַלָּח (*ḥallâ*) *cake (if pierced).* 660c זוֹלַח (*ḥallôn*) *window* (if taken as a piercing or hollow in the wall). 660d לִילַח (*ḥālîl*) *flute, pipe.* 660e לָלַח (*ḥālal*) *play the pipe.* Denominative verb. 660f הַלְחמְ (*mĕḥillâ*) *hole.* Occurs only in Isa 2:19 (parallel to cave in rocks). The verb itself is used only eight times and mainly in poetry. It usually means a fatal wounding of persons, as does the adjective *ḥālāl.* . . . In the messianic passage Isa 53:5, 'wounded' (KJV marg. 'tormented'; JB 'pierced through') follows the divine smiting (v. 4). . . . The quotation in Jn 19:12 ('they shall look on him whom they have pierced') is from Zech 12:10 but this v. uses another verb (*dāqar*) 'pierced through fatally' (usually in retribution). In Jer 51:4 and Lam 4:9 *dāqar* is used as a synonym of *ḥālal.*"

[566] Scherman, *The Chumash,* 813.

[567] The verb from which this noun is constructed is used twice in the same verse. *Rum* רוּם means "to be high" or "lift up," and the תְּרוּמָה (*terumah*) is the "thing" that is lifted up, i.e., the offering.

[568] Job 23:10 KJV.

[569] http://www.artscroll.com/Books/stoh.html.
[570] http://en.wikipedia.org/wiki/Halakha: "Halakha (Hebrew: הכלה; alternative transliterations include *Halocho* and *Halacha*) is the collective body of Jewish religious law, including biblical law (the 613 *mitzvot*) and later talmudic and rabbinic law, as well as customs and traditions. Judaism classically draws no distinction in its laws between religious and ostensibly non-religious life. Hence, Halakha guides not only religious practices and beliefs, but numerous aspects of day-to-day life. Halakha is often translated as 'Jewish Law,' though a more literal translation might be 'the path' or 'the way of walking.' The word is derived from the Hebrew root that means to go or walk."
[571] Scherman, *The Chumash*, 753-754.
[572] Ibid., 754.
[573] Ibid., 754.
[574] Ibid., 755.
[575] Ibid., 755.
[576] Ibid.
[577] Refer to the Glossary.
[578] Ibid.
[579] Micha'el Washer, *Messianic Jewish Calendar*, "Festival Commentary," 1993-1994, 5753-5754: "Bikkurim—April (Nisan-Iyar). Technically, the words 'First Fruits' in Dt 26:2 is not *bikkurim* but simply the Hebrew words for well . . . first + fruits."
[580] Chumney, *The Seven Festivals of the Messiah*, 70.
[581] Ibid.
[582] Ibid., 70-71.
[583] Carroll, *Constantine's Sword*, 294.
[584] Scherman, *The Chumash*, 755.
[585] Ibid., 755.
[586] Scherman, *The Chumash*, 755.
[587] Ibid., 757.
[588] Ibid., 758.
[589] Ibid., 757.
[590] Ibid.
[591] Ibid.
[592] Ibid.
[593] LaborLawTalk, "Dictionary," http://dictionary.laborlawtalk.com/Lucifer (accessed 01-23-05): "chief spirit of evil and adversary of God; tempter of mankind; master of Hell"; http://dictionary.laborlawtalk.com/Old_Nick (accessed 01-23-05).
[594] The History Channel, "Evolution of Santa," www.history.com/minisite.do?content_type=Minisite_Generic&content_type_id=1276&display_oder=4&mini_id=1290.
[595] Jacobs, *Deliver Us From Evil*, 41.
[596] Ibid., p. 40.

[597] The History Channel, "World Traditions," www.history.com/minisite.do?content_type=Minisite_Generic&content_type_id=1275&display_order=3&mini_id=1290.
[598] Farlex, The Free Dictionary, http://columbia.thefreedictionary.com/Lucifer.
[599] Kolatch, *The New Names Dictionary*, 189.

CHAPTER 12
Epilogue

[600] Joyner, *There were Two Trees in the Garden*, 30, 31.

Lightning Source UK Ltd.
Milton Keynes UK
UKOW04f2048110118
315980UK00001B/130/P

9 781607 911159